The Garland Library of the History of Western Music

One hundred eighty-five articles in fourteen volumes

General Editor
Ellen Rosand
Rutgers University

Contents
of
the
Set

Volume Five

*Baroque
Music
I:
Seventeenth
Century*

*Garland Publishing, Inc.
New York & London
1985*

Preface copyright © Ellen Rosand 1985

Library of Congress Cataloging-in-Publication Data
Main entry under title:

Baroque music.

   (The Garland library of the history of western music ; v. 5–6)
   Reprint of articles and essays originally published 1947–1982.
   Contents: 1. Seventeenth century—2. Eighteenth century.
   1. Music—17th century—Addresses, essays, lectures.
2. Music—18th century—Addresses, essays, lectures.
I. Series.
ML194.B23   1985   85-15982
ISBN 0-8240-7454-8 (v. 5 : alk. paper)

The volumes in this series have been printed on acid-free,
250-year-life paper.

Printed in the United States of America

Contents

Acknowledgments

Bonta, Stephen. "The Uses of the *Sonata da Chiesa*," *Journal of the American Musicological Society*, XXII (1969), 54–84. Copyright © 1969 by the American Musicological Society, reprinted by permission

Boyden, David D. "When Is a Concerto Not a Concerto?" *The Musical Quarterly*, XLIII (1957), 220–32. Copyright © 1957 by G. Schirmer, Inc., reprinted by permission

Fortune, Nigel. "Italian Secular Monody from 1600 to 1635: An Introductory Survey," *The Musical Quarterly*, XXXIX (1953), 171–95. Copyright © 1953 by G. Schirmer, Inc., reprinted by permission

Fortune, Nigel. "Italian 17th-Century Singing," *Music and Letters*, XXXV (1954), 206–19. Copyright © 1954 Oxford University Press, reprinted by permission of Oxford University Press

Hill, John Walter. "Oratory Music in Florence, I: *Recitar Cantando*, 1583–1655," *Acta musicologica*, LI (1979), 108–36. Copyright © 1979 by International Musicological Society, reprinted by permission

Hitchcock, H. Wiley. "The Instrumental Music of Marc-Antoine Charpentier," *The Musical Quarterly*, XLVII (1961), 58–72. Copyright © 1961 by G. Schirmer, Inc., reprinted by permission

Hitchcock, H. Wiley. "Vocal Ornamentation in Caccini's *Nuove musiche*," *The Musical Quarterly*, LVI (1970), 389–404. Copyright © 1970 by G. Schirmer, Inc., reprinted by permission

Horsley, Imogene. "The Diminutions in Composition and Theory of Composition," *Acta musicologica*, XXXV (1963), 124–53. Copyright © 1963 by International Musicological Society, reprinted by permission

Jackson, Roland. "On Frescobaldi's Chromaticism and Its Background," *The Musical Quarterly*, LVII (1971), 255–69. Copyright © 1971 by G. Schirmer, Inc., reprinted by permission

Moore, James H. "The *Vespero delli Cinque Laudate* and the Role of *Salmi Spezzati* at St. Mark's," *Journal of the American Musicological Society*, XXXIV (1981), 249–78. Copyright © 1981 by the American Musicological Society, reprinted by permission

Rosand, Ellen. "The Descending Tetrachord: An Emblem of Lament," *The Musical Quarterly*, LXV (1979), 346–59. Copyright © 1979 by the G. Schirmer Inc., reprinted by permission

Rose, Gloria. "The Italian Cantata of the Baroque Period," in *Gattungen der Musik in Einzeldarstellungen: Gedenkschrift Leo Schrade*, ed. Wulf Arlt, Ernst Lichtenhahn, Hans Oesch, and Max Haas (Bern: Francke, 1973), I, 655–77. Copyright © 1973 by Francke Verlag, Bern, reprinted by permission

Tomlinson, Gary. "Music and the Claims of Text: Monteverdi, Rinuccini, and Marino," *Critical Inquiry*, VIII (1981–82), 565–89. Copyright © 1982 by The University of Chicago, reprinted by permission

Walker, D. P. "The Influence of *Musique mesurée à l'antique*, particularly on the *Airs de cour* of the Early Seventeenth Century," *Musica disciplina*, II (1948), 141–63. Copyright © 1948 by Armen Carapetyan/Hänssler-Verlag, D-7303 Neuhausen-Stuttgart, No. 68.902, reprinted by permission

Preface

The Garland Library of the History of Western Music, in fourteen
volumes, is a collection of outstanding articles in musicology that
have been reprinted from a variety of sources: periodicals, *Fest-
schriften*, and other collections of essays. The articles were selected
from a list provided by a panel of eminent musicologists, named
below, who represent the full range of the discipline.

Originally conceived in general terms as a collection of outstanding articles whose reprinting would serve the needs of
students of musicology at the graduate and advanced undergradu-
ate level, the series took clearer shape during the process of
selecting articles for inclusion. While volumes covering the conventional chronological divisions of music history had been projected from the very beginning, several other kinds of volumes
cutting across those traditional divisions and representing the
interests of large numbers of scholars eventually suggested themselves: the volumes on opera, source studies, criticism, and
analysis.

Indeed, although the general objective of excellence remained
standard for the entire series, the specific criteria for selection
varied somewhat according to the focus of the individual volumes.
In the two on opera, for example, chronological coverage of the
history of the genre was of primary importance; in those on
source studies, criticism, and analysis the chief aim was the
representation of different points of view; and in the volumes
devoted to chronological periods selection was guided by an effort
to cover the various geographical centers, genres, and individual
composers essential to the understanding of a historical era.

The articles themselves were written over a period spanning
more than a half century of modern musicological scholarship.
Some are "classic" statements by scholars of the past or early
formulations by scholars still active today, in which musicological
method, intellectual vision, or significance for their time rather
than any specific factual information is most worthy of appreciation. Others represent the most recent research, by younger

scholars as well as more established ones. No general attempt has been made to bring the articles up to date, although some authors have included addenda and misprints have been corrected where possible.

Since no single reader could be fully satisfied by the selection of articles in his own field, the aims of this collection, by necessity, have had to be considerably broader: to provide not only a wide range of articles on a large number of topics by a variety of authors but to offer the student some sense of the history and development of individual fields of study as well as of the discipline as a whole. The value of these volumes derives from the material they contain as well as from the overview they provide of the field of musicology; but the series will fulfill its function only if it leads the student back into the library, to immerse himself in all the materials necessary to a fuller understanding of any single topic.

Ellen Rosand

Panel of Advisors

Richard J. Agee, The Colorado College

James R. Anthony, University of Arizona

William W. Austin, Cornell University

Lawrence F. Bernstein, University of Pennsylvania

Bathia Churgin, Bar-Ilan University

Edward T. Cone, Princeton University

John Deathridge, King's College, Cambridge

Walter Frisch, Columbia University

Sarah Ann Fuller, SUNY at Stony Brook

James Haar, University of North Carolina at Chapel Hill

Ellen Harris, University of Chicago

D. Kern Holoman, University of California at Davis

Robert Holzer, University of Pennsylvania

Philip Gossett, University of Chicago

Douglas Johnson, Rutgers University

Jeffrey Kallberg, University of Pennsylvania

Janet Levy, New York, New York

Kenneth Levy, Princeton University

Lowell Lindgren, Massachusetts Institute of Technology

Robert Marshall, Brandeis University

Leonard B. Meyer, University of Pennsylvania

Robert P. Morgan, University of Chicago

John Nádas, University of North Carolina at Chapel Hill

Jessie Ann Owens, Brandeis University

Roger Parker, Cornell University

Martin Picker, Rutgers University

Alejandro Planchart, University of California at Santa Barbara

Harold Powers, Princeton University

Joshua Rifkin, Cambridge, Massachusetts

John Roberts, University of Pennsylvania

Stanley Sadie, Editor, *The New Grove Dictionary of Music and Musicians*

Norman E. Smith, University of Pennsylvania

Howard E. Smither, University of North Carolina at Chapel Hill

Ruth Solie, Smith College

Maynard Solomon, New York, New York

Ruth Steiner, The Catholic University of America

Gary Tomlinson, University of Pennsylvania

Leo Treitler, SUNY at Stony Brook

James Webster, Cornell University

Piero Weiss, Peabody Conservatory

Eugene K. Wolf, University of Pennsylvania

Volume Five

*Baroque
Music
I:
Seventeenth
Century*

The Uses of the *Sonata da Chiesa*

By STEPHEN BONTA

IN SPITE OF THE POPULARITY of the *sonata da chiesa*, evident in the innumerable collections published in Italy from its first appearance around 1650 up through 1700, information is all but non-existent on its specific employment in the Roman Rite during this period. Attempts to supply answers on its use have been hampered thus far by inadequate consideration of the larger question of the role of non-liturgical pieces—both vocal and instrumental—in the Divine Offices in the 17th century. Those writers suggesting answers have been unable to explain adequately just how such non-liturgical pieces fitted into the service.[1] Were instrumental pieces used as preludes or postludes to liturgical chants? Were instrumental or vocal pieces used as substitutes for these chants? And, if so, what happened to the liturgical texts of these chants?

A good deal of evidence on the probable uses of the sonata, as well as on probable modes of its performance, can be found through a study of the role of free instrumental music (that is, pieces not based on a liturgical cantus firmus) in church services in the two half-centuries surrounding the period in question. The value of this evidence is greatly enhanced by the historical connections that are known to exist between canzona and sonata at the mid-century point, and between sonata and orchestral sinfonia and concerto at the end of the same century. Moreover, the fact that communications addressed *al cortese lettore* in sonata prints make no mention of how these works were to be employed in the liturgy strongly suggests that the traditions concerning the use of free instrumental pieces were already well established by 1650; the maestro would know where, when, and how to fit sonatas into existing patterns of use.

[1] See Peter Wagner, "Die konzertierende Messe in Bologna," in *Festschrift Hermann Kretzschmar* (Leipzig, 1918), p. 165; Otto Ursprung, *Die katholische Kirchenmusik* (Potsdam, 1931), p. 300; William Newman, *The Sonata in the Baroque Era* (Chapel Hill, 1966), pp. 36-37; William Klenz, *Giovanni Maria Bononcini of Modena* (Durham, 1962), pp. 128-129. On the liturgical function of Mozart's Epistle Sonatas See Orlando A. Mansfield, "Mozart's Organ Sonatas," *The Musical Quarterly* VIII (1922), p. 567; Köchel-Einstein, *Chronologisch-thematisches Verzeichnis sämtlicher Tonwerke Wolfgang Amade Mozart* (Leipzig, 1937), p. 67 (*cf.* the somewhat altered *Anmerkung* in the 6th ed. [Wiesbaden, 1964], p. 59); Emily Anderson, *The Letters of Mozart and His Family* (London, 1938), vol. I, pp. 386-387 (vol. I, p. 266 in the 2d ed. [London, 1966]; Robert S. Tangeman, "Mozart's Seventeen Epistle Sonatas," *The Musical Quarterly* XXXII (1946), pp. 591-593; Hans Dennerlein, "Zur Problematik von Mozarts Kirchensonaten," *Mozart-Jahrbuch* (1953), pp. 95-96, 104.

Although our study will be limited to free compositions, it will be well to keep in mind the obvious point that any music for use in the liturgy—a piece based on plainsong for use in alternation with the choir, or a freely composed piece—must of necessity be functional. Within fairly flexible limits, the length of a piece can be expected to be a function both of the rank of the feast for which it is intended, and of its place within the service.[2] Liturgical considerations can be expected to determine also the style of a piece designed for use in the Divine Offices: the stylistic requirements for music played at the Elevation obviously differ from those for pieces used between Epistle and Gospel. In certain cases, as we shall see, even the use of the proper ecclesiastical mode can be a factor in determining suitability.

We shall necessarily be dealing with organ music in the earlier of the two periods, since it was the organ that had traditionally borne the major responsibility for providing instrumental music in the Roman Rite from at least the 14th century. The *Caeremoniale Episcoporum*,[3] our source for the regulations dealing with the use of music in the Roman Rite, is concerned almost exclusively with the organ, mentioning only casually the use of other instruments. But there is evidence to suggest that the use of instrumental ensembles was fairly widespread during this period; and it seems probable that organ collections appearing *in spartitura* were designed to permit occasional use by such ensembles.[4] This practice would doubtless have been more prevalent in smaller parish churches and monasteries, for which these collections were primarily intended.[5] Here, use of one or two violins would have made the solemn

3

---

[2] It would appear that these limits were rather wide in some cases: the Venetians imposed a fine of one ducat on any priest who, impatient to continue the service, began to chant before the organist had finished playing. See Francesco Caffi, *Storia della musica sacra nella già Cappella Ducale di S. Marco in Venezia dal 1318 al 1797* (Venice, 1854-5; reprint, 1931), vol. I, p. 31, where he gives the date of this decree as November 28, 1564 (but see also Benvenuti, in *Istituzioni e Monumenti dell'arte musicale italiana* [Milan, 1931], vol. I, p. xlvi).

[3] *Caeremoniale Episcoporum iussu Clementis VIII. PONT: MAX:* (Rome, 1606), p. 145: "De Organo, Organista, et musicis, seu cantoribus, & norma per eos seruanda diuinis."

[4] Even though this type of ensemble performance is not suggested by its author, in one copy of Giovanni Fasolo's *Annuale* (1645), formerly used in the Monastery of the Blessed Virgin Mary in Diessen, Germany (a microfilm copy of which is presently in Isham Library, Harvard University), several of the pieces, including Hymns, Ricercares, Canzonas, and Capriccios, all of which appear *in spartitura a quattro*, have figures written in above the bass part. It seems probable that at least parts of all the organ collections that appear *in spartitura* were occasionally used for this same purpose; with their strict part-writing and the use of a style that was not markedly designed for the keyboard, they lent themselves readily to ensemble performance by any combination of from one to four instruments, the missing parts being supplied by the organ. This type of performance was, of course, common for the motet around 1600.

[5] See, e.g., François Couperin's *Pièces d'Orgue* of 1690, consisting of a *Messe pour les paroisses* and a *Messe pour les Convents*. See also the title of Banchieri's *L'Organo*

feasts a bit more festive without placing an undue strain on the limited resources at hand. Moreover, the few surviving collections of *Missae plenarium* for festive occasions, which include music for instrumental ensembles rather than for organ, indicate that the liturgical function performed by either medium was the same. In fact, the regular use of instrumental ensembles in the Divine Offices from the mid-17th century on doubtless had its origins in an appropriation of some of the liturgical functions formerly performed by the organ, in both larger and smaller churches, and for any feast on which the use of the organ was permitted.[6] It seems hardly coincidental that organ collections designed for liturgical uses, so numerous in Italy during the first half of the century, should all but cease to be published just when collections of *sonate da chiesa* began to appear in numbers.

Banchieri's *L'Organo suonarino* provides an ideal starting point for our study because of its encyclopedic character. In addition to furnishing exhaustive instructions for the "beginning organist" on his responsibilities during the services, it also contains a good deal of music meant to supply his needs. Included are a number of free instrumental pieces designated for specific points in the liturgy.

The fact that this collection was reprinted at least six times between 1605 and 1638 indicates that the practices outlined therein were indeed widespread in Italy during this period—all the more since at least six other collections, serving the same purpose, were to appear in print by the mid-century point.[7]

Banchieri makes it clear that the collection was designed to be used with "Messe di canto fermo," that is, *alternatim* Masses involving organ and choir—the mainstay of smaller parish churches and monasteries. His instructions on the use of the organ in Mass are given in Table I.[8]

---

suonarino, Opus 25 (1611): "Opera vtile, & necessaria à gli Studiosi Organisti . . . Non solo nelle Chiese de Reverendi Preti, ma in quelle de Canonici, Monaci, Frati, Monache, Suore, & Confraternite."

[6] See, e.g., Marc-Antoine Charpentier's *Messe pour plusieurs instruments au lieu des orgues.*

[7] Giovanni Matteo Asola, *Canto fermo sopra messe, hinni, et altre cose ecclesiastiche* (Venice, 1596); Adriano Banchieri, *L'Organo suonarino* (Opus 13: Venice, 1605; Opus 25 [2nd ed. rev.]: Venice, 1611 & 1620; Opus 43 [3rd ed. rev.]: Venice, 1622, 1627, & 1638); Girolamo Diruta, *Transilvano dialogo*, part II (Venice, 1610; 2nd ed., 1622); Bernardino Bottazzi, *Choro et Organo* (Venice, 1614); Girolamo Frescobaldi, *Il Secondo libro di toccate, canzone, versi d'hinni, magnificat* ([Rome?], 1627; 2nd ed., 1637); idem, *Fiori musicali* (Venice, 1635); Giovanni Salvatore, *Ricercari . . . Canzoni francese Toccate et Versi per risponder nelle Messe . . .* (Naples, 1641); Giovanni Croci, *Frutti musicali* (Venice, 1642); Giovanni Battista Fasolo, *Annuale* (Venice, 1645); Tommaso Cecchino, *Note musicali per risponder con facilità e al Choro per tutte le feste dell'anno con due sonate anco per il violino* (Venice, before 1649).

[8] *L'Organo suonarino*, Opus 25 (Venice, 1611), p. 99. *Tabella ordinata agli Novelli Organisti di quando, & quanto alternare alle Messe di Canto Fermo*

4

Setting aside for the moment the specific musical forms named, let us consider first in which parts of the Mass the organist has a role.[9] One sees

TABLE I

Table drawn up for beginning organists of when and how long to play in the Mass with plainsong

1. When the choir has finished the *sicut erat* [the *Gloria Patri*] of the Introit, the five *versetti* of the *Kyrie* and *Christe* are played.

2. When the *Gloria* has been intoned by the celebrant, it is answered in alternation [by the organ and choir].

3. When the Epistle has been finished, a short *fuga* of about forty *pause* [measures?] is played.

4. Immediately after the verse, the *Alleluia* of about twelve *battute* [breves?] is played.

5. When the *Credo* has been intoned, it is answered in alternation [by the organ and choir] (if it is used thus, or it is sung with the organ).

6. When the celebrant has said *Oremus* [following the Creed], a motet or something else is played, up to the *Orate Fratres* [the prayer before the Preface].

7. One plays twice, very briefly at the *Sanctus* [viz., in alternation with the choir].

8. At the Elevation, the sonata is piano and grave, moving [the congregation] to devotion.

9. After the *Pax Domini*, and [after] the choir has responded with *et cum spiritu tuo*, the *Agnus Dei* is played.

10. When [the *Agnus Dei*] has been repeated by the choir, a charming, but artistically elaborated Franzesina is played [viz., a Capriccio].

11 At the end, after the *Ite missa est*, or the *Benedicamus Domino*, one plays briefly [with] full [organ].

1. Finito in Choro il Sicut erat dell'Introito suonasi cinque Versetti a gli Kyrie & Christe.
2. Intuonata dal Sacerdote la Gloria, à quella rispondesi alternativamente.
3. Finita l'Epistola suonasi una fugha breve di 40. Pause in circa.
4. Immediatamente doppo il Versetto suonasi l'Alleluia di 12 battute in circa.
5. Intuonato il Credo rispondesi alternativamente (se però è uso, o cantasi nell'-Organo).
6. Detto il Sacerdote Oremus. Suonasi un Motetto ò altro fin all'Orate fratres.
7. Suonansi dui fiate brevissimamente à gli Sanctus.
8. Alla levatione grave, & Piano & suonata che muovi a devotione.
9. Doppo il Pax Domini, & risposto il Choro & cum Spiritu tuo, suonasi l'Agnus Dei.
10. Replicato dal Coro, si suona una Franzesina vaga, ma Musicale.
11. In fine doppo l'Ite Missa est, overo Benedicamus Domino, Breve & Pieno.

[9] The best studies to date on the whole question of the liturgical use of the organ in the 15th and 16th centuries, mainly in France and England, are to be found in Yvonne Rokseth, *La Musique d'Orgue au XVe siècle et au debut du XVIe* (Paris, 1930), pp. 147-152 *et passim*; Frank Ll. Harrison, *Music in Medieval Britain* (London, 1958), pp. 214-219 *et passim*; and Otto Gombosi, "About Organ Playing in the Divine Service, circa 1500," in *Essays on Music in Honor of Archibald Thompson*

that he is expected to provide a fairly continuous musical background for the service. A comparison of Banchieri's instructions with the Missal shows that the only times the organ is silent are during the Scriptural Readings (Epistle and Gospel), the Preface, the part of the Canon preceding the Elevation, the Pater Noster,[10] and all the prayers of the Proper (that is, the Collect before the Epistle, the Secret before the Preface, and the Post Communion prayers).[11] Hence we have evidence that quite extended instrumental compositions could be (and doubtless were) used in the Mass at that time, especially in the portion following the Credo.[12]

Turning now to the liturgical items mentioned, we note that *alternatim* performance is specified for the Ordinary, all five items being named. It would appear, however, that several of the elements of the Proper have been suppressed in favor of instrumental pieces: although Introit[13] and Alleluia are named, the other three items, Gradual, Offer-

---

Davison (Cambridge, Mass., 1957), pp. 51-68. All three have been extremely helpful in the present study.

[10] See the equivalent set of instructions in the third edition (1638), p. 28: "Suonasi alla Levatione suonata grave sin al Pater Noster."

[11] Banchieri's terminology is far from clear on the question of whether or not the organ was to be silent during the Post Communion Prayers [item 10]. However, the mere fact that the organist is instructed to recommence playing at the "Ite Missa est" leads one to assume that he must have stopped playing before this point. The logical place to stop would be at the end of the administration of Communion, which is marked by the Communion versicle, and followed by the Post Communion prayers, during which the Roman Church called for the organ to be silent. This is a plausible interpretation of item 10 in the third edition: "Doppo il secondo Agnus Suonasi sin fatta la Santissime Communione." See the discussion below for more on the complex problem of terminology in connection with the Communion.

[12] In view of the great interest of Venetian musicians in instrumental music, both for organ and for ensemble, it is interesting to see the Venetian manner of composing *messe concertate* as outlined by Ignazio Donati in the preface to his *Salmi boscarecci concertati à sei voci* (Venice, 1623) [See Gaetano Gaspari, *Catalogo della Biblioteca del Liceo musicale in Bologna* (Bologna, 1890), vol. I, p. 216]: "il Sanctus, & L'Agnus Dei si sono posti così semplici, & brevi alla Venetiana, per sbrigarsi presto, & dar loco al Concerto per l'Elevatione; & a qualche Sinfonia alla Communione." Giulio Cesare Arresti, writing in Bologna, omitted the Sanctus and Agnus altogether in the three masses published in his *Messe a tre voci*, opus 2 (Venice, 1663) [See Wagner, *op. cit.*, p. 164]. So, too, did Giovanni Legrenzi in the Mass setting in his Opus 9 (1667). Probably free instrumental pieces were performed in place of these two items. This practice seems to be implied by Martinus Apzileucta Navarrus in his *De Oratione et Horis Canonicis* (Venice, 1601) [cited in Georg Rietschel, *Die Aufgabe der Orgel im Gottesdienste bis in das 18. Jahrhundert* (Leipzig, 1893), p. 13]. Walter Senn in the article "Messe," *MGG*, vol. IX, col. 186, provides evidence that this is exactly what was done in Naples in the 18th century; he mentions a source that describes the Neapolitan custom of singing only the Kyrie, Gloria, and Credo. According to the preface, the organ played while the Sanctus and Agnus were recited.

[13] Banchieri gives conflicting instructions on the manner of dealing with the Introit and Kyrie. From the instructions in Table I (and in the equivalent tables in the first and third editions) it appears that the repetition of the Introit antiphon following the versicle and Gloria Patri has been suppressed, being replaced by the first *versetto* of the Kyrie. On p. 6 of the first edition, however, he includes the following statement: "avertendo in tutte le Messe, che la repetitione dell'Introito servirà per il

tory, and Communion, are conspicuously absent.[14] In each case the place
in the Mass where these items should appear has been filled by the organ.
The fact that the use of the choir is specifically mentioned in connection with the items of the Ordinary,[15] and with the Introit and Alleluia, but not at those spots where the missing Proper items should be,
clearly suggests that the pieces played by the organ at these places were
not intended to serve as prelude or postlude to a choral performance of
the chant. In the space following the Epistle, but before the Alleluia
(that is, in place of the Gradual), the organist is to play a short *fuga;*
after the Credo, but before the Preface (thus, in place of the Offertory), he is to play "a motet or something else"; and finally, following
the Agnus Dei, but before the end of the Mass (hence, in the area where
the Communion should appear), he is to play a canzona. In all three
instances it appears the vocal performance of the items of the Proper
has been suppressed in favor of organ playing.

Evidence that this is what happened is found in the first edition of
Banchieri's work, in which he includes eight free instrumental compositions to be used in the Mass, remarking that they "will be appropri-   7

primo Kyrie." A similar statement appears in the second edition [p. 6]. This suggests
that the repetition of the Introit antiphon replaces the first Kyrie: just the opposite
practice from that mentioned above. This latter practice appears to have been followed by Giovanni Croci in his *Frutti musicali* (1642); the initial sections of his three
mass settings are as follows:

> Toccata del Primo Tuono per l'Introito
> Kyrie [=Cunctipotens]
> Christe
> Kyrie
> Kyrie ultimo
>
> Introito Missa Dominicae
> Kyrie della Domenica [=Orbis factor]
> Christe
> Kirie
> Kirie ultimo
>
> Introito per la Messa Dopia
> Kyrie [=Cunctipotens]
> Christe
> Kyrie
> Kyrie

This is in contrast to Fasolo [*Annuale*] and Frescobaldi [*Fiori musicali*], both of
whom include two initial Kyries without an Introit. See Table IV, below, for a
probable use of ensemble music for the same purpose.

[14] The wording of this item in the other two editions of Banchieri's work indicates that the use of the organ (and of the Alleluia) was an occasional practice
[(1605), p. 38]: "Immediatamente doppo il Versetto si risponde all'Alleluia (occor-
rendo)"; [(1638), p. 28]: "Doppo l'Alleluia, & versetto si replica l'Alleluia (occo-
rendo)."

[15] Except the Sanctus; but Banchieri here includes music in each Mass that is
clearly intended for use in alternation with the choir.

ate for the Gradual, Offertory, Elevation, and Communion."[16] Here we have a clear indication that items 3 and 8 in Table I do not refer to improvisation by the organist on the appropriate cantus firmus, a practice still being observed at this time,[17] but rather to the use of free pieces. None of the sonatas included in the first edition show a connection with liturgical chant, nor could they be expected to if they were to serve for any Mass. So it is primarily in connection with the Proper of the Mass that free instrumental compositions appear in Banchieri's collection.

Turning to the *Caeremoniale*, we note that the use of the organ is permitted in both Ordinary and Proper, although (as with Banchieri) not all elements of the Proper have been named.[18] We also notice that Banchieri has interpreted the regulations of the *Caeremoniale* rather broadly; for although he has obviously used them as his guide, he has just as obviously enlarged the role of the organ in the service.[19] He was doubtless not alone in this.[20]

Banchieri's collection was to be used in connection with the *Messa di canto fermo*, which, as has been suggested, was the mainstay of smaller churches. What about the use of free instrumental music on solemn feasts in larger churches? Let us first examine collections of Proper settings in vocal polyphony that appeared in Italy, to see if they shed any light on the situation.[21] Polyphonic settings of the Proper appeared in Italy from about 1550 on, later by some fifty years than similar collections in Germany. But there is evidence that at least the In-

[16] P. 21: ". . . . che saranno à proposito per il Graduale, Offertorio, Levatione, & post Communione"; see below for the reasons governing this interpretation of "post Communione."

[17] See Bottazzi, *Choro et Organo* (1614), p. 9: "Avvertimento Nono: Volendo l'Organista suonare sopra alcun soggetto di Canto fermo, come sopra un Kyrie, Sequentia, Hinno, Graduale, Alleluia, ò simili. . . ."

[18] *Caeremoniale*, p. 147: "In Missa solemni pulsatur alternatim, cum dicitur [*Kyrie eleison.*] & [*Gloria in excelsis* &c.] in principio Missae; item finita Epistola; item ad Offertorium; item ad [*Sanctus, &c.*] alternatim; item dum eleuatur sanctissimum Sacramentum grauiori, & dulciori sono; item ad [*Agnus Dei, &c.*] alternatim, & in versiculo ante orationem post Communionem; ac in fine Missae." (All brackets are found in the original.)

[19] See, e.g., his reference to the *Caeremoniale* in the second edition (1611), p. 99, and the third edition (1638), p. 18.

Compare the *Caeremoniale*, which permits the use of the organ in conjunction with the "versicle before the prayers after Communion" [that is, the Communion], with Banchieri's suggestion that the organist play from a point immediately following the Agnus Dei [See Table I, item 10].

[20] The Roman Church regularly experienced difficulty in obtaining adherence to the regulations regarding the use of the organ [See Rietschel, *op. cit.*, p. 11]. Joseph Jungmann [*The Mass of the Roman Rite*, tr. F. Brunner (New York, 1951), vol. I, p. 149] states that the celebrant often confined his chanting of the Preface and *Pater Noster* to the opening words, so as to allow more time for the organ to play. He cites a condemnation of this practice by the Council of Basel as early as 1431.

[21] The information on settings of the Proper is derived from a catalogue in Walter Lipphardt, *Die Geschichte des mehrstimmigen Proprium Missae* (Heidelberg, 1950).

troit had been performed in improvised polyphony in larger churches and court chapels prior to that time.[22] Italian collections include settings for only three items of the Proper: Introit, Alleluia, and, in separate collections, the Offertory, except for those Sundays during Advent and Lent when use of the organ was not permitted.[23] In this case, the commonest pattern was to set most of the Proper.[24] The majority of the collections consisted of settings of the Introit alone, or of the Introit and Alleluia, all of them, like Isaac's famous collection, using the appropriate plainsong as a cantus firmus. (Interestingly, these are the only two elements of the Proper specifically mentioned in Banchieri's instructions in Table I.) Other collections, devoted exclusively to the Offertory and using the correct liturgical text (but not the liturgical chant as a cantus firmus), appeared rather infrequently from late in the 16th century, and evidently were closely associated with Rome.

It is highly improbable that plainsong alone would have been used to perform the missing Gradual and Communion on solemn feasts; considering the taste for sumptuous settings of the Mass, especially in the 17th century, monophonic settings of these items would have proved meager fare indeed for the worshippers. More likely, either the organ or an instrumental ensemble would have performed free compositions at these spots. Two early 17th-century prints, both quite obviously intended for festive occasions, provide us with evidence that this was so. Both prints differ from the practice seen in connection with vocal polyphonic settings of the Proper in that they include vocal pieces on nonliturgical texts as substitutes for several items of the Proper, a not uncommon practice in the seventeenth century.[25] One of the prints, by Carlo Milanuzzi,[26] consists of a *Missa Plenarium* and contains all the elements of the Ordinary, plus the following items interpolated at the proper moments:

9

[22] See the preface to Ippolito Chamaterò di Negri's collection, *Li Introiti fondati sopra il canto fermo* (Venice, 1574), cited in Ernest Ferand, *Die Improvisation in Beispielen* ("Das Musikwerk" Heft 12, Cologne, 1956), p. 9. See also *idem*, "Improvised Vocal Counterpoint in the Late Renaissance and Early Baroque," *Annales Musicologiques* IV (1956), pp. 146, 168-172.

[23] Only one known collection containing settings of the Gradual appeared in the period from 1560 to 1700 (outside of complete Offices for the services in Advent and Lent, and settings of non-liturgical texts): Giovanni Contino, *Introiti e Graduali* (1560). It has not been determined for which feasts these settings were intended.

[24] See, for example, Grammatico Metallo, *Epistola, Introiti, Offertorii, Passi, Improperii, et Messa à 4 per la settimana santa. Opus 24* (Venice, 1613).

[25] E.g., Adriano Banchieri, *Messa solenne à 8 voci dentrovi variati Concerti all'Introiti, Graduale, Offertorio, Levatione, et Communione* (Venice, 1599). See S. Bonta, "Liturgical Problems in Monteverdi's Marian Vespers" in this JOURNAL XX (1967), pp. 104-105, for a discussion of the probable reasons that Italian composers abandoned the setting of liturgical texts of the Proper in favor of non-liturgical texts as Proper-substitutes at the beginning of the 17th century.

[26] *Armonia Sacra di Concerti, Messa, & Canzoni* [See Claudio Sartori, *Bibliografia della musica strumentale italiana* (Firenze, 1952). 1622a].

Concerto a 5 [vocal]	Per l'Introito
Canzon a 5 detta la Zorzi	Per l'Epistola
Concerto a 5 [vocal]	Per l'Offertorio
Concerto a due Canti, o Tenori	Per l'Elevatione
Canzon a 5 detta la Riatelli	Per il Post Communio
Canzon a 2 alla Bastarda	Per il Trôbone, e Violino
	Per il Deo Gratias

As can be seen, this includes music for all but one section of the Proper[27] (the Alleluia being suppressed, apparently); and, interestingly—since all the vocal pieces employ non-liturgical texts—all but the Introit use the terminology employed in the *Caeremoniale*. Moreover, the only difference apparent between the contents of Milanuzzi's print and the practice outlined by Banchieri is that vocal polyphony rather than organ music is included by Milanuzzi for the Offertory and Elevation. In the other elements of the Proper, however, Milanuzzi's practice agrees exactly with Banchieri's instructions: free instrumental music is used after the Epistle and at the Communion. Milanuzzi's suppression of the Alleluia was not unusual; a very common practice in the 17th and 18th centuries was to combine Gradual and Alleluia texts in one piece, if both were performed vocally.[28] Logically then, if Gradual and Alleluia could be treated as a single unit, they could be suppressed as a single unit. A second print, by Amante Franzoni,[29] provides further evidence of the use of free instrumental pieces in the Mass. Also intended for festive occasions, it too contains a *Missa Plenarium* as well as items for Compline. In addition to the elements of the Ordinary, the Mass includes the following, again interpolated within the Ordinary:

Entrata & Ritornelli a quattro per l'Introite
Canzon Francese a quattro per l'Epistola
Laudamus Dominum, & sue Sinfonie a otto per l'Offertorio
Aperi oculos tuos a quattro per la Eleuazione
Canzon a quattro, due soprani, e due Bassi nel fine

The arrangement here is similar to that found in Milanuzzi's collection except for the apparent suppression of the Introit,[30] and the omission of

[27] The canzona "per il Post Communio" is doubtless intended to be performed at the Communion versicle. See below for the justification of this interpretation.
[28] See Lipphardt, *op. cit.*, pp. 78–81. Separate polyphonic settings of the Alleluia had ceased to appear after 1628.
[29] *Apparato musicale di messa, sinfonie, canzoni, motetti, & Letanie della Beata Vergine.* See Sartori, *op. cit.*, 1613a.
[30] The listing above is reproduced from Franzoni's *Tavola*. Within the print he includes the following items for the beginning of the Mass: Entrata; Kyrie; Ritornello; Christe; Ritornello; Kyrie.
Facing p. 1 of the Partitura, he gives the following instructions concerning this section of the Mass: "Prima dunque di cominciare la Messa, si suonara l'entrata due volte con li stromenti. . . . Finito il primo Kyrie & Christe, si ripigliaranno subito il suoi ritornello." It would appear that he is observing the first practice mentioned by Banchieri in connection with the Introit. See fn. 13, above.

the canzona at the Communion. All the instrumental pieces are intended for ensemble performance.

Significantly, both Milanuzzi and Franzoni follow the practice we have observed in polyphonic settings of the Proper; vocal pieces are not supplied for either the Gradual or the Communion. This evidence (added to that supplied by Banchieri) strongly suggests that there was a regular use of free instrumental pieces at the same liturgical spots in the Mass, whether in smaller churches and monasteries, or in cathedrals and larger secular churches; whether for lesser feasts of the Church Year, or for the more solemn ones; whether in Masses employing polyphonic settings of liturgical Proper texts, or in those using non-liturgical substitutes.[31] But one more problem must be dealt with before we state with conviction that these instrumental pieces were used as substitutes

[31] Arresti's opus 2 [see fn. 12, above] contains three Masses consisting of the following items:

Missa de Resurrectione
    Kyrie
    Gloria
    Sequentia: Victimae Paschali Laudes
    Patrem Omnipotentem
    Exultemus, laetemur
    Quid mihi est in coelo
Missa de Spirito Sancto
    Kyrie
    Gloria
    Sequentia: Veni Sancte Spiritus
    Credo in unum Deum
    O Fulgorem, o splendorem
    O Bone Jesu, o dulcis Jesu
Missa de Communi omnium festorum
    Kyrie
    Gloria
    Sonata a dui violini
    Credo
    Ad cantus ad plausus
    O quam suave

In view of the use of vocal pieces on non-liturgical texts for the Offertory and Elevation by both Milanuzzi and Franzoni it seems reasonable to suppose that the two non-liturgical vocal pieces included by Arresti in each of his three Mass settings were intended to be used for the same purpose, not (as Wagner suggests) as substitutes for the Sanctus and Agnus Dei. Strengthening the argument is the nature of the text for these two pieces in each Mass. Arresti's inclusion of a sonata in a Mass designed for use on any feast day indicates how widespread the use of music for instrumental ensemble was. His omission of the sonata from the Masses for Easter and Pentecost suggests that instrumental music may have been used primarily as a substitute for vocal music on lesser feasts. The liturgical location for which Arresti intended the sonata is not at all clear from his print. In both violin partbooks it appears following the Credo. In the organ partbook, however, it is found between the Gloria and the Credo, functioning therefore, as a substitute for the Gradual. It is so listed above. Finally, in view of the arguments presented in my "Liturgical Problems," pp. 90-91 and 104-105, concerning the changes in musico-liturgical practice in the 17th century, it is interesting to see the title of Arresti's third Mass: *Missa de Communi omnium festorum.*

for the Proper: the rather confusing use of terminology with respect to the place and role within the Mass of free pieces, whether instrumental or vocal.

As we have seen, sometimes the pieces were specifically called by the name of the Proper item they seem to replace, such as "Gradual" or "Offertory"; at other times, however, these same items appear under the more nebulous titles "After the Epistle" or "After the Credo." The greatest variety is found perhaps for what appears to have been the Communion replacement:

Canzon post il Comune	[Frescobaldi, *Fiori Musicali*]
Canzon dopo il Post Comune	[Frescobaldi, *Fiori Musicali*]
Per il Post Communio	[Milanuzzi, *Armonia sacra*]
Brevis modulatio post Agnus	[Fasolo, *Annuale*]
[per il] post Communione	[Banchieri, *L'Organo suonarino*, 1605]

Banchieri gives several other versions of the instructions on playing in the area of the Communion:

[1605]: "Replicato il secondo Agnus Dei dal Choro, si suona un Cappric-cio, overo Aria alla Francese"
[1638]: "Doppo il secondo Agnus suonasi sin fatta la Santissima Com-munione."

Before trying to straighten out the confusion found in connection with the Communion, let us consider the larger problem—why it is that two or more terms are used in connection with items that appear to fulfill the same liturgical function. This confusion doubtless results from two factors.

First of all, the Proper items were not in reality suppressed; although musical performance of the liturgical text no longer took place, the text itself was still recited by the celebrant as at Low Mass, while the free composition, either vocal or instrumental, was performed.[32] Hence, both Banchieri and the *Caeremoniale* are quite accurate in their use of terms localizing the liturgical situations in which the organ could play, since these Proper items were not suppressed, but merely recited *under* musical accompaniment. Furthermore, since these musical additions were not in actuality the Proper items, but merely their musical accompani-ment, their names, such as "After the Epistle" or "After the Credo," serve to pinpoint them in the service.

Secondly, as we have seen, Banchieri has evidently enlarged the role of instrumental music beyond that prescribed in the *Caeremoniale*.

---

[32] See "Liturgical Problems," pp. 102-103, for evidence of this practice in Italy during the 18th century, for its authorization by the Sacred Congregation of Rites, and for a discussion of the relationship between liturgical text and music in the Roman Rite.

Hence his terminology (and that of other composers following the same practice) will not agree in every detail with that of the *Caeremoniale*.

The confusion in terminology resulting from this practice of substitution is compounded by Giovanni Battista Fasolo in the preface to his *Annuale* (1645), a collection similar in design and purpose to Banchieri's print. Fasolo says "If the Graduals [or] Offertories will [prove to] be too short, a ricercar or one of the canzoni in the eight tones can be played. . . ."[33] From the makeup of his collection it is clear that by "Gradual" and "Offertory" Fasolo means not the sung Gradual or Offertory, but rather the short instrumental pieces he has included as substitutes for these items within each of his three Mass settings (see Ex. 1). The relevant pieces are labeled "Modulatio post Epistolam" and "Gravis Modulatio pro Offertorio," respectively. What he suggests is that the longer *ricercari* or *canzoni* at the end of the book could be used to replace these shorter pieces.[34]

The problem of the Communion is one of terminology. There are several possible meanings of the two terms commonly used, "Communion" and "Post Communion." "Communion" can mean either (1) that part of the Mass in which the celebrant (and possibly the congregation) partake of the elements, beginning after the Agnus Dei and ending at the Communion versicle, or (2) the Communion versicle itself. "Post Communion" can mean either (1) the Post Communion prayers, following the Communion versicle, or (2) "after the Communion," that is, at the end of the distribution of the Sacrament, where the Communion versicle appears.[35] The particular meaning intended by each composer can be determined only by a careful consideration of each example in context. For instance, Milanuzzi's collection includes the following pieces: *Concerto per l'Eleuatione; Canzon per il Post Communio; Canzon per il Deo Gratias*. It seems clear that here the first canzona must come at the end of the administration of Communion, thus coinciding with the recitation of the Communion versicle, not with or after the Post Communion prayers. If the latter were the case, it would coincide with

13

[33] See Sartori, *op. cit.*, 1645d. p. [3]: "Se le Graduali Offertorij saranno troppo brevi, potranno sonare una Ricercata ò vero una della Canzoni delli otto Toni. . . ."

[34] The validity of this interpretation is confirmed by Fasolo's wording in connection with Vespers. See "Liturgical Problems," pp. 99-100.

[35] See Jungmann, *The Mass*, vol. II, p. 397, where he cites 13th-century sources that label the Communion chant *antiphona post communionem*, and *postcommunio*. In 1710, Giovanni Battista Bassani listed as follows the compositions he was required to furnish for the Duomo at Ferrara: "gl'Introit, . . . il Graduale doppo l'Epistola, et Offertorio doppo l'Evangelo et anco il Post-Communio doppo l'Agnus Dei." [See Francesco Pasini, "Notes sur la vie de Giovanni Battista Bassani," in *Sammelbände der Internationalen Musikgesellschaft* VII (1905-6), p. 589.] In addition to his reference to the Communion as "Post-Communio," it is interesting to see how closely his terminology agrees with that found in the *Caeremoniale* and Banchieri, even including redundant references to the specific place of Proper items in the service.

Example 1

Giovanni Battista Fasolo, *Annuale* (1645): *Missa in duplicibus diebus*
    Modulatio post Epistolam

14

Gravis modulatio pro offertorio

15

Ellevatio

16

Brevis modulatio post Agnus Dei

17

17707

7707077077070

the *Canzon per il Deo Gratias*, the *Deo Gratias* being separated from the Communion versicle only by the Post Communion prayers, during which the *Caeremoniale* forbids the use of music. By the same token, Banchieri's *sonata [per il] post Communione* must coincide with the Communion versicle, since it is followed by a *ripieno* at the *Ite Missa Est*. Frescobaldi's *Fiori Musicali* includes two Masses in which the following pieces appear:

Messa della Domenica	*Messa delli Apostoli*
Toccata per la leuatione	Toccata per le leuatione
Canzon post il Comune	Recercar
	Canzon dopo il post Comune

It would appear from the context that the *Canzon dopo il post Comune* is equivalent to Milanuzzi's *Canzon per il Deo Gratias*, being preceded at the Communion by the *Recercar*. On the other hand, the *Canzon post il Comune* probably was used in place of the Communion chant, before the Post Communion prayers.

The use of instrumental music in the Mass in early 17th-century Italy is summarized in Tables II and III.[36]

All available evidence suggests that it was primarily in connection with the Proper that free instrumental music was used in the Mass. Fellerer has stated that this was customary in the Middle and Late Baroque,[37] but we find it also true at the beginnings of the era. And there

18

TABLE II

The use of instrumental music in the Mass with plainsong in Italy

Part of Ritual	Singers	Organ or Ensemble
Introit	x [antiphon & verse]	x [Kyrie I in place of antiphon repetition]
Kyrie	x [*alternatim*]	x [*alternatim*]
Gloria	x [*alternatim*]	x [*alternatim*]
Gradual		x [free instrumental composition]
Alleluia	x [alleluia & verse]	x [repetition of alleluia]
Credo	x [*alternatim* or entire]	x [*alternatim* or as accompaniment]
Offertory		x [free instrumental composition]
Sanctus	x [*alternatim*]	x [*alternatim*]
Elevation		x [free instrumental composition]
Agnus Dei	x [*alternatim*]	x [*alternatim*]
Communion		x [free instrumental composition]
Deo Gratias		x [free instrumental composition]

[36] See the similar table given in Harrison, *op. cit.*, p. 286.

[37] See Karl Gustav Fellerer, *Die Aufführungspraxis der katholische Kirchenmusik in Vergangenheit und Gegenwart* (Einsiedeln, 1933), p. 28. See also Wagner, *op. cit.*, p. 165.

TABLE III

The use of instrumental music in the polyphonic Mass in Italy

Part of Ritual	Singers	Organ or Ensemble
Introit	x [*alternatim?*]	x [*alternatim?*][a]
Kyrie	x	
Gloria	x	
Gradual		x
Alleluia	x [alleluia & verse or combined with Gradual]	x [repetition of alleluia or combined with Gradual][a]
Credo	x	
Offertory	x [or instrumental]	x [or vocal]
Sanctus	x [or instrumental][b]	x [or vocal][b]
Elevation	x [or instrumental][c]	x [or vocal][c]
Agnus Dei	x [or instrumental][b]	x [or vocal][b]
Communion		x
Deo Gratias		x

19

[a] Polyphonic settings of both Introit and Alleluia regularly involved *alternatim* performance. Doubtless this alternation in the Introit (and the repetition of the Alleluia, if it were performed as a separate entity) involved choir and organ, not choir and plainsong. A good deal of evidence for this type of performance in connection with the Introit and responsories on principal feasts is given in Gombosi, *op. cit.*, pp. 53-54. See also Bottazzi, cited in fn. 17, above. Other evidence is found in a comparison of Heinrich Isaac's settings for Doubles in the *Choralis Constantinus* with the duties expected of Hans Buchner as organist in Constance [See Hans Klotz, "Hans Buchner," *MGG*, vol. II, col. 418].

[b] See the performance practice *alla Venetiana*, fn. 12, above.

[c] Although the Sanctus and Benedictus were traditionally performed as a unit in the *Messa di canto fermo*, they were normally separated in polyphonic settings, the Sanctus being performed at its appointed spot, the Benedictus at the Elevation of the Host. The *Caeremoniale*, Bk. i, chap. 8 [See Richard Terry, *Catholic Church Music* (London, 1907), p. 25] indicates that the Benedictus was to be sung after the Elevation at Episcopal Masses. It appears, however, that during the 17th century, even in the *Messa di canto fermo*, performance of the Benedictus in plainsong was omitted by the choir in favor of organ performance at the Elevation. Fasolo's collection, which utilizes plainsong *cantus firmi*, includes for two masses pieces labeled "Benedictus & elevatio simul." Furthermore, Banchieri's three "organ masses" have music provided only for the first and third Sanctus. In addition, his *Messa de gl'Apostoli* for the Nativity (included in the third edition only), which contains not only the organ *versetti* but also the plainsong and text for the alternate verses performed by the choir, omits the Benedictus altogether. See also Couperin [Table IV, below], who includes a Benedictus in one mass, an Elevation in the other; it seems clear from the context that both pieces were to serve the same function. The priest would recite the Benedictus immediately following the Sanctus.

is every reason to believe that the practices outlined in these Tables date back to at least the late 15th century in Italy, and, in fact, arose originally because of the problem of the Proper.

Let us turn our attention now to the forms cited in Banchieri's instructions (Table I), adding in tabular form all the other available information from the 17th and 18th centuries on the use of free instrumental music in the Mass (see Table IV).

TABLE IV

Free instrumental pieces used in the Mass

Composer Work & Date	Before the Mass	Introit[a]	Gradual[b]
Banchieri L'Organo (1605) organ	—	—	*ripieno*[d] or short *fuga*
Banchieri L'Organo (1611) organ	—	—	short *fuga*, ca. forty *pause*
Franzoni Apparato (1613) ensemble	*Entrata*	—	*Canzona francese* à 4
Bernardi[g] Concerti (1615–6) ensemble	—	—	*Sinfonia Concertata*
Milanuzzi Armonia (1622) ensemble	—	Vocal Concerto à 5	Canzona à 5
Frescobaldi Fiori (1635) organ	Toccata	—	Canzona
Banchieri L'Organo (1638) organ	—	—	*Toccata breve del primo tuono* or *bizaria al graduale*[k]
Fasolo[m] L'Annuale (1645) organ	—	—	*Breve modulatio, Modulatio,* or Canzona
Couperin Pièces (1690) organ	—	—	—
Charpentier[o] (late 17th c.) orchestra	*Ouverture*[p] *per l'Eglise?*	*la simphonie*[p] *de devant le Kyrie?*	—
G. A. Perti[q] (18th c.) orchestra	*Sinfonia*[p] *avanti la messa*	*Sinfonia*[p] *avanti il Chirie?*	—
Frankfurt[r] Coronation (1711) orchestra	—	vocal motet à 4	solo vocal motet
Bologna[s] Mass (1763) orchestra	—	—	violin concerto
Montserrat[t] Mass (1790) orchestra	—	—	—

20

[TABLE IV, cont.]

Offertory	Elevation	Communion[e]	Deo Gratias
motet[d] or ricercar	piano & grave[d]	Capriccio[d] or *Aria francese*	a little ripieno[e] or the First Kyrie
motet or something else played	sonata:[f] piano & grave	*Franzesina musicale*	short & full
vocal motet & sinfonia à 8	vocal motet & sinfonia à 4	—	Canzona à 4 2 sop. & 2 bass
—	—	—	—
vocal concerto	vocal concerto à 2	Canzona à 5	Canzona à 2 alla Bastarda: violin & trombone
Ricercar or Toccata & Ricercar	Toccata or[h] *Toccata cromatica*	Canzona or *Bergamasca* or Capriccio[i]	Canzona[j]
unspecified	sonata grave	unspecified	First Kyrie of the Mass[l]
Gravis modulatio or *Ricercata*	largo *ligature & durezze*	*Brevis modulatio, More Gallico*	First Kyrie[n]
Offertoire	*Elevation* or *Benedictus*	—	—
Offerte	*Benedictus*	—	—
—	—	—	—
solo motet (vocal)	solo motet (vocal)	violin concerto	Sinfonia with trumpets
—	—	—	—
Symphony: Introduction & Allegro	—	Symphony: Andante	Symphony: Allegro

21

ᵃ See also Karl Gustav Fellerer, *The History of Catholic Church Music*, trans. Francis A. Brunner (Baltimore, 1961), p. 131: ". . . instrumental pieces that displaced the chants of the Proper, e.g., flourish or march instead of the Introit, etc." Fellerer gives no documentation for this statement.

ᵇ See also Tomáš Baltazar Janovka, *Clavis ad thesaurum* (Prague, 1701), p. 119, cited in Newman, *op. cit.*, p. 24: "Some years ago such works [sonatas] were performed in a solemn manner during the Mass after the Epistle." Further evidence on the sonata in fn. 31, above.

ᶜ See Donati's reference to "qualche sinfonia alla Communione" in fn. 12, above.

ᵈ Banchieri includes the following eight pieces, which he suggests are appropriate for the Gradual, Offertory, Elevation and Communion. (It is to be expected that the organist would select for a particular liturgical situation only those works whose style was appropriate.)

Sonata Prima.	Fuga Plagale.
Sonata Seconda.	Fuga Triplicata.
Sonata Terza.	Fuga Grave.
Sonata Quarta.	Fuga Cromatica.
Sonata Quinta.	Fuga Harmonica.
Sonata Sesta.	Fuga Triplicata.
Sonata Settima.	Concerto Enarmonico.
Sonata Ottava.	In Aria Francese.

All but one fulfill the requirements of length established for the Gradual in his second edition. The one exception, the *Aria francese*, longer than all the rest, with a repetition of the entire piece indicated, was doubtless intended to be used at the Communion. Interestingly, he has included one piece for each *Tuono*.

ᵉ Although in the second and third edition Banchieri collects all the free instrumental pieces for Mass and Vespers into a separate book at the end of the print, in the first edition these free pieces are included in the same section as the *versetti* for the various liturgical items. Hence the *Quarto Registro* here contains not only Magnificat *versetti*, but also instrumental pieces to follow the Magnificat, and includes two *ripieni per il Deo Gratias*. It is more than likely, however, that these pieces were also usable at the end of Mass. They reappear in the *Quinto Registro* in the second edition, which, as we have seen, includes pieces appropriate for either Mass or Vespers. Moreover, his instructions in the second edition [See "Liturgical Problems," p. 99] indicate that the same practice was followed for both the end of Mass and the end of Vespers. See his Opus 13 (1605), p. 7, for the use of the first Kyrie at the Deo Gratias.

ᶠ The *Quinto Registro* includes a *Toccata del Quinto Tuono plagale alla Levatione del Sanctiss. Sacr.*

ᵍ See Sartori, *op. cit.*, 1615-1616a.

ʰ It may well be that the pre-Reformation English *In Nomine* was intended for use at the Elevation, fulfilling the same function as Frescobaldi's toccatas. This use would explain the retention of its name (from the Benedictus) even though it employed the plainsong *Gloria Tibi Trinitas* as a cantus firmus.

ⁱ Although Frescobaldi does not specify a liturgical location for the *Bergamasca* or Capriccio in his *Messa della Madonna*, they both appear in an analogous position to the *Canzon post il Comune* in the *Messa della Domenica*. Moreover, he includes no piece for the Communion in the *Messa della Madonna*, which suggests that the identifying tag has merely been omitted from these pieces. [See Banchieri's use of a Capriccio at the same spot in his first edition (1605) and fn. 43, below.]

ʲ See pp. 65, 70, above.

ᵏ Banchieri's instructions in this edition [p. 28] call for the use of a *toccata breve* at this point; however, he includes in the *Quinto Registro*, among other free instrumental pieces, a *Bizaria del Primo Tuono al Graduale col Flauto all'Ottaua* [p. 135].

ˡ See p. 28: "Tabella ordinata à gl'Organisti principianti," last item: "L'Ite missa est, rispondesi Deo Gratias sopra il primo Kyrie d'ogni Messa."

ᵐ Fasolo's *Missa in Dominicus diebus* includes the following free instrumental pieces:
Brevis Modulatio post Epistolam
Gravis Modulatio pro Offertorio
Benedictus & elevatio simul: Largo assai facendo godere le ligature & durezze.
Brevis Modulatio post Agnus.

His *Missa in duplicibus diebus* contains:
Modulatio post Epistolam divisa in partes
Gravis Modulatio pro Offertorio: in tres partes divisa.
Ellevatio: Si suonera assai largo acciò si godiano meglio le ligature.
Brevis Modulatio post Agnus Dei.

Three things become immediately apparent from this table: (1) Some spots in the Mass were more favored than others for the use of free instrumental music, the commonest being the Gradual, others in descending order being the Offertory and Communion, and the Elevation. (2) Although there is some variety in the types of pieces preferred for each liturgical location, there is a good deal of consistency in utilizing common types for the same situation: the canzona or its relatives (the capriccio) or derivatives (the sinfonia and concerto) are used for three spots (Gradual, Communion, and Deo Gratias); the motet or its derivative, the ricercar, for the Offertory; slow pieces, often chromatic, are preferred for the Elevation. In other words, liturgical location determines the type of piece used. (3) The preference for a particular form is not dependent upon the medium employed; for example, one finds both organ and ensemble *canzone*, and even an orchestral violin concerto, appearing in place of the Communion.

Doubtless, then, the sonata da chiesa was used in its entirety on occasion for the Gradual, Communion, and Deo Gratias, either in a *messa di canto fermo* or in a *messa concertate*. The only sonatas for which we have any evidence of liturgical use, those of Mozart, written for

23

His *Missa de Beata Virginis* consists of :
  Brevis Modulatio in duas partes Post Epistolam :
    Capriccio alla Bastarda. Tonus Duodecimus.
    Decipit acutissimo, e gravissimo partes : compositio ad libitum.
  Gravis Modulatio pro offertorio.
  Benedictus & ellevatio : Gravis ad tempum maioris Perfectionis.
  Brevis modulatio More Gallico post Agnus.
His preface indicates that he conceived of these pieces either as short *canzone* or as short *ricercari*, for he says (p. [3]), "Le Messe contengono canti fermi trà li versi, Canzonette brevi, Ricercate brevissime" ; see Sartori, *op. cit.*, 1645d.

ⁿ See p. 79, "Deo gratias v : In primo Kyrie. . . ." See also *ibid.*, pp. 99 & 120.

ᵒ See H. Wiley Hitchcock, "The Instrumental Music of Marc-Antoine Charpentier," *The Musical Quarterly* XLVII (1961), pp. 62-69 : *Messe pour plusieurs instruments au lieu des orgues* ; *Ouverture pour l'eglise ; la simphonie de devant le Kyrie* and Benedictus (for organ) of the *Missa Assumpta est Maria* ; *Offrande pour un sacre* ; *Offertoire*. The famous *Messe di Minuit* contains the following instructions : "A l'offertoire les violons joueront 'Laissez paitre vos bêtes' en D la re sol ♯."

ᵖ It is quite possible that a distinction was made between pieces intended for the two categories here by both Charpentier and G. A. Perti ; one type being used to precede the Mass, the other to function as the repetition of the Introit following the verse, in the manner long practiced by the organist [See Gombosi's study, cited in fn. 9, above].

�q Bologna : Archivio di San Petronio, MSS Lib. P. 20 & P. 49 [see Associazione dei musicologi italiana, *Bolletino : catalogo delle opere musicali sino ai primi decenni del secolo XIX*, Serie II, *Città di Bologna* (Parma, 1910), p. 142].

ʳ Vienna : Nationalbibliothek, MS 17569 ; a collection of music performed at the Coronation Mass of Charles VI, celebrated at Frankfurt in 1711. Not included in the Table is a violoncello concerto, performed after the Te Deum [See *Tabula Codicum Manu Scriptorum . . . in Bibliotheca Palatina Vindobonensi,* vol. X (Vienna, 1899), p. 15].

ˢ Karl Ditters von Dittersdorf, *Lebensbeschreibung*, ed. B. Loets (Leipzig, 1940), p. 118 : "Bei dem Graduale spielt ich mein Konzert. . . ."

ᵗ See William Newman, *The Sonata in the Classic Era* (Chapel Hill, 1963), p. 58. Fernando Sor described the celebration of morning Mass at Monserrat : "During the Offertory they [the orchestra] performed the Introduction and Allegro of one of the symphonies of Haydn in the key of D ; during the Communion the Andante was played, and at the last Gospel, the Allegro." Since the Last Gospel immediately follows the Deo Gratias, the final Allegro evidently functioned as a substitute for the Deo Gratias.

Salzburg between 1767 and ca. 1780, were apparently used at the Gradual.[38] It was also here that Arresti's sonata was probably to be performed.

It is doubtful that the sonata was used at the Offertory;[39] besides the fact that none of the Offertory substitutes in Table IV (with the possible exception of Fasolo's collection)[40] were related to the canzona or sonata, an examination of the *Gravis modulatio* supplied by Fasolo for Doubles (the longest free composition for this liturgical situation contained within any of his Mass settings) shows that even though it contains the same number of sections as many *canzone* (and even utilizes the transformation principle), it is quite unlike the canzona in its tempo and its ricercar-like subject (See Ex. 1). Similarly, the *sonata da chiesa* would be out of character at the Elevation, although Haas suggests that a solo sonata was preferred for this liturgical spot.[41] On the other hand, one movement from a sonata would well serve as the instrumental sinfonia at the Sanctus or Agnus Dei, if the Mass were performed *alla Venetiana*.

It is also possible that several sonatas could be used in the same liturgical situation. Although we have no evidence that this was so, there is at least a suggestion that Frescobaldi had this in mind for the more solemn feasts; for although he included only one piece for each liturgical location in his *Messa della Domenica*, both the *Messa della Madonna* and the *Messa delli Apostoli*[42] (for Doubles) include several pieces that, although not assigned a liturgical position, fall between pieces which are. (Those items below that are labeled for a specific location are capitalized; the others are arranged according to their order in the print.)[43] Rather than being intended as substitutes for the labeled items, these pieces may well have been intended to supplement them; for, in general,

---

[38] See Mozart's letter of September 4, 1776, to Padre Martini [Emily Anderson, *op. cit.*, vol. I, p. 386f.; vol. I, p. 266 in the 2d ed.]: "Our Church music is very different from that of Italy, since a mass with the whole Kyrie, the Gloria, the Credo, the Epistle Sonata, the Offertory or Motet, the Sanctus and the Agnus Dei must not last longer than three-quarters of an hour." No evidence has been found to support Miss Anderson's statement on p. 386 [266], n. 2: "While the priest read the Epistle the organist played softly a sonata with or without violin accompaniment." On the contrary, all available evidence indicates that this practice was explicitly forbidden [See above, fn. 19.] Similarly, Willi Apel's statement that the Epistle sonata was "designed to be played in the church before the reading of the epistle" [*Harvard Dictionary of Music* (Cambridge, 1944), p. 247] is undocumented.

[39] No documentation has been found to support Fellerer's statement [*The History of Catholic Church Music*, p. 131] that a sonata was used at the Offertory.

[40] See fn. 33, above.

[41] Robert Haas, *Aufführungspraxis der Musik* (Potsdam, 1931), p. 207. Haas further suggests that a trio sonata was preferred for the Transformation immediately preceding the Elevation, but gives no documentation for his statement.

[42] See Sartori, *op. cit.*, 1635a.

[43] It is possible, of course, that the Bergamasca and Capriccio, since they appear at the end of the print, were not intended to be part of the *Messa della Madonna*. However, it would seem odd that Frescobaldi had supplied nothing following the Elevation in this Mass, considering the pieces included in his other Masses, as well

the length of pieces for a specific liturgical situation is a function of the solemnity of the feast. This can be seen in the two items in all three Masses for which Frescobaldi includes only one piece: the opening toccata and the Gradual canzona. It is also apparent in the free compositions included by Fasolo in his three Masses; with few exceptions the shortest pieces are those associated with the *Messa della Domenica*, the longest with the Mass for Doubles, with those for the *Messa della Madonna* falling in between.

Thinking still in terms of liturgical necessity, one might assume that on occasion one or two movements only of the *sonata da chiesa* were used within the service. Frescobaldi makes it clear in the preface to his *Fiori Musicali* that the performer had the option of playing as much as he wished (or, perhaps better, as much as was needed) of the *canzone* and *ricercari* included in his collection.[44] Within three of the pieces the point of division is indicated by the words "alio modo, si placet."[45] In two of these pieces each subdivision so indicated consists of a single tempo and character; however, in the third, the *Canzon post il Comune* from the *Messa della Domenica*, the subdivisions each include two sections contrasting in tempo and meter, analogous therefore to two movements of the later *sonata da chiesa*. Fasolo seems to imply that three of the pieces he includes within his *Messa della Madonna* and Mass for Doubles could be performed in the same manner, by sections, since their titles indicate that they are divided into *parti*.[46] In the two pieces in-

25

---

as how closely his substitutions otherwise agree with those supplied by Fasolo for the same three Masses.

	Domenica	*Apostoli*	*Madonna*
Before Mass	TOCCATA	TOCCATA	TOCCATA
Gradual	CANZONA	CANZONA	CANZONA
Offertory	RICERCAR	TOCCATA & RICERCAR CROMATICO	RICERCAR
		Altro Ricercar	Toccata & Ricercar
Elevation	TOCCATA CROMATICA	TOCCATA	TOCCATA
Communion	CANZONA	Ricercar	Bergamasca
Deo Gratias	—	CANZONA	Capriccio

[44] p. [1]: ". . . dirò solo che il mio principal fine è di giovare alli Organisti hauendo fatto tale compositione di tal stile di sonare, che potranno rispondere à Messe à Vespri, il che conoscendo esser a loro di molto profitto e potranno anco seruirsi à suo beneplacito di detti Versi, nelli Canzoni finire nelle sue Cadenze così ne[i] Ricercari, quando paressero troppo lunghi, ..." Frescobaldi's toccatas were divided in the same manner (see Sartori, *op. cit.*, 1615-1616b).

[45] *Messa della Domenica*: *Ricercar dopo il Credo* and *Canzon post il Comune*; *Messa della Madonna*: *Capriccio sopra la Girolmeta*.

[46] See the Gradual and Offertory substitutes within his Mass for Doubles, and the Gradual substitute within his *Messa della Madonna* [Table IV, fn. m, above].

cluded in his Mass for Doubles, the individual *parti* are contrasting in meter and tempo. It may not be coincidental that one of the first composers of works specifically designated as *sonate da chiesa*, Biagio Marini, used the term *parte* for the subdivisions in some of his sonatas.[47] Divided into three parts, they observe the practice found in both Frescobaldi's and Fasolo's Mass for Doubles. Moreover, a number of *parti* in Marini's sonatas include several contrasting sections, resembling therefore Frescobaldi's *Canzon post il Comune* discussed above.[48] Doubtless, sonatas by other composers, even though not divided into *parti*, could be handled in the same way, depending upon liturgical requirements. For it must be remembered that unlike the pieces of Fasolo and Frescobaldi, tailor-made for feasts of varying degrees of solemnity, none of these sonatas is designated for feasts of a particular rank. And yet we have seen that they were doubtless used in churches of all sizes, and on feasts of all kinds. Hence this divisibility would be almost a necessity to handle all liturgical situations. It is interesting to see that first movements by such composers as Merula, Cazzati, Marini, and Legrenzi regularly fall within the limits of length found for the first sections of *canzone* by Frescobaldi and Fasolo, suggesting that any of these segments could be used as Gradual-substitutes as defined by Banchieri [See Table I], since they are invariably *fughe* of about the required length. Moreover, the *canzonette* included by Fasolo for Sundays, as well as the *arie francese* Banchieri included in his first edition, are equivalent in length and character to the first movement of a *sonata da chiesa*.[49]

No conclusive answer can presently be given to the important question of whether or not these *sonate da chiesa* were ever broken down into separate sections, each section being used as a substitute for one of the Proper items. Arguing against it is the lack of consistency on the part of composers up through the 1670's in the arrangement of *tempi* between sections. On the other hand, it is known that a Haydn symphony was performed in just this fashion.[50] And it is possible that with the growing consistency in the arrangement of sections within a sonata, apparent from 1670 on, such a practice was used with the sonata on oc-

[47] *Diversi generi di sonate*, Book 3, Opus 22 (Venice, 1655). Modern reprints of several of these are to be found in Luigi Torchi, *L'Arte musicale in Italia*, vol. VII (Milan, 1908), pp. 49-59, 68-75; Joseph Wilhelm von Wasielewski, *Instrumentalsätze vom Ende des XVI. bis Ende des XVII. Jahrhunderts* (Berlin, [1874]), pp. 40-41; and *Hortus Musicus*, no. 129. See also Pietro Andrea Ziani, *Sonate a tre, quattro, cinque, et sei stromenti*, Opus 7 (Venice, 1678), in which the term *parte* is used as follows: "Sonata," "Seconda parte," "Terza parte."

[48] *Sonata per violino o cornetto e basso: seconda & terza parte; Sonata seconda: prima parte; Sonata terza: terza parte.*

[49] This practice may well be indicated by the retention of the term "canzona" for one of the internal movements of a sonata da chiesa. See Pietro Sanmartini, *Sinfonie a due violini, e Liuto*, Opus 2 [Sartori, *op. cit.*, 1688a] and Giuseppe Antonio Avitrano, *Sonate a tre, due violini e violone*, Opus 1 [*ibid.*, 1697a].

[50] See Table IV, fn. t.

casion. The pattern found in Avitrano's sonatas (as well as in most of Corelli's) lends itself nicely to the following subdivision:

Before the Mass:	Largo
Gradual:	Canzona
Offertory or Elevation:	Adagio
Communion or Deo Gratias:	Allegro

This would provide a rationale for such a late use of the term Canzona: it refers to the liturgical location ("After the Epistle") and would be recognized as such by any church musician. Yet, the fact remains that no evidence has yet been uncovered to prove that this sort of sub-division was ever made.

As for Vespers, it is primarily the items of the Proper, as one would expect, that are supplied by free instrumental music. Banchieri's instructions show that the organ, besides supplying free pieces for the beginning and end of Vespers, is also used for the antiphons following the psalms

27

Example 2

Giovanni Battista Fasolo, *Annuale* (1645)

Brevis modulatio Post Magnificat Loco Antiphonae

and the Magnificat. Fasolo's instructions confirm this,[51] and he provides a short, canzona-like instrumental piece following the *Gloria Patri* of each Magnificat, to serve as antiphon (Ex. 2).

In Fasolo's print we have our first indication that the proper ecclesiastical Tone could be a factor in determining the suitability of a free piece for a specific liturgical situation. In addition to mentioning this in his instructions, he ensures that the Tone of the antiphon-substitute included with each of the eight Magnificat settings in the collection agrees with that of the preceding canticle.[52] But, as has been discussed elsewhere,[53] in the 17th century tonal matters of this sort were apparently important only in Vespers using plainsong, not in those employing *canto figurato*.

Gathering together, once again, all the available information on the use of free instrumental music in Vespers [Table V], we see that the same historical progression occurs here as was found in the Mass. The canzona could be used as a substitute for any of the antiphons following the Vesper psalms or the Magnificat; and in the 18th century its successor, as in the Mass, was the violin concerto. We also find that the numerous *capriccii* of the 17th century could also function as antiphon-substitutes, just as they functioned in the Mass as substitutes for the Communion. For Frescobaldi suggests in his Preface to *Fiori Musicali* that the *canzone*, *capriccii*, and *Bergamasca* found in this collection were suitable for either use.[54] Doubtless the longer pieces Fasolo includes served not only for

[51] "Liturgical Problems," pp. 99-100.
[52] In one case the plagal form of the Tone has been substituted for the authentic form.
[53] "Liturgical Problems," pp. 94-96.
[54] See fn. 44, above.

TABLE V

Free instrumental pieces used in Vespers

Composer work & date	Before Vespers	Psalm Antiphons	Magnificat Antiphon	Deo Gratias
Banchieri *L'Organo* (1605) organ	*Ingresso*[a] *d'un Ripieno*	Sonatas[a] *Canzone*	*Capriccii*	*Ripieno per il Deo Gratias*
Banchieri *L'Organo* (1611) organ	*Ingresso d'un Ripieno*	short or long for occasion	Canzona or[b] whatever else	*Ripieno per il Deo Gratias*
Banchieri *L'Organo* (1638) organ	unspecified	substitute for antiphon	*Franzesa*	unspecified
Maugars[c] Rome (1639) ensemble	—	symphonies	—	—
Fasolo *Annuale* (1645) organ	—	—	Canzona or[d] *Fuga sopra gl'obligo*	—
Charpentier (late 17th c.) orchestra	*Ouverture*[e] *per l'Eglise?*	antiphon[e] for *Beati omnes*	antiphon?[e]	—
Holland[f] Vespers (1739) ensemble	—	—	—	*sonata da chiesa*
Bologna[g] Vespers (1763) orchestra	—	violin concerto	—	—
Venice[h] *Pietà* (1770) orchestra	—	—	—	symphony
Venice[i] *Celestia* (1770) orchestra	Overture	—	—	—

[a] Banchieri includes the following pieces in this print, preceding them by this information: "soggiongendovi cinque sonate in Spartitura, per l'occasione di cinque Salmi, che ordinariamente si cantano a gli Vesper :. . ."

Prima Sonata. Ingresso d'un ripieno.
Seconda Sonata. Fuga Autentica in Aria Francese.
Terza Sonata in Dialogo.
Quarta Sonata. Capriccio Capriccioso.
Quinta Sonata in Aria Francese. Fuga per imitatione.

However, it would appear from the titles of the pieces that they were not intended only the Magnificat, but also for Vesper psalms, since they include the same variety of pieces offered by Banchieri for this purpose.[55]

The only evidence we have on the use of the *sonata da chiesa* at Vespers comes from Johann Mattheson, who heard a Corelli sonata played in a church in Holland. Although we have no idea whether or not this was a church of the Roman Rite, it seems a reasonable assumption that the sonata was used at this spot in Roman churches, since a descendant of the sonata, a symphony (if one can trust Burney's use of the term), was used at the end of Vespers at the Pietà in Venice.

Hence, the *sonata da chiesa* was probably extensively used as an antiphon-substitute for both Vesper psalms and the Magnificat, as well as at the end of Vespers; and doubtless in the same fashion as at Mass, judging from the dimensions of the pieces included by Banchieri and Fasolo (that is, in its entirety for the more solemn feasts, or just the first movement for less solemn ones).

30

It remains to be seen how much earlier one can trace the use of free instrumental pieces as substitutes for certain items of the Proper in Mass and Vespers. Sources containing such exhaustive instructions as those given by Banchieri and the *Caeremoniale* appear to be non-existent before 1600. But circumstantial evidence available from Italian prints of

---

as antiphon-substitutes, but rather to fill all the necessary spots in Vespers. It is with this in mind that they appear in Table V. Banchieri also published an organ collection [*Partitura Moderna Armonia*, Opus 26 (Venice, 1612)] that consists of fifteen *canzoni*, two *fantasie*, and a Magnificat—supplying thereby most of the needs for Vespers. Ganasso's collection [*Vespertina Psalmodia in totius anni solemnitates* (Venice, 1637)] served the same purpose, containing Vesper psalms, a Magnificat, and thirteen *canzone* for organ.

    [b] "Whatever else" doubtless refers to the capriccio, included for this location in the first edition.

    [c] André Maugars is undoubtedly referring to sonata performances in his account of Vespers at the church of Minerva in Rome [*Response faite à un curieux sur le sentiment de la Musique d'Italie. Escrite à Rome le premier Octobre 1639*, ed. Thoinan (Paris, 1865), p. 28: "Dans les Antiennes ils firent encore de très bonnes symphonies, d'un, de deux ou trois Violons avec l'Orgue, et de quelques Archiluths joüans de certains airs de mesure de ballet, et se repondans les uns aux autres."].

    [d] See "Liturgical Problems," pp. 99-100.

    [e] Charpentier may well have written these pieces for this liturgical purpose.

    [f] Johann Mattheson, *Der Vollkommene Capellmeister* (Hamburg, 1739), p. 91: "Die unvergleichliche Geschicklichkeit dieses Verfassers (that is, Corelli) in der zum Kammer gehörigen Instrumental-Schreib-Art hat so was ausnehmendes, dass ich so gar in den Holländischen Kirchen, wiewol ausserhalb der zum Gottes-Dienst bestimmten Zeit, nehmlich in den Vespern, oder nach deren Endigung, seine Sonaten nicht nur von dem Organisten allein, sondern auch von einem Violinen-Concert, welches zur Ubung der Kunstbefliessenen offt angestellet wird, ehmals mit vielem Vergnügen gehöret habe."

    [g] Dittersdorf, *op. cit.*, p. 112. "Between the Psalms, Spagnoletti played a concerto by Tartini. . . ."

    [h] Charles Burney, *The Present State of Music in France and Italy* (1773), ed. Percy Scholes (London, 1959), p. 124. "They always finish with a symphony; . . ."

    [i] *ibid.*, p. 129. "I went first to that [church] of *Celestia;* the vespers were composed and directed by the *Maestro* of the Pietà, Signor Furlanetto; there were two orchestras, both well filled with vocal and instrumental performers; the overture was spirited. . . ." It appears a long Symphony in dialogue replaced the first psalm antiphon.

    [55] But see Table V, fn. a, above.

organ music strongly suggests that the practice dates from at least the early 16th century. Three of the items, mentioned by Banchieri as substitutes for Gradual, Offertory and Communion, form the bulk of free instrumental pieces in these collections: motets, canzonas, and ricercars. Two of the three types appear on occasion in the same collection,[56] but more often each is found in a separate print. And the probability is great that Italian organists used the motet or its derivative, the ricercar, for the Offertory, and the *canzona francese* (as a transcription of a vocal piece early in the century, and as a canzona "sine nomine" fulfilling the same liturgical requirements as the "missa sine nomine," at the end of the century)[57] for both Gradual and Communion, as well as for antiphons in Vespers. The argument is strengthened by the wording in the *Caeremoniale*, which in several instances indicates that the Church was recognizing and authorizing a practice already in existence.[58]

One suspects that the practice of instrumental substitutions for the Proper dates from the beginnings of the extensive cultivation of polyphony in the Mass in the early 15th century. It may not be without significance that the earliest examples of choral polyphony for both Ordinary and Proper date from roughly the same time as our earliest example of an organ setting of the Proper. According to Manfred Bukofzer,[59] Guillaume Legrant's Gloria and Credo date from the end of the third decade of the 15th century. Leo Schrade dates Dufay's *Missa Sancti Jacobi*, with its setting of the Proper designed for choral rather than solo performance, from the same time.[60] The English setting of *Felix Namque*, the Offertory for Marian Feasts, comes also from the early 15th century.[61] And it is but a short step to the abandonment of a cantus firmus and the substitution of free instrumental music in the form of

31

---

[56] See Sartori, *op. cit.*, 1523, 1543b, 1591b, and 1591c.

[57] It may not be without significance that one of the first examples of the *canzona alla francese* (that is, a piece not based on a chanson, in contrast to the *canzona francese*, which was) comes from the pen of Marc'Antonio Ingegneri, known to have been strongly influenced by the deliberations of the Council of Trent in musical matters [See Sartori, *op. cit.*, 1579].

[58] The policy of the Church concerning the use of the organ had always been that of tolerance and regulation rather than of encouragement [See Rokseth, *op. cit.*, p. 154]. See also the *Caeremoniale*, p. 147: "In Vesperis solemnibus organum pulsari solet in fine cuiuslibet Psalmi, & alternatim in Versiculis Hymni, & Cantici [Magnificat &c.] servatis tamen regulis supradictis" (brackets in the original). ("In solemn Vespers the custom of playing the organ at the end of each psalm, and *alternatim* in the verses of the Hymns and Canticles (Magnificat, etc.) may be retained subject to the above regulations.")

[59] "The Beginnings of Choral Polyphony," in *Studies in Medieval and Renaissance Music* (New York, 1950), p. 180.

[60] "Dufay et son Époque," in *Histoire de la Musique*. Encyclopédie de la Pléiade (Paris, 1960-63), vol. I, p. 954.

[61] Thurston Dart, "A New Source of Early English Organ Music," *Music and Letters* XXXV (1954), p. 201.

elaborated versions of secular pieces, or even pieces without any pre-existent model.

This is all conjecture. Supplying concrete answers here will surely be as difficult as it has been in connection with the *sonata da chiesa*. No small part of the difficulty in this case can be traced to the extensive use of improvisation by organists, which leaves us little physical evidence of what was played. But the problem is doubtless further compounded by the fact that secular pieces such as the chanson were probably extensively used as Proper-substitutes, even in the face of ecclesiastical disapproval.[62] Still, what answers there are may lie in surviving Rituales, Ordinales, and Customaries.

Hamilton College

[62] There is no question but that secular music was regularly used in the Divine Offices up through the end of the 16th century [See Rokseth, *op. cit.*, p. 156]. Its earliest known condemnation comes from Italy in 1472 [*ibid.*, p. 154n.]. As late as 1611 Banchieri included a *battaglia* in his *L'Organo suonarino*, adding by way of justi-fication [p. 41]: " . . . viene però permessa per consuetudine il giorno di Pasqua di Resurrezione suonare una battaglia che sia onesta & conforme alle Sacra Sequentia Paschale . . . ." The connection between the secular chanson and its successor, the *canzona alla francese*, is well known.

WHEN IS A CONCERTO
NOT A CONCERTO?

By DAVID D. BOYDEN

ACCORDING to Franz Giegling's article *Concerto* in Volume 2 (1952) of the currently appearing *Die Musik in Geschichte und Gegenwart,* a concerto is originally not a concerto at all but a *conserto,* the latter term "ostensibly" being transformed to *concerto* by some mysterious and unspecified "Spanish" influence in the 17th century. Giegling maintains that the word *concerto* originates solely from the Latin *consero* (*conserere, consertus*), or its Italian derivative, *conserto,* and that the term is restricted to a single meaning, namely, "to join or bind together." Furthermore, he denies the connotation of "dispute, contend, or skirmish," conveyed by the Latin *concerto* (*concertare, concertatus*), although Praetorius in his *Syntagma Musicum* (1619) lends the weight of his authority to the derivation of *concerto* from the Latin just mentioned, and says that it means "skirmish with one another" ("mit einander scharmützeln"). Giegling categorically dismisses Praetorius's explanation — and so does Hans Engel in the article *Concerto grosso* in the same volume — in spite of the fact that Praetorius enjoys a well-deserved reputation for accuracy and reliability, and is so meticulous in the case of instruments that his illustrations are drawn to exact scale in Brunswick feet. Furthermore, Praetorius's extensive knowledge of Italian music is shown by his easy familiarity with the forms of the time and by his references to an extraordinary number of Italian composers by name. Actually, in light of the evidence presented below, it appears that Praetorius defined the concerto completely and accurately as it was understood in the early 17th century and for some time thereafter.

MGG is a highly respected encyclopedia, and rightly so, but its errors should be corrected as rapidly and thoroughly as possible, particularly in view of its high authority, and because some of its information is already reaching the general public and creating a new set of fairy tales in such cases as the concerto.[1]

Contrary to the contention that *concerto* is derived from *conserto* (Lat., *consero*), I believe it can be shown conclusively that, *as regards musical usage:*

1. The word *concerto* is derived from *concerto* (*-are, -atus*).

2. The musical term *conserto* is a form of *concerto* found mainly in Tuscany and Naples approximately from 1550 to 1630.

3. The term *concerto,* as used in music, had at first (c. 1519) the *Italian* meaning "join or bind together," but late in the 16th century it acquired the additional *Latin* sense of "strive or contend with," and these two different connotations existed side by side in music from the end of the 16th to the middle of the 18th century.

I

Even on the surface of things, Giegling's position is suspect on two substantial counts: for one thing, to limit the meaning of *concerto* solely to "join or bind together" denies one of the most characteristic traits of the concerto, that of "contention, rivalry, or contrast."[2] For another thing, if *conserto* was "ostensibly" transformed to *concerto* in the 17th century, as Giegling says, we should expect to find *conserto* as the prior and prevailing form in musical usage in the 16th century. But this is not the case. The earliest and commonest instances use the "c" not the "s" form of the term.

Originally, the musical usage of the word *concerto* seems to convey merely the idea of an ensemble of voices or instruments. The earliest example now known occurs in connection with a dramatic entertainment *(intermedio)* held in Rome in 1519. A contemporary account employs the phrase *un concerto di voci in musica* for what is clearly an ensemble

[1] Giegling's opinion regarding the etymology of the word *concerto* has already found its way into Kurt Stone's notes for the complete recording by Vox of the Torelli concertos, Op. 8. Incidentally, Giegling's views were anticipated nearly fifty years earlier by Hugo Daffner in his doctoral dissertation *Die Entwicklung des Klavierkonzerts bis Mozart* (1904; published 1906), where he claims that *concerto* is derived from *conserto* and the Latin *conserere.* Daffner's *musical* evidence is even flimsier than Giegling's, citing only Agazzari's use in 1607 (see below). Still earlier, Rigutini-Bulle (*Italienisches Wörterbuch,* 1900), article *concerto,* says that *concerto* is derived from *conserto* but gives no documentation.

[2] In this connection, it is ironical that Giegling does not mention the fact that the Latin verb *consero* may also mean "to fight hand to hand." Engel (article *Concerto grosso*) remarks on this second meaning, but says no more about it.

of voices without instrumental accompaniment. Under similar circumstances in Mantua in 1542, an ensemble of four instruments is described in these words: *quattro degli stromenti cominciarono il lor concerto* (four of the instruments commenced their concerto), and the instruments involved are specified as *un violone, doi leuti, et un flauto.*[3]

A number of other instances can be cited which use *concerto* in the context of either vocal or instrumental ensemble. For instance, in a Fantasia of Francesco da Milano for two lutes (before 1550), the second lute is labelled *liuto in concerto.*[4] In 1553, Diego Ortiz published in Rome his Spanish treatise *Tratado de glosas,* which includes such phrases as *en concierto de vihuelas; concertado* [sic]; and *tañer en concierto con quatro o cinco vihuelas.*[5] In Nicola Vicentino's *L'Antica musica ridotta alla moderna prattica* (Rome, 1555), Chapter 42 of Book 4 is entitled "Regola da concertare cantando ogni sorte di compositione," and Vicentino seems to be concerned mainly with the "concerting" of singers — using "concerting" in the sense of "ensemble." There is no mention of instruments being specifically engaged in the process of "concertare."[5a] Some time later (1583), the "concert" ensemble of three famous ladies who graced the court of Ferrara — Lucrezia Bendidio, Laura Peparara, and Tarquinia Molza — is referred to by the phrase *concerto di donne.*[6]

While the earliest references involve ensembles of voices *or* instruments, the term *concerto* or its derivative *concertato* is used at least by 1565 to refer to the ensemble of voices *and* instruments. The latter term occurs in a description printed in 1566 of the marriage festivities of Francesco Medici and Johanna of Austria (1565). The first *intermedio* performed on this occasion has the direction: *La musica di questo primo*

---

[3] For these two references, see Alessandro d'Ancona, *Origini del Teatro Italiano,* Turin, 1891, II, 89 and 439 respectively.

[4] Oscar Chilesotti, *Francesca da Milano,* in *Sammelbände der Internationalen Musikgesellschaft,* IV, Heft 3, p. 400.

[5] Facsimile edition by Max Schneider, 2nd ed., Kassel, 1936: A iii recto; G ii recto; p. 72, line 2, respectively.

[5a] Vicentio Lusitano, a Portuguese theorist and composer and victor in a celebrated dispute with Vicentino (Rome, 1551), sought to consolidate his position with a treatise entitled *Introduttione facilissima, et novissima, di canto fermo, figurato, contraponto semplice et in concerto* . . . (Rome, 1553; also, Venice, 1558; Venice, 1561, 1562; the last-mentioned edition was used in this study). In this treatise the word *concerto* is used to designate the harmonious combining of voice parts in counterpoint ("soprano in concerto col basso & alto"). In view of the "join or bind together" meaning of "concerto," Lusitano's usage makes perfectly good sense, but the use of the term in the context of counterpoint is unique as far as I know.

[6] See Alfred Einstein, *The Italian Madrigal,* Princeton, 1949, II, 827.

intermedio era concertato da . . . (numerous instruments specified) and singing, dancing, and playing of instruments were involved.[7] At Ferrara, also, the Florentine ambassador described (1571) large "concert" ensembles, consisting of about 60 voices and instruments, as *concertoni di musica di circa sessanta fra voci e instrumenti* . . .[8]

While I have not found the term *concerto* (or *concertato*) used before 1565 to describe "concerts" of voices *and* instruments, I imagine that it may have been used in this sense somewhat earlier in connection with such titles as *Musica Nova accommodata per cantar et sonar sopra organi et altri stromenti* . . . (1540). In any case, it is significant that in a work of 1578 of nearly identical title, including the "cantar et sonar," the composer (Parmeggiano) refers in his preface to his pieces as "questi miei concerti."[9]

Verb forms such as *concertato,* cited above, must come from *concerto,* not *conserto* (or *consero, consertus*); and it is striking that, while *concertato* is a very common form, *consertato* (from the Italian *conserto*) is so rare that I have been unable to find this term in an exhaustive examination of titles of music and theory books of the 16th and 17th centuries. The fact is that in music the term *concerto,* its derivative forms (such as *concertato*), and the Spanish form *concierto,* outnumber *conserto* by at least 100 to 1.

The musical use of *concerto* also antedates that of *conserto* by nearly 35 years, according to the present state of our information. Giegling is on very shaky ground here. In his *MGG* article, he says that the terms *conserto* and *consertare* were in use in "the 16th century and earlier," but he gives no instance. In an earlier work, *Torelli* (1949), however, Giegling cites three musical sources that use *conserto,* the earliest of which is 1584; and he speaks of the term *conserto* occurring only "in the 16th century and partly still in the 17th century." As will appear below, there is a single earlier reference to *conserto* (1553), but none later than 1628.

The difficulty with Giegling's etymology of the word *concerto* is that he has relied on general sources (e.g., *Vocabolario della Crusca*) rather than on specifically musical works for the meaning and usage of the

37

---

[7] See Otto Kinkeldey, *Orgel und Klavier in der Musik des 16. Jahrhunderts,* Leipzig, 1910, pp. 168-9.

[8] Einstein, *op. cit.,* II, 828.

[9] See Claudio Sartori, *Bibliografia della musica strumentale italiana stampata fino al 1700,* Florence, 1952.

term. There is no doubt that *conserto* was commonly used in Italy in general (i.e., non-musical) speech prior to the 16th century, that in both *conserto* and *concerto* their meanings of "join together" or "unite" were very similar, and that these meanings persisted in general Italian usage from at least the early 16th century to the present. Giegling expended considerable labor to establish this unchallenged fact, but it is not germane to the question. The only real point at issue is what happened in music, where the musical term *concerto* came from, and what idea or ideas the term conveyed at any given time.

As we have already shown, the earliest uses of the word *concerto* in music seem to convey simply the idea of an ensemble of voices or instruments. After the middle of the 16th century, this notion is extended to mean an ensemble of voices accompanied by instruments in the sense of "per cantar e sonar." Although the original Latin term *concerto* meant "to skirmish, contend, or dispute," it lost this meaning either when or after it was taken into Italian, and acquired that of "adjust, work, or join together." Thus in the early 16th century, the *Italian* term *concerto* was perfectly adequate to describe an ensemble of the kind of music to which it was first applied in its specific musical sense.

By the end of the 16th century, however, a new style became increasingly prominent in Italian ensemble music. In this style, individual voices were employed alone or in choral groups so that such voices "contended," as it were, "in rivalry" with the other voice parts of the choral (and instrumental) mass. This manner of composing became increasingly common about 1600, and Alfred Einstein discusses it with respect to the madrigal in a chapter entitled "Concento and Concerto" in his monumental *The Italian Madrigal*. One may see other applications by examining the music of the Gabrielis, among others.

Music of this kind with solo-like parts, alone or in groups, was to be the "music of the future," compared to that of the Renaissance; and to this type of music musicians also applied the name *concerto,* a perfectly justifiable use of the term because its original Latin connotation was to "strive, contend, or compete." In this connection, one must keep in mind the aftermath of the humanistic revival; thus it was perfectly natural for musicians of the time to use the Latin meaning of the term *concerto* to describe the characteristics of the new style—a style not really identified by the Italian meaning of the word *concerto,* which conveyed only the idea of "joining together, working together, or ensemble." About

38

1600, then, the term *concerto* has two meanings that are—to borrow a telling phrase from Erwin Panofsky—"fused and confused."

In other words, *by the beginning of the 17th century there are derivations from both Italian and Latin and the two corresponding meanings for the single word concerto.* This situation is implied in Bottrigari's *Il Desiderio* (1594), and is described quite exactly by Praetorius in his *Syntagma Musicum* of 1619. Bottrigari, in discussing the etymology of *concerto,* rejects its derivation from *consero* or *conserto,* and says that *concento* is, in fact, a better term than *concerto* to describe the harmonious union of instruments about which he is talking. Nevertheless, says Bottrigari, "we will use *concento* and *concerto* without distinction." Bottrigari also explains that *concerto* means "contentione ò contrasto," and alludes to Cicero, Terence, and Pliny to support the Latin derivation and meaning.[10] But, as Einstein says:

Standing at the threshold of the new century, Bottrigari is as yet unable to bring the two concepts *concento* and *concerto* into their correct historical relationship. But for us they can throw a light on the changing relationships of the voices in the sixteenth and seventeenth centuries. In the madrigal, in the motet, the voices combine in a consonance, a *concento.* No voice stands out; each voice recognizes the rights of every other; there is a truly democratic spirit. But in the course of the century the tension of the voices with respect to one another undergoes a change: two or more voices stand out, begin to compete, and force the rest to accept a subordinate and menial role ... when two pairs of voices begin to oppose one another in a four-voiced context, the first step towards the concerto-like treatment has already been taken.[11]

Praetorius explains in some detail the two types covered by the meaning of *concerto.* He says that the Italians use the term as a synonym for terms like *concentus* and *symphonia,* meaning a harmonious ensemble of musical forces. (This part of Praetorius's explanation is not mentioned by Giegling.) In addition, Praetorius explains a second type in which the best performers are distinguished from others of the whole ensemble in such a way that the choir of such voices (i.e., *voces concertantes*) "disputes" (*streiten*) with the other (full) choir, and Praetorius says explicitly in this connection that the word *concerto* is derived from the Latin *concertare,* meaning "to skirmish with one another."[12]

[10] Bottrigari mentions that there is another Latin *consero (conserere, consitus),* meaning "to plant or sow." Of course, this has no bearing here.

[11] Einstein, *op. cit.,* II, 821.

[12] *Syntagma Musicum,* Book III: Part I, Chapter 2; Part III, Chapter 2.

39

Broadly speaking, the term *concerto* appears to be applied, at least at the end of the 16th century and early in the 17th, mostly to combinations of voices and instruments, and it is not clear whether the term is used after 1550 for unaccompanied vocal music, as implied by Einstein or by the phrase *concerto di donne* (1583), cited above. The word *concerto* is applied for the first time to a specific piece of purely instrumental music (as opposed to describing merely an ensemble of instruments) in a ricercar labelled *Ricercar per sonar* found in the *Concerti di Andrea et di Gio. Gabrieli Organisti...* (1587). Such sporadic appearances of *concerto* in connection with purely instrumental music continue to occur in the 17th century, but the instrumental concerto as such does not play an important role until about 1680, when it assumes a form and style quite different from the ricercar of Gabrieli nearly a century earlier, for which piece the term *concerto* has no formal significance whatever.

II

40

The evidence given above establishes the fact that the term *conserto* is a comparative late-comer and is relatively rare in music (see also below). Thus it is a most unlikely parent-form of *concerto*. Furthermore, there is documentary evidence that *conserto* was regarded as a dialect form of *concerto*. Bottrigari (1594) takes pains to point out that *conserto* is a Tuscan colloquialism for *concerto,* and this information explains the known instances of *conserto* found in Northern Italy.[13] Giegling (in his *Torelli,* not in his *MGG* article) mentions three authors who use *conserto*: Alessandro Striggio (1584), Agazzari (1607), and Giustiniani (1628). To this number I am able to add four more instances: Dentice (1553), a report of a *conserto* in Pisa (1589), references to *conserto* in Bottrigari (1594), as explained above, and Cerreto (1601).

The earliest of these occurs in a work by the Neapolitan theorist Luigi Dentice, who, in the second of his *Duo Dialoghi della Musica* (1553), speaks of "Alfonso della Viola who is no less miraculous in counterpoint

[13] *Il Desiderio,* p. 9, facsimile ed. by Kathi Meyer, Berlin, 1924. For pointing out to me the significance of Bottrigari in connection with the etymology of *concerto* I am indebted to Dr. Edward Lowinsky, who also furnished me the precise references to *concierto* in Ortiz, given above, and that in Dentice, given below. Einstein (*op. cit.,* II, 821) also mentions Bottrigari's point concerning *conserto*. Schering (*Geschichte des Instrumentalkonzerts, Nachträge* to p. 4) says that the appearance of *conserto* in Agazzari's *Del sonare sopra 'l basso con tutti li stromenti e dell' uso loro nel conserto* ... (1607) "may be regarded as a typographical error or a provincial colloquialism." Schering apparently did not know Bottrigari's remark on *conserto*. The *Enciclopedia Italiana* article *Concerto* picturesquely calls *conserto* an "idiotismo locale," and refers to Bottrigari.

and in composing than in playing the viola d'arco *in conserto*." Now Naples had been a Spanish possession since 1502 (and remained such for over 200 years), and there are references in Dentice's work to music in the palace of Johanna of Aragon, wife of the Spanish high constable, Arcanio Colonna. In this Spanish environment it is not surprising that the word *conserto* should emerge as a close equivalent to the sound of the Spanish *concierto,* and the word *concierto* must have been a Spanish musical term in current usage at that time because Ortiz used *concierto* in his Spanish treatise printed in Rome in the same year (1553; see above).

In the same way, one may explain the use of *conserto* by Scipione Cerreto, who published his *Della Prattica Musica, vocale et strumentale* in Naples in 1601. Cerreto uses such phrases as *il conserto delle viole da gamba* and *sola ò in conserto.*

Another 16th-century reference, *conserto di donne,* comes from a letter (1584) of Alessandro Striggio (the elder), and is used to describe the same three ladies mentioned earlier. Although Striggio was born and died in Mantua, he spent about ten years (1560-70) in Florence, the chief city of Tuscany, in the service of Cosimo de' Medici. Another instance concerns Fernando de' Medici. In 1589 he visited the city of Pisa (also in Tuscany) with his new wife, Christine of Lorraine, and among the pieces involved in celebrating this event was a ten-voiced composition performed by "52 singers, 6 trombones, 4 cornetti, and, in the middle of the *conserto,* an organ . . ."[14]

There are two more references, both from the early 17th century. Agostino Agazzari, who uses *conserto* and *concerto* interchangeably in his treatise of 1607, was a native of the Tuscan city of Siena (where he died in 1640), thus bearing out again Bottrigari's explanation of the Tuscan usage of *conserto.* The last reference is found in Vincenzo Giustiniani's *Discorso sopra la musica* (1628), probably of Roman origin. In this work are found *le Viole di conserto; un conserto di Viole ò di Flauti;* and *le tante persone al componimenti del conserto,* used in the old sense of ensemble.[15] It is impossible to say whether this usage derives from Neapolitan sources, whether it harks back to Ortiz's Roman treatise

41

[14] Kinkeldey, *op. cit.,* p. 175.

[15] Giustiniani's work is printed complete in Angelo Solerti, *Le Origini del Melodramma,* Turin, 1903, pp. 103-28. The references are on pp. 123-4 and 125, respectively.

of 1553 (*concierto* = *conserto*), or whether there is another explanation. In any case, Giustiniani's use of *conserto* is the last one known.

In sum, the overwhelming bulk of the evidence suggests that, in musical matters, far from *concerto* being derived from *conserto*, the opposite was the case. With respect to the "Spanish" influence, the transformation must have been from *concierto* to *conserto*, not, as Giegling suggests, from *conserto* to *concerto*. Since Giegling gives no particulars to support his argument, nothing further need be said on this point. Finally, the musical usage of *conserto* seems to have been relatively short-lived: from 1553 to 1628 according to the above evidence.

In passing it might be said that the English term *consort* has no discernible bearing on the argument. It is probably not derived from the Latin *consortium*, as Giegling claims, but — if one may believe the unabridged Oxford Dictionary — comes from the French term *concert* or the parent term *concerto*. In the measured prose of Oxford: "In the musical uses . . . there can hardly be any doubt that *consort* was from the beginning an erroneous representation of F. *concert*, It. *concerto*."

However, the term *consort* appears in England at least by 1586 when Marlowe writes in *Tamerlane* (Part I, IV, iv): "Methinks tis a great deal better than a consort of Musick." In Act IV of the anonymous drama *The Rare Triumph of Love and Fortune* (1589), a "Consort of Sweet Music" is called for;[16] and in 1599 Morley's *Consort Lessons* appear, followed by numerous imitators in the 17th century.

As just explained, the term *consort* appears late in the 16th century but the usage that it describes must have originated much earlier because ensembles of instruments similar to those specified by Morley's *Consort Lessons* may be found in musical and literary descriptions throughout the 16th century and earlier, and similar ensembles are also portrayed in painting. It is a striking fact—as it is with the Italian *concerti* of the 16th century—that the instruments involved are usually of different families, and there seems to be no question that the word *consort* implied ensembles of instruments of different types, at least to 1600. Thus Morley's *Consort Lessons* of 1599 are for "the Treble Lute, the Pandora, the Citterne, the Base Violl, the Flute, and the Treble Violl"; and Rosseter's *Lessons for Consort* (1609) use the same combination. Consorts of instruments of the same family occur much less frequently, and to make this meaning explicit one had to use the term "whole consort"—

---

[16] Kinkeldey, *op. cit.*, p. 177.

as opposed to "consort" or "broken" consort which meant different families—and I have been unable to find the term "whole consort" until well into the 17th century. It is true that consorts of viols became increasingly popular in the 17th century, but Francis Bacon is still equating "Broken Musick" with Consort Musick.[17] In any case, the word *consort* seems to have been used primarily to mean an ensemble of instruments (and, sometimes, voices) and not ever to have acquired the larger connotations of the word *concerto* as employed in Italy.

III

Such elaborate etymology for the word *concerto* would hardly seem worth while if it did not serve the end of expanding the existing concept of the concerto. Happily, this is the case. The dual meaning of the term in Italian and Latin, and the corresponding notions of "join together," on the one hand, and "contention, rivalry, or contrast," on the other, do serve the important function of explaining how a number of works of quite different character from about 1600-1750 could all be described with perfect propriety by the single term *concerto*. In short, during the 17th century and the first part of the 18th, the word *concerto* is to be understood, not as a fixed form with solo parts, but rather as one of two manners of setting, involving either the concept of "joining together" or "ensemble" of musical forces, or the idea of "striving, contrast, and opposition." For example, Viadana's *Cento Concerti Ecclesiastici* (1602) are "ensemble" vocal motets accompanied by organ from the figured bass, and have nothing to do with the idea of "contending." On the other hand, Monteverdi's Seventh Book of Madrigals (1619) bears the title *Concerto. Settimo libro de madrigali* ... and the music illustrates both meanings of *concerto*. At the end of the 17th century and afterwards, the term *concerto* is used to describe concertos as different as vocal concertos (voices accompanied by instruments), "orchestral concertos," *concerti grossi,* and solo *concerti*. Thus J. S. Bach uses the word *Concerto* as the title of a whole cantata, in the sense that it is an ensemble of voices and instruments. At the same time, a *concerto* may have a group of soloists (the *concertino*) in the purely instrumental *concerto grosso,* used in contrast or rivalry with the *tutti* or orchestral mass. This same rivalry and contention is intensified in the case of the solo concerto, which contrasts the superior tone, technique, and (sometimes) different thematic material of the soloist with the tone, technique, and music of the orchestra. The title *concerto* may also be applied to

43

---

[17] See *Sylva Sylvorum* (1627), Century III, No. 278.

purely instrumental works, found between c. 1680 and 1750, that have
no solo parts whatever—the so-called "orchestral" or *ripieno* concerto—
as, for example, in the Op. 7 of Albicastro (c. 1700-5); similarly, there
are numerous concertos by Corelli, Vivaldi, and Handel (among others)
in which at least one movement has no solo part(s). In this type of
concerto or movement only the idea of "joining together" is present,
not that of "rivalry, contrast, or contention."

The old "ensemble" meaning of concerto explains why, in a number
of cases, the *sinfonia* (i.e., "sounding together") resembles the concerto,
and is even equated with it at times.[18] It also helps explain why a sonata
played by the orchestra is sometimes called a *concerto,* thus becoming,
as it were, a "sonata in concerto"; and why the terms *sinfonia, sonata,*
and *concerto* are sometimes closely identified, as well as often distinguished! A particularly interesting example, illustrating the relationship
and distinction between the three terms, is afforded by Tomaso Albinoni's Op. 2 (c. 1700), the title of which reads: *Sinfonie e concerti a
cinque . . .* , and the music of which is in five real parts (2 violins, 2
violas, and cello and bass for the continuo). In the part-books, however,
each of the 6 *sinfonie* is labelled *sonata,* and each uses the four-move-
ment order (slow, fast, slow, fast) and the internal structure of the
typical *sonata da chiesa.* Thus Albinoni's *sinfonie* of Op. 2 are nothing
but orchestral sonatas. In this work Albinoni sharply distinguishes the 6
concerti from the 6 *sinfonie.* For the former there is an additional (6th)
part for a solo violin, and the order and number of movements (typically, fast, slow, fast) and the style of "rivalry and contention" between
the soloist and the five-voiced orchestral mass are plainly those of the
solo concerto. Other composers do not necessarily make such sharp
distinctions, and many single movements of concertos are indistinguish-
able in structure and style from those of the contemporary sonata.[19]

A clear distinction between *sinfonia* and *concerto* has never been

[18] Angelo Berardi, *Miscellanea musicale,* Bologna, 1689, p. 45: "Concertos for
violin and other instruments are called *sinfonie;* today one appreciates particularly
those of Sig. Arcangelo Corelli, a celebrated violinist . . ." See Marc Pincherle,
Corelli, Paris, 1933, p. 130; and Antonio Capri, *Tartini,* 1945, p. 108.

[19] Schering applied the term *concerto-sinfonia* to such orchestral sonatas without
solo parts, but the sharp distinction between *concerto* and *sinfonia,* evident in Albinoni's Op. 2, is sufficient to make Schering's term ambiguous and confusing. Bukofzer's term *orchestral concerto* is better. More recently, I suggested the term *concerto-
sonata* (see *Notes,* March, 1956, p. 330). Remo Giazotto, in his book *Tomaso
Albinoni* (1945), has anticipated me with his term *sonata-concerto* (p. 98 ff).
Another possible term is *ensemble-concerto.*

convincingly demonstrated—if indeed it is really possible to do so. All that can be said with confidence is this: 1) a *sinfonia (symphonia)* may be an independent piece for instruments alone, as in an overture or separate piece in an opera; 2) by transfer of its meaning of "joining together of sound" or "ensemble," it may be a species of concerto; and 3) an ensemble of voices and instruments (e.g., *symphonia sacra*). In view of what has been said above, it is dubious if Manfred Bukofzer's distinction with respect to the *concerti* and *sinfonie* of Torelli's Op. 5 (1692) can be maintained *generally*. In his *Music in the Baroque Era* (p. 226), Bukofzer says: "This type [the "orchestral concerto"] is characterized not by opposed groups or contrasted sections, but by melodic emphasis on a uniformly reinforced violin part and the bass. This feature, typical of continuo-homophony, explains the mystery why the pieces are called concertos: they are without exception written in concerto style, quite in contrast with the luxuriant counterpoint of the sinfonie." Apart from Torelli, the "orchestral concerto," in the sense of a concerto without solo parts, is not always characterized by "melodic emphasis on a uniformly reinforced violin part and the bass." There are numerous contrapuntal, even fugal, movements which contradict this statement. Nor is the *sinfonia* in general necessarily characterized by luxuriant counterpoint. The reverse is true in the typical *sinfonia* of Vivaldi, which closely resembles the solo concerto in homophonic texture and three-movement form (fast, slow, fast).

45

Throughout the history of the concerto, the term *concerto* has still another meaning. As an extension of its "ensemble" connotation, it suggests a musical event, ranging in importance from the simplest gathering of players to a formal symphony concert. In Italian the single term *concerto* means both "concert" as an event and "concerto" as a piece for soloist and orchestra. English and French distinguish "concert" and "concerto." The French Dictionary (Larousse), for example, defines "concert" in the sense of the English word "concert," and calls "concerto" a "mot ital.," describing it as a piece for an instrument with orchestral accompaniment. This same kind of distinction may also be found in 18th-century French treatises, where a real concerto (in the sense of a Vivaldi concerto) was called "concerto" and an assemblage of persons at a concert or a piece for a musical ensemble in general was called "concert." Hence the Couperin "Concerts Royaux" are not concertos in the modern English sense. To make the proper distinctions a French composer like Leclair used the Italian word "concerto" for his concertos modelled on the Italians. In modern German, "Konzert" means both "concert" and "concerto" but it is interesting that this form is a relatively recent spelling. J. G. Walther (1732) uses "concerto" *or* "concert" to cover both meanings, and this spelling is used well into the 19th century (cf. Weber's *Concertstück* for piano and orchestra, 1821).

And now to return *da capo* to Franz Giegling and to *concerto* vs. *conserto*. I maintain, in summary, that a concerto is really a concerto in both meanings outlined above. This view explains all cases, is based on documentary evidence germane to the specialized *musical* meaning, and above all, it does not violate a conclusion that can be arrived at inductively by any musician who examines a sufficient number of pieces of music labelled *concerto* between the years 1550 and 1750. In short, an examination of the music must inevitably lead to the same conclusion as the documents of the time that a concerto embraces the dual concept explained above: 1) an ensemble piece "joining together" different bodies of sound, vocal and/or instrumental, but having no solo parts "contending with each other"; and 2) a piece featuring the "contending rivalry, or opposition" of soloist(s) and larger, contrasting, orchestral body (the *tutti*). It goes without saying that these two meanings have a wide range of manifestations in individual concertos.

At any rate, the notion that the term *concerto* is derived solely from the Latin *consero* or the Italian *conserto* is untenable; and the complementary idea that the concerto is *limited* to the concept of "joining together" is, at best, only half the story. Besides, this half is valid only to the middle of the 18th century, after which the basic notion of the concerto as music is limited primarily to the concept of "contentione ò contrasto."

Finally, to answer the initial question "When is a concerto not a concerto?" In a word, a concerto is not a concerto when it is given the pronunciation and spelling *conserto* in colloquial-Tuscan or Spanish-Neapolitan speech. But this is a mere distinction of orthography. As regards all else, the fact is that a *conserto* is a *concierto* is a *concerto*.

46

ITALIAN SECULAR MONODY
FROM 1600 TO 1635

AN INTRODUCTORY SURVEY[1]

By NIGEL FORTUNE

MOST histories of music give an unbalanced picture of how solo song developed in early 17th-century Italy. Opera productions at Florence and Mantua fill the scene, and solo songs—if they are dealt with at all—are fitted uncomfortably into an odd corner. Caccini will be mentioned, of course, and his *Le Nuove Musiche* as well (though usually with the wrong date of publication); Peri's name will appear if we are very lucky, and Signor Parisotti's nose for the pretty trifles of Andrea Falconieri and Raffaello Rontani may earn them a disdainful line or two. But to treat Italian song in this way is to warp the facts quite wantonly. These solo songs were published not by the

[1] I would like to say how much I have profited in preparing this paper from the very generous guidance of Mr. Thurston Dart in matters of style, etc. My work in this field has also been greatly assisted and encouraged by M. Bence Szabolcsi, of Budapest; his most generous action was to type out and send to me a copy of his unpublished dissertation *Benedetti und Saracini: Beiträge zur Geschichte der Monodie*, Leipzig, 1923.

dozen but by the gross; they reached a far wider public than operas ever did; they were sung throughout Italy; and there is far more to them than Parisotti ever knew. To claim that all monody is magnificent would be ridiculous; to dismiss it as arid amateur music, dead and bloodless, is to throw away song after song of the greatest beauty.

The names in the history books are the names of opera composers —Monteverdi, Peri, Marco da Gagliano; these men put nearly all their best music into their stage works, and their monodies were often published either in miscellanies of sacred music, stage music, and songs for two or three voices, or else in collections scraped together by devoted pupils. Monteverdi's monodies, like the songs of Mozart and Haydn, form a relatively unimportant part of his total output; yet those of Peri and Gagliano are among their finest music. Opera, like a thick hedge, hides monody from the historian; it is easy for him to assume that if music is not operatic it cannot be very interesting, and easy to forget that this age, too, had its Duparcs and its Warlocks, its Zelters and its Reichardts (even if it could not produce a genius to rank with Wolf or Fauré). For instance, one fault of Leo Schrade's book on Monteverdi[2]—and if the book is to live up to its subtitle it is not an unexpected fault—is his tendency to equate Florentine monody only with the rather tedious recitative of Caccini's *Euridice;* the present survey will try to show that this stiff and severe style of vocal writing is anything but typical of monody as a whole. It is a style found only in opera, in "Lettere Amorose" (like the one in Monteverdi's seventh book of madrigals), in tragic scenas like Rinuccini's *Lamento d'Arianna* (set to music by several composers), in certain pastoral dialogues and settings of *ottave,* and in a mere handful of other songs by a mere handful of composers. Certainly the word "recitativo" was used often enough; but as Doni remarks,[3] it usually meant no more than solo song, and most monodies have little to do with the early declamatory experiments of the Florentine Camerata.

Our faulty view of monody may be ascribed to the lack of critical attention it has received; there is no study of monody in English, and there are few enough in other languages. Few monodies are available in reliable reprints.[4] Riemann was more discriminating but less comprehen-

---

[2] *Monteverdi: Creator of Modern Music,* New York, 1950.

[3] In *Trattato della Musica Scenica,* X (*De' Trattati di Musica,* Florence, 1763, II, 27).

[4] By far the most reliable are those in *La Flora,* ed. Knud Jeppesen, 3 vols., Copenhagen, 1949. This collection includes songs by several of the composers mentioned in the present study. At least one song by Caccini appears in nearly every history of music or historical anthology of music.

sive than Leichtentritt, yet Leichtentritt made some bad mistakes, and his study is often little more than a list of titles.[5] Eugen Schmitz is sounder,[6] and Einstein, Federico Ghisi, and Bence Szabolcsi have done good work on certain aspects of this music. The original list of secular song-books printed by Leichtentritt was corrected and amplified by Schmitz,[7] and I hope one day to publish an even more up-to-date list. The scholar is further handicapped by the fact that the theorists and historians of the period were so strangely quiet about monody. The prefaces to the song-books themselves sometimes contain revealing remarks, and Caccini's preface to Le Nuove Musiche was of course the manifesto of the new style;[8] Doni wrote shrewdly, but in very general terms, about it[9] (considering that he wrote so late and was not yet born when Rinuccini, Peri, and Jacopo Corsi were preparing their Dafne, he is remarkably uninformative); Severo Bonini, more detailed, lacked discrimination, and he was too narrowly concerned with his personal friends in Florence;[10] Pietro della Valle talked about popular songs and mentioned by name a cantata by Luigi Rossi.[11] But these men—and men like Banchieri, Cesare Crivellati, Vincenzo Giustiniani, and Agostino Pisa—were usually too tediously preoccupied with performers, the excellence of Gesualdo, the nature of Greek music, or problems of proportion to say anything about the monodists.

49

THE CRISIS IN ITALIAN MUSIC

Chamber monodies came into favor at a time of radical change in Italian music. It was a time when few composers still wrote placid, dia-

[5] For Riemann, cf. his Handbuch der Musikgeschichte, II: 2 (Das Generalbasszeitalter), 2nd ed., Leipzig, 1922; for Leichtentritt, cf. his chapter Der monodische Kammermusikstil in Italien bis gegen 1650 in his revised 3rd. ed. of Ambros's Geschichte der Musik, Leipzig, 1909, pp.773-892.

[6] Cf. Geschichte der weltlichen Solokantate, Leipzig, 1914, pp. 1-66; and Zur Frühgeschichte der lyrischen Monodie Italiens im 17. Jahrhundert, in Jahrbuch der Musikbibliothek Peters, XVIII (1911), 35- 48.

[7] Cf. Leichtentritt, op.cit., p.777, and Schmitz in Jahrbuch, p.48.

[8] Cf. Oliver Strunk, Source Readings in Music History, New York, 1951, pp.377-92.

[9] Cf., especially, Trattato della Musica Scenica (Trattati, II, 1-144) and part of Discorso sopra la Perfettione delle Melodie (Compendio del trattato de' generi e de'modi della Musica, Rome, 1635, pp.95-125).

[10] Cf. Prima parte de'Discorsi e Regole sovra la Musica (Biblioteca Riccardiana, Florence, MS 2218). Extract in Angelo Solerti, Le Origini del Melodramma, Turin, 1903, pp.129-39 (cf. especially pp.137-8).

[11] Cf. Della Musica dell'età nostra che non è punto inferiore, anzi è migliore di quella dell'età passata (1640). In Solerti, op.cit., pp.148-79.

tonic, linear music for voices, unsupported by instruments. They now attempted to underline the emotional words in their texts by using free declamation, bizarre harmonies, chromatic melodies, and elaborate ornaments; in fact, they treated their texts with a respect they had not shown them for years. They thought in terms of chords and no longer in terms of counterpoint. They developed a rudimentary system of tonality. Above all, they strove after contrast—contrast of rhythm, of note-values, of tone-color. Echoes and antiphonal effects are only the two most obvious devices that they employed to this end. Now, the preference for drama and contrast is by no means confined to music. One glance at the astonishing contrast of bright light and shadow in a typical painting by Caravaggio tells us that the ideals of, say, Raphael, have been thrown overboard in the quest for the dramatic, the restless, the exciting, the violent, the shocking. All the features of the music of the new century are present in the works of one man—Monteverdi. Indeed, we may hear them in the course of a single work—the Vespers of 1610; moreover, some of its pages are in the style of the 16th century. Many of these features confront us, too, in the spacious and sumptuous creations of Giovanni Gabrieli. Nothing could illustrate better the differences between the old world and the new than a comparison of Giovanni's setting of the words "timor et tremor" (after 1600) with that of his uncle Andrea (1565).[12]

Gabrieli was succeeded at St. Mark's, Venice, by musicians like Alessandro Grandi, who helped to develop the new kind of music popular in the church. This music required only a few voices to perform it, and it made use of the *basso continuo*. The birth of the *continuo* hammered, as it were, the last nail into the coffin of Palestrina. Perhaps the commonest attitude of the new century towards Palestrina and all he stood for was that of della Valle. This "famous music" and works like it, he writes, " are esteemed nowadays not for their practical value, but so that they may be preserved in a museum as very beautiful antiques."[13] And that, I may add, was written in Rome! A church composer writing in Rome or in the country could perhaps afford to sniff at the luxuriance of Gabrieli or at the queer experiments of those dilettanti in Florence; but the *continuo* had come to stay, and in the end he was forced to adopt it himself. Even those composers, like the Anerio brothers or Soriano, who professed to keep alive the traditional style of Palestrina succumbed to the new invention. They actually brought the master's work

[12] *Cf.* Manfred Bukofzer, *Music in the Baroque Era*, New York, 1947, pp.22-3.

[13] *Cf.* Solerti, *op.cit.*, p.173.

up to date. And, ironically enough, Viadana had in the first place added an organ part to his *Cento Concerti Ecclesiastici* (1602) not because he wanted to be up-to-date, but because he wanted to save all he could from the music of the past.[14] As a result of the revolution caused by the new invention, the outer parts of a composition became the dominant ones; the *continuo*-player filled in the inner parts at sight.

There had been plenty of solo vocal music in the 16th century: arrangements of frottolas and madrigals to be sung to the lute or to a consort of viols, improvised settings of stanzas from Ariosto's *Orlando Furioso,* the songs, both simple and elaborate, that were sung in masques performed between the acts of plays at the Florentine court, the brilliant displays of the three famous ladies who sang at the court of Ferrara towards the end of the century, and so on. During the 16th century, too, madrigals became more disjointed and dramatic, the upper parts began to stand out from the others, instruments mingled with the voices as well as replacing the lower ones. But madrigals were as much a dead end as Palestrina himself. The solo madrigals of the 17th century had the same form as the polyphonic ones of the 16th. All that happened was that the craze for solo songs injected new life into a dying form; the craze itself owed much more to the solo songs and madrigals of the later 16th century than to the researches of Galilei, Mei, and the rest of the Camerata into Greek music. But the effects of even the most potent injection do not last forever. When solo madrigals fell out of fashion about 1625, the madrigal as an art-form virtually died too. It was the little canzonets and ballets of men like Gastoldi and Ferretti that held the secret for the future. In their arias the composers of the early 17th century took these pieces as their models. They made their melodies more suave and rounded, and they developed the conception of tonality that we can already see in their models. In this way they paved the way for chamber cantatas, in which the art of *bel canto* reached its highest peak. Music for instruments was often just as restless and dramatic as that for voices: we have only to think of the toccatas of Frescobaldi. In new forms like the violin sonata composers tried to write idiomatically for instruments. But their first efforts were very tentative, and it would be idle to seek in them an expression of the drama and turbulence of the times.

The earliest operas were performed before distinguished audiences at ducal courts or in cardinals' palaces. But there were only very few of them, and each was heard only two or three times. If they were printed

51

---

[14] A point first appreciated, I think, in Schrade, *op.cit.,* p.164.

at all, they hardly ever went into a second edition; and, although they included a brilliant masterpiece like *Orfeo,* their influence upon the musical taste of the time can only have been small. Contrast that with the influence of chamber monodies. As soon as Caccini published *Le Nuove Musiche* in 1602, all kinds of musicians started writing songs of the same type. When they had written twenty or thirty they would get them published, usually under the title of *Musiche.* Many of these song-books went into two or more editions, and it is quite clear that it was through them and not through operas that the new style became so widely known in Italy.[15] And not only in Italy; some monodists, such as Camillo Orlandi and Francesco Rasi, worked or traveled abroad. They must have done much to introduce the "new music" to Germany, Austria, Poland, Dalmatia, and England.

The Composers

Until about 1620 nearly all the best composers of monodies were either amateurs or court musicians. The professional composers of a merchant city like Venice did not come into their own until after 1620. We would expect the amateurs to be among the most intrepid and unconventional composers of the time, and so they were. Some, like Rasi, were famous executants; some—Sigismondo d'India, for instance—held important musical posts; and others belonged to one of the professions, like the lawyers Domenico Maria Melli[16] and Desiderio Pecci. Most of them, however, were wealthy aristocrats with plenty of leisure, eager to dabble in the latest fashion: Ludovico Bellanda, Bartolommeo Cesana, Claudio Saracini, or the engaging eccentric, Bellerofonte Castaldi. A few English madrigalists—Bateson, Cavendish, and Wilbye are examples—published one or two books of madrigals when they were still quite young (just, perhaps, to be in the fashion), and then were never heard of again. So it was with these Italian amateurs. Saracini, for instance, gave up writing monodies when he was thirty-eight, though we know that he lived for another twenty-five years. The liberal courts of the Medici Grand Dukes, Ferdinand I (one of the greatest rulers in the history of the family) and his ailing son Cosimo II, in Florence and of Charles Emmanuel I, Duke of Savoy, in Turin saw the production of countless plays, ballets, and musical entertainments, for which

[15] However, we must not overlook the important part played by the lament from Monteverdi's *Arianna.* Its success was phenomenal, and Bonini tells us that every musical household had its copy (*cf.* Solerti, *op.cit.,* p.139).

[16] Melli was so early in the field that he published two books of songs in 1602, the first of which very probably appeared about two months before *Le Nuove Musiche.*

no expense was spared.[17] The composition of monodies was a sophisticated art. Small wonder, then, that it flourished in such cultivated surroundings. The song-books often contain songs that had been sung in occasional entertainments, and many other songs that do not bear the stamp of stage music may well have been sung at the festive soirées of the annual carnival. A few noble monodists held important offices at these courts (e.g. Peri and Giovanni del Turco in Florence and d'India in Turin; in fact it was the enterprising way in which d'India directed the music at Turin that put it on the musical map). Many other musicians of lesser birth helped maintain the musical life of these courts and of smaller ones like those at Modena, Parma, or Piacenza; they, too, composed many fine songs. They ranged from famous singers (Caccini and his daughters) or instrumentalists (Biagio Marini) down to the humblest employees (Vincenzio Calestani). Gradually the fortunes of these courts declined, and after 1620 the most interesting monodies were written in Venice. She had scarcely a rival. The golden age of Ferrara was over even before 1600; the Mantuans were interested mainly in operas, and even before the terrible sack of their city in 1630 they had known many years of political unrest; no artist could have found it easy to work under the harsh Spanish yoke in Naples. In cities without a court there was no monody worth mentioning: in Milan there was none at all, in Bologna next to nothing. Yet would one expect any in a center of reaction so long associated with the names of Artusi and, later, Arresti? Of course, people must have bought books of monodies in these places. But even if they liked these fashionable songs, they cannot have communicated their enthusiasm to the composers in their midst.

We need not be surprised if those professional composers who went on writing imitation Palestrina looked askance at a style practiced in the main by elegant upstarts. They must have felt like the Gothic craftsmen in England fifty years before, when Italian classicism had been taken up in exactly the same way as the composition of monodies by the princes, courtiers, and dilettanti of their own day. "Everywhere the older styles were ignored in the courtly scramble after the new, and in England the centuries-old knowledge of the master masons was driven into exile by the superficial studies of dilettanti provided with foreign

53

---

[17] Solerti dealt exhaustively with the entertainments at both courts: on Florence cf. *Musica, Ballo e Drammatica alla Corte medicea,* Florence, 1905; and on Turin cf. *Feste musicali alla Corte di Savoia nella prima metà del secolo XVII,* in *Rivista Musicale Italiana,* XI (1904), 675-724.

pattern-books."[18] It is the same story. Courtly amateurs led the drive against counterpoint and polyphony, against the music that had invaded their land from the Gothic north. Doni shows how absurd even an intelligent fanatic could become in this war against the Gothic when he scoffs at the very sound of names like Ockeghem and Obrecht to prove how barbarous these composers were. The "pattern-books" of early 17th-century music were the first books of monodies; within a few years many of their features had become stereotyped devices without which no monody was worth writing. Nevertheless, plenty of monodies were written by choirmasters who were among the most diligent church composers of the age (Antonio Cifra, Giovanni Ghizzolo), by obscure church organists (Pietro Pace, Gabriello Puliti), and by rather too worldly priests and monks (Giacomo Fornaci, Horatio Tarditi).

Nearly all these composers, from the highest court official to the lowest servant of the Church, depended upon a well established system of patronage. Each one grovelled in a fulsome dedication before his chosen protector, who might be duke, prince, or other nobleman, great lady, distinguished soldier, statesman, mayor, academician, archbishop, cardinal or lesser ecclesiastical eminence—or even one of themselves. Each was moved as much by fear of the world's harsh criticism as by veneration of his "most reverend patron." This, of course, is a familiar story throughout Europe at this time and for many years to come. The cost to the scholar of such servility is that the dedications tell him so few of the things he really wants to know.

Now, when an art-form becomes as modish as secular monodies were in the early decades of the 17th century, its very popularity may become a curse. C. S. Lewis has well described what happens: "Its characteristics are formalized. A stereotyped monotony, unnoticed by contemporaries but cruelly apparent to posterity, begins to invade it . . . In the second place, a dominant form tends to attract to itself writers whose talents would have fitted them much better for work of some other kind . . . And thirdly—which is most disastrous—a dominant form attracts to itself those who ought not to have written at all; it becomes a kind of trap or drain towards which bad work moves by a certain 'kindly enclyning.' Youthful vanity and dullness, determined to write, will almost certainly write in the dominant form of their epoch."[19] So it was with chamber monodies. Many a would-be composer, beguiled by the prospect of easy fame that the latest fashion offered him, displayed his

[18] Cf. John Harvey, Gothic England, London, 1947, p.145.
[19] Cf. The Allegory of Love, London, 6th ed., 1951, pp.232-3.

utter unfitness for the part. It was so much more profitable, after all, to offer to a publisher your latest set of "Amorous Sighs" than to write an opera that might never be produced, let alone printed. And so for every masterpiece by Saracini or d'India there are two or three insipid products of "youthful vanity and dullness." Nevertheless, the roll of important monodists is an impressive one. Manfred Bukofzer has listed them,[20] and I would quarrel with him only for including Pace, Tarditi, and the books edited by Giovanni Stefani, and for leaving out Calestani and Giulio San Pietro de'Negri. We may think, quite rightly, that Caccini is historically important; we may marvel at the radical audacities of Saracini;[21] but, in the end, one feels that the most striking of these composers is Sigismondo d'India (1562?-c.1630). I am sure that an exhaustive study of his monodies (especially the laments that he published in his last two collections of *Musiche* in 1621 and 1623), his polyphonic madrigals, his sacred works, and his occasional music would show him to be one of the outstanding European composers of his time.[22]

55

PUBLICATION AND PERFORMANCE

We would do well not to regard secular monodies as an isolated musical form. As early as 1602 and 1606, Melli and Domenico Brunetti had included dialogues and duets in their song-books. The dialogues of this period contained the germs of the chamber cantata: they included arioso passages sung by alternate voices, and they ended with a duet. There were two kinds of duet. In one kind, the lower voice doubled the *continuo;* the other kind were in a modern *concertato* style. The second type soon became so popular that publishers brought out whole books devoted to them; among these books were such masterly collections as those of d'India (1615) and Giovanni Valentini (1622). In the same

[20] *Cf. op.cit.,* p.29.

[21] Leichtentritt has many useful examples of them (*cf. op.cit.,* pp.818-32); but he made some bad slips in his transcriptions so that the harmonic acerbities sometimes seem even more startling than they really are.

[22] It is all the more astonishing, then, that of the histories of music in English that I know Prunières's *A New History of Music,* transl. by Edward Lockspeiser, New York, 1943, is the only one to mention d'India. Federico Mompellio has twice given details of his life and works: in the appendix to his edition of d'India's first book of five-voiced madrigals (*I Classici musicali italiani,* Vol. 10, Milan, 1942); and, less fully, in *Pietro Vinci, madrigalista siciliano,* Milan, 1937, pp.189-93. Stanislao Cordero di Pamparato describes in detail d'India's years in Turin and clears up some earlier misconceptions about him, in *I Musici alla Corte di Carlo Emanuele I di Savoia,* in *Biblioteca della Società Storica Subalpina,* CXXI, Turin, 1930, pp.84-93. As far as I know, not one of d'India's monodies has been reprinted.

year as *Le Nuove Musiche* Salomone Rossi published polyphonic madrigals to which a *continuo* part had been added. Within a few years collections of *continuo*-madrigals or *Musiche* for one to five or even more voices
were extremely common.[23] Monodies and madrigals clothed in the latest
fashion thus met in the same books. Francesco Turini's *Madrigali Concertati a 2-4* (1624) actually includes a solo cantata (at least Turini
calls it that, though it is really no more than a "Lettera Amorosa").
The song-books catered for violinists, too. Composers not only added
concertato parts for violins to their songs (Marini, Paolo Quagliati)
but also included a few elementary "sonatas" and toccatas (Marc'
Antonio Negri). All the same, there were plenty of enthusiastic monodists who would have no truck with *concertato*-madrigals—Bellanda
and Pietro Benedetti, for instance; yet few were quite so enthusiastic as
Saracini, who wrote book after book of solo songs in the most up-to-
date manner, accompanied only by the *continuo*.

56   The favorite voices for solo songs were soprano or mezzo-soprano
and tenor. This is hardly surprising in an age that worshipped the art
of virtuosos like Vittoria Archilei, Adriana Basile, Peri, and Rasi. They
had made their name in operas, but many of them must have sung the
latest monodies to small, distinguished gatherings at the courts of Florence, Modena, or Turin. The cardinals of Rome, too, vied with each
other to get hold of the most brilliant singers for their lavish musical
evenings. These singers sang monodies in the way the composers expected.
They "spoke in song," they enunciated every syllable clearly, they tried
to communicate to their audiences the emotions aroused by the words,
they avoided absurd gestures, and so on. Many songs, of course, were
composed for the amateur to sing in his own home: some composers
stated quite openly that they had kept their songs simple for this reason.
Monodies might also be sung in some musical academy or other. The
academies of Italy were an institution that had survived from the
Renaissance; they were clubs where cultured men met to discuss some
branch of science, art, or letters. However, far fewer academies specialized in music than in literature or philology, and, even in these few,
monodies, which needed only one or two people to perform them, were
unlikely to have the same appeal as music that required several mem-

---

[23] *Cf.* two papers by Eugen Schmitz: *Zur Geschichte des italienischen Kam-
merduetts im 17. Jahrhundert,* in *Jahrbuch der Musikbibliothek Peters, XXIII*
(1916), 43-60; and *Zur Geschichte des italienischen Continuo-Madrigals im 17.
Jahrhundert,* in *Sammelbände der internationalen Musikgesellschaft,* XI (1910),
509-28.

bers to sit round a table with their part-books.[24] If a song were written for a bass or baritone, like the virtuoso Melchior Palontrotti, it would be sure to have a very florid vocal line (which usually turned out to be a variation on the bass). The accompaniments of chamber monodies had to be realized discreetly from the *continuo* line on a harpsichord, a theorbo, a chitarrone, or a double harp. A guitar was used only for more popular songs. The bass supported the melodic line, and the accompaniment was conceived harmonically; it was quite different, therefore, from the quasi-polyphonic accompaniment of the typical lute-song. Few monodies had basses as fully figured as those in *Le Nuove Musiche;* the instructions of contemporary writers like Agostino Agazzari[25] on how to realize them are thus more welcome than ever. A few songs have survived in manuscript with realized accompaniments; the texture of these accompaniments is always chordal. I have come across a few song-books that provide a tablature for the chitarrone, and they tell the same story.

The Three Cities

57

Monodies were written in three main centers: Florence, Rome, and Venice. The songs of the three cities sometimes resembled each other, especially when they made use of certain structural devices, such as echo effects. Again, stock basses like the Romanesca, the Ruggiero, or the Gazzella were nearly always used both in Florence and Rome (though hardly ever in Venice) when *ottave* or similar poetic forms were set to music. In most respects, however, the song-styles of the three cities were very different. It is now time to see what these differences were.

(a) *Florence*[26]

Florence was the most radical center of the three. It was the place

[24] This would be less true after about 1630. In 1635 Doni still came across plenty of people who enjoyed listening to madrigals because they found monody ("Musiche Recitative") boring (*cf. Compendio*, pp.102-3); but he says that there were many others who had ears only for monody, and in 1640 della Valle could write as follows: "Nowadays fewer madrigals are being written because few people sing them, nor are there opportunities for doing so. People prefer to listen to someone singing boldly by heart to his own instrumental accompaniment than to watch four or five friends singing at a table with the music in front of them, for that is too crabbed and learned." (Solerti, *Origini*, p.171.)

[25] Agazzari's *Del sonare sopra il basso* (1607) is translated in Strunk, *op.cit.*, pp.424-31.

[26] The songs of d'India (who from 1611 to 1623 worked in Turin) and of Saracini (who came from Siena), which are among the finest of the age, resemble those of the radical Florentine composers more than those of any other city; it is perhaps a good idea, then, to regard them as "Florentine" composers.

where monodies first flourished, the one where they first died out. It was the home of Caccini and his friends, who determined the two main forms of chamber monodies: the madrigal and the aria. In the through-composed madrigal a free expressive arioso (a blend of recitative and aria) unfolded over a slowly moving bass. Madrigals were always in common time. They sometimes wandered through a wide range of "keys"—Florentine composers undermined the influence of the modes much more drastically than did their contemporaries in Rome. Composers tried to bring unity and organization to what was essentially a free form. They did this in a number of ways: by sequential or exact repetition of internal phrases or of the closing measures, by repeating constantly a striking melodic or rhythmic figure, or by introducing snatches of imitation between the vocal line and the bass (even Caccini could not manage without a *little* counterpoint). The form ABB is much rarer than some writers have supposed. The bane of the madrigal, especially in the hands of lesser men, was the temptation to punctuate the unfolding arioso with a series of emphatic perfect cadences. The end of each line of the text could no longer be concealed by polyphony, and the best madrigalists were those who managed to write their arioso in expansive phrases, which stressed only the more important poetic cadences.

The Florentines loved to clothe their extravagant texts with bizarre harmonic progressions and clashes and with expressive, truly vocal ornaments called *gorge*. These ornaments were introduced by Caccini, who had in turn made more expressive and dependent upon the text the kind of ornaments recommended in certain late 16th-century hand-books on the technique of diminution. The two commonest were the *gruppo* (the same as our trill) and the *trillo* (the same note repeated on the same syllable in ever-shortening values, generally in the last measure but one of a phrase). On the other hand, the runs and divisions in Roman madrigals were still very like their 16th-century predecessors, i.e. rather stiff and inexpressive. Many monodists (not only Florentines) also treated embellishments merely as word-painting in order to illustrate words like "waves" and "laughter." They still used all sorts of other formulas, too, to illustrate sighing, trembling, swooning, silence, and all the other stock-in-trade of madrigal verse—yes, and even "eye-music" as well when they wanted to emphasize words like "white" or "black." It was just this naive literalism that Vincenzo

Galilei had attacked so fiercely in the madrigals of the 16th century.[27]
It is easy to imagine his dismay had he lived to see it invade the new
kind of "pure" solo song which he had advocated. (We should remember, though, that it took very little to shock him: he was the grimmest
of ascetics, who believed that any pleasure that music might arouse in
the listener only distracted from its moral purpose, and was not merely
unwholesome but downright dangerous.) The more radical monodists,
however, were more careful, and seem to have used *gorge* to emphasize
less tragic passions such as intense love or pride, and to have kept harmonic asperities for grievous subjects like absence, parting, and faithlessness.

Caccini's specialty and that, too, of a few of his associates like
Rasi was an amiable but rather spineless diatonic lyricism (Ex.1):

Ex. 1.   Francesco Rasi: end of Madrigal *E sì lieto il mio core* (*Madrigali di Diversi Autori posti in Musica,* Florence, 1610, p. 3).
Words by the composer.

By indulging in such "sins" as word-painting or clef-change in the
middle of a song Caccini must have embarrassed the austerer hiero-
phants of the Camerata. But in adopting this lyrical manner he was
clearly following their advice (expressed, for example, in Count Giovanni de'Bardi's famous letter to him)[28] that he reject "the improper
practices employed today by those who search for unusual sounds."
If we listen to the tranquil, diatonic harmonies of Caccini after the
wayward passion of a d'India or a Saracini we can, I think, recognize

[27] The relevant part of his *Dialogo della musica antica e della moderna* (1581)
is in Strunk, *op.cit.,* pp.315-18.
[28] *Cf.* Strunk, *op.cit.,* p.299.

again the difference between the cloying, lachrymose sweetness of Guercino or Guido Reni and the dramatic violence of Caravaggio. Not that Caccini would have been upset to be told that his music was "sweet": Bardi had assembled for him a formidable catalogue of evidence from Aristotle, Plato, Macrobius, Petrarch, and Dante to show that that was just what music should be.[29] We shall see later that those Florentine madrigalists who went in for "unusual sounds" were historically unimportant. Bardi's phrase tells us that as early as 1580 or so such men were frowned upon by those who introduced "the new music." But at least they tried to reflect the restless spirit of the age, whereas the music of Caccini or Rasi may still seem to remind us of the music of the High Renaissance. Domenico Belli and Benedetti are the most important of those composers—we might call them mannerists—for whom no clash was too acrid, no progression too outré. The extracts shown in Ex. 2 are commonplaces in their music:

60

Ex. 2a. Pietro Benedetti: from Madrigal *Ho visto, al pianto mio* (*Musiche*, Florence, 1617, p. 17). Words anonymous.

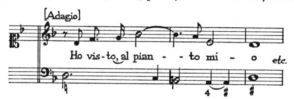

b. Sigismondo d'India: from Madrigal *Tu parti, ahi lasso* (*Le Musiche*, Milan, 1609, p. 18). Words by Giambattista Marino.

Some madrigals seem to show a compromise between the two extreme methods of Caccini and the mannerists; their dignity and grandeur make them perhaps the most striking songs of the time. I can do no better than to urge the reader to have a look at Gagliano's wonderful

[29] *Cf.* Strunk, *op.cit.*, pp. 299-300.

song *Valli profonde*.[30] After 1625 scarcely any solo madrigals were written in Florence (or, as I have pointed out, anywhere else in Italy). Another ten years or so, and Doni and Domenico Mazzocchi were lamenting that "nowadays few people compose and fewer sing madrigals."[31] They both had in mind madrigals for five voices, but they could easily have been referring to solo madrigals instead.

There were two kinds of aria, and both were settings of strophic poems. We may call the first kind strophic variations—an ugly, but a convenient, term. In these songs the instrumental bass was repeated more or less unchanged for every stanza of the poem, while the rather madrigalian vocal line varied over it from verse to verse; sometimes the variations were only very slight, as in Caccini's *Fere selvaggie*.[32] These songs were very similar to those composed over the Romanesca and other stock basses. In that type, however, one symmetrical verse (usually an *ottava*) would be split up into equal parts to form the "verses" of the song. Apart from those in *Le Nuove Musiche*, the finest strophic variations written in Florence were by Belli. The fascinating song *Occhi belli a me severi* from his *Arie* of 1616, which makes use of a ritornel, refrains, and a fairly active bass, is the earliest song to point the way to the later cantata. Strophic variations, however, were more to the taste of Roman composers; and, as we shall see below, the Venetian, Grandi, developed his cantatas out of them. There were no special kinds of texts for strophic variations; in fact the texts were often the same as those of the second kind of aria. This kind was the simple, unornamented strophic air, "scherzo" or canzonet. In these songs the bass usually moved in the same rhythm as the voice. Composers aimed at writing good, memorable tunes with interesting rhythms; they often used dance rhythms or stylized rhythms like *hemiola*. Few composers who wrote good madrigals also wrote good strophic airs; Benedetti, d'India, and Saracini certainly wrote impressive madrigals, but when it came to writing attractive tunes they were easily beaten by minor masters of the genre such as Calestani or Antonio Brunelli. Ex. 3 shows a typical song by Calestani:

61

[30] *La Flora*, I, No. 7.

[31] *Cf.* Mazzocchi's preface to his *Madrigali a 5* (1638), reprinted in Emil Vogel, *Bibliothek der gedruckten weltlichen Vokalmusik Italiens 1500-1700*, Berlin, 1892, I, 436-7. Also *cf.* note 24 above.

[32] *La Flora*, I, No. 3.

Ex. 3. Vincenzio Calestani: Aria *Damigella* (*Madrigali et Arie*, Venice, 1617, p. 35). Words by Gabriello Chiabrera.

1. Da-mi- gel- la Tut-ta bel-la, Versa, ver-sa quel bel vi-no; Fa che

ca- da La ru- gia-da Distil- la-ta di ru-bi-no!

(A ritornel follows, which is a variation on the song itself; there are five further verses.)

The lively spirit of the Florentine court is nowhere reflected more happily than in little songs like this one. But it is a spirit that was soon to fade. Florence became a musical backwater; and the music written there after 1620 is of little interest—a mere shadow, in fact, of that written in Rome and Venice. The Archduchess Christine and the Grand Duchess Maria Maddalena, ruling on behalf of the young Ferdinand II, surrounded themselves with a swarm of parasitic clerics. In material matters they were reckless and extravagant, but when money was wanted for the arts they turned into niggling puritans. Nobody would expect the arts to flourish in an atmosphere like that. Again, the more radical Florentine monodists had renounced tradition more emphatically than their contemporaries elsewhere in Italy. It is not surprising, therefore, to find that their school survived only for a bare twenty years and then itself died without founding a tradition.

(b) *Rome*

To study the songs of Roman composers after those of Florence in her prime is an unrewarding task. Nearly all the finest music composed in Rome was church music. Some of it was fostered by the assiduous Jesuits, who used it to uplift the young or to entice them from their sins (one of which, it seems, was secular music). The Jesuit censors often made life hard for the composers of secular music: if they came across a word like "beauty" used in its secular connotation they would not allow it to be printed.[33] The earliest Roman monody was sacred,

[33] The composers did not seem to object to this practice, especially if they were such good servants of Rome as Giovanni Francesco Anerio, who thought it was "just" even when he was a victim (*cf.* the preface to his *Diporti Musicali* [1617], reprinted in Vogel, *op.cit.*, I,20).

too. The first performance of Cavalieri's *La Rappresentazione di Anima e di Corpo* took place in 1600, and Agazzari's pastoral drama *Eumelio* was given at Jesuit headquarters in 1606. They were followed in 1608 by the *Arie Devote* of Ottavio Durante. The preface[34] to these first Roman monodies is worth reading by the side of Caccini's of 1602, which it follows closely. The songs themselves are full of the most lovely ideas—if only the first secular songs in Rome had been even half as striking! But at first there was nothing more substantial than the inept trifles of the conceited German nobleman Girolamo Kabsperger. He has never recovered from Ambros's amusing debunking,[35] nor, from what one has seen of his work, does he deserve to. Durante had presumably hoped to establish in Rome a taste for Caccini and other Florentine composers. But, faced by stubborn conservatism and incomprehension, he was doomed to failure. The church modes appeared to be impregnable; Roman composers seemed unwilling to develop any sense of tonality. Chromatic conceits were foreign to the solo madrigals of Rome, and embellishments often amounted to no more than the most arid passage-work, with hardly a measure's respite. The songs of Gian Domenico Puliaschi, doubtless provoked by his ability to sing alto, tenor, and bass, show us to what absurd lengths an undisciplined pen might run. Kabsperger, of course, had a great opinion of his own songs, but on the whole they were just like all the other strophic airs composed in Rome — bungling and unmelodious. There is never even a hint of the lilting tunes of Calestani or Brunelli. In the strophic variations of Stefano Landi there is a good deal of suave and dignified arioso, but even he was obviously much more at home in his operas than in his songs. However, Ex. 4 shows him at his sombre best:

63

Ex. 4. Stefano Landi: from strophic variations *Tal'hor vi porgo prieghi* (*Arie*, Venice, 1620, p. 35). Words anonymous.

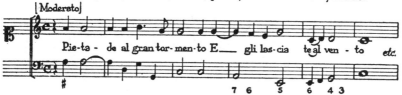

---

[34] Reprinted in Goldschmidt, *Die italienische Gesangsmethode des XVII. Jahrhunderts*, Breslau, 1890, pp.29-33.

[35] In *op.cit.*, p.469ff.

Roman composers made more use than did any of their contemporaries of stylized basses like the Romanesca. Cifra alone set thirty *ottave* over them. But these songs and others like them are so weighed down with otiose festoons of semiquavers that they might have come out of some 16th-century textbook about diminution. Now, there was without doubt a public for secular songs in Rome. Caccini tells us that Roman gentlemen were delighted with his songs and encouraged him to go on working at them.[36] D'India remarks how cardinals flattered *him* for *his* songs and how men of account despised music that was monotonous, pedestrian, and overloaded with divisions.[37] But could there be a better description than this of the common run of Roman songs? Did Their Eminences really admire the dull stuff offered by their own composers? Yet it must have been the popularity of just such music that encouraged the printers to start publishing (in 1621) miscellaneous books of songs by all kinds of Roman composers, from Frescobaldi down to the humblest Papal singer. One of the printers was Giovanni Battista Robletti, and he had an eye to business if anybody had. But these books tell the same story: they, too, are full of insignificant trifles. I think it is worth bearing in mind, though, that in Rome there had been no sharp break with tradition as there had been in Florence. We may regret that the monodists of Rome showed so little interest in the exciting ideas of the Florentines. We may regret that their songs are so tentative and dull. Yet, as we have seen, Florentine monody did not last, and we would do well to ponder whether the most gradual revolutions are not those with the profoundest consequences. There was, then, greater continuity in the music of Rome at this time of upheaval in Italian music than in that of any other city. A series of eminent professional musicians appeared there, the like of whom were hardly seen in Florence. These men, building upon the firm basis of tradition, were able to compose arias and cantatas that were among the most delightful of any music composed in Rome. In 1623 Quagliati published some appealing strophic airs with a design and melodies far more convincing than those of earlier songs. Luigi Rossi, one of Bonini's "two new swans," began to write his chamber cantatas, and soon Carissimi came to live in Rome. But unfortunately the splendors of the Roman cantata are beyond the scope of this paper.

[36] *Cf.* Strunk, *op.cit.,* p.379.

[37] *Cf.* his preface to *Le Musiche* (1609), reprinted (incomplete) in Vogel, *op.cit.,* I, 329-30.

(c) *Venice*

Most monodies were published in Venice, but at first very few were composed there. It is possible that the popularity of Gabrieli's antiphonal works or the lack of an opulent court contributed to this late start; just as it is possible that the appointment of Monteverdi as choirmaster of St. Mark's in 1613 stimulated the local composers to write more monodies. Perhaps it is significant, too, that the first Venetian composer to publish monodies (in 1611) was Marc' Antonio Negri; as the assistant choirmaster at St. Mark's he must have worked very closely with Monteverdi for about seven years. Venetian composers wrote very few solo madrigals. It is difficult to say exactly why — whether it was because they had no opportunity to do so or because they did not want to. By the time they became really interested in writing monodies the madrigal had almost had its day, and there was no point in using a dying form as the vehicle for a new means of expression. Moreover, the genius of Venice, unlike that of Florence, did not lie in the extravagant underlining of passionate texts. Venetian composers liked to write beautiful melodies and to develop them, and they were interested in problems of design. And so, in the main, they preferred strophic songs—and not only strophic airs but strophic bass cantatas as well. Grandi was the first composer to use the term "cantata."[38] He developed his cantatas mainly from two sources: from certain later madrigals, with melodies smoother and more rounded and basses more active than those of earlier madrigals; and, more obviously, from the strophic variations beloved of Roman and Florentine composers. The new cantatas, however, were much more melodious than their forerunners, and the continually varying melodies unfolded more spontaneously over the repeated basses; the basses themselves now flowed steadily in crotchets. Grandi's term was soon adopted by other composers, especially by those, like Giovanni Pietro Berti, who worked with him at St. Mark's. Unfortunately, the only cantatas of Grandi to survive into our own time were destroyed during the Second World War; thus the cantatas of his associates are now more valuable than ever to scholars.[39] Grandi, however, used the same technique in

65

[38] 1620 is the year usually quoted for this innovation; but it should be noted that his *Cantade et Arie* were only *reprinted* in that year and that the original date of publication is unknown.

[39] There are, however, convenient examples from cantatas by Grandi in Bukofzer, *op.cit.*, p.32, and in Prunières, *The Italian Cantata of the Seventeenth Century*, in *Music & Letters*, VII (1926), 41.

some of his motets, which are still extant. The new term seems to have become rather fashionable, and some composers (such as Turini in the "Lettera Amorosa" I mentioned above) used it of songs where to us it may seem inadmissible. I think it is wise to use it only to denote strophic bass cantatas like those of Grandi and Berti and chamber cantatas in several contrasting sections (which became popular only at the very end of the period covered by this survey).

Venetian composers, too, were the first to write arias over *ostinato* basses. They began to do so only about 1630—that is, later than has often been supposed. We may perhaps look upon these songs as a late Venetian counterpart to variations on basses like the Romanesca, which had been so popular elsewhere. Monteverdi and Benedetto Ferrari were the first composers to treat them with skill and resource. Ferrari and Giovanni Felice Sances and their contemporaries often used them for part of some extended lament or cantata (especially one dealing with a pathetic subject). Berti, Grandi, Guglielmo Miniscalchi, and the blind Martino Pesenti are only the best of the many Venetian composers whose strophic airs were among the most delightful—and important —of the time. Their songs were far more melodious than the Roman ones, but they were less influenced by dance rhythms than those written at the ballet-loving courts of Florence and Turin. They were mostly in triple time, they had straightforward harmonies, a clear sense of tonality, and a simple scheme of modulations.[40] It was out of these materials that the great highway of Italian song was built, and not out of the seemingly advanced audacities of the Florentine madrigal, which merely provided a recondite, if agreeable, cul-de-sac. "Throughout the sixteenth century we shall find that the incipient sense of classical tonality is always most strongly to be felt in the music which is most vigorously accented. Form, rhythm and tonality are in fact inseparably bound up with one another . . ."[41] Venetian composers of arias, too, saw that in the music of the 16th century it was the canzonets of Ferretti and his friends and not the madrigals of Gesualdo that held the secret for the future. That future had now arrived, and these Venetians (especially Berti) were quick to follow the lead that had been given them. Berti constructed his melodies in broad, sweeping phrases, and in his long refrains, which were usually quite different in char-

---

[40] I have already touched upon these songs elsewhere, with special reference to their ornamentation; cf. *A Florentine Manuscript and its Place in Italian Song*, in *Acta Musicologica*, XXIII (1952), 129.

[41] Edward J. Dent, *The Musical Form of the Madrigal*, in *Music & Letters*, XI (1930), 232.

acter from the rest of the verse, he would repeat a handful of words (often no more than the last line of the verse) over and over again. Here, indeed, were the first *bel canto* arias. Even in the earliest years of the 17th century solo madrigals had sometimes contained short sections in 3/2 time, which had usually been suggested by some reference in the text to dancing or gaiety.[42] Only after about 1620, however, did composers begin to interpret more rigidly those texts that seemed to demand a contrast among recitative and arioso and aria within a single verse. The best of the very early examples is d'India's *Torna il sereno Zefiro* (1623); to conform exactly to the poet's feelings he writes in all three styles in the course of a single verse (Ex. 5 shows how each of the three sections begins):

Ex. 5.   Sigismondo d'India: from Aria *Torna il sereno Zefiro* (*Le Musiche, libro quinto,* Venice, 1623, p. 22). Words anonymous.

Now, Venetian composers were the first to seize upon this tendency towards contrast, and to develop out of it the idea of recitative and aria. We can also see the germs of the new idea in the way in which Berti treated his refrains. The next step was for this section of the verse to become more conspicuous than ever; then it would blossom out into an aria in its own right, while the words of the main part of the verse were crowded into an introductory recitative. This is just what has happened in a song he published in 1627, called *Da grave incendio oppresso*—the first example of its kind (Ex. 6).

[42] A good example (except that the changes into 3/2 time have little to do with the text) is one of Falconieri's better songs, *Deh, dolc' anima mia* (1619); it was last reprinted in Suzanne Clercx, *Le Baroque et la Musique,* Brussels, 1948, pp.106-8.

Ex. 6.   Giovanni Berti: from Recitative and Aria *Da grave incendio oppresso* (*Cantade et Arie*, 1627, p. 5). Words anonymous.

(First six lines set in this style: 11 measures.)

(Last two lines set in this style, as a refrain. 27 measures, with a return to 4/4 at the very end. Original time-signature C, and note-values halved.)

The form of recitative and aria had come to stay. Ferrari was another composer who worked towards the same goal, although his melodies were less grateful and his touch less sure than Berti's. But Ferrari did not stop short at the aria; he applied the same technique to the nearly obsolete form of the madrigal. In his *Musiche* (1633) we are for the first time unable to tell the difference between madrigals and arias— except, of course, that the arias still have several verses. This second attempt to inject new life into the madrigal was a failure: it merely caused it to be caught up in the triumphal progress of the aria. Even the introductory recitatives had more in common with the recitatives of the early operas than with the solo madrigals of the previous thirty years. Truly "nowadays few people compose . . . madrigals"—at any rate in the form in which they had so recently been familiar.

THE TEXTS

The texts of solo madrigals were often the same as or similar to those set to music by the polyphonic madrigalists of the 16th century. Batista Guarini, a court poet of Ferrara whose pastoral drama *Il Pastor Fido* had endeared him to musicians, lost none of his popularity. He more than any other poet evolved the form of the pastoral dialogue, of which his own *Tirsi morir volea* is the classic example. Its structure gave composers plenty of opportunities for contrasts and refrains, and it was thus another impetus behind the gradual development of the

aria and cantata. A startling new talent, Giambattista Marino, rivaled
Guarini as the most popular poet with the song-writers of the early
17th century. Marino was the leading Italian poet of his day, and, assisted by a horde of imitators, gave his name to a new poetic fashion.
Not that all this is as splendid as it sounds. Marino was no Ariosto and
certainly no Tasso. His talent shone the brighter merely because he
happened to live during the first years of that vast sequence of Italian
poetry which has continued to our own century, whose practitioners
(Leopardi alone excepted) have usually given themselves over to bom-
bast, false heroics, sentimentality, and insipid persiflage. But in spite of
their false taste, insincerity, concealed obscenity, and artificiality, Marino
and his attendant poetasters delighted the composers of madrigals.
For the former held several trump cards, too: they wrote sensual and sophisticated conceits, and they peppered them with fanciful antitheses,
grotesque hyperbole, and opportunities for word-painting. No wonder,
then, that their verses were set to music over and over again. Some
composers—Bartolommeo Barbarino, Castaldi, and Rasi were three—
wrote their own words, or asked their friends to write them. All of them,
however, wrote in the style of the age—the style of Marino. Much
of this verse was patently "poetry for music," and perhaps even more
was written to order than we are apt to think. The endless complaints
of "dying" lovers, the invocations of Phyllis and Cloris, the exaggerated
pains of absence and parting, the nauseating way in which kisses are
discussed—all these features soon become intolerable when we divest
them of their music. At the same time, however, the new domination
of word over music at the beginning of the 17th century kept alive an
interest in poetry more valuable for its own sake. For instance, the
monodists were just as fond of setting sonnets to music as the 16th-
century madrigalists had been. They took a new interest in the sonnets
of older poets like Pietro Bembo and Jacobo Sannazaro, and to anyone
reading the texts of monodies from a purely literary standpoint the sonnets of Petrarch must seem very oases. There seems to have been some
convention that made only a few of them admissible, but
these were set to music time and again. However, it was useless for
Doni to try to lure composers away from their amorous trivialities and to
suggest that they write music for noble and heroic poetry like Petrarch's
Italia mia.[43] Dante had been quite forgotten; the high seriousness of
Tasso's *La Gerusalemme Liberata,* however, is another example of
literary quality that was still admired. From it composers selected several

[43] *Cf. Compendio,* p.122.

of the *ottave* that they set to music over stylized basses.[44] They usually
turn out to be those stanzas that have a certain "baroque" feeling and
that were therefore more to the taste of the new century. Roman composers, though, seem to have been blind to literary quality and to have
used these *ottave* merely to get in a little practice at diminution. It
must have been in this spirit of "anything goes" that Cifra went on
setting Ariosto long after other composers had forgotten about *Orlando
Furioso*.

Marinism had little influence over the poems of strophic songs. At
the turn of the century the dominant poet in this field was Gabriello
Chiabrera. In using intricate and attractive rhythms, which musicians
found irresistible, he was a true successor to Ronsard and the Pléiade.
In his turn Chiabrera strongly influenced Ottavio Rinuccini, the most
successful musical poet of the time. Chiabrera had an enviably light
touch, wit, and a sense of fun, at least in his canzonets—he is a fear-
some bore in heroic mood—but few of his contemporaries knew how
to emulate him. The texts of other strophic songs included a few very
charming spring- and hunting-songs, but on the whole they were quite
worthless as literature and often improper or even downright silly. As
music recovered its old status in the Venetian arias of Berti, Ferrari,
and their successors the words came to matter even less; they did, however, begin to deal with more serious subjects, which once had been
more appropriate to madrigals. Quite early in the 17th century popular
books of canzonets began to appear, often without music; the most
familiar of these collections is that of Remigio Romano. They
usually gave letters for the Spanish guitar and suggested that certain
poems might be sung to music associated with other poems. Such music
was presumably well known. It may even have been folk music, which
at times influenced even the most serious monodists; or it may have
been familiar from *laude spirituali*. No important poet contributed
to this torrent of verses. By 1620 nearly all the texts of monodies were
anonymous, and we have no hope of finding out who wrote them—
as if it mattered! Many of them were of a "regional" nature: one poem
was set by seven Roman monodists and by no others, another attracted
two or three Venetians only, and so on—there are plenty of similar
examples. Again, many verses enjoyed only a very short vogue; they
were set many times during four or five years and were then super-
seded by the latest frivolities.

---

[44] Of the useful list of *ottava*-settings compiled by Einstein in *Notes*, VIII (1951),
cf. pp.629-30.

*   *
*

The object of this paper has been merely to give a general picture
of Italian secular monodies in the first third of the 17th century— to
put into proper perspective a class of music that has never received
the attention it deserves. I have not thought this the place to offer new
biographical details, or to launch into detailed analysis of individual
madrigals and arias. But I have tried to show, among other things, that
we should not allow the operas of the time to hide monodies from us
in the way that students of 16th-century Italian music used to allow
the infallible figure of Palestrina to blot out the madrigalists. I have
tried to stress, too, that the songs composed in various parts of Italy
were very different from each other: how Florence, the most important
center for monodies early in the century, soon became unimportant;
how Roman composers got off to a slow start in this field, but came into
their own in the heyday of the chamber cantata; how the monodies
of Venice were the most influential of all, and pointed the way to the
future. In fact, if we have not studied the songs of Grandi and Berti,
of Ferrari and Francesco Mannelli, and those of many other Venetian
composers, we cannot expect to see the achievements of Monteverdi
in their correct perspective.

71

ITALIAN 17th-CENTURY SINGING

By Nigel Fortune

THIS paper arises out of a study of Italian secular monodies. More than 200 books of these solo madrigals and arias were published in the first forty years of the seventeenth century, and they were among the most popular music of the day. Most of my quotations are taken from the prefaces to these song-books and from those to volumes of monodic motets, which were also very popular. The prefaces to operas and polyphonic madrigals are sometimes worth quoting, too; nor can one ignore the opinions of contemporary theorists and chroniclers like Doni and della Valle. To avoid footnotes I shall begin by listing the principal sources:

(a) Prefaces to the following books of secular monodies:

Antonio Brunelli: 'Arie, scherzi, canzonette, madrigali à 1–3', (Venice, 1613.)

Giulio Caccini:
    'Le Nuove Musiche', (Florence, 1602).
    'Nuove Musiche e nuova maniera di scriverle', (Florence, 1614).

Bellerofonte Castaldi: 'Primo Mazzetto di fiori musicalmente colti dal giardino bellerofonteo', (Venice, 1623).

Sigismondo d'India: 'Le Musiche', (Milan, 1609).

Giovanni Domenico Puliaschi: 'Musiche varie à una voce', (Rome, 1618).

(b) Prefaces to the following books of monodic motets:

Bartolommeo Barbarino: 'Motetti à voce sola, libro secondo', (Venice, 1614).

Giovanni Bonachelli: 'Corona di sacri gigli', (Venice, 1642).

Ignatio Donati: 'Secondo libro de' Motetti à voce sola', (Venice, 1636).

Ottavio Durante: 'Arie Devote', (Rome, 1608).

Horatio Modiana: 'Primitie di sacri concenti', (Venice, 1623).

Francesco Severi: 'Salmi passaggiati per tutte le voci', (Rome, 1615).

(c) Prefaces to the following operas and madrigals:

Marco da Gagliano: 'Dafne', (Florence, 1608).

Domenico Mazzocchi: 'Madrigali à 5', (Rome, 1638).

Jacopo Peri: 'L'Euridice', (Florence, 1601).

(d) Essays and Treatises:

Giovanni de' Bardi: 'Discorso mandato . . . a Giulio Caccini detto Romano sopra la musica antica e'l cantar bene', (c. 1580).

Severo Bonini: 'Prima parte de' Discorsi e Regole sovra la Musica', (after 1642 but before 1663.)

Cesare Crivellati: 'Discorsi musicali', (Viterbo, 1624).

Giovanni Battista Doni: 'Discorso sopra la Perfettione delle Melodie o de' Concenti'. In 'Compendio del trattato de' generi e de' modi della Musica', (Rome, 1635), pp. 95–125.

Vincenzo Giustiniani: ' Discorso sopra la Musica de' suoi tempi ',
   (1628).
André Maugars: ' Response . . . sur le sentiment de la musique
   d'Italie ', (Rome, 1639).
Pietro della Valle: ' Discorso della musica dell'età nostra . . . ',
   (1640).

Caccini's first preface, Peri and Bardi are translated in Oliver
Strunk's ' Source Readings in Music History ' (London, 1952), and
I have used his translations in this paper; Bonini, Gagliano, Gius-
tiniani and della Valle may be read in Angelo Solerti's ' Le Origini
del Melodramma ', (Turin, 1903); Bonachelli, Donati, Durante,
Mazzocchi and Modiana may be read, in part or complete, in
Hugo Goldschmidt's ' Die italienische Gesangsmethode des XVII
Jahrhundert ', (Breslau, 1890).   Most of the prefaces may be read
in the catalogue, by Gaetano Gaspari and others, of the Liceo
Musicale, Bologna, 4 vols. (Bologna, 1890–1905); and most of those
to secular works are reprinted, in part or complete, in Emil Vogel's
' Bibliothek der gedruckten weltlichen Vokalmusik Italiens, 1500–
1700 ' (Berlin, 1892).   Maugars's essay was reprinted in Paris in
1865 and translated into English by J. S. Shedlock in ' Studies in
Music ',, ed. Robin Grey, (London, 1901).

    Nine monodies out of ten were written for a high voice, soprano,
mezzo-soprano or tenor; the clefs most often used are the soprano,
tenor and treble, in that order.   But clefs are not a very reliable
guide to the voice that a composer had in mind when he wrote a
song—if indeed he had one in mind at all.   Some composers wrote
songs specially for their friends or for eminent singers; for example,
Giovanni Pietro Bucchianti wrote one in 1626 for Francesca Caccini,
and Nicolò Fontei composed the whole of his ' Bizzarrie Poetiche '
(1635 and 1636) for that other celebrated soprano-composer,
Barbara Strozzi.   As a rule, though, the same songs were meant to
be sung by men and women alike.   Nobody troubled much in the
seventeenth century about the incongruity of a tenor's singing the
lament of a forsaken maiden; besides, we may remember Campion's
remark in the preface to his ' First Booke of Ayres ' (c. 1613):
" treble tunes . . . are but tenors mounted eight notes higher."
Because he interpreted the clefs so literally Doni was trapped into
making irrelevant criticisms on these lines of Monteverdi's " lettere
amorose ".   Castaldi is on safer ground when he remarks that it
seems to him " laughable that a man with the voice of a woman
should set about proposing to his mistress and demanding pity of
her in the voice of a falsetto ".   Castratos and contraltos do not
seem to have been very popular with the admirers of secular music;

73

certainly very few monodies were written in the alto clef—if that is any guide. There was at least one castrato at the Medici court in Florence; towards 1640 the castrato Loreto Vittori, who also composed operas and cantatas, was one of the most noted singers in Italy; Giustiniani and Maugars report that there were many altos and castratos in the churches of Rome, and della Valle mentions three or four " falsettos " by name: Lodovico, Orazietto and Giovanni Luca (Conforto—who wrote a book on vocal ornaments?); Puliaschi, who was a papal singer, sang also at the Medici court in 1620 (and tenor and bass as well).

Doni, the soundest and most interesting Italian theorist of his day, had nothing but contempt for the contralto voice; he dismisses it as " unnatural and too feminine ". On this point, then, he agrees with Castaldi and Caccini, two champions of secular music. Caccini says that a singer should " sing his clear and natural voice, avoiding feigned tunes of (*sc.* or?) notes ", and should save his breath, not for these offensive sounds but " to give the greater spirit to the increasing and diminishing of the voice, to exclamations and other passions ". He concludes: " From a feigned voice can come no noble manner of singing, which proceeds from a natural voice, serving aptly for all the notes which a man can manage according to his ability, employing his wind in such a fashion that he may command all the best passionate graces used in this most worthy manner of singing ". Of all voices Doni—and, I suppose, Caccini, too—preferred the tenor, and he singles out for special praise the Roman tenor Francesco Bianchi. Most of the other famous singers of the time were sopranos, and it is therefore surprising to find that in Doni's hierarchy these occupy only third place—one place above the altos. For next to tenors Doni liked basses.

Doni hated indiscriminate graces and divisions and I feel sure he meant to qualify his predilection for basses with some such words as these: " Of course I do not mean those who seek only to show us how low they can sink, alike in the notes they sing and in their lack of taste which impels them to feed their ignorant admirers upon ridiculously florid runs ". Except Puliaschi, secular composers do not seem to have been at their best in their bass songs. Charon's music in ' Orfeo ' and Pluto's in ' Il Ballo delle Ingrate ' is not vintage Monteverdi as the solos written for Gostling are sometimes vintage Purcell. There is not a monody written for a bass but lapses after a few bars into an empty series of divisions on the continuo line. Some of the finest and most radical monodists—Pietro Benedetti and Claudio Saracini, for instance—wrote no bass songs at all, probably because they knew that this would mean sacrificing their artistic personalities to hollow conventions.

Caccini was particularly pleased with two songs that he published in 1614. Although they are written for a tenor they " seek out notes more proper to a bass ". He mentions them boldly on his very pretentious title-page, which was probably intended to bolster up his fading reputation at the Florentine court. This was a much more serious business than following the sound advice of Giovanni de' Bardi. Had not Bardi years before counselled him " never to pass from the tenor to the bass, seeing that with its passages the bass takes away whatever magnificence and gravity the tenor, with its majesty, has bestowed "? In his preface Caccini admits that the lower notes of these two songs should be freely ornamented, so as to give them a little more bravura; for he knew well enough that " the bass register is less able than the tenor to move the passions ". Maugars remarks how few really deep bass voices there were in Rome. Of all the singers listed by della Valle and Giustiniani, Melchior Palontrotti is the only one who we know was a bass; in fact, he seems to have been the most famous bass of his time. He was a nobleman who was at once a member of the papal choir and a leading figure in the operatic life of Florence and Mantua. He must surely have sung some of the bass songs composed by monodists who lived at these courts. We know one song that he sang and also how he sang it: " Muove si dolce " from ' Il Rapimento di Cefalo ' (1600), which Caccini printed in ' Le Nuove Musiche ' with all its original divisions.

I turn now to the sopranos and tenors who were the musical idols of the age. Della Valle alone mentions fifteen sopranos who were well known at Rome, and he refers to several others who came from nunneries in and around Rome. He tells us that some of them belonged to the retinues of music-loving cardinals like Borghese and Montalto. Probably only very few of these singers were known outside Rome, but he mentions three who were famous throughout Italy: Vittoria Archilei, Adriana Basile and Francesca Caccini (Giulio's daughter). Adriana is best remembered for her glittering performances in the operas produced at Mantua and in Rome. Francesca (affectionately known as " La Cecchina ") was the most versatile of the three. She was a pupil of her father, and she made her début in 1602 at the age of fifteen; she could play the harpsichord and theorbo; she wrote ballets and monodies (not very good ones, it is true) and some of their texts as well. But it was her voice which for twenty years brought her fame; night after night she delighted the Medici with her singing, and she won the admiration of Monteverdi, too. Even so, the connoisseurs of singing reserved

their most generous plaudits for Vittoria Archilei. There is hardly
a Florentine composer, hardly a contemporary writer on music,
who has not mentioned her in terms of extravagant flattery. For
Peri, she was " that celebrated lady whom one may call the Euterpe
of our age "; for d'India, whose songs she admired as the most
" powerful " she had ever heard, she was most excellent beyond
any other singer and also one of the most intelligent of all. Della
Valle writes: " She was no beauty, but one of the foremost singers
of the time ". D'India gives a delightful picture of her. One day
in 1608, when " the world's leading singers " were rehearsing in
Caccini's house for the festivities which graced the marriage of the
future Cosimo II, Grand Duke of Tuscany, Vittoria " turned away
from the rehearsal and honoured my songs with the sweetness of
her singing voice ".

Della Valle mentions one or two Roman tenors, Verovio and
Ottaviuccio, for example. Incidentally, the fact that singers are
referred to so often by their Christian names only or by the diminu-
tive forms of these names is another indication of their popularity.
Most of the best-known tenors of the day—Caccini, Giuseppino,
d'India, Peri and Francesco Rasi—were also famous composers of
monodies. Caccini was proud, vain, conceited and hot-tempered;
and a number of indiscriminating admirers lavished on him any
amount of half-baked praise. But he was obviously a fine singer.
His art may probably be summed up in the one word " elegance ".
His contemporaries tell us that he was more elegant and refined
than Peri, though he lacked Peri's ability to go straight to the
hearts of his audience. And he deserves to be remembered for his
attempts to replace with graceful, subtle, even whimsical ornaments
the aimless divisions which disfigured the vocal music of his time;
it was for his " industry " in this matter that Doni particularly
admired him. The publishers of both d'India's third set of
' Musiche ' (1618) and Peri's ' Le Varie Musiche ' (1609) agree upon
one thing—that nobody can appreciate the perfection of these
songs unless they have heard them sung by the composers themselves. We know very little about d'India as a singer and not very
much about his life. He was a Sicilian nobleman, and he held
only one important musical appointment; this was from 1611 to
1623, when he was director of music at the court of Savoy at Turin.
Next to Monteverdi, he was, I think, the finest composer of vocal
music in Italy. Gagliano mentions the " estrema esquisitezza " of
Peri's singing; and his words are echoed by many other writers, not
least by the dithyrambic Bonini, who also notes Peri's particular
success in writing and singing of tearful matters; in fact " his talent

would have moved to tears the stoniest of hearts ". But it seems that for sheer beauty of tone no one could touch Rasi; his singing in Peri's 'Euridice' and Gagliano's 'Dafne' transported his hearers. Francesco Rasi, says Bonini,

> sang elegantly, and with great passion and spirit. He was a handsome, jovial man, and he had a delightfully smooth voice; there was in his divine, angelic singing something of his own majesty and cheerfulness.

There remains Giuseppino. Is this a familiar name for the papal singer Giuseppe Cenci, as some writers—Doni for one—seem to imply? An interesting passage in della Valle's essay—I shall quote it later—in which he says that Giuseppino's singing seemed to consist of one long division, suggests that it is; for this definition of Giuseppino's singing also sums up Cenci's only known printed song. On the other hand, della Valle says that this Giuseppino wrote most of the villanelles which he learned in his youth (say, between 1590 and 1600) from Stefano Tavolaccio; and these songs were lewd and technically rudimentary. It is one thing for a papal singer to go off to Florence and sing in the operas of aristocrats, as Palontrotti did; it is quite another for him to go around the country composing and singing uncouth villanelles. Whoever he was, Giuseppino was no elegant singer like Caccini and Rasi. To paraphrase della Valle: " Giuseppino's voice was not a good one, yet he had a tremendous personality. His knowledge of music was nothing to write home about, but making divisions was second nature to him ". 77

Mersenne drew a rather arbitrary and artificial distinction between Italian and French music. The Italians, he says,

> represent for all they are worth the passions and affections of the mind and the soul, for example, anger, fury, rage, spite, swooning and several other passions, and they do this with incredible violence . . .; whereas our French composers are content to tickle the ear and to use all the time in their songs a sweetness which is inimical to strength.

To a compatriot of Guédron's all this may have seemed true. But it is only half the story. Granted, there is no violence in the French music of Mersenne's day, but there is much more sweetness in the Italian than he knew of. In fact, it is not too much to say that in the art of singing Italian composers and writers looked mainly for two things: sweetness and divisions. We may embroider that and say that on the whole it was the intelligent listeners who looked for sweetness, elegance, refinement, for discreet and subtle embellishments of the vocal line; while the untutored wanted only to be thrilled by extravagant roulades, by piercing high C's from sopranos

and by cavernous low C's from basses.   But that is not the whole
story, either, for it does not take into account the treatment of the
passions, which Mersenne recognizes as a peculiar Italian quality.
Caccini devotes a good deal of his prefaces to the means whereby
music can be made more emotional, more passionate; and some of
the finest solo madrigals abound with ecstatic exclamations and
with lugubrious, not to say morbid, harmonic progressions.   However, few other writers say anything very flattering about passion,
and it is worth noting that no book of monodies that contained
many passionate madrigals was ever reprinted.   Mersenne merely
admired with a touch of envy a feature of Italian music which was
quite foreign to the music of his own country, and it was one which
was not treated very seriously by the Italians themselves.

The encomiums of early seventeenth-century Italian singers are
full of adjectives like " soave ", " leggiadro ", " dolce ", " angelico "
and so on.   These are always the first adjectives to come to the
writer's mind—not " appassionato " or " energico ".   According
to Crivellati,

> in churches you sing differently from music-rooms; in churches you
> sing with a loud voice, in music-rooms with a subdued voice,

though sometimes you must sing more loudly to conform to the
sense of the words.   The editor of Giovanni Croce's ' Sacrae
Cantilene Concertate ' à 3, à 5 and à 6 (Venice, 1610) also says:
" where the voices sing, it (the organ?) must not be very loud,
except in the part where it is marked TUTTI, which must be sung
loudly to make a beautiful sound ".   Puliaschi warns the singer
that even when he is singing loudly " his voice should not lose its
sweetness ".   Even Severi, who is writing for people who sang
in churches, insists that their tone should be " ferma e soave ".   The
most authoritative opinion is Bardi's:

> the nice singer will endeavor to deliver his song with all the suavity
> and sweetness in his power, rejecting the notion that music must
> be sung boldly, for a man of this mind seems among other singers
> like a plum among oranges.

He assembled for Caccini a series of quotations from Aristotle,
Plato, Macrobius and Dante to prove that music could have no
more persuasive quality than sweetness, and he concludes:

> From these things one may gather that music is pure sweetness and
> that he who would sing should sing the sweetest music and the
> sweetest modes well ordered in the sweetest manner.

Divisions are, to quote Caccini, " those long windings and
turnings of the voice " which

> have been invented, not because they are necessary unto a good
> fashion of singing, but rather for a certain tickling of the ears of
> those who do not well understand what it is to sing passionately;

for if they did, undoubtedly divisions would have been abhorred, there being nothing more contrary to passion than they are.

They consist as a rule of florid festoons of notes of equal value; they were used indiscriminately; and they would sound just as well on instruments. We find them in a number of songs in the elaborate masques produced at Florence towards the end of the sixteenth century and in the madrigals for one to three voices by Luzzasco Luzzaschi. If we compare them with the new, subtle, essentially vocal ornaments evolved by Caccini (in some cases from examples quoted in sixteenth-century handbooks on ornamentation) we shall see why intelligent music-lovers found them so distasteful.

These music-lovers seem to have regarded divisions as a necessary evil, and an evil so firmly entrenched that they gave up trying to combat it. After all, many people obviously doted on them and would have protested violently if composers had stopped writing them. The philistine always makes more noise in defending something he likes or in attacking something he suspects than does his intellectual opponent, who usually adopts the resigned and faintly exasperated tone that Bardi adopts in the following passage:

> To make divisions upon the bass is not natural, for (as we have said) this part is by nature slow, low and somnolent. Yet it is the custom to do this. I know not what to say of it and am not eager to praise or to blame it, but I would counsel you to do it as little as possible and, when you do, at least to make it clear that you do it to please someone.

Della Valle writes further of Vittoria Archilei: " She ornamented the written monody with long flourishes and turns which disfigured it but were very popular ". Doni is less inclined to blame the composers than the singers, like Archilei, who devised divisions at sight, and the " stupid adulation of the ignorant mob, who often applaud things which deserve only cat-calls "; while the sensitive listener feels, as he endures some interminable division, as if he is hanging on a string and is waiting for it to snap. Giuseppino, an ignoramus himself, was obviously a man after the heart of the ignorant mob. In attacking him della Valle elaborates Caccini's point about divisions being " contrary to passion ", and puts his finger on their fundamental defect:

> . . . usually he inserted divisions where they were inappropriate. You never could tell whether his singing was supposed to be sad or gay, since it always sounded the same; or rather, it was always gay, because he always sang so many notes and sang them so fast. And I am sure he did not know himself what notes they were.

In fact Giuseppino, who knew how to sing divisions and therefore sang almost nothing else, was like that painter, of whom Gagliano

79

writes, who, knowing well how to paint cypresses, painted them all the time.

Donati provides some rules for the education of boys and girls in the art of singing. Here is one of them:

> Hold the head high and look straight ahead, with your mouth half open so as not to lose too much breath; try not to arch the eyebrows, to move the lips or to make unseemly gestures with your face.

Durante advises the singer

> not to make gestures with his body or his face while he is singing; but if he really wants to he must do so gracefully and in accordance with the sense of the words.

He must certainly not dance about the stage until his strength fails him, as Doni has seen some singers do. Crivellati must have seen this kind of singer, too, for he decries the use of gesture as more appropriate to the actors of comedies. There is an interesting letter from Rasi on this matter, which also throws some more light on the differences between the Italian and the French methods of singing at this time. He is writing to the Duke of Mantua, who has ordered Rasi's sister and pupil, Sabina, " to learn to sing in the French manner " (" imparar a cantar francese "). Rasi objects that " she will lose all the charm of the Italian way of singing " and adds:

> the Spanish style of singing adds to the charm of the Italian style as much as the French style detracts from it, filling it with many ugly gestures, like moving the mouth and the shoulders, and so on.

Here, surely, Rasi is talking about that " canto alla francese " which Monteverdi is said to have introduced into Italy in 1599. This expression seems to me to denote a method of singing and not a kind of music; if this definition is accepted by those writers on Monteverdi who have attempted to explain " canto alla francese " by dragging in red herrings like " musique mesurée ", I think they will concede that their discussions of the problem are a little heavy-handed.

The most important part of the preface to Caccini's ' Le Nuove Musiche ' is that in which he lays down the foundations of good singing. I want to consider his points in turn and support them, where appropriate, with the remarks of other Italian writers. It is profitable, too, to compare these opinions on singing with the advice that Frescobaldi offered to organists in the preface to his ' Toccate ' (Rome, 1614). Arnold Dolmetsch translated it in his book on interpretation (pp. 4–6). At the same time, though, one wonders if there were any very marked regional differences in the art of singing in Italy at this time. Did the Romans, for example, take to Caccini's emotional kind of singing? Was Severi's way of singing quavers acceptable to the Florentines?

The most important thing to learn first of all is correct intonation (" tuning of the voice "). Caccini says that in his day it was the custom to achieve this in one of two ways: " in the tuning of the first note " to " tune it a third under "; or to " tune the said first note in his proper tune, always increasing it in loudness ". He favours the second method (Durante does, too), except that he prefers to diminish the sound rather than to increase it. This latter practice " oftentimes becomes harsh and insufferable to the hearing "; " but in the diminishing of the voice it will work quite a contrary effect, because when the voice is slackened, then to give it a little spirit will always make it more passionate ". It is almost impossible to grasp from the written notes the passionate effects a fastidious composer like Caccini expected from his singers. The most important of these are exclamations (" the principal means to move the affection "), which may be either languid or lively. Caccini prints an example, ' Cor mio, deh, non languire ', showing two kinds of exclamation, which have been employed to imitate the words; " deh! " (" alas! ") calls for a more passionate exclamation than does " cor mio " (" my heart "). Exclamations may be used " in all passionate musics " on all dotted minims and dotted crotchets which move to a lower note; they will be much more effective on these notes " than they can be in semibreves, in which it will be fitter for increasing and diminishing the voice without using the exclamations ".

81

This last practice anticipates two devices introduced by Mazzocchi which are also to be used on long notes. In the first of them, the " messa di voce ", the singer should gradually increase both breath and tone; in the second the singer has

> sweetly to increase his voice in liveliness but not in tone; then he should gradually quieten it and make it smooth until it can scarcely be heard and seems to be coming from the depths of a cavern.

Incidentally, there are only very few dynamic markings in monodies, and they are always either ' P(iano) ' or ' F(orte) '; as one might expect, these few are nearly always found in echo-songs. Caccini has pointed out that his graces are to be used in " passionate musics "; he then makes it clear that " in airy musics or courantes to dance, instead of these passions there is to be used only a lively, cheerful kind of singing which is carried and ruled by the air itself ". This seems to have been the view of every monodist, for songs like this are hardly ever embellished and they are anything but languid and passionate.

Caccini also asks us to note how much more graceful are the last four notes in the fourth bar of ' Cor mio ' as they are written in his example than if they had been written as four equal quavers. Brunelli's views on singing are similar to Caccini's. Many people, he remarks, vainly presume to sing (they still do!) who know nothing about exclamations and ornaments and, especially, about the right way to sing quavers. Quavers, says Brunelli,

> must be sung in such a way that each one is detached from the next, and they must be formed in the throat and not in the mouth, as many people do. And when these people come across a group of quavers or semiquavers they enunciate only the first and the last of the group, while those in between are lost to the winds.

Caccini goes on to describe the different kinds of embellishment he has used in his songs. The two commonest ones were the " gruppo ", which was like our trill, and the " trillo ", in which one note, usually the last but one of a phrase, was repeatedly sung to the same syllable in ever-shortening values. Composers rarely troubled to write them down; usually they indicated them with the letters g and t, or left it to the singer to insert them in the appropriate places. Durante says that ornaments should never be added to the opening bars of a song or to the last syllable of a word; they are to be sung only on the vowels A, E and O (I and U are " odious vowels"); and the singer must ensure that he takes enough breath to complete a roulade without breaking it (unless, of course, the composer has broken it himself to illustrate some word like " sigh " in the text). Crivellati, who likens roulades on I and U to quacking and howling, agrees with him on these points; in fact he some-times seems to have copied Durante word for word. Donati sides with Durante, too; and, like Brunelli, he also wants all the notes in a roulade to be clearly enunciated and to be equal in volume. The finest monodists nearly always followed these instructions. Other monodists were not so careful, especially when they indulged in word-painting; for instance, in Italian a roulade illustrating laughter inevitably falls on the letter I. The normal unit of a roulade is the semiquaver. Severi says that roulades should come from the chest and not from the throat—otherwise the singer will fill his listeners with " confusione et disgusto "; and what is more, they should be taken as fast as possible. Severi is here uncomfortably close to the dangerous ground on which Giuseppino founded his art. But at least he seems to have realized the fact, for he admits that some people will find his roulades extravagant and difficult; but they should also find them natural and spontaneous. Donati probably agreed with Severi that runs should be sung as fast as possible, but he recommends young singers to take them quite slowly at first and to work up a good speed later; in this way they will learn to sing them in one breath, as Durante expected them to be sung. Modiana says that you should always slow down towards the end of a roulade; this is also what Frescobaldi used to to do when he played his toccatas.

The more elaborate embellishments were probably sung only by professional singers who had been trained to cope with them. Some composers kept their songs on the simple side for the benefit of the less expert amateurs; " facili per cantare ", they proclaim on their title-pages. They were following the advice succinctly phrased by Durante: " make your music singable and as easy as possible and then, as well as being more beautiful, it will be sung and listened to more readily ". Before they published their songs composers and their patrons sometimes passed copies of them round among their friends; d'India, for example, says that Cardinal Farnese has distributed some of his songs to many admiring musicians in Rome. Barbarino, who has handed out copies of his songs, is annoyed because some lazy and impatient souls have simplified the more difficult roulades and have then passed off the songs as their own. He specifies one roulade which was beyond the powers of these ordinary amateurs—a simple passage in dotted quavers. It does not say much for the standard of amateur singing at this time if amateurs could not manage to sing even the right notes of a simple roulade, let alone sing them as Severi says they should be sung. In future Barbarino knew better and, just as Monteverdi printed two versions of Orpheus's great song ' Possente spirto ', so did Barbarino publish two versions of his solo motets: a plain one and an ornamented one. The first was for those who did not like divisions and also for those who did but were skilled enough to devise their own; the second was also for those who liked divisions but lacked the skill to devise them according to the rules.

Caccini mentions one last important attribute of good singing: rubato (his word is " sprezzatura "). Unlike the other points that I have discussed it is not merely a matter of technique. In fact, in his 1614 preface he links it to two rather elusive qualities as one of the three things essential to anyone who wants to sing solo. The other two are the ability to arouse the passion of one's listeners and the ability to arouse different passions in the course of the same song as the words demand. Rubato, then, says Caccini,

> is that gracefulness in singing which, if applied in the right place (as it might be during a sequence of quavers or semiquavers passing through various harmonies), takes away from the singing a certain constricting stiffness and dryness and makes it pleasing, free and airy; just as in ordinary speech an eloquent delivery makes the things one says sweet and agreeable.

83

Caccini is here remembering the advice of Bardi, who says that the singer should " contract or expand the time at will, seeing that it is his privilege to regulate the time as he thinks fit ". A number of later writers also insist that solo songs should be sung with the utmost freedom; rigid and insensitive singing robs them of half their charm. Donati, for example, says " you should never beat time at all ", but should aim only " at singing in the broadest possible manner ". And there is no need to sing your song " with fear and anxiety ", for the accompanist has his own copy of the music and will always wait for you. The remarks of Bardi and Donati give us a good idea of the latitude allowed to the singer; they also emphasize the subservient rôle of the accompanist, who must content himself with playing a few discreet chords. Caccini believed that the best way to perform a song was for the singer to accompany himself.

Monteverdi stipulates that his " lettere amorose " are to be sung " senza battuta ". Other composers worry less about rubato than about setting a tempo to suit the words. Modiana leaves the singer to decide " whether (the words) call for a slow or a quick beat ". Bonachelli says the same thing, only more elaborately. It was only after about 1610 that composers began to add tempo directions to their monodies; the first that Curt Sachs has found are in Banchieri's ' L'organo suonarino ' (1611). At first, composers were content with obvious directions like " adagio " and " presto ", but later they ventured " mesto ", " vivace " and others still in use. And if Cenci is in fact Giuseppino it is no surprise to find that the roulades in his only published song are marked " fugace ".

If the composer and the singer obeyed all the instructions I have quoted in this paper they would be well on the way to achieving that most important quality, according to most theorists of the time, of solo vocal music: the complete audibility of the entire text. Vincenzo Galilei, Bardi, Caccini, Crivellati, Doni: all these men rage against polyphonic madrigals because half the words are incomprehensible. What kind of music is this, declares Doni, that makes nonsense of great poetry and has to fall back repeatedly on feeble love lyrics? These theorists nearly always write from the point of view of the listener, and they are among the first writers on music to do so. They seem to forget that sixteenth-century composers wrote their madrigals solely for the enjoyment of performers; they did not expect to find Galilei sitting at the back of the room picking holes in their counterpoint because he could not catch all the words. The kind of vocal music that the reformers recom-

mended—songs for a single voice accompanied by a single intrument
—is music that people could listen to, confident that if the composer
and the singer were worth their salt they would be able to hear all
the words. The singer must always sing in the spirit demanded
by the words and remember Gagliano's sound advice: " scolpire le
sillabe ". And that—and every other technical point I have
mentioned—goes, too, for the singer of today who wishes to sing
early seventeenth-century Italian songs in the only way that does
them justice.

THIS PALE SPRING

To be in the countryside
This pale Spring
Is like being under the sea:
Grey-blue water,
White surf,
Wan shadows,
Stark silhouettes
Of branched coral reefs,
Green seaweed,
Geometrical patterns
Of filtered sunlight,
Bright fish
Still or on the move,
But whether flowers in flight
Or birds rooted I know not,
I know only *Addunt robur stirpi*
And, " Je trouve bien! "
" Je trouve bien! "
" Je trouve bien! "
Only the unfinished solo of the blackbird
—Herald of high summer,
The tardy bicyclist
And Richard Adeney on the air
Sophisticated,
Piping with tender eloquence
Passages in A major
From the Musical Offering of J. S. B.
Do not belong to
My painted sub-sea world,
This pale Spring.
Elizabeth Godley.

85

Oratory Music in Florence, I: *Recitar Cantando*, 1583–1655 *

JOHN WALTER HILL (URBANA/ILLINOIS)

The cultivation of *recitar cantando*, acting while singing, in Florence toward the end of the sixteenth century can be placed in a broader historical perspective through the following examination of documents that shed light simultaneously in several directions. They reveal previously undetected activities of some of those who were associated with Giovanni Bardi's *camerata* and of other Florentine composers and poets who were their direct successors. They also describe the emerging practice of performing sacred musical dialogues in Florence, and thus help illuminate the early history of the oratorio in Italy.

The oratory in question here was the consecrated prayer hall of a religious confraternity of laymen called the Compagnia dell'Arcangelo Raffaello.[1] This company, which traced its origins to 1406,[2] had for its original purpose the religious education of adolescent boys not destined for the clergy. For their indoctrination and inspiration it relied principally upon sermons preached by the boys themselves and by clerics, *laude* sung by all, and *sacre rappresentazioni* acted by the young members. The boys administered their own company under the final authority of an adult layman (*Guardiano*) and a priest (*Padre Correttore*). They came from every social class, but relied on the patronage of the wealthier fathers of members for the support of the elaborate music and drama that they produced. In these and in several other respects the Compagnia dell'Arcangelo Raffaello was typical of several other boys' companies established in Florence during the fifteenth century.[3]

During the sixteenth and seventeenth centuries these companies began to include men over the original age limit of twenty. At first these older members may have

* Research for this, the first of three projected articles touching on the history of the oratorio in Florence, was carried out with assistance from a University of Pennsylvania Faculty Research Grant, 1973; a grant from the American Philosophical Society, 1974; and a fellowship from the American Council of Learned Societies, 1976–77. All dates in this article falling between January 1 and March 24 inclusive have been modernized by the addition of one year to compensate for the old Florentine calendar, which began the year on March 25. The following *RISM* sigla are used to denote libraries and archives: B:Bc–Brussels, Conservatoire Royal de Musique; I:Bc–Bologna, Civico Museo Bibliografico Musicale; I:Fas–Florence, Archivio di Stato; I:Fc–Florence, Conservatorio di Musica Luigi Cherubini; I:Fl–Florence, Biblioteca Medicea-Laurenziana; I:Fm–Florence, Biblioteca Marucelliana; I:Fn–Florence, Biblioteca Nazionale Centrale; I:Fr–Florene, Biblioteca Riccardiana; I:MOe–Modena, Biblioteca Estense.

[1] The full, formal name, Scuola et Compagnia della Natività del Noṣtro Signor Giesu Christo, chiamata la Compagnia dell'Arcangiolo Raffaello, ò vero della Scala, appears, with slight variations in orthography, at the beginning of this company's earliest surviving constitution, I:Fas, Capitoli delle compagnie religiose soppresse, 752 (Dec. 28, 1559) and record books, I:Fas, Compagnie religiose soppresse (Comp. rel. sop.), 160, 162, and 163.

[2] This date is given in the constitution of 1559 cited in footnote 1, although it conflicts with a slightly later date given by Trexler (see fn. 3).

[3] This information and its sources can be found in RICHARD C. TREXLER, *Ritual in Florence: Adolescence and Salvation in the Renaissance*, in: *The Pursuit of Holiness in Late Medieval and Renaissance Religion: Papers from the University of Michigan Conference*, ed. CHARLES TRINKAUS and HEIKO A. OBERMAN, *Studies in Medieval and Reformation Thought* 10 (Leiden 1974), p. 200–264, the most comprehensive study to date of Florentine religious companies for boys.

been technically alumni,[4] but eventually they were admitted directly.[5] In the Compagnia dell'Arcangelo Raffaello, this development was reached by the middle of the sixteenth century, although it was not recognized by a revision of its constitution until about 1640.[6] The significance for us of this change is that while the educational and inspirational purpose of the company's musical and dramatic productions remained oriented toward the boys, the older members provided a reservoir of artistic experience and invention and financial support that helped elevate those productions. Furthermore, the long term of membership of several important musician-members, often reaching from early boyhood to the end of their lives, must have encouraged continuity. Thus it will be all the more relevant to examine earlier productions in order to understand the nature of later ones.

The Compagnia dell'Arcangelo Raffaello, like the other Florentine boys' companies, possessed its own premises. They included a small chapel and a larger room each with its altar.[7] Mass and an Office were heard at pre-dawn and mid-morning company assemblies on most Sundays and on many holidays throughout the year. From at least the mid-sixteenth century, the older members also congregated after sunset on Sundays and other holidays from All Saints' Day to Easter.[8] These evening assemblies included sermons and often some very interesting music and drama.

87

[4] The constitution of the Compagnia dell'Arcangelo Raffaello, cited in footnote 1, contains the provision (fol. 13[r]) that, although a member normally leaves the company at the age of 22, exceptionally 24 or 25, those who have "left" can attend meetings and take communion, but cannot vote or hold office.

[5] The Compagnia della Purificazione della S.ma Vergine Maria e di S. Zanobi detta di S. Marco, one of the four companies of the Christian Doctrine reorganized in 1442 by S. Antonio, then prior of S. Marco, formed, about 1528, a special sub-group of youths who attended secret early-morning meetings (I:Fas, Comp. rel. sop., 1646, no. 7, fols. 297[v]–280[v]). From 1541 to 1576 the members who were admitted to this *tornata segreta* ranged in age between 12 and 21, most being 14–16 years old. But in 1577, the entering members were between the ages of 16 and 30 (I:Fas, Comp. rel. sop., 1646, no. 7, fols. 295[r]–307[v]; and 1647, no. 9, fol. 365[r]). From 1594 to 1685 the ages of entering members ranged from 14 to 42 (*ivi*, 1647, no. 10, *passim*). Another of the original four companies, that of S. Niccolò del Ceppo, recognized two *tornate* in its new constitution of 1563. One was for *giovanetti*, the other for *persone più mature* over the age of 18, who would meet in the evening (I:Fn, Conv. sop., D.3.270, fols. 7[v] and 19[v]). The companies of Arcangelo Raffaello and of S. Giovanni Evangelista were the other two companies of the Christian Doctrine.

[6] The constitution (I:Fas, Capitoli delle compagnie religiose soppresse, 627) is not dated, but was approved by Archbishop Piero Niccolini whose tenure was from 1632 to 1652. It mentions no maximum age for members, but does specify a minimum age of 30 for certain important offices. This change in the nature of these boys' companies has gone entirely unnoticed by general and literary historians, who have uniformly focused their attention on the companies activities in the fifteenth century. For references see Trexler, *Ritual in Florence*, *passim*.

[7] An inventory of documents in the possession of the Compagnia dell'Arcangelo Raffaello made in 1591 (I:Fas, Comp. rel. sop., 164, no. 38 [*olim* 36], fols. 9[r]–11[r]) outlines the succession of locations used by the company. From 1533 to its suppression in 1786, the company occupied rooms fronting on the piazza S. Maria Novella, immediately to the left of the porter's lodge of that cloister. The site is occupied by a modern hotel today. That there were a smaller and a larger prayer hall, each with altar, is evident from descriptions of assemblies on pages cited below and among the documents at the end of this article. Descriptions of the premises of this and some other boys' companies can be found in [GAETANO CAMBIAGI], *L'antiquario fiorentino o sia guida per osservar con metodo le cose notabili della città di Firenze*, 2nd ed. (Florence 1771), p. 64, 125, 145; in FERDINANDO LEOPOLDO DEL MIGLIORE, *Firenze città nobilissima illustrata* (Florence 1684), p. 306; and in WALTER and ELISABETH PAATZ, *Die Kirchen von Florenz: Ein kunstgeschichtliches Handbuch* IV (Frankfurt 1952), p. 392–98.

[8] In 1581–82, for example, assemblies were held before dawn, during the day, and after sunset on every Sunday from November 5 through Easter (April 15) and on the feasts of All Saints (Nov. 1), St. Andreas (Nov. 30), Holy Conception (Dec. 8), St. Thomas (Dec. 24), Christmas, St. Stephan (Dec. 26), St. John the Evangelist (Dec. 27), St. Silvester, for which the company always substituted their feast of Archangel Raphael (Dec. 31), Holy Circumcision (Jan. 1), Epiphany (Jan. 6), Purification (Feb. 2), Annunciation with its vigil (March 24–25),

The features enumerated so far, typical of Florentine boys' companies, distinguish these companies from those of the *laudesi* whose earlier musical activities have been described.[9] They help explain the cultivation of certain kinds of music and drama during the seventeenth century which were apparently not fostered by those other companies. But the Compagnia dell'Arcangelo Raffaello was distinguished from even the other boys' companies by its membership.

Giulio Caccini entered the company in about 1575. At about the same time Piero Strozzi joined, as did Filippo, the eldest son of Giovanni Bardi, the organizer of the *camerata fiorentina* with which Caccini and Strozzi were associated. Somewhat later Camillo and Cosimo, two of Bardi's younger sons, also joined.[10] The participation of Giovanni Bardi himself is therefore probable.[11] If he had been a member in his own right, he would probably have joined before 1562, when the surviving membership records begin. The same is true of Vincenzo Galilei, whose

Friday of Quaresima (April 5), Palm Sunday (April 8), Wednesday, Thursday, Friday and Saturday of Holy Week (April 11–14) – in all, thirty-nine days. Easter Monday began the vigil of the Forty Hours discussed elsewhere below. Then only morning assemblies were held on the fourth and fifth Sunday of April, feast of Sts. Philip and Jacob, first, third, and fourth Sunday of May, feasts of the Holy Spirit, Corpus Domini, and St. John the Baptist, first Sunday of July, St. Mary Magdalene, first and second Sundays in August, Assumption, August 15 (elections of officers), first and second Sundays of September, and St. Francis (I:Fas, Comp. rel. sop., 162, no. 22 [*olim* 21], under the dates cited). The calendar of feasts changed constantly but this list is generally representative of the schedule of assemblies for all the former boys' companies during the sixteenth and seventeenth centuries.

[9] The *compagnie dei laudesi* whose musical activities in the fourteenth and fifteenth centuries have been thoroughly documented by FRANK A. D'ACCONE, *Le compagnie dei laudesi in Firenze durante l'ars nova*, in: *L'ars nova italiana del trecento: Secondo convegno internazionale 17–22 luglio 1969*, ed. F. ALBERTO GALLO (Certaldo 1970), p. 253–80; and D'ACCONE, *Alcune note sulle compagnie fiorentine dei laudesi durante il quattrocento*, in: *Rivista italiana di musicologia* X (1975), p. 86–114, were made up of adult members. They did not possess their own premises, but met in chapels within large churches. They did not hear and recite sermons, and they did not stage dramas. These factors, which distinguish them from the boys' companies, do not seem unrelated. The *laudesi* studied by D'Accone seem not to have sponsored performances of sacred dialogues in the seventeenth nor oratorios in the eighteenth centuries; at least their surviving records make no mention of them. The musical activities of other types of Florentine lay companies, i.e., the *disciplinati*, the *compagnie cogli stendardi*, and the *compagnie della notte*, if any, have not been studied.

[10] The name "*Giulio di Michelang.o Caccini m.co di S. A. S.*" is written in a chronologically ordered list of entering members, without date, but directly after an entry with the date 1575 and directly before another with the date 1576 (I:Fas, Comp. rel. sop., 164, no. 38 [*olim* 36], fol. 70ʳ). The same list gives the entries "*m[esser] Piero di Matteo Strozzi, 1575*" (fol. 83ᵛ), "*Filippo del Sig.re Gio. de Bardi di Vernio*" near the date 1575 written elsewhere (fol. 64ʳ), and "*Camillo del Sig.re Gio. de Bardi di Vernio, 1581*" (fol. 58ᵛ). "*Cosimo del Sig. Giovanni Bardi di Vernio*" entered on Jan. 1, 1591 (n.s.) (I:Fas, Comp. rel. sop., 165, no. 48 [*olim* 40], fol. 32ʳ).

[11] The fact that fathers of young members took an active part in the company is evident throughout the surviving descriptive records; it is recognized, e.g., on the title page of JACOPO CICOGNINI'S *sacra rappresentazione Le celeste guida* (Florence 1625), which is dedicated to the *honorandi padri e Fratelli* of the Compagnia dell'Arcangelo Raffaello. Pietro de' Bardi named Vincenzo Galilei and Giulio Caccini as musicians who frequented his father's circle. And Piero Strozzi appears as Bardi's disciple in Galilei's *Dialogo . . . della musica antica et della moderna* (Florence 1581), the most extensive document reflecting the ideas developed by the camerata (CLAUDE V. PALISCA, The "*Camerata Fiorentina*": *A Reappraisal*, in: *Studi musicali* of the Accademia Nazionale di Santa Cecilia, Rome I [1972], p. 203–208). Strozzi was the composer of the solo madrigal "*Fuor dell'umido nido*" sung by Caccini on the *Carro della notte* in 1579, which has been considered the earliest surviving example of music linked to the *camerata* (NINO PIRROTTA, *Li due Orfei da Poliziano a Monteverdi* [Turin 1969], p. 252–55). Caccini, in 1602, reckoned that he had entered the service of Cosimo I ca. 1565, but the record of his matriculation into the Compagnia dell'Arcangelo Raffaello in 1575 or 1576, with its annotation "*m.co di S. A. S.*," is now the earliest corroborating documentation of his status as Florentine court musician. Less direct corroboration of Caccini's presence in Florence during the 1560s is offered by a salary roll for the grand-ducal court, which notes that "*Cipione delle palle*," i.e., Scipione delle Palle, whom Caccini later named as his teacher in Florence (H. WILEY HITCHCOCK, *A New Biographical Source for Caccini*, in: *JAMS* XXVI [1973], p. 145–47), died on Oct. 20, 1569 (I:Fas, Depositeria generale 1516, opening 48). This payroll does not, however, include the name of Giulio Caccini.

grandson Vincenzo entered the company sometime before 1615.[12] We know for certain, however, that the mentor to the *camerata*, Girolamo Mei, had joined either before 1549, when he left Florence, or on some brief return visit, as in 1568, for example.[13] In 1587 the company included Jacopo Corsi,[14] whose association with Giovanni Bardi as fellow Accademico Alterato[15] and whose friendship and support of Giulio Caccini and Piero Strozzi,[16] on the one hand, and of Jacopo Peri and Ottavio Rinuccini on the other,[17] make him a key link in establishing continuity between the speculations and musical styles of Bardi's circle and the earliest experiments with opera in Florence.[18] Of the other Alterati, "pioneers in the theory

[12] I:Fas, Comp. rel. sop., 162, no. 22 [*olim* 21], fol. 33ʳ.

[13] The name "*Girolamo di Pagholo* [i.e., Paolo] *Mei*" is found, without indication of date, on a membership list (I:Fas, Comp. rel. cops, 164, no. 38 [*olim* 36], fol. 67ʳ) that gives no dates earlier than 1562. Mei's name, however, is near the head of the entries under the letter "G" and precedes by a good deal the first given date, 1566. The most detailed account of Mei's life is found in the introductory study of CLAUDE V. PALISCA, *Girolamo Mei (1519–1594), Letters on Ancient and Modern Music to Vincenzo Galilei and Giovanni Bardi,* Musicological Studies and Documents 3 ([Rome] 1960), p. 15–34. Mei's key rôle, as correspondent, in supplying Galilei and Bardi with information about Greek music and ideas for the reform of modern music is thoroughly documented by this study of Palisca's and in his earlier article *Girolamo Mei, Mentor to the Florentine Camerata,* in: MQ XL (1954), p. 1–20. In The *"Camerata Fiorentina,"* p. 208, Palisca places the height of activity of the *camerata* between 1577 and 1582, during which years Mei wrote five of six surviving letters to Galilei and Bardi. Mei himself estimated that he and Galilei had exchanged thirty letters (PALISCA, The *"Camarata Fiorentina,"* p. 214). It would appear, on the basis of the following newly-found letter from Bardi, that most of the lost letters were sent weekly to Galilei during the first half of 1577 and that they perhaps formed the basis of regular weekly meetings of the *camerata* at Bardi's house during that period (I:MOe, Autografoteca Campori, s.v., "Bardi, Giovanni," from Florence, Nov. 2, 1577, to Giovanfrancesco di Lodovico Ridolfi in Rome): "*Molto Mag:co M[esser] Giovanfrancescho / il desiderio che o di servirla, et l'amorevolezza sua mi da animo a darle una briga, la quale è questa, ch'io vorrei che la si pigliasse cura, che le l[ette]re che scrivve m[esser] Girolamo Mei (il quale, sta costi, dovve voi) venissero ogni settimana in mano die M[esser] Vincentio Galilei. Questo li sarà facile perche la potra farle venire ogni settimana a m[esser] Giovanfrancesco Strozzi V[ost]ro amico et mio con il quale io mi intendero, et cosi verra adempiuto il mio desiderio, io vi do questa briga perche da due mesi in qua non abbiamo mai le sue l[ette]re in tempo come desidereremo, la potra tutto conferire con M[esser] Girolamo, e intanto racomandarmi a M[esser] Giovanfrancesco et a madonna Portia assai et tenermi in sua gratia / di Firenze alli dua di novembre 1577 / s.re [?] di V. S. e parente / Giovanni Bardi di Vernio*"

[14] An account book relating to the joint inheritance of Jacopo and his brother Bardo Corsi, I:Fas, Guicciardini–Corsi–Salviati, libro 408, contains the following entry dated April 9, 1587 (opening 42, left): "*A Jacopo Corsi L. 2 contanti a Dom.co di Jac.o servo della Compagnia del Angiolo Raffaello di via Maffia per limosina acolta della soscrizione fatta detto Jac.o nostro addi primo d'aprile passato.*" The books of the company omit recording Corsi's inscription for some reason. However, on April 22, 1593, the Corsi account book (ibid., opening 7, left) records Jacopo's contribution of twenty-eight lire toward expenses incurred by the "*Compagnia dell'angiol Raffaello*" during Holy Week. Finally, in a review made by the company in 1620, it is revealed that Jacopo Corsi had suggested that new bellows be added when an organ had been purchased from Galileo Galilei about twenty-four years earlier (I:Fas, Comp. rel. sop., 156, fascio A, note dated Oct. 3, 1620).

[15] CLAUDE V. PALISCA, The *Alterati of Florence, Pioneers in the Theory of Dramatic Music,* in: *New Looks at Italian Opera: Essays in Honor of Donald J. Grout,* ed. WILLIAM J. AUSTIN (Ithaca, N.Y. 1968); p. 9–38.

[16] Of Corsi's friendship with Caccini I have found a single but eloquent testimony from the period immediately following the departure for Rome of Caccini's mentor and patron Giovanni Bardi (I:Fas, Guicciardini–Corsi–Salviati, libro 408, [fol. 230ʳ] – Nov. 22, 1592): "*A m[esser] Jac.o Corsi L. 14 resi a Dom.co spenditore tanto disse averele date a detto m[esser] Jac.o per pagare un medico per Giulio romano.*" Libro 432 of the same series contains records of a series of payments from Corsi to Piero di Matteo Strozzi stretching from Dec. 8, 1581 to some time in 1602.

[17] Corsi's artistic association with Peri and Rinuccini is, of course, well known. However, a contract dated Nov. 1, 1600 (I:Fas, Guicciardini–Corsi–Salviati, Filza 1a, no. 27) made Corsi and Peri business partners in the wool trade. Professor Jordan Goodman, an economic historian to whom I am gratefully indebted for my introduction to the Corsi archive, with which he has been working for some years, tells me the Jacopo Corsi became one of the wealthiest men in Florence, and that Peri seems to have become rich as well. Toward the end of his life (1600–1602) Corsi also made enormous payments to Ottavio Rinuccini (I:Fas, Guicciardini–Corsi–Salviati, libro 432).

[18] Bardi seems to have befriended Corsi and Rinuccini by taking them along on one of his musical scouting expeditions to Ferrara in February of 1590; see ANTHONY ADDISON NEWCOMB, *The Musica Secreta of Ferrara in the 1580s,* (Ph. D. diss. Princeton University 1969), p. 340. Perhaps the Bardi and Corsi circles were

of musical drama," Piero and Carlo Ruccellai became members, while Filippo Strozzi and Nero del Nero were represented by their sons.[19] (Other musicians, poets, and supporters of the new monodic style who entered later will be mentioned in due course.) Obviously during the later sixteenth century the Compagnia dell'Arcangelo Raffaello had every means and every encouragement for the cultivation of *recitar cantando*.

Most Florentine lay companies kept financial, legal, and descriptive records of their activities. In the case of the Compagnia dell'Arcangelo Raffaello, the official called the *sotto provetittore* was required to write a description of each assembly in order to note policy decisions, record the generosity of benefactors, and help insure the continuance of traditional practices. In many cases of detailed descriptions of music and drama, one senses that the diarist also wished to preserve for posterity at least a vestige of the glory of these productions.

The surviving descriptions of the assemblies of the Compagnia dell'Arcangelo Raffaello start in 1556. But detailed accounts begin only after a gap between 1573 and 1581 during which no records were kept.[20] Shortly after the descriptions resume, we read the following account of the company's assembly on June 1, 1582, feast of the Holy Spirit:

> And the Ave Maria having rung [at sunrise], and [everyone] having been seated in the large hall, a youth and a Tobias dressed as a pilgrim came out, and after a long discourse between them the said Tobias cast off his pilgrim's costume and revealed who he was. And, having put fresh heart into the youth, he began the prayer to Archangel Raphael. And when it was finished, the said Archangel Raphael came out accompanied by angels and a musical chorus. And they began to sing a madrigal. When it was finished, Tobias was counseled by Archangel Raphael. And from the hands of the angels, each [member] was given a printed card with this message. (Doc. 1)

An abbreviated catechism follows, and then the diarist copies the text that had been recited.

This single scene, complete in itself, differs from any *sacra rappresentazione* of the fifteenth or sixteenth century described or transcribed in the major works on the genre.[21] Although it uses eleven-syllable lines, the rhyme scheme is irregular; it is

---

not quite as disjunct as has been intimated by NINO PIRROTTA, *Temperaments and Tendencies in the Florentine Camerata*, in: MQ XL (1954), p. 183. For further on this issue see BARBARA RUSSANO HANNING, *The Influence of Humanist Thought and Italian Renaissance Poetry on the Formation of Opera*, (Ph. D. diss. Yale University 1968), p. 1–117.

[19] These were among the members of the Accademia degli Alterati who delivered discourses in Florence during the 1570s and '80s concerning the affective power of music and the efficacy of accompanied solo singing in imitation of what were thought to have been the characteristics of ancient Greek music and drama. See PALISCA, *The Alterati of Florence*, p. 9–38. I:Fas, Comp. rel. sop., 165, no. 48 [*olim* 40] records the initiations of Piero Rucellai on April 16, 1591 (fol. 34ᵛ), Carlo Rucellai on Jan. 6, 1593 (fol. 40ᵛ), Alfonso di messer Filippo Strozzi on March 1, 1592 (fol. 38ʳ), and Filippo di Nero del Nero on Jan. 15, 1620 (fol. 122ʳ).

[20] I:Fas, Comp. rel. sop., 160 contains the diaries of assemblies for 1556–1563 (no. 7 [*olim* 6]), and 1563–1573 (no. 8 [*olim* 7]). Comp. rel. sop., 162, no. 22 [*olim* 21] contains the records for 1581–1610. Comp. rel. sop., 160, no. 9 [*olim* 8], a summary of a few highlights extracted from several diaries, begins with this observation: "*Fornito il Libro A sino 10 Lug:o 1575* [really 1573], *comincia il Libro B à di p:o 9bre 1581. Nel termine di questi sei Anni non si trovano ricordi particolare per nigligenza tralasciati.*" A similar observation was made by the new recordkeeper in 1581 (I:Fas, Comp. rel. sop., 162, no. 22 [*olim* 21], fol. 1ᵛ).

[21] ALESSANDRO D'ANCONA, *Sacre rappresentazioni dei secoli XIV, XV e XVI* (Florence 1872); D'ANCONA, *Origini del teatro italiano*, 2nd ed. (Turin 1891) I, p. 27–49, 391–94, 421; VINCENZIO DE BARTHOLOMAEIS, *Le origini della poesia drammatica italiana* (Bologna 1924), p. 456–61; BARTHOLOMAEIS, *Laude dramatiche e rappresentazioni sacre* (Florence 1943).

not *ottava rima*. It consists of 238 lines, and therefore is far shorter than any known *sacra rappresentazione* of the time. It has two speaking rôles rather than a dozen or more, has no internal divisions, has no scenery specifically erected for the drama, is not introduced by a prologue, or *annunzio*, nor concluded with an epilogue, or *licenzio*, and therefore has much more continuity with what preceded and followed it in the assembly. Given the state of the surviving records of the company, one can only say that a similarly brief and simple dramatization was performed as early as 1563.[22] At least one other Florentine boys' company produced such brief spoken dialogues during the seventeenth century.[23] It is one type of earlier dramatic production to which later musical performances seem to be related.

Another traditional practice of the company that provides the background for later musical performances is the decoration of their large hall with a catafalque, that is, a large false tomb or sepulcher, erected for the observances of Holy Week and the Forty-Hours vigil, in which cases it represented the sepulcher of Christ, and for All Saints' Day, when it commemorated the souls in purgatory and was meant to impress the young members with the brevity of human life.[24] In the presence of just this type of *apparato* the following performance took place in the company's large hall on Thursday of Holy Week, April 7, 1583:

91

> In the evening, the usual office was said with the usual music, and further, at the Benedictus there was one of our brothers who played a large musical harp, accompanying himself and a little boy [*putto*] in the responses; and at the Miserere [they sang while the one was] playing a large *lira*. And in truth the people were well satisfied. And Tenebrae finished, everyone was dismissed. (Doc. 2)

This description is suggestive of an early experiment in the new style of accompanied singing. One thinks of the lamentations and responses for Holy Week set by Vincenzo Galilei in 1581 or 1582.[25] The identity of the singers perhaps bears on this matter. It seems to be revealed in the description of the assembly for All Saints' Day, November 1, 1584:

> At a half hour after sunset, the office was begun, 2 youths of age [i.e., between the ages of 25 and 40][26] who were good musicians having been entrusted [with the music]. And all the lessons [were sung] by adolescent musicians instructed by messer Rafaello Gucci, [the

---

[22] I:Fas, Comp. rel. sop., 160, no. 8 [*olim* 7], fols. 8ᵛ–9ʳ. The records of the company describe similar, single-scene dramatizations in 1587, 1592, 1594, 1623 and 1624 (I:Fas, Comp. rel. sop., 162, no. 22 [*olim* 21], fols. 84ʳ, 148ʳ⁻ᵛ, 171 bisᵛ; no. 23 [*olim* 22], fols. 103ʳ, 115ʳ⁻116ʳ).

[23] The Compagnia di S. Jacopo del Nicchio in 1602, 1604, 1605, 1606, and 1618 (I:Fas, Comp. rel. sop., 1246, no. 8, fol. 94ʳ; no. 9, fols. 9ᵛ, 24ʳ, 36ᵛ, and 131ᵛ).

[24] The practice was general throughout Catholic Europe during the seventeenth century. For illustrations see MARK S. WEIL, The Devotion of Forty Hours and Roman Baroque Illusions," in: *Journal of the Warburg and Courtauld Institutes* XXXVII (1974), p. 218–48; GIOVANNA GAETA BERTELÀ and ANNAMARIA PETRIOLI TOFANI, *Festi e apparati medicei da Cosimo I a Cosimo II: Mostra di disegni e incisioni*, Gabinetto Disegni e Stampe degli Uffizi, 31 (Florence 1969); and PER BYURSTÖM, *Baroque Theater and the Jesuits*, in: *Baroque Theater: The Jesuit Contribution*, ed. RUDOLF WITTKOWER and IRMA B. JAFFE (New York 1972), p. 104–105.

[25] The famous letter of Pietro Bardi to Giovanbattista Doni, which mentions the lamentations, is reprinted in ANGELO SOLERTI, *Le origini del melodrama: Testimonianze dei contemporanei* (Turin 1903), p. 145. The passage in question is translated into English by OLIVER STRUNK, *Source Readings in Music History* (New York 1950), p. 364. Galilei's settings were composed in 1581 or 1582 according to further information presented by PALISCA, The "Camerata Fiorentina," p. 39.

[26] The traditional age classifications are explained in TREXLER, *Ritual in Florence*, p. 201, fn. 2.

company] no longer having a *maestro di cappella*.[27] And messer Giulio Caccini, musician of His Most Serene Highness [Grand Duke Francesco de' Medici] and our brother, rehearsed the three madrigals that were sung last year. They [were] all sung by our brothers. And the Miserere was sung to the accompaniment of a *gran lira*[28] by him [Caccini] together with a little castrato of his [*un suo putto castrato*] whom [Caccini] maintains in his house by requisition of His Most Serene Highness, and whom he teaches.[29] There having been set up in the middle of the hall a tomb in which [Caccini] entered without being seen, he sang and played there. And there was a response by the musical chorus, [all of] which, in truth, made a beautiful sound. Thus [also] the Benedictus was sung. (Doc. 3)

In the context of All Saints' Day, the singing inside the tomb evidently represented the voices of souls in purgatory confessing sin, praying to be purged and cleansed, and begging not to be banished from God's presence (*Miserere* – Psalm 50), then looking forward to the salvation of "those who live in darkness" (*Benedictus*–Luke I, 69–79). In this respect it is *recitar cantando* of a sort.

Admittedly it is not clear in the descriptions of 1583 and 1584 (Docs. 2 and 3) as to whether Caccini and his *putto* sang simultaneously or separately. However, Caccini had evidently sung his own music alone on All Saints' Day a few years earlier. Giovanni Bardi, in his *Discorso* (in a passage omitted from Strunk's translation) describes the earlier occasion – it was in the year 1577 or 1578 according

92

---

[27] The *maestro di cappella* since 1563 had been one Jacopo Mollazzi, about whom nothing more is known. His duties, and those of his successors, were to provide music for all the company's assemblies and to teach singing to ten boys or adolescents who were members. He was paid by a member, one Girolamo di messer Luca during this period (I:Fas, Comp. rel. sop., 160, no. 8 [*olim* 7], fol. 4ᵛ).

[28] Giulio Caccini was almost certainly the anonymous brother who sang and played the harp and *gran lira* on April 7, 1583 (Doc. 2). Here, evidently, he again plays the *gran lira*. Caccini is known to have played the harp during the fourth intermedio of 1589 (D. P. WALKER, ed., *Les Fêtes du mariage de Ferdinando de Médicis et de Christine de Lorraine, Florence 1589*, Vol. I: *Musique des intermèdes de "La Pellegrina"* [Paris 1963], p. xlvi). He is credited with playing both harp and *lira* by the Este ambassador to the Medici court in 1588; see NEWCOMB, *The Musica Secreta of Ferrara*, p. 360. Howard Brown reports that he played a *lira da braccio* on the *Carro della notte* of 1579 (HOWARD MAYER BROWN, *Psyche's Lament: Some Music for the Medici Wedding in 1565*, in: *Words and Music: The Scholar's View: A Medley of Problems and Solutions Compiled in Honor of A. Tillman Merrit by Sundry Hands*, ed. LAURENCE BERMAN [Cambridge, Mass. 1972], p. 7 and 10–11), although the original published description that Brown cites says that Caccini played a viol (see the reprint in ANGELO SOLERTI, *Musica, ballo e drammatica alla corte medicea dal 1600 al 1637* [Florence 1905], p. 10). Perhaps Brown reached his conclusion after scrutinizing the engraving of the *carro* with (presumably) Caccini on board (reprinted, e.g., in A. M. NAGLER, *Theatre Festivals of the Medici, 1539–1637* [New Haven, Conn. 1964], plate 31; and PALISCA, *The "Camerata Fiorentina"*, after p. 218). Concerning the chord-playing capabilities and problems of the *lira* and *lirone*, see HOWARD MAYER BROWN, *Sixteenth-Century Instrumentation: The Music for the Florentine Intermedii*, Musicological Studies and Documents, 30 ([Rome] 1973), p. 39–49 and the literature cited there. A *lira* had been used to accompany singing in the Compagnia dell'Arcangelo Raffaello as early as 1560 (I:Fas, Comp. rel. sop., 160, no. 7 [*olim* 6], fol. 26ᵛ).

[29] The *putto castrato* must be the same *putto* mentioned in 1583 (Doc. 2). A notice from 1587 (Doc. 9) joins the names of Giulio Caccini and Rafaello Gucci (see above) with those of Lelio Ghirlanzoni and "Niccolo Castrato." This Niccolo would seem to be the *putto castrato* of Documents 2 and 3. The list of musicians employed by Grand Duke Ferdinando in 1588 includes one "Niccolò Bartolini da Pistoia, Eunuco," and the list of singers for the first intermedio of 1589 includes a "Niccolò Castrato" (ABY WARBURG, *I costumi teatrali per gli intermedi del 1589: I disegni di Bernardo Buontalenti e il libro di conti di Emilio de' Cavalieri: Saggio storico-critico* [1895], repr. in his *La rinascita del paganesimo antico*, ed. GERTRUD BING [Florence 1966], p. 107 and 77 respectively). Lelio Ghirlanzoni, mentioned in Document 9, thus joins the list of Caccini's associates. Ghirlanzoni's association with Jacopo Corsi is established by his having received the rather large sum of 350 lire from Corsi on March 16, 1589 (I:Fas, Guicciardini–Corsi–Salviati, libro 408, opening 114, left). Shortly after this, Ghirlanzoni appears in the chapel of the Duke of Ferrara, where he served, in 1592, as the vehicle for transmitting to that musical establishment twelve madrigals by Piero Strozzi (LORENZO BIANCONI, *L'officina cacciniana di Pietro Maria Marsolo*, in: PIETRO MARIA MARSOLO, *Secondo libro dei madrigali a quattro voci, opera decima, 1614, un madrigale a cinque voci, 1604, sei concerti a una, due e tre voci, 1620–1624*, ed. LORENZO BIANCONI, *Musiche rinasciamentali siciliane 4* [Rome 1973], p. xviii–xix).

to Palisca's dating of the treatise,[30] which is addressed to Caccini:

If you act according to my judgment, remembering the extraordinary satisfaction that the Florentine people had at the commemoration of last All Saints' Day because they well understood the words of your musical compositions, you will take great care that [the words] are clearly understood [in all your other music].[31]

The context of Bardi's remarks makes it clear that he is describing Caccini's solo singing. It seems reasonable to suppose that these clearly declaiming solo madrigals or motets of Caccini's were heard by Bardi in the Compagnia dell'Arcangelo Raffaello, since Caccini had recently joined it and since the company sooner or later developed a tradition of solo singing on All Saints' Day.

The accounts of 1583 and 1584 may be ambiguous in some degree, but the descriptions of subsequent solo performances by Rafaello Gucci,[32] who had shared instructional duties with Caccini for the 1584 commemoration, are free of any confusion in this regard. During the years 1584–1586 there are five reports of Gucci singing by himself to the accompaniment of his own harpsichord (Docs. 4–8). On All Saints' Day of 1585 he sang while concealed within the catafalque (Doc. 7), just as Caccini had done.   93

Accompanied solo singing and dramatic enactment were visibly combined on the feast of Archangel Raphael, December 31, 1591:

The day [having arrived], [the brothers] waited for the hour in which the Most Serene Grand Duchess, Our Lady, gave us to understand she wanted to visit our festivity. There was provided a selection of youths with excellent voice and singing ability, who, from one side, formed a chorus. And messer Raffaello [Gucci], who was the other chorus, sang alone, but [was accompanied] by various sounds of instruments. And immediately upon the entrance of the Most Serene Lady, the Holy Vespers was begun with great applause and devotion on the part of those attending. This finished, certain curtains of thin silk, which concealed the chorus, were drawn aside. [This] unexpectedly revealed three lavishly dressed angels, one of which was Bernardo Carraresi, who by himself sang a newly-composed madrigal in praise of our protector [Archangel Raphael], the personage which he represented. Before the song began, many very delicate cascades of [instrumental] notes preceded, after which the angel, who held in his hand a silver vase, [sang] with such a delicate voice and manner, more angelic than human, that by the sweetness of it the souls of those attending were suspended. (Doc.10)

The Grand Duchess was so impressed with this *colpo di scena* that she immediately enrolled her first son, the future Grand Duke Cosimo II, as a member of the company.[33]

---

[30] PALISCA, The "Camerata Fiorentina," p. 218, argues, convincingly in my view, that Bardi's treatise must have been written after January of 1578, but before May 15, 1579. The translation by STRUNK, Source Readings, p. 290–301, had suggested a date of ca. 1580 for the Discorso.

[31] Discorso mandato da Gio: de' Bardi a Giulio Caccini detto Romano sopra la musica antica, e'l cantar bene, in: De' trattati di musica di Gio. Battista Doni patrizio fiorentino, tomo secondo, ed. ANTON FRANCESCO GORI (Florence 1763), p. 246: "Se voi farete a mio senno, rammemorandovi della straordinaria soddisfazione, che ebbe il Popolo Fiorentino nella solennità d'Ognissanti passato, perchè bene intese le parole delle vostre musiche, averete gran riguardo, che s'intendano, chiaramente . . ." PALISCA, The "Camerata Fiorentina," p. 215–19, and elsewhere, relies on an earlier, manuscript copy of Bardi's treatise (I:Rvat, Barberinianus latinus 3990, fols. 4ʳ–13ᵛ), which, he says, does not differ substantially from the printed version given above.

[32] Gucci, like Caccini and Niccolo castrato, sang in the famous intermedi of 1589 (WARBURG, I costumi, p. 77), but, unlike those two, he apparently never served in the grand-ducal chapel. His association with Jacopo Corsi predates even the notice given above, since he sold a strumento, presumably a harpsichord, to Corsi on August 23, 1580 (I:Fas, Guicciardini–Corsi–Salviati, libro 433, opening 12, left). Nothing further is known about Gucci's musical activities outside of the Compagnia dell'Arcangelo Raffaello.

[33] I:Fas, Comp. rel. sop., 162, no. 22 [olim 21], fols. 143ʳ–143ᵛ.

Elements of action, scenic effect, and dialogue were added to solo singing in the performance at the Easter Monday assembly of 1592:

A curtain was drawn back that covered the entire architecture that had been erected for the sacrament [i.e., the catafalque], and there were seated many angels and prophet-sibyls. And each in turn was revealed, and each recited some verses. Then came the three Marys saying that they wished to visit the sepulcher. And the sepulcher was revealed to have an angel upon it who sang a madrigal that said that the Lord had risen. And the Chorus of angels sang a madrigal at the beginning and at the end. (Doc. 11)

Although this presentation resembles some medieval *visitatio sepulchri* dramas in certain respects, it has not been possible to find a continuous link between it and the earlier traditions.

While spoken dialogue continued to be combined with *recitar cantando* in the company's brief dramatizations well into the seventeenth century,[34] the first of many that were entirely sung was presented on December 31, 1593:

The office being finished, five angels came to the altar, in the midst of whom was our Archangel Raphael, and they sang a madrigal with instruments, and the [arch]angel [sang] a solo. (Doc. 12)

94

A solo madrigal that fits this description, or that of December 31, 1591, or both, is found, without ascription, in each of the two largest manuscript collections containing the earliest surviving examples of Florentine *recitar cantando*, I:Fn, Magl. XIX, 66 and B:Bc, 704.[35] The text has been ascribed to Ottavio Rinuccini, who is identified as the author of other texts sung at the Compagnia dell'Arcangelo Raffaello in later years.[36] The words are obviously those of an archangel, one who alone can speak directly with God. He addresses his words to angels who sing "hymns and praises," and he carries aloft the prayers of the mortals assembled:

Angel' divin' da luminosi giri
Divine angel(s?) from the luminous spheres,

spiego le penn'aurate
I spread my golden wings

mentr'Inni e lodi al Re del Ciel cantate.
while you sing hymns and praises to the King of Heaven.

Indi per l'alto polo
Then to heaven

[34] The single-scene dramatizations listed in footnote 22 all included singing, usually both solo and ensemble.
[35] These manuscripts are discussed by FEDERICO GHISI, *Alle fonti della monodia: Due nuovi brani della "Dafne" e il "Fuggilotio musicale" di G. Caccini* (Milan 1940), p. 9–48; NIGEL FORTUNE, *A Florentine Manuscript and its Place in Italian Song*, in: *AMl* XXIII (1951), p. 124 and 134–36; WILLIAM V. PORTER, *The Origins of the Baroque Solo Song: A Study of Italian Manuscripts and Prints from 1590–1610*, (Ph. D. diss. Yale University 1962), p. 63–70; and PORTER, *Peri and Corsi's Dafne: Some New Discoveries and Observations*, in: *JAMS* XVIII (1965), p. 173. The same manuscripts contain settings of the texts "Lasciate pastorell'," "L'alto fattor che l'universo regge," and "Ecco dal sommo trono,", each of which are the words of an angel announcing to the shepherds the birth of Christ. The first two of these are strophic, and two stanzas from either would have sufficed for the angel who sang from heaven at the Christmas assembly of 1613, for example (Doc. 15). The Florence manuscript also contains two texts suitable for All Saints' Day, "Mentre di negre tenebre, s'adombra," which refers to souls in purgatory who return, for one night, to their former bodies, and "Alme cui divin' foco incend'e coce," which are the words of an angel who is rescuing souls from purgatory.
[36] The text is found in I:Fn, Palat. 249, fol. 64[r], within one of the portions of the manuscript designated as written in Rinuccini's hand by LUIGI GENTILE, *Cataloghi dei manoscritti della R. Biblioteca Nazionale Centrale di Firenze, I: Codici palatini* I (Rome 1889), p. 372–85. Rinuccini as poet of texts sung at the Compagnia dell'Arcangelo Raffaello is mentioned in 1609 (see fn. 43) and 1612 (Doc. 13).

porto su l'ali i dolci cant'à volo.
I swiftly carry the sweet songs on my wings.
Su dunque alme devot'alme ben nate.
Up then, devoted souls, well-born souls!
Seguit'i preghi ch'io
Follow the prayers that I bring back
al Ciel ritorn'e gli consacro a Dio.
to heaven and consecrate to God.

The music (Ex. 1) shows traits more characteristic of Caccini's early solo madrigals than those that survive of Peri's. Among these traits are the dotted rhythms in two of the melismas, the extensive musical repetition incorporated into the reprise of the last three lines of poetry, the lack of syncopation, and the bass line that does not remain on the same pitch for longer than one breve. The monotone recitation and first ornament on the word *"giri"* recall Caccini's setting of *"Perfidissimo volto"* (*Nuove musiche*, p. 8–9), which he claims to have composed about 1585.[37]

95

I: Fn, Magl. XIX. 66, fols. 1^r–2^r

---

[37] Caccini's claims are found in the prefaces to his *Euridice* and *Nuove musiche*, translated into English in STRUNK, *Source Readings*, p. 370–72 and 377–92.

96

cr'à Di - o.

From 1594 to 1609 there are no detailed descriptions of music and drama in the
record books of the company due to the admitted lack of interest in his duty on the
part of the *sotto proveditore* during most of that period.[38] However, in 1607 this
office passed to Lionardo da Gagliano, who soon had special reason to report
performances in detail. On December 2, 1607, the company voted to replace Baccio
Malespini, who had served since 1591,[39] with a new *maestro di cappella*, Lionardo's
brother Marco da Gagliano, who had been a member since 1589 when he was six
years old.[40] This replacement seems to have run afoul of court politics, and there
ensued an exchange of letters about it between young Prince Cosimo de' Medici and
Cardinal Ferdinando Gonzaga of Mantua.[41] Finally, on June 28, 1609, Malespini
yielded his position to Gagliano, who held it for the next thirteen years.

Although Gagliano continued to present traditional productions, such as angelic
visitations,[42] he introduced, for the first time as far as the surviving descriptions
record, an important new type of brief musical Christmas pageant in 1612:

> In the evening the office [was sung] with beautiful music, and afterward there was revealed
> the crèche, which was covered with a taffeta curtain. And the said curtain [having been]
> raised, there was a perspective [i.e., a scenic backdrop or flat] of a wooded countryside. And
> certain shepherds recited. And afterward there appeared an angel in a cloud, who sang alone.
> And then a chorus of shepherds sang in music. And afterward the heaven opened, and the
> angels sang in various ways. And during this [singing] the wooded countryside disappeared,
> and one saw the manger with a most beautiful perspective and a beautiful *apparato*
> throughout the hall, such that this feast pleased all the people greatly. (Doc. 14)

Other such brief dramatizations, but entirely sung without any spoken dialogue,
were performed for the company at Christmas time in 1613, 1614/15, 1616, 1618,

---

[38] I:Fas, Comp. rel. sop., 162, no. 22 [*olim* 21], fol. 205ʳ (Dec. 25, 1597): *"La sera la tornata grandissima di
popolo, e con music[h]e, e molte circostanze le quali, non occore farne menzione."* Ibid., fol. 214ᵛ: *"Lascio
discrivere tornata per tornata come se fatto per a dietro perche non è seguito in nostra compagnia se non tornato
solito, e non aver che dire particolari lascio tre mesi passati."*.
[39] His appointment on April 21, 1591 is recorded in I:Fas, Comp. rel. sop., 162, no. 22 [*olim* 21], fol. 133ʳ.
[40] Marco di Zanobi da Gagliano entered the company on Feb. 24, 1589 (n.s.) (I:Fas, Comp. rel. sop., 165, no. 48
[*olim* 40], fol. 22ᵛ).
[41] This episode has been thoroughly illuminated by EDMOND STRAINCHAMPS, *Marco da Gagliano and the
Compagnia dell'Arcangelo Raffaello in Florence: An Unknown Episode in the Composer's Life*, in: *Essays
Presented to Myron P. Gilmore*, ed. SERGIO BERTELLI and GLORIA RAMAKUS (Florence 1977), p. 473–87.
I should like to thank Professor Strainchamps for allowing me to consult the proofs of his excellent article, and to
offer respectfully one addition and one minor correction. Cardinal Ferdinando Gonzaga had a special interest in
the affairs of the Compagnia dell'Arcangelo Raffaello, having been granted membership in it at his personal
request during his visit on Nov. 1, 1605 (I:Fas, Comp. rel. sop., 165, no. 48 [*olim* 40], fol. 87ᵛ). Strainchamps
reports that Gagliano entered the company on Feb. 24, 1588 (p. 475), overlooking in this instance that the
Florentine calendar year began on March 25. Thus the year of Gagliano's entry was 1589 by the modern
calendar, which means that he was six and a half when he joined, not five and a half as Strainchamps reckons.
[42] These were produced in 1610, 1612, 1613, 1614, 1616, 1617, and 1618 (I:Fas, Comp. rel. sop., 162, no. 23 [*olim*
22], fols. 6ʳ, 13ʳ, 25ʳ, 32ʳ, 48ᵛ, 56ʳ, and 62ʳ).

and 1619 (Docs. 15–20). In each case the singers were costumed and scenic effect
was provided by the traditional crèche.

Only one composition sung for the company during Marco da Gagliano's term as
maestro seems to survive. It matches a description of Christmas, 1609, which
mentions a "beautiful lauda" written by Ottavio Rinuccini and sung by Giulio
Caccini's son Pompeo.[43] There is, in fact, a lauda, "*Pastor levate*," by Rinuccini, set
as strophic variations in Gagliano's *Musiche a una due e tre voci* (Venice 1615),
which may have been among the pieces that he had already composed before March
of 1608.[44] It has been published in a modern edition by Putnam Aldrich.[45] The words
could be those of an angel, though the description of the assembly does not mention
a costume. The crèche, of course, was in place and could not have been avoided by
the singer.

During the period of Marco da Gagliano's activity in the company, a new
generation of musicians had become members: Giovanni, Orazio, and Giulano del
Franciosino, Giovanni del Turco, Alessandro Ghivizzani, Giovanni Battista Signorini, Domenico Belli, Francesco Nigetti, and, a little later, Giovanni Battista
dell'Auca.[46] Several of these names are found on the pages of early Florentine
monody manuscripts.[47] Most are included in the roles of the grand-ducal chapel.[48]
As members of the company, they presumably sang or played in some of the
productions that Gagliano provided.

98

---

[43] I:Fas, Comp. rel. sop., 162, no. 22 [*olim* 21], fol. 285ʳ. This notice is transcribed by STRAINCHAMPS,
Marco da Gagliano, p. 476. Although I cannot find the name of Pompeo Caccini on membership lists, I note that
his son Jacopo had just joined the company on Dec. 21, 1609 (I:Fas, Comp. rel. sop., 165, no. 48 [*olim* 40], fol.
100ʳ) and that his brothers Michelangelo, Giovanni Battista, and Giulio di Giulio Caccini had entered on Nov. 1,
1607 (the first two) and May 3, 1609, respectively (ibid., fols. 93ʳ and 98ᵛ).

[44] Gagliano's newly-composed music for one, two, and three voices is mentioned in his letter of March 8, 1608,
from Mantua, to the poet Michelangelo Buonarroti, Jr. in Florence (I:Fl, Arch. Buonarroti 46, fol. 686ʳ).

[45] PUTNAM ALDRICH, *Rhythm in Seventeenth-Century Italian Monody With an Anthology of Songs and
Dances* (New York 1966), p. 168–70.

[46] I:Fas, Comp. rel. sop., 165, no. 48 [*olim* 40] records the matriculations of Giovanni del Franciosino, March 17,
1591 (fol. 32ᵛ), Orazio and Giuliano del Franciosino, Feb. 27, 1594 (fol. 44ʳ and 44ᵛ), Giovanni del Turco, Dec. 21,
1601 (fol. 74ʳ), Alessandro Ghivizzani, March 25, 1605 (fol. 83ʳ), Giovanni Battista Signorini, Nov. 1, 1604 (fol.
85ᵛ), Domenico Belli, Aug. 10, 1607 (fol. 92ᵛ), Francesco Nigetti, Jan. 1, 1613 (fol. 109ᵛ), and Giovanni Battista
dell'Auca, Dec. 22, 1630 (fol. 148ᵛ).

[47] Solo songs by Ghivizzani, Nigetti, and Auca are included in I:Bc, Q 49, which is the subject of FORTUNES's
A Florentine Manuscript. One aria of Belli, from his *Arie* of 1616, is included in the Barbera manuscript (I:Fc)
described by FEDERICO GHISI, *An Early Seventeenth Century Ms. with Unpublished Italian Music by Peri,
Giulio Romano and Marco da Gagliano*, in: *AMl* XX (1948), p. 46–60; and in the *Postscript: A Note on Some
Other Florentine Monodic Manuscripts*, in FORTUNE, *A Florentine Manuscript*, p. 134–36. BELLI's *Primo
libro dell'arie* (Venice 1616), p. 26–27, contains an echo-dialogue on a religious text, "*Anima peccatrice ch'al
regno alto*," suitable for All Saints' Day. New evidence concerning the relationship between Giovanni del Turco
and Marco da Gagliano is presented by EDMOND STRAINCHAMPS, *New Light on the Accademia degli
Elevati of Florence*, in: *MQ* LXII (1976), p. 507–535. Although Signorini was a composer, none of his works is
known to survive (see SOLERTI, *Musica, ballo e drammatica*, p. 102).

[48] Giovanni, Orazio, and Giuliano, students of Franciosino, appear on the salary list of 1603 (I:Fas, Depositeria
generale 1517, openings 56, 77, and 91). Giovanni Battista Signorini, later husband of Francesca Caccini,
appears as another student of Franciosino in the 1604 list (dep. gen. 1518, opening 67). These students of
"Franciosino," i.e., of Bernardo Pagani, were trained primarily as wind players (WARREN KIRKENDALE,
L'Aria di Fiorenza id est il Ballo del Gran Duca [Florence 1972], p. 51, fn. 20). Alessandro Ghivizzani was in the
grand-ducal chapel at least by 1610, the year he left Florence with his wife Settimia Caccini (Dep. gen. 1520,
openings 36 and 101). Domenico Belli joined the rôles some time before 1626 (Dep. gen. 1523, opening 133).
Giovanni Battista dell'Auca joined them on June 19, 1623 (FREDERICK HAMMOND, *Musicians at the Medici
Court in the Mid-Seventeenth Century*, in: *Analecta musicologica* XIV [1974], p. 164). Giovanni del Turco was
superintendent of music at the court from about 1614 to about 1625 (*MGG*, s.v. "*Turco*").

In 1622 the records of the company first mention the name of Jacopo Peri, who composed music for one of their performances in that year.[49] In 1633, at Peri's death, the diarist describes him as a brother.[50] But the surviving membership records do not record his joining, as is also the case with Jacopo Corsi (see footnote 14). Either he could have joined the company during the period 1575–1581 when no records were kept, or his membership could have been subsumed under those of his sons Antonio and Dino, who joined in 1613.[51] Shortly after Jacopo Peri's two sons joined, the two sons of Jacopo Corsi, Peri's patron and collaborator, likewise became members.[52]

Marco da Gagliano's last recorded service to the company was on March 14, 1622, when he provided music for the funeral of Cosimo II.[53] He was succeeded in the position of *maestro di cappella* by his younger brother Giovanni Battista.[54]

In 1622 also, the company was joined by the important poet and dramatist Jacopo Cicognini.[55] From 1615 to his death in 1633, Cicognini produced a series of his *sacre rappresentazioni* for the Compagnia di S. Antonio di Padova in Florence as well as for the Compagnia dell'Arcangelo Raffaelo with music by Giovanni Battista da Gagliano, Francesca Caccini, Filippo Vitali, Jacopo Peri, and Agnolo Conti.[56] These religious plays expanded the tradition of using musical dialogues as intermedi, ànd, hence, belong peripherally to our present topic. But for reasons of space, it will be better to discuss them in another place.

99

Cicognini's most notable contribution to the company's series of brief musical dramas was performed on All Saints' Day in 1622 by singers, perhaps unseen, but in the presence of the traditional sepulcher commemorating the souls in purgatory (compare with the performances of Nov. 1, 1584 and 1585 cited above):

In the evening the Office of the Dead was sung with very good music for two choirs. And before and after the said office, a short dialogue [*uno Dialoghetto*] in music was sung, for which [the singers] pretended to be souls in purgatory which [souls] were begging to be free from their pains. And the angel, consoling them, promised [deliverance] to them by means of the Office that was [about] to be celebrated. And after [the Office] was finished, the angel

[49] I:Fas, Comp. rel. sop., 162, no. 23 [*olim* 22] reveals that Peri provided some music for intermedi in productions of Giovanni MARIA CECCHI's La beneditione di Jacob, Nov. 11–26, 1622 (fol. 95ʳ), of JACOPO CICOGNINI's Il gran mistero della redentione humana, Dec. 25, 1622 (fol. 98ᵛ), and of CICOGNINI's La celeste guida, Feb., 1624 (fol. 111ᵛ).
[50] I:Fas, Comp. rel. sop., 162, no. 24 [*olim* 23], fol. 61ʳ.
[51] I:Fas, Comp. rel. sop., 165, no. 48 [*olim* 40], fol. 109ʳ; and Comp. rel. sop., 164, no. 38 [*olim* 36], no foliation, second alphabet, under the letter "D."
[52] Giovanni and Lorenzo di Jacopo Corsi entered on March 10, 1613 (I:Fas, Comp. rel. sop., 165, no. 48 [*olim* 40], fol. 110ʳ).
[53] I:Fas, Comp. rel. sop., 162, no. 23 [*olim* 22], fol. 83ʳ.
[54] Giovanni Battista di Zanobi da Gagliano became a member of the company on July 24, 1599 (I:Fas, Comp. rel. sop., 165, no. 48 [*olim* 40], fol. 65ᵛ). The first mention I find of him as *maestro di cappella* is on Christmas of 1622 (I:Fas, Comp. rel. sop., 162, no. 23 [*olim* 22], fol. 97ʳ), although the terms of former maestri always began on November 1.
[55] I:Fas, Comp. rel. sop., 165, no. 48 [*olim* 40], fol. 129ʳ.
[56] Cicognini's activities on behalf of the Compagnia di S. Antonio are detailed in GIUSEPPE BACCINI, Notizie die alcune commedie sacre rappresentate in Firenze nel secolo XVII (Florence 1889), but the reader is warned that nearly all of Baccini's dates are wrong, partly because of his failure to correct for the old Florentine calendar. The notices that he transcribes are found in I:Fas, Comp. rel. sop., 134, no. 3 [*olim* 2]. CICOGNINI's sacre rappresentazioni were acted and sung by members of the Compagnia dell'Arcangelo Raffaello in 1622, 1623, 1624, and 1629 (I:Fas, comp. rel. sop., 162, no. 23 [*olim* 22], fols. 93ᵛ–95ʳ, 97ʳ–98ᵛ, 103ʳ, 108ʳ–111ᵛ, and 162ʳ–164ᵛ).

repeated that they [the souls] had been liberated, and thus they flew to heaven, thanking the brothers for the prayers and suffrages offered. The whole was the composition of messer Jacopo Cicognini, which inspired great devotion in everyone. (Doc. 21)

The remarkably effective text of this composition survives under the title "*Coro d'anime del Purgatorio*" in a manuscript that indeed ascribes it to Cicognini:[57]

[*Anime purganti*:]	*O tenebroso orrore*
	Oh gloomy horror
	o insopportabil pena
	oh insupportable pain!
	chi ne soccorre, ohime, chi ne scatena.
	Who relieves us from it, alas, who unchains us from it?
Una voce [*del vivente:*]	*Quai voci flebili*
	Those mournful voices
	tra noi rintonano.
	resound about us;
	Son forse l'anime
	they are perhaps the souls
	che in fiamme orribili
	who, in horrible flames,
	dolenti piangono.
	weap sorrowfully.
	Che mano angelica
	What angelic hand
	ormai le liberi
	may free them now
	dal duro carcere
	from the harsh imprisonment
	ohime, che spezzaci
	alas, which breaks
	a tante duol per gran pietà il core.
	our hearts out of great pity for such pain?
Coro [*d'anime:*]	*O tenebroso orrore,* [*ecc.*]
	Oh gloomy horror, etc.
Anima [*purgante:*]	*Deh voi, che ancor vivete*
	Pray you, who still live,
	in questo basso Mondo
	in this world here below,
	dal nostro duol profondo
	from our profound grief
	omai senno apprendete.
	at last learn wisdom.
	Son fumi, e vanitade
	But pride and vanity are
	giovinezza, e beltade.
	youth and beauty.

100

---

[57] I:Fn, Magl. VII, 358, fols. 110ʳ–112ᵛ.

Ahi come nebbia il vento
Alas, like clouds in the wind

si dilegua il contento
contentment vanishes,

e come al sol le Nevi.
like snow in the sun.

Quasi lampo, o baleno
Like lightning or thunder

ogni pompa vien meno.
every display dies away.

Oggi in vita festosi
Today joyful in life,

doman sottera ascosi.
tomorrow concealed under the earth.

Un'altra [anima purgante:]	*O fragil voglie* Oh frail wishes,
	o debil possa. oh little power!
	Ecco v'accoglie Behold
	l'orrida fassa. the horrid grave welcomes you.
Un'altra [anima:]	*Ahi mal si passe* Ah, badly the heart is wounded
	di speme il core. with hoping.
	Oggi rinasce Today it is reborn,
	doman si muore. tomorrow it dies away.
Coro [d'anime:]	*O tenebroso orrore [ecc.]* Oh gloomy horror, etc.
Angelo:	*Non più duol non più lamenti.* No more grief, no more lamenting.
	Son celeste messaggiero. I am a heavenly messenger.
	Scendo a voi dall'alto Impero I come down to you from the kingdom above,
	e vi tolgo a rei tormenti. and I remove you from your cruel torments.
	Han placato il Re del Cielo The King of Heaven has been appeased
	de viventi i caldi pr[i]eghi by the ardent prayers of the living.
	Ne pietà sia, che si nieghi Nor is it mercy that would deny
	a si puro, e sacro zelo. such pure and holy fervor.

101

Coro [d'anime:]   *Su lasciamo, i regni ardenti.*
                             Up, let us leave the fiery realms!

                             Non più duol, non più lamenti.
                             No more grief, no more lamenting.

                             Lieti cantiamo
                             Let us sing joyfully.

                             Ratti voliamo
                             Quickley let us fly

                             ov'e gioir eterno
                             to where there is eternal joy,

                             da questo Inferno.
                             away from this inferno.

                             Speghiamo l'ali
                             Let us spread our wings

                             tra gl'Immortali.
                             among the immortals.

                             Non più lamenti.
                             No more lamenting.

                             Formiam beati accenti
                             Let us exclaim happy words.

                             Non più non più lamenti
                             No more, no more lamenting.

102

The division of this dialogue, mentioned in the description of its performance, obviously comes after all or part of the angel's verses, which indeed refer to the prayers, hence the office, offered by the living brothers. This would, therefore, easily be the earliest known sacred dialogue for an oratory to be divided into two parts, albeit divided by an Office for the Dead rather than a sermon as in later decades.[58] In length, the composition is above the average of the dialogues printed in G. F. Anerio's *Teatro armonico spirituale* of 1619.[59] It is slightly longer than Pietro della Valle's *Oratorio della Purificatione* performed in Rome *ca.* 1640.[60] Another dialogue was performed for the company on All Saints' Day of 1626 (Doc. 23), but the description of the assembly is too sketchy to permit any comparison with Cicognini's of 1622 (Doc. 21).

[58] Domenico Mazzocchi's setting of the *Coro di Profeti* and the text by Francesco Balducci to *La fede*, both dating from the 1630s, according to accepted views, are, otherwise, the earliest known multi-partite sacred dialogues or oratorios (WOLFGANG WITZENMANN, *Domenico Mazzocchi, 1592–1665, Dokumente und Interpretationen*, in: *Analecta musicologica* 8 [Vienna 1970], p. 22–24, 124–41; DOMENICO ALALEONA, *Storia dell'oratorio in Italia*, 2nd ed. [Milan 1945], p. 142–45, 289–303; GUIDO PASQUETTI, *L'oratorio musicale in Italia* [Florence 1906], p. 205–228; ARNOLD SCHERING, *Geschichte des Oratoriums*, Kleine Handbücher der Musikgeschichte nach Gattungen, ed. HERMANN KRETZSCHMAR 3 [Leipzig 1911] p. 54–55 and *Anhang*, p. vii–xii). The first part of GIACOMO CARISSIMI's *Oratorio della Santissima Vergine* is based on Balducci's text *Il trionfo*, and therefore it could also date from the 1630s (LINO BIANCHI, ed., *Giacomo Carissimi: Oratorio della SS.ma Vergine*, Istituto Italiano per la Storia della Musica, *Monumenti* 3, vol. 8 [Rome 1964], p. xiii).
[59] WAYNE CLANTON HOBBS, *Giovanni Francesco Anerio's* Teatro Armonico Spirituale di Madrigali: *A Contribution to the Early History of the Oratorio* (Ph. D. diss. Tulane University 1971), p. 288.
[60] AGOSTINO ZIINO, *Pietro della Valle e la "musica erudita": nuovi documenti*, in: *Analecta musicologica* IV (1967), p. 102.

Cicognini also contributed to the company's repertoire of musical-dramatic dialogues that include the personage of its Archangel protector (Doc. 22) and to the series of musical Christmas pageants sung in costume in front of the crèche (Doc. 24). In these latter two cases the music was probably composed by Agnolo Conti, who had succeeded G. B. da Gagliano as *maestro di cappella* of the company as of November 1, 1625.[61]

Although little survives of Conti's music, we have it on the authority of Antonio Biscioni that "he published much church music, such as masses, vespers, sacred motets, and spiritual festivities [*Veglie spirituali*], presented in the Compagnia dell'Arcangelo Raffaello, called della Scala, and other compositions."[62] He served as *maestro* of the company for his remaining seventeen years. Like Peri and the Gagliano brothers, he was a theorbist who served the grand-ducal court (1631–1642).[63]

Conti was probably the composer of the elaborate musical drama that was sung "in place of a motet" after Christmas Mattins in 1639 (Doc. 26). The text of that musical drama may have been by Girolamo Bartolommei who joined the company in 1636 and served as its *Governatore* in 1638.[64]

103

Bartolommei was certainly the author of the text of the *Trionfo d'amori celesti* sung in honor of the birth of Cosimo, the first born of Vittoria della Rovere and Grand Duke Ferdinando II, on August 24, 1642. The company's records call the composition a motet (Doc. 27). The libretto printed for the occasion styles it a *dramma sacro*.[65] But it was reprinted among Bartolommei's *Dialoghi sacri musicali* in 1657, and sacred dialogue is the name music historians would now give it.[66] The personages are Archangel Raphael, two *amori celesti*, and a chorus of *amori*. In substance it belongs to the type of musical dialogue, produced by the company in previous decades, in which the archangel responds to and encourages the pious aspirations of those present, offers himself as spiritual guide (as he did to Tobias), and carries to heaven the prayers of the brothers. This dialogue is 197 verses long and has thirteen textual divisions. Presuming the poet's stated intentions were carried out, the solo portions would have included recitatives that contrasted in style with the choruses and, presumably, the arias.[67] The text is dramatic and reflective,

---

[61] I:Fas, Comp. rel. sop., 162, no. 23 [*olim* 22], fol. 128ᵛ.

[62] I:Fn, Cl. IX, 69, ANTONIO MARIA BISCIONI, "*Giunte e correzioni alla Toscana letterata del Cinelli*," vol. I, p. 57. ANGELO (alternate form of "Agnolo") CONTI's *Motetti a due, quattro, cinque, sei & otto voci per concertarsi nell'organo, & altri strumenti* (Venice 1639) contain no dialogues. The name "Agniolo" given in the Florentine monody manuscript I:Bc, Q 49, fols. 3ᵛ and 12ᵛ, quite likely refers to Agnolo Conti. His printed collection of masses (Venice 1634) and three books of madrigals à 4 (*ivi* 1635–1639), now lost, were reported in F[RANÇOIS]-J[OSEPH] FÉTIS, *Biographie universelle des musiciens et bibliographie générale de la musique*, 2nd ed. vol. II (Paris 1875), p. 349.

[63] HAMMOND, *Musicians*, p. 158 and 162.

[64] I:Fas, Comp. rel. sop., 165, no. 48 [*olim* 40], fol. 159ʳ; 162, no. 24 [*olim* 23], fol. 136ʳ.

[65] *Trionfo d'amori celesti nella nascita del Serenissimo Principe di Toscana: Dramma sacro offerta de fratelli della Compagnia della Scala* (Florence 1642), exemplar in I:Fm, Misc. 205.8. PASQUETTI, *L'oratorio*, p. 379, calls this a cantata, and misdates it as 1645.

[66] GIROLAMO BARTOLOMMEI GIÀ SMEDUCCI, *Dialoghi sacri musicali intorno a diversi suggetti, opera nuova di* . . . (Florence 1657), exemplar in I:Fn, Palat. 29.2.6.39.

[67] BARTOLOMMEI, *Al benigno lettore*, in: *Dialoghi sacri*: "*Io procurai perciò di disporne in tal maniera questi miei Sacri Dialoghi, che vaglia in essi in più guise scherzare lodevolmente la Musica, valendosi or del modo recitativo ne' soliloqui, ed ora de' suoi vaghi passeggi nel pieno de' Cori.*"

although it describes no plot or action. In every respect the composition is within the norms that apply to works that were called "oratorios" in mid-seventeenth-century Italy.[68] The composer was Baccio Baglioni, who had been named *maestro di cappella* of the company in 1642.[69]

The *Trionfo d'amori celesti* seems to have been the first dialogue or brief musical dramatization performed in the company with neither costumes nor scenic effect. The reason for this innovation may lay in physical changes in the company's prayer hall that had recently been carried out under the direction and at the expense of Alberto del Vivaio, the aristocrat and dilettante composer who had been elected the company's superintendent of music on May 25, 1641.[70] In that year, Vivaio had an elevated balcony with attached rehearsal room constructed, both at the mezzanine level, to accommodate the musicians.[71] This, it was observed, would keep the brothers and the musicians from getting in each others' way.[72] It could not be used, of course, while singing dialogues in front of the crèche, inside the catafalque, or at the altar, as had been the custom. Only one more description after 1641, of a *dialogo in musica* in 1644 (Doc. 28), permits an interpretation that includes a staged presentation, though even in this case costumes and scenic effect are not mentioned explicitly. The next two descriptions of dialogue performances, of 1654 (Doc. 29) and 1655 (Doc. 30), would seem to have been carried out in the fashion considered normal for oratorios in the mid-seventeenth century. The last one, called a *Mottetto à forma del Dialogo in musica*, receives the title *Il giudizio universale*; its music was by the company's *maestro di cappella* of that time, Giovanni Battista Comparini.[73]

This convenient point of arrival coincides with the last descriptions of elaborate music performed for the Compagnia dell'Arcangelo Raffaello before a third gap in its surviving descriptive records, 1658–1686, intervenes. Although it is possible to establish continuity between the company's activities during the 1650s and its

104

[68] HOWARD E. SMITHER, *What Is an Oratorio in Mid-Seventeenth-Century Italy*, in: *IMS, Report of the Eleventh Congress, Copenhagen, 1972* (Copenhagen 1974) II, p. 657–63.

[69] I:Fas, Comp. rel. sop., 163, no. 26 [*olim* 25], fol. 9ʳ. Baglioni was another theorbist, became *maestro di cappella* of the Cathedral of Livorno, and died on Aug. 30, 1649, as we learn from notices transcribed by BIANCA BECHERINI, *Catalogo dei manoscritti musicali della Biblioteca Nazionale di Firenze* (Kassel 1959), p. 15. He was succeeded as *maestro di cappella* of the Compagnia dell'Arcangelo Raffaello by Niccolò Sapiti on Nov. 1, 1644 (I:fas, Comp. rel. sop., 163, no. 26 [*olim* 25], fol. 39ʳ). The opera *Celio* that Baglioni and Sapiti composed together has been studied recently by LORENZO BIANCONI and THOMAS WALKER, *Dalle* Finta Pazza *alla* Veremondo: *Storie di Febiarmonici*, in: *Rivista italiana di musicologia* X (1975), p. 445–54.

[70] I:Fas, Comp. rel. sop., 162, no. 24 [*olim* 23], fol. 158ʳ. Biscioni, I:Fn, Cl. IX, 69, fol. 198ʳ tells us that Vivaio was a mathematician as well as a composer. Being the last of his family, he left the Compagnia dell'Arcangelo Raffaello, on his death in 1659, a large endowment for musical performances (I:Fas, Comp. rel. sop., 156, fascio C, "*Comp.a dell'Arcangiolo Raffaello d.a la Scala e Capperelli e PP. di S. Giuseppe*"). Biscioni says that Vivaio published a book of madrigals in Florence, but all that is known of his music are the madrigals included in the collections of Santi Orlandi (1602 and 1605) and Filippo Vitali (1616 and 1629).

[71] I:Fas, Comp. rel. sop., 162, no. 24 [*olim* 23], fols. 188ʳ and 194ʳ.

[72] I:Fas, Comp. rel. sop., 163, no. 26 [*olim* 25], fols. 2ʳ–4ʳ.

[73] Comparini had been a member of the company since Dec. 25, 1620 (I:Fas, Comp. rel. sop., 165, no. 48 [*olim* 40], fol. 126ʳ) and could therefore remember the dialogues sung in costume with *apparati* under the direction of Marco and G. B. da Gagliano, Agnolo Conti, and Baccio Baglioni. He was elected *maestro di cappella* on Nov. 1, 1653 (I:Fas, Comp. rel. sop., 163, no. 26 [*olim* 25], fol. 142ᵛ). His contemporary GIOVANNI CINELLI, *La Toscana letterata, parte prima, ovvero storia o catalogo degli scrittori fiorentini per ordine dell'alfabeto dei nomi* (I:Fn, Cl. IX, 66), p. 802, reports of him: "*Gio: Batt[ist]a Comparini Musico: fu Maestro di Cappella del nostro Duomo, e successe nella carica a Filippo Vitali. Compose molte opere buone per la Cappella come la Magnificat, molti Mottetti, Messe e Vespri di diversi, li quali componimenti vanno manoscritti attorno per le mani de' professori. Morì nel 1659 l'anni 48.*" One motet by Comparini survives in I:Fc, E.177.

previously-known oratorio productions that were formerly thought to have begun about 1690,[74] that discussion can wait for a separate study. The earlier documents cited above, meanwhile, raise several questions and issues.

*

Since the dramatic compositions described in the company's records of 1612–1639 were sung with costumes, scenery, or both, is it accurate to call them sacred dialogues, "incunabula of the oratorio?"[75] While the terms *"dialogo"* or *"dialoghetto"* appear six times in the company's descriptions of musical performances, more often the diarist omits a generic name, as on Christmas of 1639 when he wrote, "and in place of a motet, some shepherds appeared." The two surviving texts linked to specific performances are in every respect like the texts of dialogues used to illustrate the history of the oratorio. In other instances we must rely on descriptions. The most detailed of these, for the fully staged performance of Christmas, 1612, presents an outline not unlike that of the dialogue *"Voi ch'ai notturni"* in G. F. Anerio's *Teatro armonico* of 1619, except that it seems to have been preceded by some spoken lines. Later performances did away with speaking, but retained similar outlines. None resembled operas in length, division into acts and scenes, number of interlocutors, or complexity of action.

105

Performance with costumes, visual representations, or both is not incompatible with the content of any Italian-language, sacred musical dialogue before Anerio's of 1619 which have been described so far by writers about this genre. They all do without the *testo*, a figure apparently more commonly encountered in the earliest Latin dialogue motets.[76] Even most of Girolamo Bartolommei's dialogues, published in 1657, have no narration, just possibly reflecting the earlier manner of performing them in the company of which Bartolommei was a member.[77]

[74] PASQUETTI, *L'oratorio musicale in Italia*, p. 378–79.

[75] The term "incunabula of the oratorio" is SCHERING's (*Geschichte des Oratoriums*, p. 43) and has been revived by HOWARD E. SMITHER, *A History of the Oratorio*, Vol. I: *The Oratorio in the Baroque Era: Italy, Vienna, Paris* (Chapel Hill, N.C. 1977), p. 118–42.

[76] The texts of five pre-1619 Italian-language sacred musical dialogues are printed in ALALEONA, *Storia*, p. 122–24; or in SMITHER, *History* I, p. 96–102. Of the sixty-one Latin dialogue motets listed by HOWARD E. SMITHER, *The Latin Dramatic Dialogue and the Nascent Oratorio*, in: *JAMS* XX (1967), p. 429–33, twenty-one use narration.

[77] The period of Bartolommei's membership in the Compagnia dell'Arcangelo Raffaello, 1635–1662, includes years in which there were performances of dialogues in costume with representational *apparato*. In fact, the performance of August 24, 1644 (Doc. 28) corresponds in outline and cast to some dramatic poetry by Bartolommei – not one of his sacred dialogues, but the third act of *Maddalena al sepolcro*, published in his *Drammi musicali morali* (Florence 1656), II, p. 209–31, but with this interesting comment within the preface to this individual *dramma*: "*Spero per ciò, che possa la Benignità di V. A. parimente gradire il presente Componimento, quantunque molto semplice, e breve; e più somigliante a Dialogo Musicale, che a Dramma; e più, che per pubbliche Scene, acconcio per cantarsi ne' privati Oratorij.*" However, while Bartolommei here distinguishes between *drammi musicali* and *dialoghi musicali* on the basis of length and complexity, in the preface to his *Dialoghi sacri* (1657) he says that *drammi musicali* require scenery while *dialoghi* do not. On the other hand, he does not say that *dialoghi* were not or should not be performed with scenic effect: "*Non ha dubbio, che l'Azioni più pompose, partorirne vagliano effetti maggiori di diletto, e d'utilità, concorrendo con l'udito la vista per una tale commozione d'affetti, che da essa ne derivi l'umana Felicità. Ma chi non sa con quanta fatica, e quanto dispendio pervengano a farne fra' Teatri pompa di loro stessi a gli Spettatori, a cui per ciò si rappresentino di rado? la qual cosa non segua ne' Dialoghi, li quali appagandosi nell'esser solamente ascoltati nel contenuto loro in breve giro di parole ristretto, ritrovano pronta in ogni loco la Scena loro, e singolarmente i Sacri tra' frequentati Oratori, tra' quali possano con aggradevole dilettazione eccitarne una divota pietade, se venghino addolciti da proporzionata armonia di note musicali.*" These two statements and the variety of generic

The visual representations employed by the Compagnia dell'Arcangelo Raffaello for these dialogue performances differed from the scenery the company used for their longer, largely spoken *commedie sacre* during the same period.[78] These plays used theatrical sets adapted to each scene so as to give the illusion of the proper time and place. The dialogues, on the other hand, with two exceptions (Docs. 14 and 25), used *apparati* consisting of objects, such as the crèche and catafalque, unchanging flats or backdrops, pictures of angels, virgins, cadavers, etc., as well as non-representational decoration (Docs. 22 and 29). These *apparati* pertained to the holiday more than to the dialogue, and they remained in place before and after the performance. They are like the *apparati* set up on special holidays in churches, especially Jesuit churches, all over Catholic Europe during the seventeenth century.[79] Sacred dramatic music must have frequently been seen performed in front of such *apparati*, as we know it was occasionally in Rome and Vienna during the Baroque era.[80]

106

Granted, then, that Italian-language, sacred musical dialogues were performed in the Compagnia dell'Arcangelo Raffaello, 1612–1655, what connection is there between these dialogues and early *recitar cantando* presented by the same company? Since so little music survives, our main clues are again in the documents.

The musical performances described in detail by the *sotto proveditori* of the Compagnia dell'Arcangelo Raffaello, 1583–1655, share a great deal in common, and this to a remarkable extent considering the time span involved and the absence of liturgical restraints. By far most of the detailed notices describe performances that took place on All Saints' Day or at Christmas time, including the feast of Archangel Raphael (Dec. 31). Four of the seven performances in the period 1582–1586 took place during Holy Week but were similar to the two on All Saints' Day during the same period. Naturally, therefore, the themes and personages involved remained relatively constant. Furthermore, until 1642 all of the performances took place in a dramatic setting with costumes, visual representation, or both.

Throughout the period 1583–1655 we find testimony to the emotional and moral fervor that these musical-dramatic presentations inspired. Surprise and spectacle

names given to BARTOLOMMEI's *Trionfi d'amori celesti* – motet, *dramma sacro*, and *dialogo sacro* (see fns. 65 and 66, and Doc. 26) – seem to reflect the fluid terminology of a time of rapid and fundamental change within an emerging genre.

[78] The scenery for CICOGNINI's *commedie sacre* (*sacre rappresentazioni*) is described in the archival notices cited in fn. 54 and in the printed libretti for his *Il martirio di S. Agata* (Florence 1624), I:Fn, Magl. 3.5.231; *La celeste guida dell'Arcangelo Raffaello* (Florence 1625), I:Fn, Magl. 3.5.229; *Il gran natale di Christo* (Florence 1625), I:Fn Magl. Misc. 1262.6; and *Il trionfo di David* (Florence 1629), I:Fn, Magl. 3.5.223.

[79] WEIL *The Devotion of the Forty Hours*, p. 220–21, fn. 4; BJUSTRÖM, *Baroque Theater*, p. 104–105. Early Florentine use of pictorial *apparati* is described in seventeenth-century record books of the Jesuits there (I:Fas, Com. rel. sop., 991, nos. 78–80; 992, nos. 81–83) and in some correspondence of 1618 (I:Fas, Mediceo del principato, filza 6110, fol. 977ʳ). For references to descriptions of performances of music in front of or above similar *apparati* in the grand-ducal palace in Florence during the second two decades of the seventeenth century, see SMITHER, *A History of the Oratorio* I, p. 377–78.

[80] A[UGUSTO] BEVIGNANI, *L'Arciconfraternità di S. Maria dell'Orazione e Morte in Roma e le sue rappresentazioni sacre*, in: *Archivio della R. Società Romana di Storia Patria* XXXIII (1910), p. 133–34, reports on Roman performances in 1646. A summary is given by SMITHER, *A History of the Oratorio* I, p. 164–65. RUDOLF SCHNITZLER, *The Sacred Dramatic Music of Antonio Draghi* (Ph. D. diss. University of North Carolina, Chapel Hill 1971), p. 59–105, 286–95, and the literature cited there, discusses late Baroque, Viennese performances. See SMITHER, *A History of the Oratorio* I, p. 261–74 for a survey with illustrations of the original studies of Roman oratorio performances with *apparati* during the early eighteenth century.

played their parts, but there continued to be great reliance on solo singing as a means of stirring human passions. This reliance, of course, was consonant with the opinions about the affective potential of music held by certain members of the company in common with other Florentines during the late sixteenth century. From 1612 onward *recitar cantando* was clearly the prevailing mode, but also many of the earlier descriptions strongly suggest that the performers sang the words of the personages they represented. The continuity of these performances is but one aspect of the tendency to preserve tradition that is apparent in all the activities of the company during the 250 years covered by its records.

But within this continuity there was obviously a series of changes. From 1583 to 1585 one heard liturgical texts sung from within the catafalque. From 1587 to 1612 solo and ensemble singing were frequently added to spoken dialogue. After Christmas of 1612, thirteen of the sixteen described performances were completely musical dialogues. The general pattern seems to be that singing first replaces spoken verse, then visual representation as the predominating medium of communication as one type of production supersedes another.

These supersessions resulted largely from the selections, from available music and poetry, made by the *maestro di cappella*, probably in response to the wishes of the superintendant of music and of other interested members of the company. To this extent the innovations within the continuity of performances reflect changing taste. The *maestri di cappella*, two or more poets who were members of the company, and, perhaps, other Florentine artists produced at least some if not most of the works performed. To this extent we may presume that changing taste affected musical and poetic style. What resulted from this interaction between taste and style? Dialogues that are not among those described in the records of the Compagnia dell'Arcangelo Raffaello, but that are similar to them, were composed by members of the company itself and by other Florentines before 1655. Some were performed elsewhere in Florence. Some may have been performed before the company, but were not singled out in the descriptions of assemblies. The music or at least the poetry of a few survive.

107

G. B. da Gagliano, a member of the Compagnia dell'Arcangelo Raffaello from 1599 to his death in 1651, published one Italian-language sacred musical dialogue, on a Christmas theme. It is included in his *Varie musiche* (1623), which appeared in the middle of the three years (1622–1624) during which he served as the company's *maestro di cappella*.[81] The younger Gagliano's *Mottetti* of 1626 include one Latin dialogue, also for Christmas; and his second book of motets of 1643 contains another three.[82]

---

[81] This dialogue, "*O notte amata*," like the "*Coro d'anime del Purgatorio*" of 1622 (see fn. 57), is musically structured by recurring material. It begins with seven sections of solo and duet singing that include interlocking repetitions and alternations between metrical ($^3/_2$) *ariette* and rhythmically freer passages, in which seven sections the words of two angels and a shepherd are set ("*O notte amata . . . O notte luminosa et ammirabile*"). The concluding chorus, sung by angels *à 5*, "*Gioite ò selve ò colli*," tells the shepherds to follow the star ("*seguite l'ormora*"). Although the components of this dialogue are listed as separate items in the print's index, their texts clearly reveal that together they form a continuous whole.

[82]The dialogue "*Angelus ad Pastores dixit*" in G. B. DA GAGLIANO's *Mottetti per concertare a due, tre*

Ottavio Rinuccini wrote several sacred dialogue texts. Angelo Solerti has published a description of two performances of one, in 1620, with scenery.[83] Another Florentine, Alessandro Ginori († 1615), has left texts of four dialogues for Holy Week.[84] Benedetto Rigogli, an active member of the Compagnia dell'Arcangelo Raffaello from 1612 to 1630,[85] wrote texts for at least two Christmas dialogues.[86] Another two for the same holiday by the Florentine Benedetto Buonmattei (1581–1647) are dated 1622.[87]

Carlo Dati (1619–1676), one of the most important Florentine men of letters of his day, left five dialogue texts in an autograph collection of his poetry.[88] One, entitled *"Per S. Giovanni Evangelista, per la musica, 1641,"*[89] was almost certainly performed in Florence. During the winter of 1641–42, Dati was especially active as a member of the Compagnia dell'Arcangelo Raffaello, having completed a term as *Governatore* on December 8, 1641 and having taken his turn during the prayer vigil of the Forty Hours on April 20, 1642.[90] On the feast day of St. John the Evangelist, December 27, 1641, the Compagnia dell'Arcangelo Raffaello sent a delegation of its members to the evening celebration of its brother company of S. Giovanni Evangelista. This celebration would appear to have been the occasion for which Dati wrote the text.[91]

Less precisely datable are thirty-five dialogue texts for a variety of church feasts, but mostly for Christmas time, contained in a manuscript that apparently served as an inventory of a collection of scores. Nearly every text is followed by the comment

quattro, cinque, sei, & otto voci (Venice 1626) is made up of three short sections. The tenor precedes the words of the angel (canto), which are followed by a concluding narrative sentence sung à 6. GAGLIANO's *Il secondo libro de motetti a sei et otto voci per concertarsi nell'organo, & altri strumenti* (Venice 1643) contains the Latin dialogues *"Audivi vocem de caelo," "Crux fedelis,"* and *"Laudem Domino cantemus,"* but these are not dramatic in the sense of using identifiable personages. None of these four dialogues is listed by SMITHER, *The Latin Dramatic Dialogue.*

[83] ANGELO SOLERTI, *Gli albori del melodramma* (Milan 1904) II, p. 347–50. Solerti prints, without explanation, what I take to be four more independent texts after the chorus of angels that concludes on p. 350 with the verse, *"Cantino eterni secoli."* The next text, *"Spiega pur le bell'ali,"* refers to the birth of Christ, then *"Fuggite l'empio! o quanti"* concerns the flight into Egypt. *"Ecco splendere in ciel quel di giocando"* relates again to the Nativity, and *"Lasciat'i campi luminosi a tergo"* is another text for the Annunciation. The first text includes thirty-two verses in two divisions: Gabriel's solo and the reflective response of the choir of angels.

[84] The manuscript containing all four, I:Fu, Magl. VII, 818, fols. 131ᵛ–132ᵛ and 146ᵛ–147ᵛ, is dated 1622 on the title page. Ginori's passion dialogue uses a guardian angel and a soul as interlocutors. It contains forty-two verses in eight divisions, as compared to the twenty-six verses in ten divisions set by Quagliati in his dialogue *"Quando sarà quel giorno"* for angel, soul, and chorus of angels.

[85] I:Fas, Comp. rel. sop., 162, no. 23 [*olim* 22], fol. 16ᵛ; no. 24 [*olim* 23], fol. 3ᵛ.

[86] I:Fn, Magl. VII, 625, fols. 25ᵛ–23ᵣ. The second of these (fols. 26ᵛ–28ᵣ), *"Poi che del nato Dio l'alta novella,"* with the narrator, shepherds, and angels, contains sixty-three verses in six divisions.

[87] The dialogue *per al presepio* (for in front of the crèche), entitled *"Inteneriti il seno,"* uses a chorus and three soloists who are not given names. It is narrative and reflective, rather than dramatic, sixty-four verses in length, and divided into eleven sections (I:Fn, Palat. 243, fols. 19ᵛ–20ᵛ). The other, in Italian also, but entitled *"Pastores loquebantur ad invicem,"* uses three shepherds who sing alone and together (forty-six lines, twelve divisions).

[88] I:Fn, Magl. VII, 472, fols. 1ᵣ–8ᵣ, *"Cantico sacro, e morale fatto per i PP. della Chiesa Nuova di Roma 1652;"* fols. 9ᵣ–11ᵣ and 161ᵣ–162ᵣ, *"Cantico per lo Santiss.o Sacramento dell'Altare;"* fols. 71ᵣ–74ᵣ, *"P[er] S. Giovanni Evangelista, per la musica 1641;"* fols. 143ᵣ–144ᵣ, *"Coro d'Angioli custodi;"* fols. 145ᵣ–146ᵣ, *"La Religione solve."*

[89] Narrative and relective, three recitatives for unnamed soloist(s), two choruses, fifty verses.

[90] I:Fas, Comp. rel. sop., 162, no. 24 [*olim* 23], fols. 136ᵛ and 139ᵛ; Comp. rel. sop., 163, no. 25 [*olim* 24], fol. 5ᵛ.

[91] I:Fas, Comp. rel. sop., 162, no. 24 [*olim* 23], fol. 140ᵛ. The records of the Compagnia di S. Giovanni Evangelista were destroyed during the flood of 1966.

"*Questo l'ò in musica.*"[92] Most of the texts in the manuscript do not exceed the length of those set by Anerio. One of the earliest of them, on a Christmas theme, but not a dialogue, is described as a "*madrigale del S.r Cava[liere] del Turco*" (fol. 34^r), referring evidently to Giovanni del Turco, a member of the Compagnia dell'Arcangelo Raffaello since 1601 and a student of Marco da Gagliano. Although most of the compositions of which the manuscript preserves the texts are anonymous, three of its sacred dialogues are ascribed respectively to Jacopo Melani, Giovanni Battista Benvenuti, and Buonaventura Cerri, all of whom were active in Florence beginning about the middle of the seventeenth century.

By far the largest group of sacred dialogue texts by a Florentine poet are the seventy-five that make up Girolamo Bartolommei's *Dialoghi sacri musicali intorno a diversi suggetti* (Florence 1657). Bartolommei was an active member, from 1635 to his death in 1662, of the Compagnia dell'Arcangelo Raffaello, which as we have seen, presented in 1642 one of the dialogues included in this printed collection. Another of them was copied into the large manuscript anthology of texts discussed in the preceding paragraph, with the annotation "*e l'o in musica*" (fols. 56^r–60^r). Bartolommei must have written some of the texts soon after joining the Compagnia dell'Arcangelo Raffaello, since Galileo Galilei sent some of them to the composer Giovanni Giacomo Porro in Munich in 1638. Porro was eager to set Bartolommei's texts, and if he did, they would easily qualify as the earliest known Italian-language sacred dialogues to have been set to music in a German-speaking country.[93]

109

Naturally the taste and style of early-seventeenth-century Florentines did not develop independently of currents felt all over Italy. In spite of the continuity fostered by the Compagnia dell'Arcangelo Raffaello, no one can argue that later dialogues developed directly and exclusively out of Caccini's early *recitar cantando* performed for the company. But while it is not fair to say that the sacred dialogue was invented by the *camerata fiorentina*, the evidence presented here at least ought to make us reexamine some accepted assumptions concerning the oratorio, namely that the genre first emerged in Rome, that it arose in the context of religious practices and institutions introduced there by Filippo Neri, and that it was spread largely by the Padri della Congregazione dell'Oratorio di S. Filippo Neri, as they were established in other Italian cities during the seventeenth century.[94] Cavalieri's *Rappresentazione di anima e di corpo* (1600) and Anerio's *Teatro armonico* (1619) actually had very few immediate precedents and successors in the repertoire of the

---

[92] I:Fn, Magl. VII, 432. The first page of the manuscript bears the inscription, "*Questo libro è della Lucia che serve la Ser.ma Sig.ra Principessa Anna.*" The princess is obviously Anna de' Medici (1616–1675), who left Florence in 1646 for Innsbruck, where she married Archduke Ferdinand Carlo of Austria. The dialogue texts, however, are in a second hand. It seems probable that the book, having been started by Anna's servant, was left behind in Florence and used by someone else at the court later.

[93] In his letter of January 8, 1638 (GALILEO GALILEI, *Le opere*, Vol. XVII [Florence 1937], p. 253–54), Porro asks Galilei for "*Qualche dialoghi, o spirituali o morali, per cantar in camera . . . che di queste cose li SS.ri poeti fiorentini non hanno pari.*" In his next letter of April 2, 1638 (ibid., p. 323), Porro thanks Galilei for the "*parole mandatemi, belle tutte invero, ma bellissime quelle del Sig.r Bartolomei, al qual vivo obligatissimo.*"

[94] These assumptions underlay the narratives by ALALEONA, *Storia*, p. 187; PASQUETTI, *L'oratorio*, p. 45, 279; SCHERING, *Geschichte des Oratoriums*, p. 50; and SMITHER, *A History of the Oratorio* I, p. 24, 29, 75, 145, and 258.

Oratorian's Chiesa Nuova.[95] And it would seem that regular production of sacred dialogues, or nascent oratorios for various Roman oratories was well under way only by the mid-1630s and 1640s with the works of Mazzocchi, Della Valle, Carissimi, Marazzoli, and Rossi.[96] Up to that time, the cultivation of the sacred musical dialogue in Florence, beginning in 1612, if not in 1593 (Doc. 12), would seem to have been at least comparable to that in Rome in terms of chronology and textual features of the works. So by the time the Florentine Congregazione dell'Oratorio (established in 1632) formally decided, in 1652, to follow the custom of the Roman congregation by preceding and following their evening sermons with music, including, at least upon occasion presumably, one or two dialogues,[97] other Florentines had already been composing and performing such dialogues on their own for at least forty years.

Even the deep background of the oratorio, supposedly traceable to the religious practices of S. Filippo Neri, is not strictly Roman. Lay sermonizing and lauda singing were important activities of Florentine companies like that of Arcangelo Raffaello before Filippo Neri was born.[98] On the basis of a statement attributed to Neri, it has even been suggested that he had been a member of one of these companies during his boyhood in Florence, and that some of his institutions were based on traditions he encountered there.[99] Again, we should not presume Florentine origins, but leave open the possibility of a pan-Italian oratorian movement, of which the Oratorians were but a part. Nevertheless, the traditions of Florentine lay piety had profound historical importance. Kristeler finds in them important roots of Renaissance humanism.[100] These two aspects of Florentine culture – piety and humanism – once thought separate, even antagonistic, are now viewed as complementary.[101] Even the reorganization and revitalization of the Compagnia

110

[95] SMITHER, A History of the Oratorio I, p. 79–90; 118–42. Of the four composers of Italian-language dialogues discussed in the places cited in fn. 76, two, Pietro Pace and Antonio Cifra, held posts at Loreto, not Rome. Of the twenty-two composers of Latin dialogues, 1600–1630, listed by SMITHER, The Latin Dramatic Dialogue, p. 429–33, thirteen, including the first four to publish them, had no known position in Rome. SCHERING, Geschichte des Oratoriums, p. 17, pointed out the large number of the earliest Latin dialogues composed by northern Italians, but did not pursue the consequence of his own observation.
[96] SMITHER, A History of the Oratorio I, p. 145–206.
[97] The decision, which is recorded in Florence, Archivio della Congregazione dell'Oratorio in S. Firenze, Libro di ricordi ordinari A, p. 22, will be discussed in another place.
[98] See fn. 3. Two other practices associated with S. Filippo Neri were already known in the Compagnia dell'Arcangelo Raffaello by the mid-sixteenth century: the Forty-Hours vigil and evening assemblies on Sundays and holidays from All Saints' Day to Easter. The first Forty-Hours vigil recorded in the company's surviving books, May 29, 1558, included sermons, prayers, lauda singing, and an apparato that represented paradise (I:Fas, Comp. rel. sop., 160, no. 7 [olim 6], fols. 4ᵛ–5ᵛ). The first description of evening meetings comes from 1559 (I:Fas, Comp. rel. sop., 160, no. 7 [olim 6], fols. 12ᵛ–13ʳ), when such an assembly was already described as "usual."
[99] ANTONIO CISTELLINI, San Filippo Neri e la sua patria, in: Rivista di storia della chiesa in Italia XXIII (1969), p. 64–66, who supports this interpretation of Neri's words, cites the Florentine tradition of lauda singing as a source of Neri's institutions. Lay sermonizing, even by boys, in Florence is given as one of Neri's remote inspirations by Giovanni Incisa della Rocchetta and Nello Viano, eds., Il primo processo per San Filippo Neri, vol. III, Studi e testi, 196 (Vatican City 1958), p. 324–25, fn. 1645.
[100] PAUL OSKAR KRISTELLER, Lay Religious Traditions and Florentine Platonism, in his Studies in Renaissance Thought and Letters (Rome 1956), p. 99–122.
[101] Two recent affirmations of this view are found in CHARLES TRINKAUS, The Religious Thought of the Italian Humanists, and the Reformers: Anticipation or Antonomy? and PAUL OSKAR KRISTELLER, The Rôle of Religion in Renaissance Humanism and Platonism, both in: The Pursuit of Holiness, p. 339–66 and 367–70 respectively. See fn. 3.

dell'Arcangelo Raffaello and of its three brother companies were instigated by the humanist Pope Eugenius IV during his stay in Florence following the great council of church reunification.[102] The council, of course, gave great impetus to the study of Greek history and writings in the West because of the scholars and manuscripts that arrived with the retinues of Patriarch Joseph and Emperor John VII of Byzantium. Now we can see how, in turn, lay piety received new support from the humanistically inspired Florentine cultivation of *recitar cantando*.

Appendix of documents

Each of the following notices is found in one of the series of descriptive record books (*ricordi*) of the Compagnia dell'Arcangelo Raffaello, found in the Archivio di Stato di Firenze, Compagnie religiosi soppresse, with the *filza*, book, and folio numbers given below.

Doc. 1. 162, no. 22 [*olim* 21], fols. 12ᵛ–13ʳ, June 1, 1582: E sonata che fussi l'Ave Maria e ferm.si a sedere nello stanzone, vene fuori l.o giov.ne e Tobbia vestito in forma di pellegrino, e doppo un lungo lor' discorso il detto Tobbia gettato via l'habito del Pelleg.no si li dim.ro quello che egli erà, e riconfortato al quanto il giov. ne cominciò a far q.a or.ne all'Arc. Raff.lo e finita che fu vene fuora il detto Arc. Raff.lo accomp.to dai Ang.li e l.o coro di Musica e cominc.no à cant.re l.o Madrig.le il qual fornito dall'Arc. Raff.lo fù cons.to Tobbia, e per mano dei Ang.li datte à ciasc.no l.a carta stampata di questo Tenore.

Doc. 2. Ibid., fol. 26ᵛ, April 7, 1583: La sera si disse il solito hufitio con le solite musiche et di piu ci fu al benedictus, uno de n[ost]ri fratelli che nella risposta sonava una grande Arpe musichale cantandovi sopra lui et un putto et al Miserere sonando una Gran Lira che in vero il populo ne resto molto soddisfatto et fatto le tenebre ciaschuno fu licenziato.

Doc. 3. Ibid., fols. 53ᵛ–54ʳ, Nov. 1, 1584: A mezza hora di notte si dette principio al uffitio havendo fatto imporre a 2 giovanni [sic] di età e quale buonissimi musici, et tutte le letioni da Giovannetti musici struiti da m. Rafaello Gucci non havendo piu m.o di cappella, et da m. Giulio Caccini musico di S. A. S. et n[ost]ro fratello fu concertato e tre madrigali che l'anno passato si cantorno tutti cantati da n[ost]ri fratelli e da lui fu cantato insieme con un suo putto castrato che a requisitione di S. A. S. tiene in casa, et l'insegnià il Miserere sonando una Gran lira havendo achomodato nel mezzo di compagnia una archa dove egli entratovi dentro senza che fussi visto quivi cantava, et sonava, et dal coro di musica era risposto, che in vero fece un bel sentire cosi si canto il beneditus.

Doc. 4. Ibid., fol. 54ʳ, Nov. 4, 1584: La sera si disse l'ufitio intero de morti per l'anime di tutti e Guardiani Corretori et fratelli della casa si come e usanza fare ogni prima dom.a doppo la festività di tutti e santi havendo fatto alquanto d'aparato, et dal n[ost]ro Amorevole fratello Rafaello Gucci fu cantato il Miserere, et il Beneditus sur uno buonacordo, et il coro rispondeva, quale dette molto contento a fratelli, et altri che per loro divotione erano venuti per sentire.

Doc. 5. Ibid., fol. 55ʳ, Dec. 8, 1584: Rafaello Gucci n[ost]ro amorevole fratello haveva fatto condurre un suo strumento di tasti, sonò et cantò il Te deum, et la Gloria et il Beneditus.

Doc. 6. Ibid., fol. 61ʳ, April 19, 1585 (Good Friday): Et mentre s'andava ala cia[. . . cut off] Rafaello Gucci cantava e sonava il suo strumento e soliti versetti.

Doc. 7. Ibid., fol. 70ʳ, Nov. 1, 1585: Et venutone la sera dove era acomodato il parato secondo li altri anni, et fatto il catafalcho in compagnia si dette principio al santo lufitio quale fu imposto da dua de n[ost]ri fratelli buoni musichi et le letioni anchora, et rispetto al tempo piovoso mancho alcuni de fratelli che dovevano cantare e soliti Madrigali delli altri anni dove

---

[102] The historical signifiance of this reorganization and revitalization within the context of Renaissance Florentine culture was first recognized by EMILIO SANESI, *Sant'Antonino e l'umanesimo*, in: *La rinascita: rivista del Centro Nazionale di Studi sul Rinasciamento* III (1940), p. 105–116.

il n[ost]ro Amorevole fratello Rafaello Gucci soperi lui cantando et sonando in buonacordo il Miserere, et benedictus, quale non era visto sendosi acomodato dentro al catafalcho.

Doc. 8. Ibid., fol. 75ᵛ, April 2, 1586 (Wed. of Holy Week): Al beneditus et Miserere si fece dua Cori uno di 5 viole et voci , et l'altro Rafaello Gucci col suo strumento.

Doc. 9. Ibid. fol. 92ʳ, Nov. 1, 1587: La sera essendo fatto suntuoso apparato nella Compagnia grande e con grandissima Musica di madrigali cantati dal S.r Giulio Romano, S.r Lelio Ghirlanzoni, m. Raff.lo Gucci, Niccolo Castrato.

Doc. 10. Ibid., fols. 143ᵛ–144ʳ, Dec. 31, 1591: Il giorno di poi aspettan.o l'ora, nella quale la Serenissima Gran' Duc[h]essa Nostra sig.ra ci haveva fatta intendere di voler visitare la festa nostra. Si provedero l.a scelta di alquanti giovani di voce e di pratica nel canto eccelenti che da l.a banda facessero coro. E m. Raff. Gucci quale dal al[t]ro coro cantava solo ma da diversi suoni di strumenti acompagnato. E subito entrata la Sereniss.ma Sig.ra dattosi principio al S.to vespro con grande aplauso e devozione de circostanti il quale finito e tirato certe cortine di ermisi che celavono il coro rimase scoperto inaspettatamente tre angeli molto sontuosamente vestiti l.o de quali era Bern.o Carraresi quale solo cantò l.o madrig[ale] nuovo composto in lode del nostro prottetore la persona del quale rapresentava. Avanti cominciassi il canto precedette molte delicatissime tirate di suoni doppo i quali l'ang.lo che in mano teneva l.o vaso d'argento con una voce e modo tanto delicato piutosto angelico che humano dalla suavita del quale li animi de circonstanti furono sospesi.

Doc. 11. Ibid., fols. 148ʳ⁻ᵛ, [March 29], 1592 (Easter Monday): Si tiro l.a cortina che copriva tutta l'ordine che sera fatta per il sacramento e quivi accomodat. molti angeli e sibille profete e tutti in hordine si scoperse e si recitorno ciascuno alquanti versi. Di poi venne le tre Marie e quelle dicendo di volere andare a visitare il sepolcro e quello si scoperse il sepolcro che v'era l.o angiolo sopra e cantato l.o madrigale disse ch'il Sig.re era resuritato e'l coro delli angeli cantorno l.o altro madrigale nel principio e nel fine.

Doc. 12. Ibid., fol. 171bisʳ, Dec. 31, 1593: E finito l'uficio venne all'altare cinque angeli che nel mezzo era il Nostro Arcang. Raff. e quelli cantorno con strumenti l.o madrigale e l.o solo l'angiolo.

Doc. 13. 162, no. 23 [olim 22], fol. 13ʳ, March 18, 1612: E la sera si canto l'ufitio con buona musica e doppo apparve all'altare uno coro di angioli che in mezzo viene l'angiolo Raffaello che cantoruno di musica certi versi composti da Sig.re Ottavio Rinuccini molto belli.

Doc. 14. Ibid., fol. 18ʳ, Dec. 25, 1612: La sera l'ufitio con buona musica e doppo si scopersse il presepio il quale era coperto con una cortina di tafetta e levato detta cortina resto una prospetiva di paese boscherecio e recitorno certi pastori al quanto e doppo aparsse uno angiolo in una nugola che cantò solo e di poi canto di musica un coro di pastori e doppo si aperisse il cielo e gli angioli cantorno in diversse maniere e in questo stante sparì il paese boscherecio e si vedde il presepio chon bellissima prospetiva e uno bello apparato per tutta la Compagnia talmente che questa festa piaqque asai a tutti e popoli.

Doc. 15. Ibid., fol. 25ʳ, Dec. 25, 1613: E la sera l'ufitio con buonissima musica e doppo si aperse il cielo che era sop:a il presepio e canto uno a[n]giolo solo dua stanze di lauda e poi canto[rono] tre angioli insieme.

Doc. 16. Ibid., fol. 32ʳ, Dec. 31, 1614: La sera si canto l'ufitio della Gloriosa V. M.a molto solennem.te con buona musica e doppo aparve cinque angiolo [sic] davanti al presepio e cantorno di musica molto gentilmente. (See Doc. 17.)

Doc. 17. Ibid., fol. 32ᵛ, Jan. 6, 1615: E la sera l'ufitio con buona musica e doppo aparve cinque angioli come la sera della n[ost]ra festa [Doc. 16] e cantorno certe stanze di musica molti belli e prima cantava solo il n[ost]ro P.re S. Raff: Arca[n]g e di poi gli altri a dua e tutti insieme e molti strumenti dietro e voce che fece uno belissimo sentire e vedere perche erano vesti richamente.

Doc. 18. Ibid., fol. 48ᵛ, Dec. 31, 1616: La sera si canto il matut:o con musica a dua cori e doppo l'ufitio cantò davanti al presepio cinque angioli con diversi strumenti sonati da ciascuno di essi.

Doc. 19. Ibid., fol. 62ʳ, Dec. 31, 1618: La sera si cantò il santo Mattutino con musica a dua cori, e doppo l'uffitio sei angioli accanto al presepio tre da una banda, e tre dall'altra cantorono insieme e da per se molto gentilmente.

Doc. 20. Ibid., fol. 69ᵛ, Dec. 25, 1619: La sera il santo Mattutino con buona musica al quale intervenne infinito numero di popolo, e dopo l'Uffitio sei Pastori avanti al Presepio tre da una banda, e tre dall'altra cantorono insieme, e da per se molto gentilmente.

Doc. 21. Ibid., fols. 95ᵛ–96ʳ, Nov. 1, 1622: La sera si cantò l'Ufitio de Morti con buonissima musica et a due cori, et avanti, et dopo d.o Uffitio si cantò uno Dialoghetto in Musica, per il quale si fingevono l'anime del purgatorio, che domandavano essere libere dalle pene, et l'Angiolo consolandole gle lo promettava mediante l'Uffitio, che si doveva celebrare, et di poi quello finito replicò l'Ang.lo che erano state liberate, et così se ne volarono al Cielo ringratiando i fratelli delle preci, et suffragio portoli, che il tutto fù compositione di m. Jac.o Cicognini la quale apportò a tutti grandissima devotione.

Doc. 22. Ibid., fol. 130ʳ, Dec. 31, 1625: A poco terminato l'uffitio si aperse, et si vedde uno Coro di Angeli rappresentanti il nostro P.re Arc.lo Raffaello con Tobbia, et Michaello, Gabbriello, et Uriello, che avanti erono stati richiamati alle preghiere di quei fratelli rappresentati da una voce, che si sentì celatam.te et formò un'ecco molto bello e a proposito. Gl'Arcangioli cantorono tutti da per se figurando loro medesimi, e mostrando a preghi di Raffaello essere discesi a quel Sacro Tempio, dove si celebravono le sue lodi in questo giorno solenne, et per protegere quell'animi, et inviarli al Cielo, et con un corpo pieno terminò poi così bella vista, et con questa devotione si diede fine alla festa, et la composizione fù del Dottore Cicognini nostro fratello altrove nominato.

L'apparato di quest'anno perche fù fatto con buon disegno è parso degno di memoria. Dal Palco alle Cornice delle Manganelli erono distese vasce di colore incarnato che rigiravono a torno a torno, et divisa la muaglia in convenienti spazzi vi erano attaccate alcune figure huroglifiche in onore del Nostro Padre, et Protettore, et dell'Insegna di nostra Compagnia, et quelle tramezzate da alcune pitture antiche con ornam.to di legno intagliato, e dorato in forma circulare et erono Immagini della Beatissima Vergine, et ciascuna pittura era sotto, et sopra ornata di festone formato da vasce bianche, e gocciole, che terminavono in uno festone di Bambagia orpellato che posava in su le Cornice delle Manganelle, et sopra terminava con alcune rame d'abeto, et le manganelle erono tutte parate di Arazzi. Il primo stanzone altre a paramenti d'Arazzi e pitture reguardevoli haveva l'Altare tutto Adorno de soliti Reliquiari, e l'altare grande tutto bene corredato, e ricco di lumi come si può immaginare, si che il tutto parsò con ogni dovuto onore.

Doc. 23. Ibid., fol. 159ᵛ, Nov. 1, 1626: La sera l'uffitio generale per tutti i Defunti, qual fù cantato devotam:e e solennem.te et con Musica a due cori, et quello finito fù terminata la tornata con uno Dialogo in Musica bellissimo lassando tutti i fratelli satisfatissimi.

Doc. 24. Ibid., fol. 140ᵛ, Dec. 25, 1626: Et la sera il Mattinuto della Beata Verg.e con buonissima musica terminando con una Rappresentazione di Pastori cantata dentro con ritornello fatto con instrum.ti pastorali.

Doc. 25. Ibid., fol. 156ʳ, Nov. 1, 1639: La sera essendo parata tutta la Compagnia e lo Stanzone fino alla volta di lavori, et saie nere e Rappresentato sopra la scena nella quale si era nella Primavera passata recitata la Tragedia a suo luogo nominata Uno Purgatorio ove si vedevono l'Anime Purganti, et Diversi Angioli, che parti di quelle per aria sollevono, et conducevono alla Gloria del Paradiso, dall'apparenza del quale restavono che l'amerava atterriti, et compunti apportando spavento, e timore, et eccitando grademente alla devotione, et alla compassione di quelle Povere Anime.

113

Doc. 26. Ibid., fol. 158ʳ, Dec. 25, 1639: Si canto solennemente il Mattutino con bonissima musica. Et in fine in luogo di Mottetto comparserò Alcuni Pastori riccamente vestiti alle loro usanza cantando insieme, et da per se con maraviglia, et ammiratione della luce, et splendore che vedevono apparire nella mezza notte, et nel medesimo tempo si vedde apparire una Nugola ove posava un' Angiolo che annuntiò alli medesimi il Nato Messia, et arrivato al mezzo della scena sparve da loro con ascondersi fra le Nugole. Et eglino appresso scoprendo il Santo Presepio genuflessi adorarono il Santo Bambino, et in stile recitativo da per se, et unitamente insieme con parole dimostrarono l'affetto, et devotione che in loro si svegliava, et l'allegrezza che sentivono, et le proferivono con tant'affetto, che forzavono li ascoltanti a lacrimare per devotione unendo ancora al canto ritornelli con Instrumenti Pastorali che facevono bellissimo sentire. Et nell'ordinare la Partenza si vedde ad un tempo aprirsi il Paradiso et molti Angioli in esso Avisi con diversi Instrumenti, et unitamente con d.i Pastori fecero un' coro ricchissimo, et bellissimo, unito con dett'Instrumenti tutti ammirati et con desiderio di rivedere di nuovo detta Rappresentazione stimandola degna di essere di nuovo rivista per satisfare ancora a gl'altri che non erono stati presenti.

Doc. 27. 163, no. 26 [olim 25], fol. 9ʳ, Aug. 24, 1642: Nell'istessa mattina in ringraziamento della Nascita del Ser.mo Gran Principe fù cantato il Te deum solennemente in musica, et una messe grande solenne havendo l'ordine che app.o. . . . Diedero motivo di m. Girolamo Bartolommei, Guglielmo Altoviti, et Agnolo Galli i quali trovatisi insieme con Alberto del Vivaio sopraintendente delle nostre musiche stabilirono, che da Baccio Balgioni Maestro della Nostra Cappella sos[titui]to si componesse par la Messa una solenne musica . . . Fù arrichito il sacrifizio, e la musica da un vago mottetto messo in musica dal medesimo Baglioni cantato in fine della messa composizione del d.o m. Girolamo Bartolommei, nel quale si cantavono le lodi de Genitori, e si faceva preludio alle alte speranze del loro Prima Genito.

Doc. 28. Ibid., fol. 35ᵛ, July 24, 1644 (feast of St. Mary Magdalen): Et dopo [il Vespro] fù rappresentato un' Dialogo in Musica cantato da Tre fanciulli nostri fratelli quali furono Girolamo Bernardi, in apparenza d'Ortolano figurante n[ost]ro Sig.re resucitato, l'altro Gio: Filippo Rucellai rappresentante S. Maria Mad.a dolente per non havere ritrovato nel sepolcro il suo Sig.re, et Gio. B.a Vantucci l'altro figurante l'Angiolo con Coro di Musici dentro, et tutti si portarono benissimo, et tutti segui con applauso, et lodi universali.

Doc. 29. Ibid., fol. 152ᵛ, Nov. 1, 1654: La sera si diede principio alle nostre Veglie Spirituale, et si fece tornata numerosissima alla quale fù cantato solennem.e l'Uffizio Generale per tutti li fedeli Defunti con bonissima Musica fatta del N[ost]ro Maestro di Cappella [G. B. Comparini], terminando in fine con uno Mottetto in forma di Dialogo alludendo alla liberazione, et sollievo dell'anime del S.to Purg.o.

Doc. 30. Ibid., fol. 163ʳ, Nov. 1, 1655: Il Giorno di Tutti li Santi da sera si diede principio alle nostre Veglie Spirituale facendo la nostra prima Tornata assai numerosa, alla quale si cantò l'Uffizio Generale per tutti li fedeli defunti con buona musica fatta dal Nostro Maestro di Cappella Gio: Bat. Comparini in hoggi Maestro di Cappella del Duomo, et doppo si fatto devoto Discorso sopra l'anime Purganti nel Santo Purgatorio dell'Istesso Bart.o Talenti nostro fratello giovanetto molto spiritoso, et attissimo in simili impieghi, e da sperarne ogni buona riuscita, terminando la Tornata con Mottetto à forma del Dialogo in Musica rappresentante il Giudizio Universale.

THE INSTRUMENTAL MUSIC OF
MARC-ANTOINE CHARPENTIER

By H. WILEY HITCHCOCK

NEVER attached directly to the court of Louis XIV, Charpentier had no opportunity to write suites or *simphonies* for the *Vingt-quatre violons*. Not an instrumentalist but a singer, he had no occasion to compose *pièces de viole* or *de clavecin* to demonstrate his virtuosity in the *concerts du dimanche*. He was a composer for the Church — for the chapels of the Duchesse de Guise and the Dauphin; for the church of the Jesuits; for various convents; and for the Sainte-Chapelle. And he was a composer for the theater — for the private entertainments of the duchess; for the Latin plays of the Collège de Clermont; for the Théâtre du Palais-Royal of Molière.

In these capacities, Charpentier produced over two hundred orchestral and chamber works in four broad categories: 1) preludes to motets, psalms, and other choral works; 2) liturgically functional compositions, such as an instrumental Mass, versets of hymns and antiphons; 3) dramatic music — overtures, dances, and *entr'acte* pieces; and 4) miscellaneous works for various purposes.

All of Charpentier's instrumental music is written for ensemble or orchestra, and this survey may begin with a consideration of his instrumentation and orchestration. His voluminous manuscripts[1] are, in

---

[1] "Mélanges autographes," Paris, Bibl Nat., Ms. Rés., Vm¹ 259 (28 volumes, in-folio). Microfilms of these holographs, which comprise virtually the complete works of Charpentier, were the primary source for this study. In addition, films of the 1694 Ballard publication of *Médée*, Philidor's copy of *David et Jonathas* (Bibl. du Conservatoire, Rés. F 924 [Coll. Philidor No. 44]), and copies made by Sébastien de Brossard of other works were consulted. The only independent instrumental work not available for the study was a *Sonate à huit instruments* (MS, Bibl. Nat., Vm⁷ 4813) attributed to Charpentier. If the sonata is indeed by Charpentier, it is his only work including theorbo in its instrumentation. See Lionel de la Laurencie, *L'École française de violon*, Paris, 1922-24, I, 98.

fact, a treasure-house of information on late 17th-century French taste in these matters — or Italo-French, granted Charpentier's Italianate background. In contrast to the usually sketchy French scores of his period, which often omit not only instrumental specifications but even the inner *parties de remplissage,* Charpentier's manuscripts are detailed and illuminating.

Charpentier writes for ensembles ranging from two treble parts without continuo (a fanfare for two trumpets) to double orchestra with eight real parts. The Italianate trio instrumentation of two trebles and bass predominates in the preludes. But it is rivaled there by four-part scoring (V, S, MS, B),[2] and the majority of the liturgical and the stage works are written for four-part orchestra. The five-part writing typical of Lully occurs infrequently.

The instruments mentioned in Charpentier's manuscripts are those found in other French sources of the period: strings of the violin family, including *basse de violon;* viols, including both *basse de viole* and *violone;* flutes, both end-blown and transverse; oboe, bassoon, *cromorne,* and serpent; treble and bass trumpets; kettledrums; *clavecin* and organ.[3] Although the list is an impressively varied one, it has elements of conservatism: one is faintly surprised by the Italianate Charpentier's maintenance of the viols as occasional orchestral instruments, and one looks in vain for the hunting horns that Lully employs occasionally.

117

In small ensembles of three or four parts, Charpentier favors like instruments: two flutes with continuo or two violins with continuo, or a four-part ensemble of strings alone. But the orchestra he prefers when he has the resources at hand is one of strings doubled by woodwinds. Such doubling is often explicitly required; elsewhere the term *tous* carries this meaning, especially when it appears in contrast with other terms like *violons seuls* or *flûtes seules.* Equivalent in meaning to *tous* is the term *grand choeur.* Borrowed from the *grands motets* of Dumont,

[2] Clefs are indicated in this article as follows: V = French violin; S = soprano; MS = mezzo-soprano; A = alto; T = tenor; B = bass.

[3] The *piva* (discant shawm) mentioned in *Epithalamio in lode dell'Altezza Serenissima Elettorale di Maximiliano Emanuel Duca di Baviera* (Vol. VII, fol. 54ᵛ of the "Mélanges") is perhaps simply an oboe. All instrumental citations in this work, which has an Italian text, are Italian themselves (*primo violino, prima tromba,* etc.), and "piva" is probably Charpentier's choice of an equivalent for "hautbois." One is tempted to cite, with the drums, the *mortiers* (apothecaries' mortars) which appear as rhythmic accompaniment to the chorus of surgeons and apothecaries in the third *intermède* of *Le Malade imaginaire.*

Lully, and Delalande, where it stands for full vocal chorus as opposed to the *petit choeur* of vocal soloists, the *grand choeur* in Charpentier's orchestra is equivalent to the *concerto grosso* of the Italians. Similarly, *petit choeur* is his adaptation of *concertino*. For Charpentier, trumpets and drums are elaborative additions to the basic orchestra; their parts are always carefully written out or precisely cued in.

In works calling for both strings and woodwinds, Charpentier's choice of the particular parts to be doubled by members of both families reflects a typical 17th-century view of the relative importance of the parts. Outer parts are the ones most frequently doubled. Almost as commonly, two treble parts and the bass are doubled, while inner parts are either left to the continuo realization (in the pieces *à 3*) or to single instrumental voices. Thus an amphonic or a trio-sonata texture is emphasized, even in the works for four or more parts. Even when instrumental specifications are lacking, the bass has a fundamental importance and presumably is to be doubled by keyboard and melodic instruments. Notes by the composer, stipulating not only the types of instruments for each part but also their numbers, confirm these preferences. One of the compositions *Pour un reposoir* (I, 64)[4] is scored in five parts (V, S, MS, A, B) in the *tous* passages, which alternate with passages for a *petit choeur* of four parts; Charpentier specifies the number of players in the *petit choeur* as *3 dessus* (V), *1 haute-contre* (S), *1 taille* (MS), and *2 quintes* (A). An *Allemande grave,* which concludes the same set of *reposoir* pieces, includes a *petit choeur* of two *dessus,* one *dessus,* and two *basses.*[5] The fundamental importance of the bass is emphasized in one of the versets of a *Pange lingua,* scored for a three-part *petit choeur* with two pairs of treble strings and a quadrupled bass.[6]

---

[4] Location of works among the "Mélanges autographes" is indicated by volume and folio numbers (Roman and· Arabic numerals, respectively).

[5] Similar distribution is specified in Kyrie 5 of the *Messe pour . . . instruments* (I, 67ᵛ-78) for the *violons du petit choeur* in three parts: 2 first violins, 1 second violin, 2 bass violins. See also *Ouverture, Pour un reposoir* (XX, 14-14ᵛ). Charpentier's emphasis of outer parts seems to have begun with the act of composition, as we might expect. One dance in the "Satires du prologue de *L'Inconnu*" (XVII, 51ᵛ) has treble and bass parts written out for eight measures, with blank staves between them for two other parts. In measure 8 the two-voice framework gives Charpentier some trouble and he crosses out what he has written, to begin afresh on the next page.

[6] "In supremae pour le petit choeur," *Simphonies pour un reposoir* (XV, 103ᵛ-104). Kyrie 4 of the *Messe pour . . . instruments* is written for flutes, with the following numbers specified: "2 flûtes douces et une d'allem[agne] [V], flûte d'allem[agne] [S], flûte d'allem[agne] [MS], quatre basses de flû[te] [B]"; here the intention is probably to emphasize a *cantus firmus* in the bass part.

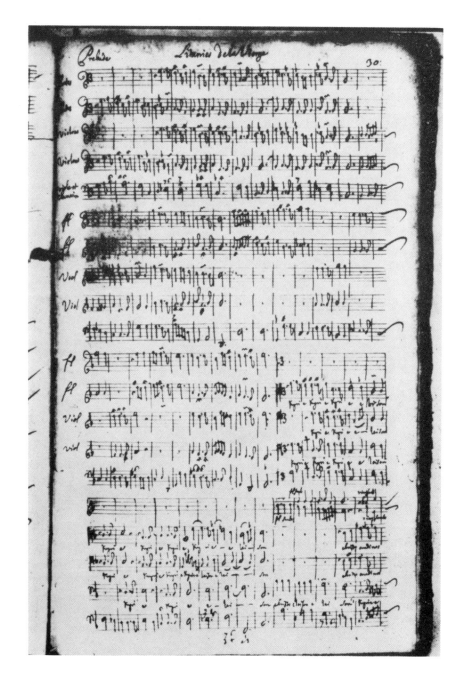

Plate I
Prelude and beginning of Kyrie in Charpentier's
Litanies de la Vierge

(Paris, Bibl. Nat. Ms. Rés., Vm¹ 259, Tome XXIII, fol. 30)

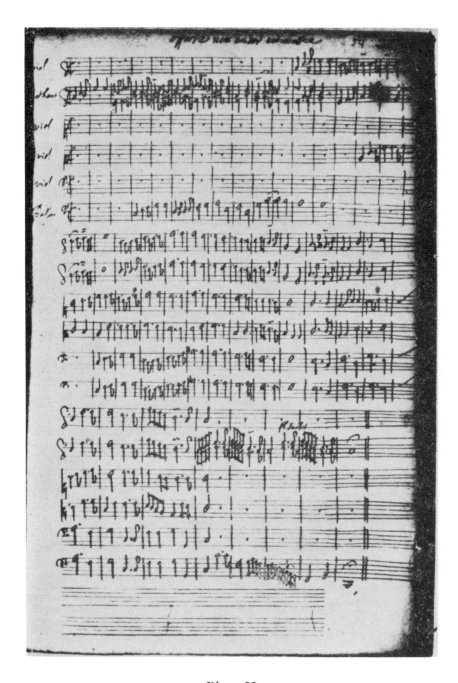

Plate II

First movement of Charpentier's *Offerte*
non encore exécutée

(Paris, Bibl. Nat. Ms. Rés., Vm¹ 259, Tome XVII, fol. 54)

As an orchestrator, Charpentier was distinctly a colorist. Although he wrote no concertos as such, the heart of his orchestration technique is the concerto principle of opposed instrumental combinations. In his most characteristic exploitation of concerto-like contrasts, Charpentier alternates a *tous* of strings and doubling woodwinds with an unmixed group from one or the other family; no reduction in forces in either group is demanded. In a prelude to *Litanies de la Vierge* (XXIII, 30), for example, one three-part group of violins and continuo and another of flutes and continuo are contrasted with each other and with the whole ensemble of doubled violins and flutes. (See Plate I.) For even greater contrast, Charpentier often scores the *grand choeur* in four or more parts, the *petit choeur* in three (almost invariably two trebles and bass).[7]

Naturally, it is the majestic *pièces d'occasion* and some of the *grands motets* that exploit trumpets and drums. Here one might speak, not of a *grand* and a *petit choeur,* but of a *grand* and an *encore plus grand choeur*: to the normal *tous* of strings doubled by woodwinds are added trumpets and drums; this impressive mass is then contrasted with the less noisy string-and-wind ensemble.[8] Elsewhere, the combined forces of strings, winds, brasses, and drums alternate with *petits choeurs* of strings or of winds or, alternately, of each.[9]

The distinction in timbre between violins and viols is explored occasionally by Charpentier. In the prelude to an elevation motet (XX, 24-24ᵛ), two treble violins alternate with two viols (the latter in tenor range) over a continuous bass part for bass violin and harpsichord; in the series of *Ritornelles pour la p[remiè]re leçon de ténèbres du vendredi s[ain]t* (IV, 22ᵛ-23ᵛ), a trio of two violins (V, V) and continuo tends to alternate with one of viols (A, T) and continuo.

Still another type of concerto-like contrast, the most archaic of all, is a polychoral treatment of two equal orchestras. Two versions of a prelude to the oratorio *Josue* (XI, 23-24; XVII, 42-43) and preludes to both parts of the oratorio *Caecilia Virgo et Martyr* (III, 35ᵛ-36ᵛ, 42ᵛ-44) are scored for double orchestra, a *premier choeur* of four parts and a *second choeur* with the same instrumentation.

119

---

[7] E.g., Prelude, *Laudate Dominum omnes gentes* (XXVI, 25-25ᵛ).

[8] Typical is the prelude to a *Te Deum* (X, 73ᵛ); this may be heard in a recording issued by the Haydn Society (HSL-2065).

[9] *Second air de trompettes* . . . (X, 52-53), recorded *ibid.; Epithalamio* . . . (VII, 54ᵛ-55); *Marche de triomphe* (X, 51ᵛ-52); *Marche de triomphe* (XVII, 38-38ᵛ).

Charpentier seems to have been comparatively uninterested in the possibilities of a solo instrument set off against an ensemble. However, one work, the cantata *Orphée descendant aux enfers* (VI, 11), uses solo violin, for programmatic purposes: accompanied by a chamber group of violin, treble recorder, transverse flute, and continuo (gamba and harpsichord), the "violon d'Orphée" plays preludes for the cantata as a whole and for the opening solo of Orpheus.[10]

Although Charpentier's *basse continüe* is in general precisely that — a continuous bass — he sometimes stipulates that the melodic *basses du choeur continüe* should not play in passages for a *petit choeur* of flutes and continuo; furthermore, the keyboard player is told to double the parts in such passages.[11]

Like Lully, and perhaps following his example, Charpentier is one of the first composers to call for mutes. *Sourdines* are specified, in all the string parts, in night-scenes *(sommeils)* in three of the oratorios.[12]

Special attention should be called to one work, the *Messe pour plusieurs instruments au lieu des orgues* (I, 67ᵛ-78), because of its varied and colorful orchestration. It seems almost to have been a test piece in which Charpentier wished to demonstrate his skill at handling diverse combinations of instruments. In all, ten different ensembles are employed in the Mass, which is scored as follows:

KYRIE

Kyrie 1 ....4-part *tous* (strings doubled by woodwinds)
Kyrie 3 ....Trio (2 oboes and continuo)
Christe 2 ....Trio (2 solo violins and continuo)
Kyrie 4 ....4-part wind band (combined recorders and transverse flutes)
Kyrie 6 ....4-part *tous*

[10] See also "Quoniam pour le cromorne," in the Gloria of the *Messe pour . . . instruments* (I, 71-71ᵛ), where the principal melodic line is given to *cromorne,* with a background of *octaves, flûtes douces,* and *basses de flûte.*

[11] "Quand les flûtes jouent, l'orgue joue leurs mêmes parties," *In Assumptione Beatae Mariae Virginis* (IX, 18). Similar instructions for doubling flute parts in the organ appear in three *antienes* for orchestra (IX, 31-31ᵛ, 36ᵛ-37; XVII, 27-28).

[12] *Nuit,* in *In Nativitatem D[omi]ni Canticum* (IX, 55ᵛ-56); *Nuit,* in *Dialogus inter Angelos et Pastores Judeae* (XXVIII, 28-29); prelude to Part II, *Judicium Salomonis* (XXVII, 28-28ᵛ). The first of these has been edited by Guy-Lambert in *Musiques françaises,* No. 8 (Geneva, 1949).

Gloria

Et in terra ....4-part *tous*

Benedicimus Te ....Trio (2 oboes and continuo)

Glorificamus Te ....4-part string orchestra

Domine Deus Rex ....Trio (2 treble recorders and continuo)

Domine Deus Agnus ....4-part wind band

Qui tollis ....4-part *tous*

Quoniam ....4-part wind band (obbligato *cromorne* with recorders, including *octave* and *basse de flûte*)

Tu solus altissimus ....Duet (oboe and *cromorne*)

In Gloria ....4-part *tous*

Offerte

Bi-choral: $\begin{cases} \textit{Choeur des instruments à vent} \text{ (V, S, MS, B)} \\ \textit{Choeur des violons} \text{ (V, S, MS, B)} \end{cases}$

Sanctus

4-part *tous*

[Agnus Dei?][13]

[4-part *tous?*] (V, S, MS, B)

121

* *

*

The majority of Charpentier's works for instruments are preludes; they number about 150 and are diverse in length, form, style, and degree of independence from the works they introduce.

The preludes range in length from seven to more than seventy measures, but most are from twenty to thirty measures long and are in the tradition of the brief preludial *sinfonia,* whose function is to establish tonal atmosphere without much elaboration of themes. More often than not, the prelude is dependent for thematic material on the work it introduces — but this, it should be recalled, was a novel procedure in the 17th century.

Most commonly, a single theme anticipating the first vocal entry is presented in one or two points of imitation leading to a tonal cadence. The texture is pseudo-contrapuntal; a compromise between the *stile antico* and the more modern, bass-directed homophony, it threatens at any moment to harden into true homophonic writing. The style is

[13] This movement is incomplete; only the last page, which lacks title and instrumental specifications, remains.

reminiscent of the more serious movements of a sonata *da chiesa* by Legrenzi or even Corelli. A lovely example of this most common type of prelude introduces a setting of the Ash Wednesday tract, *Domine, non secundum* (XXVI, 51-51ʳ). Characteristic of Charpentier's mature style are the graceful theme and the *bel canto* lyricism of the first part, and the chromaticism — kept within strict tonal bounds by the bass — of the last part (Ex. 1).

122

For more elaborate vocal works — the *grands motets,* the larger oratorios, polychoral Magnificats and Te Deums — Charpentier's light counterpoint often thickens into an amphonic texture with dense and active but basically non-thematic inner parts, or into a majestic, turbulent homophony such as one hears in the first sections of Lully's overtures or in the *grands motets* of Henry Dumont.[14]

Related to the multi-sectional canzona and to the canzona-derived Lullian overture are several preludes in two or three sections, the first

[14] A good example is the prelude to one *Magnificat* for two choirs (XI, 4ᵛ), which may be heard in a Haydn Society recording (HSL-102).

usually in duple meter, the second in triple, and the third (if there is a third) in duple again.[15] Also in the canzona tradition, especially as modified in the solemn homophonic style of the Venetian operatic *sinfonia,* is the prelude to a motet celebrating the return to health of the Dauphin; even the old opening dactyl is preserved (Ex. 2).[16] The

Ex. 2   Flûte

123

flavor of the polychoral sonata style of Giovanni Gabrieli pervades the prelude to *Josue* (XI, 23-24), where two four-part orchestras vie with each other in massive antiphonal interplay.[17]

A few of the preludes are obviously dance-derived. Except for the lack of repeats, a prelude to a motet *In Assumptione Beatae Mariae Virginis* (IX, 18) might serve as a sarabande in a ballet (Ex. 3). Gavotte-derived is a prelude, in ₵ meter marked "guay," to the second part of a motet for a *reposoir* ceremony (XII, 2ᵛ-3). Another prelude (XVII, 46-46ᵛ), to be played "devant l'ouverture" of some unspecified work, is a miniature suite with an opening *alla breve,* a *menuet* in binary form without repeats, and a *passepied* with repeats. The impressive *Te Deum* in Volume X[18] is prefaced by a march in *rondeau* form with two *couplets.*

[15] See especially two alternative preludes (V, 8ᵛ, 9) for a setting of Psalm 19 (XI, 15ᵛ), the second an interesting expansion *à 4* of the first, which is *à 3.*

[16] *Gratiarum actiones ex sacris codicibus excerptae pro restituta Serenissimi Galliarum Delphini saluta* (IV, 109ᵛ). Cf. *Prelude pour "Quare fremuerunt gentes" à 8 voix* (XVII, 41-41ᵛ), which begins similarly.

[17] The first page of the manuscript is reproduced in *The Musical Quarterly,* XLI (1955), facing p. 45. Another, similar prelude for *Josue* (defaced by the composer with huge X's on each page) appears in XVII, 42-43.

[18] See above, note 8.

Ex. 3 [VI.1]

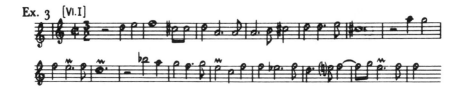

Militant motets "pendant la guerre" or "pro pace," settings of those psalms that sing of the might of Jehovah, honorific pieces in praise of the King of France, oratorios concerning struggles between Israelites and Philistines — all these kinds of works are apt to be preceded by the type of prelude often called by Charpentier "rumor bellicus," a brief piece usually in C major featuring fanfare themes and other appurtenances of the *stile concitato*.[19] Similarly programmatic in intent are the lullaby-like preludes of several oratorios, which draw on the Lullian tradition of the *sommeil*,[20] and the expressive laments found as preludes to an obituary motet and a *De Profundis* (XX, 28ᵛ-29, 48ᵛ-49), both written for the funeral of Queen Marie-Thérèse.

*   *

*

Musically more independent than the preludes are the liturgical works for instruments, about 35 in number. These comprise sets of *simphonies* for Corpus Christi processions and for consecrations of bishops; offertories and versets for the Mass, including the *Messe pour . . . instruments;* antiphons for Office services; an *Ouverture pour l'église;* and several *noëls*.

These works for the Church reflect the mélange of sacred and secular, of traditional and novel, in the religious life of Paris under Louis XIV. In a set of compositions for a *reposoir,* or street-altar used in processions of the Fête-Dieu (Corpus Christi), we find side by side a French overture, versets of the hymn *Pange lingua* set in *cantus-firmus*

[19] Typical preludes to each of these types of works are found as follows: *Rumor bellicus,* in *Canticum pro pace* (II, 19ᵛ); Prelude, *Psalmus 147: Lauda Jerusalem* (VI, 37); prelude to *In Honorem Sancti Ludovici Regis Galliae* (VI, 7); *Rumor bellicus,* in *Mors Saulis et Jonathae* (IV, 119ᵛ).

[20] *La Nuit,* prelude to Part II of *Judith* (II, 10ᵛ); *Praeludium,* in *In Nativitatem D[omi]ni Canticum* (IX, 51ᵛ); prelude to *In Circumcisione D[omi]ni: Dialogus inter Angelum et Pastores* (XX, 11); prelude to Part II of *Judicium Salomonis; Nuit,* prelude to Part II of *Dialogus inter Angelos et Pastores Judeae.*

style, and a dance movement (allemande). Operatic overtures introduce the sets of compositions for bishops' consecrations; according to one title, the overture was to be played during the bishop's robing.[21] The Midnight Mass at Christmas was an especially jolly affair: Charpentier's *Messe de Minuit* (XXV, 62-77) is a *missa carminum* based largely on *noël* tunes; a note of the composer specifies that "for the Offertory, the strings will play *Laissez paître vos bêtes* in D major."[22] Four of the orchestral antiphons are sober pieces, in the same style as the more serious preludes, but the fifth — *Antiene; après "Beati omnes"* (XVII, 28-29) — is a fast, triple-meter dance movement in binary form with repeats; only a fugal beginning lends it a touch of learned seriousness (Ex. 4).

Ex. 4

125

The most ambitious liturgical work is the *Messe pour . . . instruments.* Its movements are diverse in style, as they are in instrumentation. Kyrie 1 is a *cantus-firmus* movement; the bass, in whole notes throughout, is a Gregorian Kyrie (Ex. 5). Kyrie 3 and Christe 2 are free, while Kyrie 4 and Kyrie 6 return to the *cantus firmus* of the first verset. The versets of the Gloria similarly alternate between archaic *cantus-firmus* technique and a more modern free style. The bi-choral Offertory, in three contrasting sections, is derived from the Italian canzona-sonata.[23]

[21] "Ouverture pendant qu'il s'habille" (III, 115ᵛ-117).

[22] "A l'offertoire les violons joueront 'Laissez paître vos bêtes' en D la re sol ♯." The music is not provided in the manuscript of the Mass. An instrumental setting of the carol does appear in IX, 61ᵛ, untitled except for "autre noël," but it cannot be the setting planned for the Mass since it is in C major and calls for flutes as well as strings. For the *noël* melody, see Jan Reinier Hendrik de Smidt, *Les Noëls et la tradition populaire,* Amsterdam, 1932, p. 140.

[23] Although unpublished, this *Offerte à deux choeurs* (I, 72ᵛ-77ᵛ) may be heard in a Haydn Society recording (HSL-102). Besides the Mass for orchestra, Charpentier wrote eleven choral Masses. Six of these include substantial orchestral move-

Ex. 5 Premier Kyrie: Tous les instruments

Two of the three sets of compositions for Corpus Christi street-altar
ceremonies comprise an overture, instrumental versets for a hymn, and
an allemande; the third set is made up of an overture and a motet.
Each set is unified by key and by instrumentation. From Charpentier's
notes, one gets a good picture of a Parisian Fête-Dieu of the 17th
century. One must imagine a temporary altar placed on a supporting
stand *(reposoir)* at some prominent street-corner. Near it is the orchestra
— strings, flutes, and harpsichord.[24] Down the street comes the procession, a banner at its head, with priests bearing the Holy Sacrament.
"As soon as the procession appears,"[25] the orchestra begins an overture.
"Things must be worked out so that the Holy Sacrament is placed [on
the altar] before the conclusion of the . . . overture, which then will
serve as prelude to the motet [or hymn] that follows."[26] After the motet
or hymn, a benediction is said. Then the procession moves on. "After
the benediction, and when the priests are far enough away not to hear
them, the strings are to play an allemande."[27]

---

ments, some of them preludes — e.g., "la simphonie de devant le Kyrie" of *Missa
Assumpta est Maria* (XXVII, 1) — and others integral parts of the liturgical structure — e.g., Agnus Dei 1 and 3 of the *Messe de Minuit.*

[24] Specified in *Ouverture, Pour un reposoir* (XX, 14-14ᵛ).

[25] *Ibid.* The subtitle reads, "dès que la procession paraît." In the *Simphonies
pour un reposoir* (XV, 102ᵛ-105), the first title reads, "Ouverture dès qu'on voit
la bannière."

[26] "Il faut faire en sorte que le St Sacrement soit posé avant que l'ouverture
précédant finisse, ce qui servira de prelude au mottet suivant" (XX, 14ᵛ). Another
overture (XV, 102ᵛ-103) is followed by the instruction, "Passez au 'Pange lingua'
suivant quand on posera le St Sacrement sur l'autel du reposoir."

[27] "Après la bénédiction et que les prêtres seront assez loin pour ne les plus
entendre, les violons joueront une allemande" (note at the end of the "Amen pour
les violons," XV, 105).

The general tone of these processional pieces is serious and ceremonious. The orchestral hymn-versets are almost all *cantus-firmus* settings, designed to alternate with the chant of the priests. The overtures are all related to the Lullian opera overture (as are the overtures for consecrations of bishops and the *Ouverture pour l'église* [XX, 23ᵛ-24]).

The orchestral offertories, like the overtures, are rooted in the Italian canzona-sonata tradition. One of them, "non encore exécutée" (XVII, 54-55ᵛ), is among Charpentier's most brilliantly and carefully orchestrated works. In three sections, it is emphatically concerned with coloristic values, with frequent alternations of different kinds of trios and the *grand choeur* of strings and winds (see Plate II).[28]

In addition to the *simphonies* of the *Messe de Minuit* — all based on carol melodies — ten independent *noël* settings are found among Charpentier's manuscripts (V, 21ᵛ-24ᵛ, 30ᵛ-33; IX, 61-63). Lively and straightforward, set in the manner of dance pieces with some *doubles,* these *noëls* are among the most charming of Charpentier's orchestral movements. They deserve a place alongside the *noëls* for organ of Charpentier's contemporaries.

127

*   *
*

The Académie Royale produced only one opera by Charpentier *(Médée)*. Nevertheless, in his positions with the Jesuit colleges, with the Duchesse de Guise, and with the theater of Molière (and of Thomas Corneille and Donneau de Vizé, after Molière's death), Charpentier wrote vocal music and overtures, dance movements, and *entr'acte* pieces for more than twenty-five stage works — pastorales, divertissements, intermezzos, comedies, comedy-ballets, and tragedies.

The overtures are all related to that abstraction called the "French" type. The majority (fifteen of twenty-four) are in two sections, a moderate duple section cadencing on the dominant followed by a faster section, usually in contrasting meter. Seven other overtures add a third section, almost invariably in the meter and mood of the first and functioning as a sort of epilogue.[29] Otherwise, like the ballet and comedy overtures of Lully (in contradistinction to the later opera overtures),

---

[28] See also *Offrande pour un sacre* (III, 117-120); *Offertoire* . . . (V, 54).

[29] The *Ouverture du prologue de L'Inconnu* (XVII, 47-48) is in four sections, with the meters 2, 3, 6/4, and 2 again. The *Ouverture de l'opéra d'Actéon* (XXI, 28ᵛ-29) has five sections (¢, 3, 6/8, 2, and 6/8).

Charpentier's are not particularly stereotyped. The opening section is usually a serious, even march-like expression. The second section is usually fugal and based on minuet or gigue rhythms (but in several overtures the texture is homorhythmic and the style is that of a sarabande). In the three-part overture of *Circe* (XVII, 1-1ᵛ), it is the last part that is contrapuntal.

About 110 dances make up the bulk, if not the weight, of Charpentier's instrumental music for the theater. Including the many movements that bear no dance titles but are classifiable, the following dance types occur (in order of decreasing frequency): *menuet, marche, gigue, sarabande, gavotte, chaconne, bourrée, loure, gaillarde, passecaille, passepied, courante,* and *canaries.* Allemandes are not once cited by name, but distantly related to the allemande are several ballet *entrées* of demons, phantoms, furies, and the like. Fanfare motifs are the basis of some ten combat dances.

Except for the chaconnes and the passacaglias, which are all in continuous variation form with occasionally a final return to the opening *ritornelle,* the dances are mostly in the usual two-part dance form. The two parts may be perfectly balanced — eight plus eight measures is not uncommon — but more frequently the second part is longer than the first. Charpentier is fond of repeating the last few bars of a dance movement in a *petite reprise,* in addition to the *grande reprise* of the entire second part. Virtually all the dance types appear also *en rondeau,* which Charpentier composes with but one or two *couplets.* In contrast to the two-part forms, which are often built up by phrases of interestingly uneven lengths, Charpentier's *rondeaux* are four-square in the extreme; with but few exceptions, the *rondeau* proper as well as each of the *couplets* is an eight-measure double period.

Compared to Lully's dances, Charpentier's seem somewhat artless, even naive, but their surface simplicity is belied by the carefully led inner parts and the balanced spacing of voices. They are light in texture, buoyant, and full of delicate nuances of chromaticism and rhythmic interplay between the parts. In contrast to the preludes and the liturgical works, instrumentation is seldom specified in the stage works.[30] These features, as well as the distinctively melodious and structurally powerful bass line typical of Charpentier's music, may be exemplified by the

[30] This may well be a reflection of the restrictions on stage orchestras outside the Académie after the estrangement of Lully and Molière in 1672.

sarabande en rondeau that serves as an *entr'acte* in *Circe* (1675; see Ex. 6).

Ex. 6

129

*   *

*

The instrumental works that must be designated as "miscellaneous" comprise the following: programmatic *simphonies* in five oratorios and in *Orphée descendant aux enfers:* orchestral interludes in occasional and honorific works; and independent compositions — overtures, marches, minuets, a *caprice,* a *fanfare* for two trumpets, a *simphonie* (chaconne) for three flutes or three violins, and a *Concert pour quatre parties de violes*. Of these miscellaneous compositions, the most noteworthy are three triumphal marches for large orchestra and the *concert*.

The triumphal pieces include two grandiose *rondeaux*, both titled *Marche de triomphe* (X, 51ᵛ-52; XVII, 38-38ᵛ), and an equally martial *rondeau* in triple time titled simply *Air*.[31] All are scored for Charpentier's largest orchestra, with treble and bass trumpets as well as timpani added to the usual four-part ensemble of strings and doubling winds. A pompous, ceremonial atmosphere infuses every measure of these works, which seem perfectly to symbolize the ritualistic monarchical splendor of France in the *ancien régime*. The *concert* for viols,[32] on the other hand, is an intimate dance suite in six movements: *prelude, allemande* (untitled), *sarabande en rondeau, gigue angloise, gigue françoise,* and *passecaille*. The rhythmic appeal of the several dances is combined with Charpentier's feeling for line and equality of voices in a work of more than casual attractiveness.

130

*   *

*

Restricted only by the relatively narrow circumstances for which it was written, Charpentier's instrumental music bespeaks a composer fully the equal of the more celebrated Lully. These works for varying instrumental ensembles already display the inquisitiveness about orchestral color that would remain a principal trait of French music. And they are an important harbinger of the *goûts réunis* on which Couperin would pride himself, for they admirably reconcile contrapuntal and harmonic styles, combining Italian lyricism with French grace, clarity, and occasionally splendor and circumstance.

---

[31] *Second air de trompettes, vio[lo]ns, fl[ûtes], et hautb[ois] et timb[ales]* (X, 52-53). This work follows the *Marche de triomphe* of Vol. X; thus the latter is presumably the "premier air" implied in the title. Both have been issued on records by the Haydn Society (HSL-2065).

[32] See *Notes*, 2nd Series, XVI, No. 4 (Sept., 1959), 619-620, for a review of a recent edition of the *concert*. An earlier edition is that by Guy-Lambert in *Musiques françaises*, No. 16 (Geneva, 1952).

VOCAL ORNAMENTATION IN CACCINI'S *NUOVE MUSICHE*[*]

By H. WILEY HITCHCOCK

EVERYONE is aware that in his preface to *Le nuove musiche,* that "manifesto of the new style" of Italian solo song of the late 16th century,[1] Giulio Caccini speaks at considerable length about vocal ornamentation. Less well understood is that in discussing ornamentation he speaks from the viewpoints of three very different kinds of persons: composer, singer, and voice teacher. To understand the nature and application of Caccini's principles of vocal ornamentation we must separate these alter egos, for we must be clear about when Caccini is explaining what he has composed (that is, written out in his songs), when he is explaining how to interpret what he has composed, and when he is describing how he trains the voice. The aim of this article[2] is to attempt such a clarification and thus to aid in an appropriate interpretation of Caccini's songs.

Let us dispose of Caccini the voice teacher first.[3] In *Le nuove musiche* he speaks only once about his teaching: when he discusses the *trillo* and the *gruppo* (his terms for the tremolo and the trill, respectively). He prints the following examples (Ex. 1, to be found on the next page). These two illustrations, reprinted many times in discussions of early Baroque ornamentation,[4] have become a kind of canon law for the per-

[1] Nigel Fortune, "Italian Secular Monody from 1600 to 1635; An Introductory Survey," *The Musical Quarterly,* XXXIX (1953), 171-95.

[2] Adapted from a paper read before the Greater New York Chapter of the American Musicological Society in New York, October 18, 1969.

[3] He was a successful and famous one: among his students were singer-composers like Ottavio Durante and the noted tenor Francesco Rasi as well as the castrato Giovanni Gualberto Magli, who created the title role in Monteverdi's *L'Orfeo.* He also had a habit of both marrying and fathering great singers, whom he trained — his first wife, Lucia, and his second, Margherita; his daughters Francesca and Settimia; and his son Pompeo.

[4] Most recently by Fortune, in Chapter 4 ("Solo Song and Cantata") of *The New Oxford History of Music,* IV (London, 1968), 158, where, however, the *trillo* is incorrectly transcribed.

Ex. 1

formance of the tremolo and the trill in Caccini's music (and in much other 17th-century music); that is, they have been read as examples of how the ornaments should be sung. But here is the context in which they are introduced by Caccini:

I must now demonstrate first how the tremolo and the trill are written by me, and how I teach them to those of my household who are concerned with such matters. ... The tremolo written by me on a single note is demonstrated in this way for no other reason than that, in teaching it to my first wife and now to the one who is living with my daughters, I observed no other rule than that which is written out for both [ornaments]: i.e., to begin with the first quarter-note, then restrike each note with the throat on the vowel à, up to the final double-whole-note; and likewise the trill. How excellently the said tremolo and trill were learned by my late wife with the above rule may be adjudged by those who heard her sing during her lifetime. ... I can state with some assurance that no better way to teach them can be found, nor a better way to describe it, than is here given for both [ornaments].[5]

This passage is obviously that of a voice teacher, not a composer or even a singer: Caccini is illustrating a "rule," a *regola* — an exercise, in this case — by which he trains his students' voices to achieve the proper speedy articulation of the two ornaments. That being so, we may question whether in performance the tremolo and the trill should be effected with the regular acceleration, in measured rhythms, that makes such good sense as a vocal exercise. Robert Donington, among others, has relieved us of the necessity to answer for the trill: he has demonstrated persuasively that trills are not to be measured, and, furthermore, that even when trills appear written-out they are to be read as symbols for real trills.[6] The same principles may be applied to the performance of Caccini's tremolo. Ex. 2 is a passage from the song "Filli mirando il cielo"; it contains two

[5] My translation from *Le nuove musiche* (Florence: Marescotti, 1602), prepared for an integral new edition of the entire work (Madison: A-R Editions, Inc., in press). Unless otherwise noted, all quotations from Caccini herein are from his preface "To the Readers" (without pagination in the original). Two facsimile editions of *Le nuove musiche* have been published, both at Rome (1930 and 1934).

[6] "Ornaments," *Grove's Dictionary,* 5th ed. (London, 1954).

Ex. 2

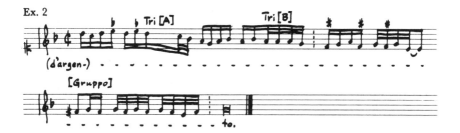

of the very few specific indications for tremolos to be found in *Le nuove musiche* (and, at the end of the phrase, a written-out trill). The indication at B might possibly be descriptive: "This is a tremolo." But the indication at A can hardly mean this; it must be prescriptive: "Here make a tremolo." But how? Surely not by following Caccini's *regola* and making a measured, accelerating tremolo on the single sixteenth-note value indicated. The marking at B must also be prescriptive and symbolic, as is that at A and as is the written-out *gruppo* at the end of the phrase. In sum, except for the *regola*, the exercise, of Ex. 1, all the evidence points to Caccini's tremolo as being no more than a "trembling voice," as Zacconi had defined it simply in 1592 without saying anything about acceleration, let alone measured rhythm.[7] Where the note to be "trembled" is long enough, perhaps some acceleration of the tremolo is stylish: Bovicelli, for instance (who also describes the tremolo as "nothing but a trembling of the voice on a single note"), says explicitly that it "demands that the notes go by degrees,"[8] i.e., accelerate, and some of the few written-out tremolos in *Le nuove musiche,* even if they are probably symbolic, include acceleration. However, the tremolo with regular acceleration in measured rhythms (as we have often been hearing it in performances of Seicento music) is without foundation, except as the training exercise favored by Giulio Caccini in his role as voice teacher.

Tremolos and trills are basically cadential ornaments. In one of the two model songs Caccini includes in his preface (a setting of Chiabrera's madrigal "Deh, dove son fuggiti"), which he furnishes liberally with indications for ornamentation (unlike the songs of the collection proper), tremolos are suggested at three of the four cadences in which the voice falls by step to the tonic note. In the body of the collection, however, not a single cadential tremolo is indicated, and the interpreter may add one

[7] Lodovico Zacconi, *Prattica di musica,* I (Venice, 1592), fol. 60.

[8] "Il tremolo nondimeno, che non è altro, che un tremar di voce sopra ad una stessa nota, ricerca, che le note vadino sempre per grado." Giovanni Battista Bovicelli, *Regole, passaggi di musica . . .* (Venice, 1594), p. 12.

133

whenever the voice falls from second degree to tonic. Cadential trills, on the other hand, are written into the music — in fact, at every single cadence where the voice rises from leading tone to tonic. This difference in the treatment of the two cadential ornaments — one left for the singer to add, the other indicated explicitly (if symbolically) by the composer — leads us to inquire which of the many other ornaments discussed, illustrated, or mentioned in Caccini's preface may be read in his songs and which must be read into them.

There is little doubt about several devices involving sonorous expressivity. Caccini speaks of these as would a vocal coach; they are almost never indicated in his songs, and the interpreter must add them. They are *l'intonazione della voce, l'esclamazione,* and *il crescere e scemare della voce.*

Caccini discusses *l'intonazione della voce* at some length. His first sentence about it suggests that he uses the term in two senses: "The first and most important foundation is a vocal intonation on all the notes not only such as to avoid flatting or sharping but to have a good style." "Avoidance of flatting or sharping" is intonation in our modern sense, that of pitch placement. "Having a good style" of intonation involves the approach to a note, the attack, and, in the discussion that follows, *l'intonazione della voce* has the meaning of "manner of attack" at the beginning of a song or of a phrase.[9] Caccini cites three such modes of attack. The first begins a third lower than the written note, then rises to it. He deprecates this attack on the grounds that the third below is often discordant, that "even where it can be used it has become by now . . . a commonplace," and that it often lacks grace since "some stay too long on the third below, whereas it should scarcely be suggested."[10] Caccini voices a preference for two other kinds of attack, both made directly on the

---

[9] In a broader but related meaning, *intonazione* is familiar to us from the 16th-century Italian organ repertory: the improvisatory *intonazioni* or "mode-setting" pieces used as preludes. From Caccini's discussion one can initially draw the inference that he is speaking only of the very first vocal attack, at the beginning of a song: he speaks only of the "first note." But the context, and the later discussion and illustrations of *esclamazioni,* make it clear that it is the first note of a phrase as well that is being discussed.

[10] As Caccini suggests, such a mode of attack must have been as common in his time as the singer's calculated "scoop" in ours. Bovicelli writes out examples of "bad" and "good" attacks from below, saying: "To lend grace to the voice . . . you begin a third or fourth below [the given note] depending on the harmony of the other parts . . . [and] the longer you hold the first note, the shorter the second, the more grace will the voice gain" (*Regole, passaggi,* p. 11). Despite his strictures against the attack from the third below, Caccini actually writes out such attacks (although infrequently) in the songs of *Le nuove musiche.*

given note. In one, the singer is to begin on "the first note at its actual pitch and make a gradual crescendo." In the other, a decrescendo is to be made, as is illustrated in Caccini's model madrigal, where he writes "scemar di voce" ("diminishing of voice") over the first note. This last mode of attack, with a decrescendo, Caccini prefers above all, for it permits the singer to move gracefully on to an *esclamazione*: "I have found to be a more affective manner an attack that is the opposite of the other; that is, to begin singing with a decrescendo, then on to an exclamation, which is the most basic means of moving the affect." This third type of attack, then, really involves two things: the attack itself, with a decrescendo, and another vocal device, the *esclamazione*.

The *esclamazione* is explained none too precisely by Caccini. He says only that "an exclamation is really nothing but a certain strengthening of the relaxed voice" and that "at its point of relaxation, giving [the voice] just a bit more spirit will make it ever more affective." Thus the exclamation would seem to be a kind of light, quick crescendo made from a point of low vocal intensity, itself achieved by a preliminary decrescendo. Exclamations may be more or less forceful depending on the expressive aim; Caccini gives as an example a setting of the opening line of Guarini's madrigal poem "Cor mio, deh, non languire," in which different degrees of exclamations ("languid" and "more lively") are called for, depending on whether the note falls by step or by leap (Ex. 3):

135

Ex. 3

Exclamations may be made on all moderately long notes that descend, but are not to be made on whole-notes.[11] The latter injunction is perhaps not to be taken too seriously, however, since Caccini himself calls for exclamations on whole-notes twice in his model madrigal. The exclamation as an attack-ornament at the beginning of a phrase seems to have been almost *de rigueur* for Caccini: he calls for an exclamation at the beginning of nine of the ten lines of the model madrigal poem. In the twenty-odd songs of *Le nuove musiche*, however, exclamations are indicated only

[11] "[Esclamazioni] si possono usare in tutte le mimime, e seminiminime col punto per discendere.... Non [si] faranno nelle semibrevi." Caccini's first remark is ambiguous: it may be read either as "exclamations may be used on all half-notes and dotted quarter-notes that descend" or (especially in the light of his illustrations [Ex. 3]) as "exclamations may be used on all dotted half-notes and quarter-notes that descend."

twice (neither time at the beginning of a poetic line); thus they must be added by the interpreter, and as we have seen he may be quite lavish with them, especially when a phrase begins with a longish note that will descend.

The other ornament of vocal expressivity mentioned by Caccini is the crescendo-and-diminuendo. That this is a single thing in his mind, involving both the increasing and abating of volume, is suggested by his use, never of "il crescere ed il scemare della voce," but always of "il crescere e scemare della voce." He says only one thing about it, and that by indirection: the reason for not using exclamations on whole-notes is that such notes "offer more room for a vocal crescendo-and-diminuendo without using exclamations." This implies that in Caccini's style the crescendo-and-diminuendo takes more time than the exclamation; it may be made comfortably on whole-notes, thus, logically, on notes still longer. Otherwise, we are left in the dark as to where the crescendo-and-diminuendo may stylishly be added to the songs, since Caccini neither illustrates it in his preface nor indicates it in his music. He does, however, rule out the use of the crescendo-and-diminuendo (and of exclamations, in general) in "airy pieces or dance songs, [where] one should rely only on the sprightliness of song, as usually conveyed by the air itself; although occasionally some *esclamazione* may occur, the same sprightliness should be maintained, with no affect smacking of lethargy introduced."

Caccini discusses a number of other devices of vocal ornamentation in his preface. We must continue to ask: are they written into his songs or are they to be added? To put it the other way: are they discussed by Caccini the composer or Caccini the singer and coach? Helpful in answering such questions are comparisons between the songs as published in the 1602 print of *Le nuove musiche* and versions of many of them as found in various manuscripts of the late 16th and early 17th centuries.[12] Ex. 4 gives the vocal part of the *aria seconda,* "Ardi, cor mio" (Rinuccini), as it appears in *Le nuove musiche* and, below that, in two manuscript versions (the only known ones).

The manuscript versions are almost identical, so close as to suggest a common source (about which we shall be inquiring shortly). Caccini's printed version is considerably different from them; it is much more

---

[12] Especially Brussels, Bibliothèque du Conservatoire, MS 704 (with versions of fifteen of the songs of *Le nuove musiche*); Florence, Biblioteca Nazionale, MS Magliabechiana XIX.66 (with versions of ten); Tenbury Wells, St. Michael's College Library, MS 1018 (with versions of six); Florence, Biblioteca del Conservatorio Cherubini, Barbera MS (with versions of four); and Modena, Biblioteca Estense, MSS Mus.F.1526 and Mus.F.1527 (with versions of two).

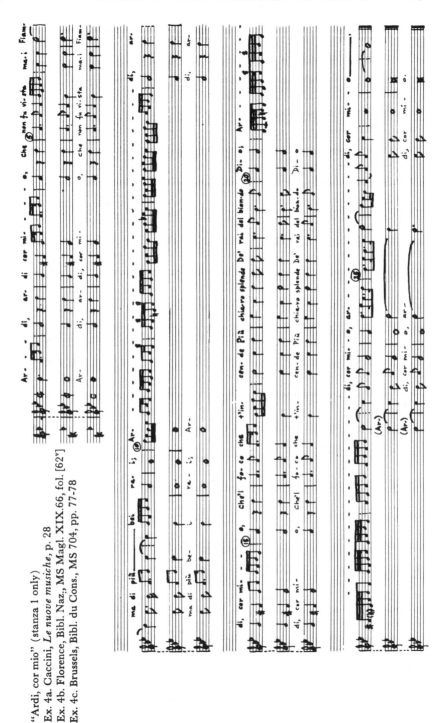

"Ardi, cor mio" (stanza 1 only)
Ex. 4a. Caccini, *Le nuove musiche*, p. 28
Ex. 4b. Florence, Bibl. Naz., MS Magl. XIX.66, fol. [62ᵛ]
Ex. 4c. Brussels, Bibl. du Cons., MS 704, pp. 77-78

137

elaborate and, in fact, includes most of the devices he discusses in his preface:

(1) uneven-note patterns ("dotted rhythms"), which he considers to have more grace than even notes (measures 1, 3, 7, 16, 24-25);
(2) roulades (*giri di voce, passaggio*-like divisions and diminutions), of the four kinds he cites:
    (a) "simple" (*semplici*), of eighth-note values (measures 24-25; Caccini "graces" the eighths by making them uneven);
    (b) "double" (*doppi*), of sixteenth-note values (measures 11-12);
    (c) "redoubled" (*raddoppiate*), of thirty-second-note values (measure 21);
    (d) "intertwined with each other" (*intrecciate, l'una nell'altra*) — eighths and sixteenths in measures 10-12, eighths, sixteenths, and thirty-seconds in measures 21-22;
(3) "restriking with the throat" (*ribattuta di gola*), a kind of slow trill in uneven rhythms, beginning on the principal note (measure 25);
(4) the fall (*la cascata*) in its "single" (*scempia*) form (measure 26).

The little flourishes in measures 1, 3, 5, 8, 14, and 16 are related to the diminutions of *passaggi*. In his essay, Caccini feels himself obliged to rationalize such improvisatory spurts: "For a bit of decoration I have sometimes used, mainly on short [i.e., unaccented] syllables, a few eighth-notes for as long as a quarter of one tactus or a half at the most [♩ and ♪ respectively, in the transcription of Ex. 4a]. These are permissible since they pass by quickly and are not *passaggi* but [give] merely an additional bit of grace." Another device written into the songs of *Le nuove musiche* is the "fall to retake a breath" (*la cascata per ricorre il fiato*): the manu-

Ex. 5
Caccini, *Le nuove musiche*, p. 17
Moderna, Bibl. Estense, MS Mus.F.1527

script version shown in Ex. 5 lacks the rest inserted by Caccini in the published version to permit a catch-breath before the *cascata*. Both versions may illustrate Caccini's "double fall" (*cascata doppia*), which he neither explains nor discusses but simply uses as a heading for two musical examples differentiated from the *cascata scempia* only by the fall's dropping below the anticipated arrival-note before rising to achieve it finally. In sum, all the devices of ornamentation mentioned in this paragraph are demonstrably written out by Caccini in his songs as printed in *Le nuove musiche*. In his discussion and demonstration of them in the preface he must be speaking as composer and not simply counseling singers how to improvise such flourishes as additions to his music.

In the foregoing, all the devices of vocal ornamentation mentioned by Caccini have been considered. By way of summary the following table shows which ones seem to be the concern of Caccini as voice teacher, which of Caccini as coach, and which of Caccini as composer..

139

Vocal Devices Cited in the Preface of *Le Nuove Musiche*	Caccini as voice teacher	Caccini as coach	Caccini as composer
1. *Il trillo*	x		(x)
2. *Il gruppo*	x		(x)
3. *L'intonazione della voce*			
a. from third below to main note		x	(x)
b. main note with crescendo		x	
c. main note with decrescendo		x	
4. *L'esclamazione*		x	
5. *Il crescere e scemare della voce*		x	
6. Uneven-note patterns			x
7. *Lunghi giri di voce* (*passaggi*)			
a. *semplici* (♪)			x
b. *doppi* (♪)			x
c. *raddoppiate* (♪)			x
d. *intrecciate, l'una nell'altra* (♪, ♪, ♪ mixed)			x
8. Brief *passaggio*-like flourishes			x
9. *La ribattuta di gola*			x
10. *La cascata*			
a. *scempia*			x
b. *doppia*			x
c. *per ricorre il fiato*			x

The table shows that Caccini the composer produces a music of considerable elaborateness, incorporating in print a great many devices of vocal ornamentation that had previously been improvised in performance (nos. 6-10 in the table). This, in fact, is one of the great novelties of *Le nuove musiche*. Oddly, Caccini makes no mention of this departure in his essay of 1602. However, twelve years later he published another collection of "New Music," this one with an amplified title: *Nuove musiche e nuova maniera di scriverle*. Now, the "new way of writing" is not a matter of the musical notation, for there is absolutely nothing new or unusual about that. But, in the preface to the 1614 collection, Caccini remarks on "my solo singing style, which I write exactly as it is sung" [13] — and this is what is new about the writing.

* * *

There remains for us to inquire about the principles on which Caccini bases his written-out ornamentation. To do so is to approach the heart of Caccini's musical style and to reveal his ingenious reconciliation of two apparent opposites in his musical life: his career as a virtuoso singer and his commitment as a member of the Florentine Camerata.

At the time when Bardi's academy was flourishing, Caccini was very young but already a famous singer.[14] His active performing career seems to have been finished by the turn of the century; when the early Florentine operas were produced, he was conducting them, not singing in them.[15] However, as we have seen, he was by then a celebrated teacher of singers. It was an era of extraordinary vocal virtuosity in Italy: the era of the famous "three ladies of Ferrara" for whom Wert and Luzzaschi composed spectacular madrigals; of the tenors Rasi and Peri at Florence, and the sopranos Vittoria Archilei and Francesca Caccini (Giulio's daughter, nicknamed La Cecchina, "the little magpie"); of the great Melchior Palantrotti, basso of the Papal Chapel; of the expert coloratura voices available to Monteverdi at Mantua for pieces like the air "Possente

[13] "Questa mia maniera di cantar solo, la quale io scrivo giustamente, come si canta."

[14] In a letter of 1634 to Giovanni Battista Doni, Pietro de' Bardi speaks of Caccini as having been "very young of age" during the Camerata years; the court chronicler of the festivities of 1579 for the marriage of Francesco de' Medici and Bianca Capello calls Caccini, who performed in the *intermedi*, "famous for singing." See, respectively, the reproduction of Bardi's letter in Angelo Solerti, *Le origini del melodramma* (Turin, 1903), pp. 143-47, and Raffaello Gualterotti, *Feste nelle nozze del Serenissimo D. Francesco Medici . . . e della . . . Signora Bianca Capello* (Florence, 1579), p. 31.

[15] See Solerti, *Musica, ballo e drammatica alla corte medicea dal 1600 al 1637* (Florence, 1905), *passim*.

141

The title page of Caccini's collection of 1614,
Nuove musiche e nuova maniera di scriverle.

spirto" of *L'Orfeo*. Such virtuosos were expected as a matter of course to add improvised embellishments of all kinds to the written music. Manuals teaching how to do so were appearing: Dalla Casa's *Il vero modo di diminuir* (Venice, 1584), Conforto's *Breve e facile maniera d'essercitarsi a far passaggi* (Rome, 1593), Bovicelli's *Regole, passaggi di musica* (Venice, 1594), and others. A singer's reputation could rest on his ability to elaborate the music before him: Caccini remarks in his preface that precisely "because of these [*passaggi*] some have been extolled by the hoi polloi and proclaimed mighty singers."

It was as a young tenor, in this age of virtuosity and improvised ornamentation, that Caccini joined that group of humanists which was Bardi's Camerata. Nothing could have seemed more at odds with the fashionable vocal virtuosity of the era than their Platonic ideal of music as "naught but speech, with rhythm and tone coming after" (as Caccini phrases it). Caccini must have faced a real dilemma when he became one of the Bardi group: how to reconcile virtuoso singing (on which his reputation rested) with the Camerata's ideals of speech-dominated song. He sought, and found, a means of reconciling them.

First of all, he accepted the idea that music was primarily a matter of "speech," but he interpreted the notion of "speech" in a special way. In his songs, he did not turn to recitative; thus "speech" for him was not a naturalistic matter of monotonous parlando declamation (although his concept of *una certa nobile sprezzatura di canto* — "a certain noble negligence of song" — included a freedom of rhythm more like speech than traditional singing).[16] However, Caccini paid the closest attention to the

[16] Rubato-like freedom on the singer's part — extending as far as "often halving the values of the notes" — was one of two means whereby Caccini sought to achieve his "noble negligence." The other was a question not of interpretation but of composition: Caccini points to his "negligent" dissonance-treatment in which he occasionally permits himself "several dissonances while still maintaining the bass note"; that is, not resolving the dissonances by changing the bass and its harmony in the usual way.

Caccini neatly summarized the aims and techniques of his *sprezzatura di canto* in the preface to his 1614 volume of *Nuove musiche e nuova maniera di scriverle:* "*Sprezzatura* is that charm lent to a song by a few 'faulty' eighths or sixteenths on various tones, together with those [similar slips] made in the tempo. These relieve the song of a certain restricted narrowness and dryness and make it pleasant, free, and airy, just as in common speech eloquence and variety make pleasant and sweet the matters being spoken of."

One might recall that the ideal of *sprezzatura* was not original with Caccini but had been upheld in Italian courtly life and art at least since Castiglione's *Il Cortegiano* (1528), where it is defined as "that virtue opposite to affectation ... whence springs *grazia*." See Baldassare Castiglione, *Opere,* ed. Carlo Cordié (Milan, 1960), I, no. 28; John Shearman, *Mannerism* (Harmondsworth, Middlesex, 1967), p. 21.

structure, the syntax, and the accentuation of the poems he set; he seems to have equated their "speech" with their structural integrity. No one could call "Amarilli mia bella" an example of *recitativo,* but it is hardly less thoroughly conceived in terms of the "speech" of the poem, in this special sense. Guarini's seven-line madrigal is based on an alternation of seven- and eleven-syllable verses (*settenario* and *endecasillabo*). These are accented poetically as shown by the acute accents added to the poem below; the primary accent, on the penultimate syllable in any Italian verse line, is shown in italics. The column to the right shows the rhyme and meter scheme, and the division of the poem into two complete sentences.

[1] A-ma-ríl-li mia *bél*-la,	a⁷	
[2] Non cré-di, o dél mio cor dól-ce de-*sí*-o,	b¹¹	
[3] D'és-ser tú l'a-mor *mí*-o?	b⁷	
[4] Cré-di-lo púr, e se ti-mór t'as-*sá*-le,	c¹¹	
[5] Prén-di qué-sto mio *strá*-le,	c⁷	143
[6] Á-pri-m'il pét-to, e ve-drai scrít-to il *có*-re:	d¹¹	
[7] A-ma-ríl-li è'l mio a-*mó*-re.	d⁷	

By forming cadences at the line-endings and by setting the accented syllables to long notes, Caccini projects clearly the linear and accentual structure of the poem. Furthermore, at only two points does his music cadence on the tonic note: at the end of the third line and the end of the last line. These are the two sentence-endings, thus his music mirrors the larger structural organization of the poem. In two interlocked ways, then (agogic accents and harmonic-rhythmic cadences), Caccini's music respects the "speech" of the poem.

Had Caccini stopped there, all of the songs in *Le nuove musiche* might be similar to "Amarilli." They are not: outside of "Dovrò dunque morire," which is close in style and structure to "Amarilli," and a few of the *arie* based on dance rhythms, all the songs of *Le nuove musiche* include more elaborate *giri di voce,* more frequent flowerings of brief decorative diminutions, more *cascate* and *ribattute di gola* than we find in "Amarilli." These songs reflect vividly Caccini's abilities as a virtuoso singer; to understand how their florid ornamentation is related to the Camerata's ideals, we must read Caccini's commentary closely. The main reason he gives for publishing *Le nuove musiche* is that singers were misinterpreting his songs and his new style of singing:

If I have not heretofore published the musical studies I made after the noble manner of singing . . . nor other compositions . . . it is because I esteemed them but little:

it seemed to me that these pieces of mine had been honored enough ... by being constantly performed. ... But now I see many of them circulating tattered and torn; moreover, I see ill used those single and double roulades — rather, those redoubled and intertwined with each other — developed by me to avoid that old style of *passaggi* formerly in use. ... And I see the vocal crescendo-and-diminuendo, exclamations, tremolos and trills, and other such embellishments of good singing style used indiscriminately. Thus have I been forced (and also urged by friends) to have these pieces of mine published.

Caccini is particularly harsh on those singers who, seeking to be fashionable, have turned to solo singing to the lute or harpsichord, but without changing their style of ornamentation; he rails at their "solos sung to one or another string instrument, wherein not a single word has been understood for the multitude of *passaggi* on both short and long syllables and in every sort of piece." His own singing, he implies, is infinitely more respectful of the text, and he enunciates some general principles that guide him in the formation of improvisatory decorations. Buried in a passage that deals also with compositional matters, these principles are expressed in this way (my emphasis):

144

I have formed chords on the long syllables, avoiding them on the short; *and I have observed the same rule in making passaggi*, although for a bit of decoration I have sometimes used, mainly on short syllables, a few eighth-notes for as long as a quarter of one tactus or a half at the most. ... *Passaggi* were not devised because they are essential to good singing style but rather, I believe, as a kind of tickling of the ears of those who hardly understand what affective singing really is. If they did understand, *passaggi* would doubtless be loathed, there being nothing more inimical to affective expression. Thus did I speak of those long vocal roulades as being ill used, even though *they are indeed adopted by me for use in less affective pieces, also on long syllables — not short! — and in final cadences.*

Reading between the lines of this somewhat cloudy statement, we can interpret Caccini as saying that as a Camerata member he reviles the mindless and indiscriminate invention of *passaggi* by the singers of his time, but as a virtuoso singer himself he is unwilling to give them up and has found a way to preserve such passage-work in conformity with the precepts of the Camerata. He forms roulades on "long" syllables — that is, accented ones — and in final cadences; and he is freer with *passaggi* in "less affective pieces" — that is, in settings of less high-flown and less serious poems. This helps to explain how he could view as agreeing with the Camerata's ideals such flourishes as we find at the line "I vivi ardori miei" in his setting of Rinuccini's "Sfogava con le stelle" (Ex. 6a): he decorates with a spectacular roulade the strongly accented second syllable of "ardori," leaving unemphasized the more weakly accented "vivi" (which any madrigalist interested in word-painting as such would probably have chosen to emphasize). His principles explain also the flowery final cadence of "Amarilli"; even more characteristically elaborate are the final cadences of "Dolcissimo sospiro," another affective madrigal poem by Rinuccini (Ex. 6b) and of Guarini's "Vedrò'l mio sol" (Ex. 6c), a madrigal Caccini cites in his preface as having been extremely well received during the Camerata years.

Ex. 6a.

Ex. 6b.

Ex. 6c.

Caccini's principles also help to explain why he sets a simple strophic canzonet like "Ardi, cor mio" (see Ex. 4a, above) so much more elaborately than the madrigal "Amarilli," with its poetic artifice and conceits, in an otherwise strange reversal of 16th-century procedures: the less affective poem, according to his view, can bear more of the "ear-tickling" superficiality of *passaggio*-like decoration than can the more affective one. (And, incidentally, since the decoration is made according to word ac-

centuation, not according to word meaning in a madrigalesque way, it
will be valid for all the stanzas of the air.)

One conclusion to be drawn from this interpretation of Caccini's work
is that his songs will hardly allow for *further* ornamentation of the sort
we have been discussing. The point is important, since some have read
Caccini's preface as if it were a manual for improvised ornamentation,
like Conforto's or Bovicelli's — that is to say, as if it were the product
exclusively of Caccini as singer and coach — and have found in it license
to add all sorts of decorative passage-work to Caccini's songs.[17] But such
additions merely destroy the subtle balance between decoration and declamation achieved by Caccini; they also deny Caccini the composer his
"new way" of writing music, "as it is sung."

Another conclusion to be drawn from this interpretation relates to the
puzzlingly plain character of most of the manuscript versions of Caccini
songs that have come down to us. Most of them are virtually bare of
decoration, mere skeletons. One specialist in monodic music of Caccini's
period has said that "it is almost impossible to decide whether [such plain
versions] are Caccini's own early experiments or 'maimed and spoiled'
copies sung by those who were baffled by the unfamiliar style of the final
versions." [18] Most probably, however, these manuscript versions, if not
exactly "early experiments," represent the way Caccini first wrote out his
songs, leaving the ornamentation to be improvised in performance, as was
the practice of the later 16th century. This would explain the remarkable
likeness between the various manuscript copies of single songs (as between
Ex. 4b and c, above), and their generally uniform simplicity. Other singers must have ornamented the songs differently; they did so badly, according to Caccini's views, by adding "a multitude of *passaggi* on both
short and long syllables" and by using other ornaments indiscriminately.
This led Caccini to his "new way of writing" music and to the embodi-
ment in print of his new kind of virtuoso song.

146

[17] See, for example, Arnold Schering's edition of "Amarilli, mia bella," *Geschichte
der Musik in Beispielen* (Leipzig, 1931), no. 173.

[18] Fortune, *The New Oxford History of Music*, IV, 155-56. The quotation
"maimed and spoiled" is from Playford's 17th-century translation of Caccini's preface
(reprinted with some emendations in Oliver Strunk, *Source Readings in Music History*
[New York, 1950], pp. 377-92); cf. my "tattered and torn" in the next-to-last quotation given above.

This connection with contrapuntal technique is further established in the writings ascribed to the well-known *ars nova* theorist, Jean de Muris,[3] where contrapuntal style is divided into two classes—*simplex* (note-against-note) and *diminutus*. The same relation between ornate and simple style is maintained, the diminuted version being derived from a note-against-note skeleton. But his treatment of *contrapunctus diminutus* is a disappointment because he is primarily concerned with rhythmic and mensural problems, and because his examples by no means approach the complexity found in contemporaneous works.

David Hughes[4] has shown that these *ars nova* compositions can be reduced to a simple note-against-note skeleton, but has concluded that they most probably were not composed in the prescribed order. The relation between the simple and ornate structures remains valid, nevertheless, as a description of the style; perhaps also it is the result of a common pedagogical process. It is a relationship not unlike that between the harmonic skeleton of a classical symphony and the finished work. It is inherent in the style, and the composer does not need to follow the process to ensure the correct result.

When virtuoso transcriptions for keyboard of *ars nova* works are compared with the originals a procedure similar to that described by de Muris can be detected. Here the simple form is already a finished work in *contrapunctus diminutus* which, in turn, becomes the basis of a more ornate version.[5] There is evidence, here and there, of the arranger reverting to a simpler form of the composition before putting in his diminutions. A section of the melody is removed, apparently reduced to a single long note, and a new passage moving through different intermediate notes inserted. It is clear that the arranger considered it legitimate to reduce at least a section of the work to a simpler form before applying diminutions—a concept in accord with de Muris' definitions and the analyses of Dr. Hughes.

By the sixteenth century these processes were more distinctly defined. Theorists continued to divide contrapuntal technique into *simplex* and *diminutus* (or *floridus*) but the second type was no longer conceived as directly derived from the first.[6] The dominant style, an outgrowth of the choral style of the Netherlanders, was remarkably close to the rules given by theorists. The quarter note was the smallest value treated by the theorists, and it was the smallest used to any extent by composers. Until the third quarter of the century, eighths were used sparingly in the common ¢ notation; madrigals printed in the new *note nere* (with the signature C), where the quarter rather than the half was the unit, used eighths where the older notation used quarters, and these eighths followed the same restrictions as did quarters in the

149

---

[3] Coussemaker, *Scriptores* III p. 62—68. Correct form of examples and discussion of other sources of treatise in: David G. Hughes, *A View of the Passing of Gothic Music; Line and Counterpoint, 1380—1430* (Diss., Harvard 1956) p. 37—40.

[4] Ibid., p. 66 ff.

[5] See: Dragan Plamenac, *Keyboard Music of the 14th Century in Codex Faenza 117* in: JAMS IV (1951) p. 179—201; and Arnold Schering, *Das kolorierte Orgelmadrigal des Trecento*, in: SIMG XIII (1911—1912) p. 172 ff.

[6] Claude V. Palisca, *Kontrapunkt*, in: MGG 7, 1532 ff.

¢ notation. This was merely a change in appearance, not in actual duration of sounds. Extremes of rhythmic motion were not sought by composers of the time.

But virtuoso singers and instrumentalists continued to demand fast, showy passages; and the rapprochement of theory and composition was paralleled by a pedantic systematization of the technique of improvising diminutions. Since these diminutions were improvised in the performance of polyphonic works, the instructions given for their application in the many manuals on ornamentation published at the time showed a common concern for maintaining the correctness of the original counterpoint. Two general procedures were followed: either the diminution began and ended on the pitch of a single long note for which it was substituted, or it began with that note and approached the next note (of the original work) by scalewise motion. The first usage preserved the counterpoint of the original work intact. In the second case, it was expected that speed and smoothness of movement would conceal any resulting errors in counterpoint.

Often, however, the new passage replaced more than one note of the original. In that case, according to the examples given (no manual specifically discussed this situation), the same two principles were applied. Either the embellishment began on the first note of the original passage and ended on its final note, or else it began on the first note of the original and moved directly on to approach by step the note immediately following the passage being ornamented. Only Ganassi includes examples of these usages. (Example 1)[7] Each of the original patterns, considered by Ganassi as a perfect fourth, includes an intermediate note which is not counted as a part of the interval. Treated in the ordinary way, each note would be used separately as the basis for a diminution, but here Ganassi prefers to use the whole note as the time unit being ornamented. This results in the melody being reduced to an even simpler structure of which the intermediate note was already an ornament. The intermediate note may either act as an end to the diminution, or be eliminated entirely while the diminution moves from the beginning of the first whole note to the beginning of the second by stepwise, or predominantly stepwise, motion. In the first instance, (excerpts from *Regola Prima* 9, nos. 1, 4; *Regola Secunda* 6, no. 3) dissonances might occur within the passage, but the beginning would still be consonant and there would be no parallels in the approach to the following note. In the second, (*Regola Prima* 9, no. 7; *Regola Secunda* 6, nos. 4, 7) the dissonance treatment would be similar, but parallels might occur in the approach to the next note.

Other manuals give only simple intervals as prototypes in their lists of diminutions, but their models showing ornamented versions of actual compositions follow the procedure shown in Ganassi. The choice as to which time value would be the temporary unit of ornamentation was left to the taste of the performer or arranger, and this made possible a wide number of variants. Short excerpts from two ornamented versions of de Rore's *Di tempo in tempo* (Example 2)[8] show the different

150

---

[7] SYLVESTRO GANASSI, *Opera intitulata Fontegara* (Venice 1535). Selected from *Regola Prima* and *Regola Secunda*.
[8] From GIROLAMO DALLA CASA, *Il vero modo di diminuir* (Venice 1584) *Parte prima*, p. 67—71.

effects produced in ornamenting note by note or in substituting an embellishment for two or more notes of the original.

The interrelation of ornamentation and contrapuntal technique is emphasized pointedly by certain writers. Ganassi[9] warned the student violist that, just as a knowledge of intervals was necessary for a correct performance of the original work (cosa positiva), so also was a knowledge of counterpoint essential to the proper making of diminutions. In the early seventeenth century, when many opere passeggiate were being published to satisfy the growing appetite for virtuoso compositions, Bartholomeo Barbarino explained in the preface to his Secondo libro delli motetti (Venice 1614) that he was giving two versions of each motet—a simple one for those who could not sing coloratura passages, or for those who could sing them, but knew counterpoint well enough to make their own diminutions; and an embellished version for those who wanted to sing virtuoso passages but, knowing no counterpoint, could not create them for themselves. In the instructions at the beginning of his Breve et facile maniera (Rome 1593), Giovanni Luca Conforto gave rudimentary information for those untrained in theory who might be afraid to improvise or write out opere passeggiate and marked certain of his passaggi that would work whether the first note made an octave, tenth, or twelfth with the bass.

Conforto's mention of written-out opere passeggiate is significant, for by his time diminutions were not only written out frequently in arrangements of popular works, but they were again becoming a part of the composer's vocabulary. As a result, the shorter note values were discussed by early seventeenth-century theorists. Although by this time theorists were well aware of the secunda prattica, it is in the strict contrapuntal style that the treatment of eighths and sixteenths was first codified. In his treatment of this stile osservato in the second section of Book II of Il transilvano,[10] Girolamo Diruta stated emphatically that eighths and sixteenths were to follow the same rules as quarters: the beginning and second half of the beat (notes one and three) should be consonant, and all skips should be consonant. Zarlino's pupil, Lodovico Zacconi,[11] gave similar rules.

The stile osservato, an extension of conservative Renaissance theory, remained a highly idealized and artificial concept throughout the seventeenth century.[12] Its rules differed not only from seventeenth-century practice but also from the practices that Vincenzo Galilei[13] recorded as characteristic of the 1580's—that when notes smaller than the half followed each other stepwise, consonance and dissonance alternated without regard to placement in the beat. Diruta recognized the existence of another style, freer than the osservato style, which he called contrapunto com-

151

---

[9] GANASSI, Lettione secunda (Venice 1543) Cap. XVII. Facs. repr. with Regola Rubertina (1542) ed. M. SCHNEIDER (Leipzig 1924).
[10] GIROLAMO DIRUTA, Seconda parte del transilvano ... nel quale si contiene il vero modo, + la ver regola d'intavolare ciascum canto, semplice, + diminuito (Venice 1622; 1st ed. 1609) p. 11.
[11] In: Prattica di musica II (Venice 1622) p. 93.
[12] PALISCA, Kontrapunkt, and RALPH H. ROBBINS, Beiträge zur Geschichte des Kontrapunkts von Zarlino bis Schütz (Berlin 1938).
[13] PALISCA, Vincenzo Galilei's Counterpoint Treatise, in: JAMS IX (1956) p. 83.

mune.[14] Adriano Banchieri[15] accepted this division of counterpoint into two styles, but pointed out that the *contrapunto commune* had not yet been reduced to rules, apparently resting solely on the judgment of the composer. Banchieri's ideal training for the composer would include experience in both styles; he should learn first the strict style, using Zarlino and Artusi as his masters, and then move on to the freer usage. This conception was to permeate most pedagogical theories set forth in the seventeenth century.

Diruta's treatment of diminutions was equivocal. He did not discuss eighths and sixteenths in the section on *contrapunto commune* despite their inclusion in his rules for strict counterpoint, but in the first part of the same treatise[16] he went into detail about their use in making florid arrangements for keyboard. For him, also, this technique was closely related to composing. He maintained that it was impossible to make good intabulations without a knowledge of counterpoint and that to achieve perfection in this *bella scienza* it was necessary also to be a *prattico compositore.* Yet the strict rules of *osservato* counterpoint evidently did not apply to what he called *il diminuire osservato.* Here the rules were precisely the same as those given in the sixteenth-century manuals for improvising diminutions, and the aim was the same—to preserve the basic consonances of the work being ornamented. No rules for dissonance treatment were given, and his models for *il diminuire osservato* (Example 3)[17] show a much freer treatment than that permitted in *osservato* counterpoint. Diruta had already justified this type of dissonance treatment in an earlier publication[18] when discussing the freer dissonances found in the fast passage work in toccatas: the dissonances passed so swiftly that they did not disturb the ear—and the beauty and lightness of the diminutions were more important than the observation of contrapuntal rules.

Some of the dissonances in Diruta's first example (Example 3) are no different from those found in ornament textbooks published before the end of the sixteenth century, but others—especially the *b-flat* on the first of four sixteenths and the skip from *b* to *g* over an *f*-chord, are less characteristic. Similar dissonances, however, are found in sixteenth-century instrumental tablatures. The close correlation apparent between theory and practice in Renaissance choral music was not characteristic of instrumental music. This was particularly true of music for lute and keyboard instruments, where the departure from strict counterpoint included a freer use of dissonance on long notes as well as the writing in of coloratura passages. Knud Jeppesen has pointed out in his study of the organ tablatures of Andrea Antico (1517) and Marco Antonio Cavazzoni (1523)[19] that, while some early sixteenth-century vocal works may occasionally depart from the prescribed rules for dissonance treatment, in the organ tablatures of the period there is even greater freedom

---

[14] *Seconda parte del transilvano*, p. 14 ff.
[15] In: *Cartella musicale* (Venice 1614) p. 165 ff.
[16] *Secunda parte del transilvano* p. 1—21.
[17] Ibid., Examples arranged in modern score.
[18] *Il transilvano, dialogo sopra il vero modo di sonar organi* (Venice 1625; 1st ed. 15ʳ7) p. 62.
[19] *Die italienische Orgelmusik am Anfang des Cinquecento* (Copenhagen 1943).

in the treatment of quarters and also "unlawful" dissonances in longer notes. He does not mention shorter notes, no doubt because theorists of that time gave no rules for their use, and perhaps also because they are clearly ornamental in nature. But in these fast passages we find dissonances treated with greater freedom than was shown in the models for diminutions published in the textbooks on embellishment.

As the sixteenth century moved on, the treatment of longer notes in instrumental music approached more nearly the ideals of theorists, although the advent of the early Baroque came before complete correlation was accomplished. But the treatment of dissonance in fast passages remained relatively free. While diminution manuals before Diruta were aimed at singers, and wind and string players, two Renaissance treatises on improvised counterpoint for keyboard instruments include, in contrast to conventional theory texts, contrapuntal models using fast notes and florid passages as well as diminutions applied to simple melodic intervals.[20] In Conrad Paumann's *Fundamentum organisandi* (1452), both the examples of florid counterpoint over long notes (Example 4a)[21] and those pieces using virtuoso *passaggi* in counterpoint use dissonances freely. Dissonances appear on any part of the beat and are often left by skip. The melodic movement, however, is mainly scalewise, and skips larger than a third are rare. In his *Arte de tañer fantasia* (*Valladolid* 1565), Tomás de Santa Maria lists diminutions (*glosas*) in the manner of ornament manuals, as embellishments of unaccompanied melodic intervals, and his models of forms and styles for improvising use few fast notes. But here and there are found examples using eighth notes which exhibit a freedom in treatment of dissonance not found in his works in slower notes. (Example 4a)[22]

153

*

Although the employment of written-in diminutions and the freer use of dissonance in lute and keyboard music were important in the development of Baroque style, it was in the realm of vocal polyphony, and especially in the madrigal, that the rebellion against strict counterpoint was first consciously manifest. It is here, too, that the battle with the theorists was fought. The primary concern of the theorists was the irregular use of dissonance in the commonly used note values. Diminutions were not part of the controversy, yet their absorption into the composer's vocabulary was also an important element in the transformation of the *ars perfecta* into the several new styles of the Baroque.

---

[20] Two works on *a la mente* counterpoint likewise include examples of long passages of eighths against a *cantus firmus* in whole notes, when regular theory books are not yet discussing them — VICENTE LUSITANO, *Introduttione facilissima et novissima* (Venice 1561) f. Dv° and Dllr°, and the manuscript treatises on improvised counterpoint of Giovanni Maria and Giovanni Bernardino Nanino, f. 25v ff. Facsimiles in: ERNEST T. FERAND, *Improvised Vocal Counterpoint in the Late Renaissance and Early Baroque*, in: *Annales Musicologiques* IV (1956) between p. 144 and 145; quotations from the Nanino treatise pp. 161—163. Dissonance treatment strict in both, with some use of passing dissonance on the 3rd of 4 eighths in the Nanino work.

[21] From *Conrad Paumanns Fundamentum organizandi* ed. HEINRICH BELLERMANN and L. W. ARNOLD, in: JfMW (1867) p. 183.

[22] f. 25v. Rhythmic exercise for playing simultaneous eighths and quarters.

The process began, of course, in improvised performance, where the expression of solo virtuosity made necessary the introduction of coloratura. When a soloist embellished a single line of a polyphonic work, he was creating an antecedent of vocal or instrumental monody. When several soloists performed, each taking a turn in ornamenting his part, they transformed the old contrapuntal style into what the succeeding century was to call luxuriant counterpoint.

The latter practice appears to have reached its climax first, both in improvisation and in its adoption into the written style by composers. Only three of the sixteenth-century authorities on ornamentation—Hermann Finck (1556), C. G. Maffei (1562), and Girolamo dalla Casa (1584)—give specimens of their ideal improvised versions,[23] but these have enough in common to give a general idea of the style. The most obvious change from the effect of the original work is the increased range in note values used, with the fast notes predominating.[23a] The works ornamented by Finck and Maffei, with a half note getting the beat, use many passages in eighths; dalla Casa's, also using the half as the unit, include long passages of sixteenths. In Finck and dalla Casa, once the opening measures are past, ornaments are used so consistently (in one part or another) that a steady fast movement is felt. Maffei uses diminutions more conservatively, increasing the motion only at the ends of sections.

Both the use of dissonance and extension of melodic range are more conservative in these polyphonic ornamentations than in the monodic ones, no doubt for practicality in performance. Except for ornamented cadences (Example 2, bars 23 and 58) and suspension (Example 5, in bracketed section of soprano), the beginning of the half-note beat is always consonant. Dissonance commonly appears on the second half of the beat, as the third of four eighths or the fifth of eight sixteenths. If two eighths follow a quarter, or two sixteenths an eighth, the first of the pair is often dissonant. In one frequently used four-note pattern—the downward skip of a third followed by two upward steps—the third note usually dissonates. Skips do not appear often; when they do, both notes are consonant. Only dalla Casa uses skips larger than a third, and these are rare in his polyphonic arrangements.

The use of embellishments in relation to structure is significant. While Finck rarely adds ornaments in the lowest part, both Maffei and dalla Casa insert fast passages in the bass, dalla Casa ornamenting it as often and as freely as the upper parts. Diruta[24] opposed the ornamentation of imitations. If they were to be ornamented, he insisted that all entrances should have similar embellishments. In the models given by Finck, Maffei, and dalla Casa, the heads of themes in the

---

[23] Those from Finck and Maffei, and one from dalla Casa in: FERAND, *Improvisation in Nine Centuries of Western Music* (Köln 1961; German ed. 1956). Note values reduced. In this paper I refer always to the original notation.

[23a] The addition of faster notes in improvised performance was, no doubt, one of the elements bringing about the change in the concept of rhythmic organization which came about at the turn of the century, although none of the diminution treatises discuss the problem. This change from a rhythmic system based on a fixed *tactus*, to that based on a beat in various tempos is detailed in: HARALD HECKMANN, *Der Takt in der Musiklehre des 17. Jahrhunderts*, in: AfMW X (1953) pp. 116—139.

[24] *Seconda parte del transilvano* p. 10.

beginning of each imitative section are often left unornamented, although diminutions usually appear in the same part of the theme when used, and often are inserted before the whole of the melodic subject is finished. These ornaments are rarely all alike melodically, but are usually rhythmically identical. Dalla Casa's embellished version of de Rore's *Selve, sasse* (Example 5)[25] shows a characteristic treatment of imitation.

Nor is exactness of ornament commonly found in keyboard and lute music in the sixteenth century, either in ornamented transcriptions or in original works. Much of the time the heads of the themes are not decorated, but when they are, there is less consistency shown than is found in the ornamented vocal models, as can be seen from the examples quoted in Example 4b.[26] Not until the seventeenth century do composers treat diminutions as an integral part of their themes, using the same ornament in the same place each time the theme appears. This is no doubt due to the increasing acceptance of these ornaments as a part of musical language—a feeling that must also have been behind Diruta's dictum about consistency in ornamentation.

155

Apparently it was the demand for virtuoso compositions brought into being by the famed three singers of Ferrara — Lucrezia Bendidio, Laura Peperara, and Tarquinia Molza—that increased the use of composed coloratura in the madrigal. Composers of conservative as well as progressive bent who had contact with the court produced works for this trio, introducing sections of florid writing into their works. In Giaches de Wert's eighth book of five-part madrigals (Venice 1586) are found works containing virtuoso passages for three sopranos; in some sections the diminutions penetrate the entire texture. Likewise Benedetto Pallavicino's fourth book of madrigals à 5 (Venice 1588) contains long sections of coloratura, although here the diminutions are concentrated in the bass and soprano parts. In both collections the virtuoso madrigals are written in the C notation, the quarter note getting the beat, and the eighth often carrying a syllable; the coloratura passages are in eighths, with a few sixteenths (generally in pairs), so that this change was not radical rhythmically. Short passages in eighths had been used in this notation, but those found in Wert and Pallavicino were longer and more pervasive, and clearly virtuosic in character. Melodically, they were conservative, moving smoothly in scales with a few small skips, and with steady rhythmic motion. Contrapuntally, too, they were conservative. Except for a few dissonant cadential ornaments they followed the rigorous rules of strict counterpoint.

In addition to this firm contrapuntal control, these early specimens of luxuriant counterpoint show certain distinct contrasts with their "improvised" counterparts. First, the florid passages are not used indiscriminately, but in harmony with the text. They appear only on words such as *cantare*, *fuoco*, *ardere*, *soave*, where they

---

[25] *Il vero modo*, II, p. 46.
[26] From: Luys de Narvaez, *Fantasia VI*, in: *Delphin de musica* (Valladolid 1536) ed. Emilio Pujol, *Monumentos de la Musica Española* VII (Barcelona 1949) p. 12; and Valentin G. Bakfarc, *Fantasias*, in: *Premier livre de tabelature de luth* (Paris 1564) ed. Adolf Koczirz in: DTÖ Jahrg. XVIII Bd. II (1911). A, p. 70; B, p. 72.

not only avoid confusing the expression of the text,[27] but have the positive advantage of pointing it up more effectively according to conventional standards. This concentration of fast passages on certain sections of text also resulted in more contrast in rhythmic movement, an important element in the style of the late sixteenth century.

A second and important difference is the simultaneous use of diminutions in several parts, something impossible of attainment in ensemble improvisation on a precomposed work. As far as embellishment of imitations is concerned, the ornaments tend to be exact in form and placement, but not always so. A new usage was evolving—the unification of a polyphonic section by free imitation within the embellishing diminutions. A section from a work in Wert's eighth book of five-part madrigals, *Rallegrati mio cor*, shows this technique in an elementary form. (Example 6) The entrances of the different parts on *"in gioia"* are not in exact imitation, though all involve the use of ornament. The diminutions differ in length and overall shape, but two short four-note motives predominate and, while not particularly distinctive in character, give unity to the section.

156   Few of the many compositions and arrangements made for the famous trio survive, having been kept from circulation by Duke Alfonso, but the madrigals for one, two, and three sopranos composed for the court by Luzzasco Luzzaschi, and published a few years after the death of the Duke, illustrate the more progressive type of music performed there. Although text is important, and long sections of declamation are included, ornamentation is not rigorously limited to words where it might amplify the text. In style the madrigals are close to the embellished versions of madrigals found in diminution textbooks. This is immediately apparent when the keyboard accompaniments are compared with the vocal parts, as, for the most part, they double the voices. Where the voices are ornamented, the keyboard plays a simple version. While at times more freedom is expressed—as is appropriate in free writing—most of the time these simple keyboard parts hold the same relation to their florid counterparts that the plain lines of the composed madrigals held to their embellished versions.

It is in the three-part madrigals that the relation of the simpler contrapuntal structure to its "luxuriant" modification is most obvious. (Example 7)[28] Although the ornaments are applied according to *il diminuire osservato*, so that the consonances on the beginnings of the beat in the keyboard part are kept (except for cadential trills), a few dissonant clashes between voices occur within the beat as the result of simultaneous ornamentation. Clashes sometimes occur within the beat between voice parts and accompaniment when the ornaments clash with the long notes they are ornamenting, although unless the accompaniment was played on an organ, the fading of the keyboard tone would ameliorate this. Such clashes must

---

[27] Nicola Vicentino complains that the improvised diminutions make sad music sound happy by replacing long notes with fast passages. See: *L'Antica musica ridotta alla moderna prattica* (Rome 1555) Cap. XXXXII.

[28] "O Dolcezze amarissime d'Amore" from: L. Luzzaschi, *Madrigali per cantare, et sonare* (Rome 1601) p. 20—25.

have been common when soloists improvised ornaments upon a madrigal and the original work was played by lute or keyboard as accompaniment.

Toward the end of the century similar dissonances appear in instrumental ensemble music in the virtuoso style. A single measure from Giovanni Gabrieli's *Canzon duodecima à 10* (with two organs concertante),[29] is enough to show a like use of diminutions in a different musical situation. (Example 8) The basic rule for diminutions is followed—consonance on the beginning of each beat—and the dissonant clashes result from the use of simultaneous *passaggi*. But here there is no pre-existent contrapuntal skeleton. The framework is harmonic, and, while the choice is still limited, any member of the chord may be chosen as the beginning and end of a "diminution." This way of composing was not new. It had been a common procedure in lute and keyboard variations using a harmonic progression as the theme since the second quarter of the century,[30] and its introduction into ensemble music shows its growing importance in the development of Baroque style.

Although their most obvious intrusions into the serious polyphonic style were in the interests of virtuoso singers and instrumentalists, during the last two decades of the sixteenth century the diminutions were gradually becoming a part of the musical language of the madrigal composers. Expression of text was their primary motivation, and short passages of fast notes were used to point up the text by visual reference—as on the word *arco* in Marenzio's *Chi vuol veder Amor* (Example 9a)[31]—or to express mood by quickened motion—as in a short section from Gesualdo's *A voi mentre mio core.* (Example 9b)[32] These also provide distinctive motives for expansion of the contrapuntal texture.

157

The use of faster notes in the madrigal coincided with its rhythmic transformation and the loss of the distinction between the C- and ¢-signatures. By the mid-nineties the C signature was the one commonly used, but without its old significance. Using it, composers wrote sections in which the eighth note was the unit carrying the syllable and others in which the half was felt as the basic unit; rhythmic contrasts were important and clearly delineated by notes. The range of note values used, from very long to very short, was expanding. As has been stated, the *coloraturae* in the madrigals of Wert and Pallavicino were predominately in eighth notes. Sixteenth notes, which were used in the old *note nere* as were eighths in the ¢-notation, were at first used rarely in the "new" madrigals of the nineties, and then usually in pairs. This is characteristic of Marenzio. Although his use of paired sixteenths (especially in melismas) increases from the publication, in 1594, of his sixth book of five-part madrigals, they seldom appear in groups of more than two, and the use

---

[29] From: *Sacrae symphoniae* (Venice 1597) ed. GIACOMO BENVENUTI, *Istitutioni e Monumenti dell'Arte Musicale Italiana* II (Milan 1932) p. 118. Canzone not numbered in original print.

[30] I. HORSLEY, *The Sixteenth-Century Variation and Baroque Counterpoint*, in: MD XIV (1960) p. 159—165.

[31] Ninth madrigal from his fifth book of five-part madrigals (Venice 1585) in: A. EINSTEIN, ed. *Luca Marenzio, sämtliche Werke* II (Leipzig 1931).

[32] Fifteenth madrigal from his fourth book of madrigals (Ferrara 1596) in: WILHELM WEISMANN, ed. *Gesualdo di Venosa, sämtliche Madrigale für fünf Stimmen nach dem Partiturdruck von 1613* III (Hamburg 1958).

of a run of four sixteenths (as that filling in a fifth in *Clori mai, Clori dolce*, the twelfth madrigal in book six) is not common. In this instance it is a special effect, a rapid fall after an emphasized climax. The sixteenths do not attain thematic identity.

Gesualdo's love of rhythmic contrast leads him to use groups of four sixteenths as part of the thematic structure beginning with the third book of madrigals (Ferrara 1595), although it is not until his fifth book (Gesualdo 1611) that extended passages in sixteenths are found. While Marenzio is conservative, following the *osservato* rules for eighths and sixteenths in groups of four or more, Gesualdo is concerned primarily with the melodic and rhythmic effect his passages produce. In a single section the same pattern may appear with different consonance-dissonance arrangements, and he often uses dissonance on the beginning of the beat. (Example 9b) This is in harmony with his general style. From the first he uses dissonance on the beat—dissonance on the first of two descending eighths, each carrying a syllable, is common, as are accented passing tones in quarter notes. But, while he is radical in the rhythmic placement of dissonance, he is usually careful to approach and leave it by step, especially when using it on the strong part of the beat.

Monteverdi uses little coloratura in his first two books of madrigals (Venice 1587 and 1590), and that limited to short *passaggi* on appropriate words. These are conservative rhythmically, using only eighths and paired sixteenths. They are also conservative polyphonically—as in Marenzio's madrigals, the first of paired eighths or sixteenths may dissonate, but longer groups of eighths follow the rules of strict counterpoint. His third book (1592) uses more ornamentation and includes sections of virtuoso style in several of the madrigals. The dissonance treatment here is usually conservative, but not consistently so, and this is in keeping with a slightly freer use of dissonance in non-melismatic sections. This trend is carried further in his fourth book (1603); long virtuoso sections are included, and dissonances in *passaggi* appear at times on the beginning of the beat. Monteverdi's tendency to incorporate improvised ornaments in his melodic line is further seen here in the use of short ornaments drawn from new monodic style. [33] The madrigals in his fifth book put less stress on virtuosity for its own sake. A few isolated groups of four sixteenths had been used in book four, but here, for the first time, sixteenths become part of a theme and are thus used consistently enough to dominate a section. The effectiveness of such quickened motion can be seen in the famous *Cruda Amarilli* from this collection. (Example 9c) The freer use of dissonance found in book four continues here. But in view of the swiftness of its passing, the dissonance on strong beats in *passaggi* cannot have had the special emotive purpose that freer dissonance had when used in longer note values. The free use of dissonance in fast passages

---

[33] Such as attacking a melodically important note by starting a third below the note (on the beat) and sliding up to it. See *Svogava con le stelle*, m. 2; *Luci serene e chiare*, m. 7. The rhythmic form used here by Monteverdi approximates the form approved by G. B. Bovicelli in *Passaggi, regole di musica* (Venice 1594), a form which Caccini condemned in the preface to *Le nuove musiche* (Florence 1601). Bovicelli held the first note, gliding quickly over the second to the main note; Caccini preferred both notes of the slide to be touched lightly.

must be considered more the result of the loosening of the old conventions, and the new stress on the shape of the melodic line as more important than its contrapuntal relation to other parts.

The direct absorption of diminutions into polyphonic composition of itself tended only to expand the possibilities of the madrigal style rather than to destroy it. But the use of dissonance on the strong beat in *passaggi* coupled with a freer use of dissonance on longer notes marked the end of the old conception of the diminution technique. It was no longer a question of inserting fast passages into a stable and consonant contrapuntal structure. The free use of dissonance demanded by expression soon found musical stability in a system ordered by harmonic control, and the luxuriant counterpoint of the Baroque was permeated by chord structures. Those madrigals in book five to which Monteverdi has added the *basso continuo* stand in direct contrast to the first seven, and show the liberating effect which a harmonic framework has upon his melodic and contrapuntal style. In the highly virtuoso lines of these concertato madrigals sixteenths are used freely, even carrying syllables, and dissonances in *passaggi* appear on any part of the beat and may be approached or left by skip. The highly florid style of these madrigals is in direct contrast to his earlier works and is clearly not derived from them. It comes in part from the concertato of the Venetian school, and more particularly from the monody and the types of ornamentation associated with it.

159

Those elaborately ornamented versions of polyphonic works intended for solo performance which appeared in sixteenth-century diminution manuals and which anticipated the vocal and instrumental monody of the seventeenth century were even more destructive of the *ars perfecta* than the embellished polyphonic versions. The close relation of these arrangements to personal virtuosity is made apparent in the wide variety of styles used, and the change of style from one manual to the next. As the century moved to its close there was a constant increase of rhythmic and melodic complexity and a steady growth in the technical demands made upon the performer. In those arrangement intended for singers,[34] thirty-second notes appeared first in the ornaments given by Bovicelli (1594) and were even there used sparingly; in those intended for string and wind players,[35] sextuplets of sixteenths as well as thirty-second notes appeared as early as dalla Casa (1584) and these faster notes remained characteristic of this form. Although there is a great difference between the vocal and instrumental arrangements — the instrumental versions having a wider range, more skips, and moving at a consistently faster speed — they have elements in common. Most important from the point of view of style is the

---

[34] Found in: DALLA CASA, *Il vero modo*; RICHARDO ROGNIONO, *Passaggi per potersi essercitare nel diminuire* (Venice 1592); LUDOVICO ZACCONI, *Prattica di musica* (I) (Venice 1594) Cap. LXVI; and BOVICELLI, *Passaggi, regole*. In addition to the manuals, solo arrangements may be found in: GIOVANNI BASSANO, *Motetti, madrigali et canzone francese ... diminuiti* (Venice 1591) and *Intermedii et concerti fatti per la commedia rappresentata in Firenze nelle nozze de Serenissima Don Fernando Medici ...* (Venice 1591).

[35] Found in: DIEGO ORTIZ, *Trattado de glosas* (Rome 1553) repr. ed. M. SCHNEIDER (Kassel 1936); DALLA CASA, *Il vero modo*; R. ROGNIONO, *Passaggi per potersi*; GIOVANNI BASSANO, *Ricercate, passaggi et cadentie* (Venice 1585); G. B. SPADI, *Libro de passaggi* (Venice 1609).

concentration on one part and the reduction of the others to the role of accompaniment.[36] The freedom this reduction of the polyphonic element allows in the use of dissonance is seen when these versions are compared with those ornamented in all parts and meant for ensemble performance. The first of four eighths or of eight sixteenths is sometimes dissonant, and very often the third of four eighths or the fifth of eight sixteenths—in fact, any of the notes may be dissonant and these dissonances are often approached or left by skip. But the frequency of such dissonance is not great, as can be seen in the excerpts from five different versions of the soprano part of de Rore's *Anchor che col partire*. (Example 10a)[37] Compared with that found in contemporary keyboard music (Example 10b),[38] it is rather conservative. The most startling effect of the madrigal arrangements is the complete transformation of the melodic line. The original melody can be picked out of the embellished version with little difficulty, but there is little relation between the overall effect of the simple and ornamented lines—even the setting of the text has been rearranged in the versions by Rogniono and Bovicelli. The other parts of the madrigal are entirely subordinate and represent an anticipation of the role of the continuo in monody proper.

160

The continuo, by giving harmonic definition to the melody, intensified the possibilities of expressive dissonances, and certain of the *effetti*—short ornaments which emphasized significant melodic and textual points—were dissonant in character, delaying the arrival of the chord tone in the melody. Dissonance could also be used without inconvenience in any part of a diminution, so long as the line as a whole was dominated by chord tones and the non-chord tones were at least approached or left by step. But the diminutions were used much less freely in monody. Their role was defined by Caccini in *Le nuove musiche*. The *effetti* carried the burden of expression. Diminutions were concentrated at the cadences and in varied repetitions, and where they could ornament the line and give vent to virtuosity without interfering with the projection of the text.

The role of diminutions remains ambiguous throughout the Baroque. The *opere passeggiate* published in the late sixteenth and early seventeenth centuries[39] which so often give the effect of mechanically written-out passages aiming at a stylish display of technique gradually disappear from the scene as the diminutions become an essential part of the thematic structure of arias, sonatas, choral works,—the

[36] The manuals give only the parts ornamented. If we are to follow Luzzaschi (1601) who gives simple and ornamented parts to be played together, the whole madrigal would be played along with the embellished version. Ortiz (1553), however, states that when the soprano is ornamented it is more graceful if the cembalo player omits the soprano part when he accompanies the soloist. (*Trattado*, p. 72).
[37] Version of the original from *The Madrigals of Cipriano de Rore for 3 and 4 Voices* ed. GERTRUDE P. SMITH, *Smith College Archives* VI (Northampton, Mass. 1943) p. 45—47. Ornamented works from: DALLA CASA, *Il vero modo* II p. 35; R. ROGNIONO, *Passaggi per potersi* p. 60, 61; BOVICELLI, *Passaggi, regole* p. 42—49; and SPADI, *Libro de passaggi* p. 28—30.
[38] ANDREA GABRIELI, *Fantasia Allegra per organo* from *Il Terzo libro de ricercare* (Venice 1596) as reproduced in: TORCHI, ed. *L'Arte Musicale in Italia* III p. 67.
[39] Listed in: MAX KUHN, *Die Verzierungs-Kunst in der Gesangs-Musik des 16.—17. Jahrhunderts* (Leipzig 1902).

whole of Baroque musical production. The diminutions became an integral part of the composer's vocabulary; their use is one of the outstanding characteristics of Baroque melody. Yet a comparison of the monodies from Caccini's *Le nuove musiche* with the manuscript copy of their unornamented versions[40] shows that the published form was primarily a model for the effective performance of the songs, showing the correct way to add *effetti* and diminutions. Innumerable treatises on ornamentation, instrumental and vocal tutors, embellished transcriptions, and examples of written-out ornamentation published during the Baroque show that soloists were expected to add diminutions in performance, especially in slow movements, at cadences, and in sectional repeats.

Their treatment in pedagogical texts reflects this ambiguity. There is the usual time lag between the appearance of new composition procedures and their rationalization by theorists. To our ears the harmonic basis of the music is obvious, melodic notes dividing themselves into chord tones and non-chord tones, and it seems strange that, with the almost universal adoption of the continuo, the harmonic basis should not be emphasized by theorists. Yet during the seventeenth century "composition" continued to be equated with counterpoint, whether strict or free, and treatises on the *basso continuo* related mainly to performance and similar pragmatic considerations.

161

Another development that may have slowed down the relating of diminutions to harmonic structure was the growing tendency to crystallize ornaments into fixed patterns and thus to associate them with melodic units. In the last two decades of the sixteenth century this process begins in the diminution manuals where certain diminutions associated with cadence patterns assume fixed forms.[41] At the same time ornaments of a new type which anticipated the *effetti* put in their appearance.[42] These tendencies continue in the works of Caccini, Diruta, Banchieri,[43] and Francesco Rogniono.[44] The Italian style was adopted enthusiastically by the Germans and the process continued there. In 1619 Michael Praetorius described, with examples, the Italian manner of ornamentation,[45] and Johann Andreas Herbst, depending heavily on Praetorius organized it into a pedagogical method in *Musica Practica ... eine kurtze Anleitung zum singen ... auff die italienisch Manier* (Nürnberg 1642). A second edition of this book, *Musica moderna prattica* (Frankfurt 1653) included a greatly expanded section of examples, including material from Italian sources — Banchieri, and Richardo and Francesco Rogniono. A third printing followed in 1658, and this text became the basis of another manual on singing and ornamentation, George Falck's *Idea boni cantoris* (Nürnberg 1688).

---

[40] Ms. 1018 in Library of St. Michael's College, Tenbury, England. See: NANCY L. MAZE, *The Printed Manuscript Sources of the Solo Songs of Giulio Caccini* (M. A. Thesis, Univ. of Illinois 1956). This does not include complete transcriptions from the Ms.

[41] In: DALLA CASA, *Il vero modo*; BASSANO, *Ricercate, passaggi*; and CONFORTO, *Breve et facile*.

[42] In: R. ROGNIONO, *Passaggi per potersi*; BOVICELLI, *Passaggi, regole*.

[43] *Brevi documenti musicale* (Venice 1609).

[44] *Selva de varii passaggi* (Venice 1620). This also includes solo arrangements for voice and for instruments in the Baroque style of works by older composers such as de Rore and Palestrina.

[45] In: *Syntagma musicum* (Wolfenbüttel 1619) III p. 229 ff.

Although certain of the Italian *effetti*, such as *accenti* and *tremoli*, could be classified as *agrément* types—being of small range and fixed shape, and tending to emphasize one note—most Italian and German authors classified them as diminutions along with the freer *passaggi*. The forms of particular ornaments may vary with different authors, but in the second half of the century the Italian types—*tremolo*, *groppo*, *tirata*, etc.—are fixed by German writers and attempts are being made to pick out and classify other forms found in the freer *passaggi*. The list given by Wolfgang Caspar Printz in his *Compendium musicae*[46] is the most useful for this study since it contains the basic forms and types included in later theoretical works.

A quick glance at these (Example 11)[47] is enough to attest their frequent appearance in Baroque compositions, although they are given in the *Compendium* as a list of ornaments to be added in performance. The *groppo* (*Waltze, Kugel*), *tremolo*, *tirata mezza*, and *circulo mezzo* are fixed shapes appearing in only two forms, ascending and descending. A combination of both forms of the *circulo mezzo* makes a complete *circulo*. Other figures have several possible forms: the *accentus* (sic) uses in some form the note above or below a given note; the *tirata* is a direct scale. While the above figures come from Italian sources there are several new types first defined by Printz. These have distinct characteristics but can appear in many forms—*salto semplice* is the singing of one syllable in a skip; *salti composti* means any group of four fast notes separated by skips; *messanza* (*misticanza*) uses four fast notes of which two are on the same pitch and others may shake (i. e. use auxiliary) or go by step or skip; *figura corta* simply means a group of three fast notes; and *figura suspirans* is a *figura corta* with a rest on the beginning of the beat.

Printz defines these diminution patterns as fixed figures,[48] and for him they are allied also to the art of composition. In his *Phrynis mitelenaeus oder satyrischer Componist*[49] he devotes the first part to counterpoint, the art of composing. The strict rules for counterpoint are given for the treatment of notes smaller than a quarter, but soon tempered by an intelligent discussion of the freer dissonance treatment practiced by composers, including a summary of their justifications of this freedom. The second part includes a section on variation and invention for the aid of the composer,[50] and here Printz lists in great detail the types of diminution figures found in the *Compendium*, with examples of many variants. He suggests varying them further by using dots or different rhythmic proportions, points out those particularly appropriate for voice or instruments, and shows how the different types of figures may be combined. Over a descending major tetrachord he writes a hundred variations made up of different combinations and variants of these figures. For their use in composition he outlines the process that has always been associated with

---

[46] Published: Leipzig and Dresden 1668, 1689 and 1714.
[47] From 1714 edition, *Cap. V*.
[48] Ibid., „*Eine Figur ist in der Musik ein gewisser Modulus, der entstehet aus einer oder auch etlicher Noten Diminution und Zertheilung . . .*“.
[49] Published: Leipzig and Dresden 1676—1677 (in 2 parts), and 1696; references here to 1696 edition.
[50] Ibid., *Ander Theil*, p. 45—90.

diminutions. The composer must first make a simple version, from which he will remove all intervals unsuitable because of range, etc., and then he will insert suitable figures.

In using the terms *variatio* and *inventio* Printz had reference to terms then associated with rhetorical compositions. Although distinctly separated from the musical figures by which German theorists of the Baroque attempted a musico-structural parallel to figures of speech,[51] these diminution figures were often associated with the musical-rhetorical figures. This may be because, while they did not have the structural significance of the musical-rhetorical figures, they were fixed patterns and, like the rhetorical figures, represent an addition to, or alteration of, a simpler musical construction.

An earlier instance of this is found in the study notes of Christoph Bernhard (c. 1660)[52] which include without differentiation among the figures used in the "luxuriant style" both those that are clearly rhetorical in origin (such as *ellipsis*) and those derived from improvised vocal ornaments *(superjectio, multiplicatio)* as well as simple diminutions *(variatio)*. In his examples he shows all of these as variants of a simple contrapuntal skeleton. The composition process implied here not only follows that long used in making diminutions but shows, as well, a parallel relationship between a musical phrase conceived in strict counterpoint and a stylistically freer version.[53] It is interesting to note that Bernhard records an historical explanation of the development of this technique.[54] After a summary of the conservative rules for the treatment of dissonance, some of the figures are listed again,[55] this time prefaced by a short history of their introduction into the old style. First, the composers of the preceding century had heard them only in performance; then, realizing that what can be sung can be written as well, they began to include them in their works, and what was formerly inadmissable became accepted by the ear.

Certain observances in Johann Samber's *Continuatio ad manuductionem organicum* (Salzburg 1707) are similar to Bernhard's notes and several of the same figures are listed. Johann Walther gives the same historical summary and many of the same figures found in Bernhard's notes in his *Praecepta der musicalischen Composition*,[56] but his *Musicalisches Lexicon* (Leipzig 1732) includes also all the figures listed by Printz. Most later writers follow the clear division into figures of the rhetorical type and fixed diminution figures inherent in Printz's instructions, and the metaphorical relation between musical and rhetorical composition still dominates their thinking.

163

---

[51] HANS-HEINRICH UNGER, *Die Beziehungen zwischen Musik und Rhetorik im 16.—18. Jahrhundert.* (Würzburg 1941). See also ARNOLD SCHMITZ, article *Figuren, musikalisch-rhetorische*, in: MGG 4, 176 ff.
[52] J. M. MÜLLER-BLATTAU, ed. *Die Kompositions-Lehre Heinrich Schützens* (Leipzig 1926).
[53] HELLMUT FEDERHOFER, *Der strenge und freie Satz und sein Verhältnis zur Kompositionslehre von H. Schütz . . .* in: *Beiträge zur musikalischen Gestaltanalyse* (Graz—Innsbruck—Wien 1950) p. 61 ff.
[54] Ibid., p. 147.
[55] Ibid., p. 148—153. In this section they are listed under *"superficial figures"*.
[56] Ms. in Weimar Landesbibl. ed. PETER BENARY, *Jenaer Beiträge zur Musikforschung* Bd. 2 (Leipzig 1955).

In one interesting parallel between music and rhetoric, Mauritz Vogt describes the old technique of adding diminutions to a simple preexistent skeleton. In *Conclave thesauri magnae artis musicae* (Prague 1719)[57] he suggests that the composer start with a *phantasia* (simple musical framework in long notes)—which, like a text for a speech, is susceptible to artifical development—and then proceded to elaborate the *phantasia* by using the fixed melodic figures. This process he applies both to single lines and contrapuntal bases, and he shows how a simple note-against-note canon can be developed into a florid one. (Example 12) He admits, however, that some types of music, such as recitatives, cannot be developed in this way, and includes a sample of another type of music not derived from a *phantasia*. (Example 12) Later, in his *Tractatus musicum compositorio practicus* (Augsburg 1745),[58] Meinrad Spiess uses the rhetorical terms *inventio, dispositio, elaboratio,* and *decoratio,* and equates the musical-rhetorical figures, fixed diminution figures, and the *Manieren,* with *decoratio,* adding that the *Manieren* and the fixed diminution figures may be either improvised or written into the music.

164

But by this time the theories of Rameau had begun to make themselves felt. His conviction that harmony was the most important element in musical conception caused him to place little stress on the treatment of non-harmonic tones, which he lumped together as *notes de goût*[59]—notes necessary to make the melody pleasing, but not an essential part of its basic structure. The German theorists, with their emphasis on counterpoint, kept their concern for rationalization of dissonance use when adopting Rameau's theory, and recast the contrapuntal dissonances as various types of non-harmonic tones. At the same time the ideal of melodic creation was being transformed. Melody was conceived as made up from single tones,[60] and was expected to follow the grammatical divisions of speech (word, phrase, sentence) and to achieve structural balance and logical coherence. This new concept of melody as based on periodic form[61] brought with it a feeling for the significance of even the smallest melodic unit having within itself the potential of meaningful developments and relationships. The diminution process was a more mechanical method of melodic construction.

The principle of diminution lingered on as a part of the system of improvised ornaments, but the fixed patterns of Baroque diminutions dropped out of vogue.[62] In composition they were shifted into subordinate positions, appearing mainly in sections of figuration such as those found in transition passages. They are still listed in some theory books. F. W. Marpurg lists them in his *Anleitung zur Musik,* relating them to harmonic structures. Likewise, J. A. Scheibe, in *Über die musikalische Com-*

---

[57] p. 140 ff.
[58] p. 135.
[59] J.-P. RAMEAU, *Traité d'Harmonie* (Paris 1722) p. 311.
[60] JOHANN MATTHESON, *Kern melodischer Wissenschaft* (Hamburg 1737) p. 31; and J. N. FORKEL, *Über die Theorie der Musik* (Göttingen 1777) p. 13 ff.
[61] LEONARD G. RATNER, *Eighteenth-Century Theories of Musical Period Structure,* in: MQ XLII (1956) p. 439—454.
[62] MATTHESON scorned them as old fashioned in *Kern melodischer Wissenschaft* p. 143.

position (Leipzig 1773) and E. W. Wolf in *Musikalischer Unterricht* (Dresden 1788), analyze them minutely, and show them to be made up of harmonic and non-harmonic tones of various sorts. Resolved to these component parts, and having fallen from favor as figures, they eventually disappear from pedagogical works. But the ideate basis of the diminutions—the elaboration of line by insertion of embellishments— being inherent in melody itself, remained as one of the ways of creating melody, especially in the variation of a simple melodic idea. The division of melody notes into chord members and non-harmonic tones merely provided a looser framework within which freer ornamentation could be invented.

165

Examples see pp 141-153

Ex. 1 Ganassi: Model and selected Diminutions for descending fourth

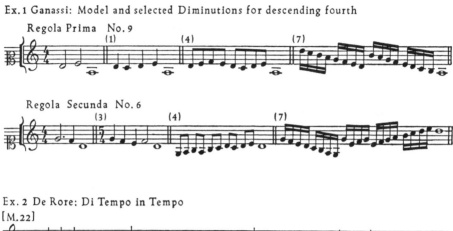

Ex. 2 De Rore: Di Tempo in Tempo

166

Ex. 3 Sogetto

Minuta sopra la parte del soprano

Alio modo

167

[sic]

Ex. 4a Paumann: Ascensus per tercias

etc.

Santa Maria

168

Ex. 4b
Narvaez: Fantasia VI sobre fa, ut, mi, re

Bakfark: Fantasias
A.

B.

etc.

Ex. 5 Dalla Casa: Diminutions on de Rore's Selve, Sassi, Compagne

169

Ex. 6 Wert: Rallegrati mio cor

170

Ex. 7 Luzzaschi: O Dolcezze amarissime D'Amore

171

Ex. 8 Giovanni Gabrieli: Canzon Duodecimi Toni á 10

172

Ex. 9 a. Marenzio: Chi vuol veder Amor

b. Gesualdo: A voi, mentre il mio core

173

c. Monteverdi: Cruda Amarilli

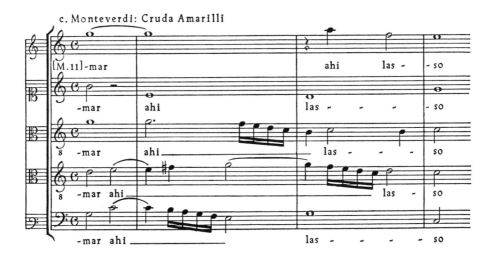

Ex. 10 a. Diminutions on the soprano of De Rore's *Anchor che col Partire*

174

175

b. A. Gabrieli: Fantasia allegra per organo

[M.24]

[M.32]

etc.

Ex. 11 Printz: Accentus

176

Ex. 12 Vogt: Phantasia Simplex

177

etc.

ON FRESCOBALDI'S CHROMATICISM
AND ITS BACKGROUND

By ROLAND JACKSON

AUGUST AMBROS was among the first to draw attention to Frescobaldi's unusual chromaticism, remarking that "he occasionally burned his fingers, but often succeeded in creating the most powerful of effects." [1] Here one observes already that blend of fascination and puzzlement that has typified descriptions ever since. Frescobaldi's technique has been characterized as "bold," "sensitive," or "revolutionary," but little attempt has been made to analyze it or to relate it to earlier or contemporary practice. An attitude underlies many of the writings that it might better be looked upon as an expression of personal fantasy than as an outgrowth of what earlier composers had done. André Pirro, for instance, wrote concerning Frescobaldi's chromatic compositions: "How is one to recognize in these vague experiments, which so captivate us, the outcome of the problem so neatly posed by Vicentino? Frescobaldi prefers the dream to calculation and the strong sensation to the ingenious solution. He turns his back on savants to embrace practitioners endowed with good sense." [2]

Certainly a wide gulf separates Frescobaldi's sensitively colored chromatic lines from the rather stiff models set forth in Vicentino's treatise. Yet there may have been more calculation in Frescobaldi's art than Pirro suspected, and more connection with earlier composers. As Paul Henry Lang has observed, "Frescobaldi's style absorbed the revolutionary chromaticism of the early baroque and he used this modern idiom with more boldness than perhaps anyone else." [3] But what was the nature of early Baroque chromaticism? And what did Frescobaldi "absorb" from it? These questions will form the basis of the present essay.

[1] *Geschichte der Musik,* IV (Leipzig, 1881), 441.

[2] *Les Clavecinistes* (Paris, 1925), p. 48.

[3] *Music in Western Civilization* (New York, 1941), p. 363.

I

To begin, we might inquire which composers were the most influential on Frescobaldi. Music historians have suggested, from among the madrigalists, Vicentino, Luzzaschi, Marenzio, and Gesualdo and, from among keyboard musicians, Macque, Mayone, Ercole Pasquini, and Trabaci. Willi Apel in an early study on the Neapolitan keyboard school [4] built up a case for Mayone and Trabaci, in whose toccatas "the harmonies step beyond the small center of balance and safety, begin to waver and to move suddenly in distant and surprising directions. A glance at any one of Frescobaldi's Toccatas is sufficient to show the close relationship between them and those of the Neapolitan composers." [5] Van den Borren, on the other hand, declared that "the first rank among predecessors of Frescobaldi clearly belongs to Macque, judging by the publication of volume IV of the [Belgian] Monumenta." [6]

In regard to chromaticism, however, Trabaci seems to have made the strongest impression on Frescobaldi. Ex. 1 can serve as a starting point. Here are presented three excerpts by Macque, Trabaci, and Frescobaldi that have a remarkably similar quality. In each a mood was cultivated directly antithetical to that of most keyboard music written in the preceding generation (ca. 1560-1590). In place of decisiveness and assurance we encounter a deliberate vagueness and ambiguity: the harmonies are indefinite and suggestive, the chromatic lines sinuous and marked by unexpected turns, and the sudden and unpredictable chromatic lowering of certain tones contributes to an indecisive wavering in the melodic lines.

In Macque's Capriccio,[7] measure 5, the note E is pointedly lowered to E-flat (then B to B-flat, and F-sharp to F), a procedure that seems the more surprising because of its being combined with a conventional trill (on the third quarter) which implies a cadence to F (on the third half). The subsequent avoidance of the resolution, the resulting feeling of tonal aimlessness, the harmonic succession from a major to a minor triad on the same tonal degree are aspects of Macque's chromaticism that boldly intimated a new direction to be taken by his immediate followers.

Chief among these followers, of course, was the Neapolitan court organist and choirmaster Trabaci, whose two published keyboard vol-

---

[4] "Neapolitan Links between Cabezon and Frescobaldi," *The Musical Quarterly*, XXIV (1938), 419.

[5] *Ibid.,* p. 436.

[6] Charles van den Borren, *Geschiedenis van de Muziek in de Nederlanden* (Amsterdam, 1949), p. 406.

[7] *Monumenta Musicae Belgicae,* IV, ed. Joseph Watelet (1938), 33.

Ex. 1a   Macque: *Capriccio sopra re fa mi sol*

Ex. 1b   Trabaci: *Consonanze Stravaganti* (Book of 1603)

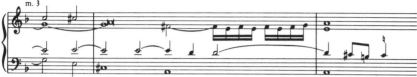

Ex. 1c   Frescobaldi: *Toccata Quarta* (Book of 1627)

181

umes of 1603 and 1615 formed the indispensible link between Macque and Frescobaldi. In the example cited here (Ex. 1b), which is taken from Trabaci's *Consonanze Stravaganti* of 1603,[8] one observes a strong tie to Macque in the half step lowering of the leading tone on C-sharp. At the same time Trabaci points to Frescobaldi by placing the chromatic change within a more solidly defined tonal context. The slow succession of chords (V_5^6-I_4^6-V-v), markedly underscoring the tonality of D major, causes the abrupt change to C-natural in measure 5 to stand out the more forcefully.

Frescobaldi's opening [9] (Ex. 1c) seems to some extent indebted to Macque's Capriccio, particularly in its use of a stereotyped trill on the leading tone C-sharp, the resolution of which is unexpectedly negated by a chromatic lowering. In most other respects, however, it seems to have drawn its substance from Trabaci. Notice especially the descending line E-D-C♯-C, with the brief suspension on D; the background of complex chords: four-note combinations, inversions, sustained dissonances (far

[8] Luigi Torchi, *L'Arte Musicale in Italia*, III, 372. For a transcription of all of Trabaci's keyboard music see Roland Jackson, "The Keyboard Music of Giovanni Maria Trabaci" (University Microfilms, Ann Arbor: 1965, no. 64-13, 023), Vol. II.

[9] Girolamo Frescobaldi, *Orgel- und Klavierwerke*, IV, ed. Pierre Pidoux (Kassel, 1948), 16.

more advanced than Macque's purely triadic basis); the almost identical succession of the harmony (D: V^6_5·I-v); and the well-established tonality, which makes the chromatic alteration more prominent than Macque's. These elements he seems to have gained through direct contact with the keyboard music of Trabaci.

How and to what extent the style of Frescobaldi felt the impact of the late Italian madrigal deserve a more detailed treatment than can be accorded it here. I should like merely to single out one rather peculiar chromatic pattern that appears at least as far back as Marenzio's book of 1587 and that Frescobaldi later enlisted as the basis of certain tonally restless passages in his toccatas. This was a distortion of the normal syncope cadence (7-1 — 7|1), ubiquitous in late-sixteenth-century music. In Marenzio's *Se la mia vita* [10] this cadence (Ex. 2a) is implied by the 7-1 (G-sharp to A) in the upper line coupled with a *quarta consonans* on beat two and suspension on beat three, but is then suddenly thwarted by the falling back of the melody to G (perhaps as a play on the word "pauroso"). The pattern appears also in certain experimental keyboard pieces from around the turn of the century (e. g., in a *Durezze e Ligature* by Macque [11] and one by Ercole Pasquini.[12] Frescobaldi's later use of it in the opening of his *Toccata Chromaticha per l'Elevatione* [13] is more extensive than in these earlier examples in that there the pattern is stated three times in immediate succession, each time with the implication of a different tonality (D, G, and C). The strange chromatic waverings, C♯-D-C, F♯-G-F, B-C-B-B♭, and the tonal ambiguity attending them probably seemed to Frescobaldi an appropriate means for suggesting through music the mystery of the Elevation. The source of Frescobaldi's idea in this instance seems to have been the opening of Trabaci's *Durezze et Ligature* of 1603,[14] where one encounters the identical threefold succession (for comparison Frescobaldi's excerpt, Ex. 2b, has been transposed a fourth higher). Trabaci's piece (Ex. 2c), among the most audacious experiments of early Baroque music, caused Pirro to exclaim that "they had a weakness for strange music in Naples at that time." [15] The strangeness of the chromaticism is much enhanced by the augmented triad placed at the

[10] Cited in Alfred Einstein, *The Italian Madrigal* (Princeton, N. J., 1949), p. 665.

[11] Watelet, *op cit.*, p. 38 (mm. 1, 2).

[12] Ercole Pasquini's collected keyboard works: W. Richard Shindle, ed., *Corpus of Early Keyboard Music*, XII (Dallas: American Institute of Musicology, 1966), 14.

[13] Frescobaldi, *op cit.*, V, 18.

[14] Torchi, *op. cit.*, p. 370.

[15] Pirro, *op. cit.*, p. 45.

beginning of measures 3 and 4. It is this sonority especially that makes appropriate the word *durezze* ("harsh dissonances")[16] in the title.

Ex. 2a   Marenzio: *Se la mia vita* (Book of 1587)

Ex. 2b   Frescobaldi: *Toccata Cromaticha* (Fiori Musicali) transposed up a fourth

183

Ex. 2c   Trabaci: *Durezze et Ligature* (Book of 1603)

Frescobaldi in this example adopts Trabaci's lines but not his colors, preferring a softer palette of sonorous seventh chords. Perhaps he felt that Trabaci's harmony, especially the augmented triad, was too momentarily startling and detracted from an impression of detachment or of endless motion. At the same time the change reflects a general tendency. Whereas early in the century new devices and techniques were more eagerly seized upon and ostentatiously presented, by the 1630s they had come to be used more unobtrusively as part of a larger musical continuity.

II

During the latter part of the sixteenth century a distinctive new keyboard genre made its appearance, the composition based entirely on a

[16] Robert Haas defines *durezze,* as they appear in Trabaci's book of 1603, as suspension dissonances (*Vorhaltsdissonanzen*); *Die Musik des Barocks* (Potsdam, 1928), p. 93. It seems more likely that Trabaci associated the term in this instance with the augmented triad, thereby distinguishing it from *ligature* (suspensions).

chromatic subject. Such pieces were often entitled as such, e. g., *ricercare cromatica, fantasia cromatica, verso cromatico,* and almost invariably relied upon a chromatic subject bounded by the interval of a perfect fourth.[17] The vogue for such themes probably owed its origins to Vicentino, who in his famous treatise had described the chromatic genus of the Greek as consisting of two continuous semitones plus the melodic leap of a minor third.[18] In numerous late-sixteenth-century pieces, however, the entire fourth came to be filled in with half steps. This latter procedure received theoretical justification by Scipione Cerreto, who even went so far as to proclaim its superiority: "The chromatic genus may be employed in a different way, that is by proceeding consecutively through five semitones that together form a tetrachord. This is the true manner of proceeding in the chromatic genus." [19]

184

Themes of both types (which will here be distinguished as the Greek tetrachord and the chromatic fourth) are encountered frequently in the keyboard works of Frescobaldi. Occasionally, however, one discovers a chromatic theme that is curiously divergent from the regular patterns prescribed by the theorists — such a theme as that of the *Ricercare dopo il Credo,* the *Capriccio Cromatico,* or the *Recercar Chromatico.* These have been cited numerous times as evidences of the more bizarre or capricious side of early Baroque music. Pirro, for example, says of the *Fiori Musicali* that "in the chromatic pieces the desire to surprise is at times a bit too apparent." [20]

But is there not perhaps a more precise manner of accounting for such themes? Do they not in fact spring from experiments of a similar nature found in earlier composers? Let us consider the theme (Ex. 3b) of the *Ricercare dopo il Credo,*[21] which is, of course, actually not difficult to relate to Cerreto, since in it an underlying motif of an ascending chromatic fourth is immediately discernible. Here Frescobaldi could in fact quite consciously have been influenced by such a madrigal as *Quivi sospiri* (Ex. 3a) by his own teacher Luzzaschi, in which at "al cominciar ne lagrimai" [22] an ascending fourth on the same tonal degrees, D-G, as

[17] Alan Curtis has compiled a list of such pieces, *Sweelinck's Keyboard Music* (London and Leiden, 1969), p. 135. He remarks (p. 136): "it always seems to consist of a chromatic fourth .... its intervallic boundary seems to remain intact even when adopted for chaconnes, passacaglias, and operatic laments."

[18] Nicola Vicentino, *L'Antica musica ridotta alla moderna prattica* (1555), p. 14.

[19] Scipione Cerreto, *Della Prattica Musica vocale e strumentale* (1601), p. 173.

[20] "L'Art des organistes," *Encyclopédie de la musique et dictionnaire du Conservatoire,* Partie II, p. 1263.

[21] Frescobaldi, *op. cit.,* V, 54.

[22] Cited in *The History of Music in Sound,* IV (New York, 1954), 15.

well as the accompanying harmony of successive "dominant" chords (V of F, V of G)[23] seems clearly to anticipate the thematic material of the ricercare. A relationship such as this could have prompted Hans Redlich to remark that "Luzzaschi in Ferrara, who remained in close contact with progressive artists like Gesualdo and Vicentino [is, with Trabaci] among the chief spiritual ancestors of Frescobaldi's art."[24]

A bold digression from Luzzaschi, however, may be seen in the insertion of the note B-flat near the beginning of Frescobaldi's theme — an insertion it might be added that singlehandedly raises Frescobaldi's melody out of the commonplace or stereotyped. Can any explanation be offered for this unusual alteration of the conventional chromatic pattern? Perhaps a clue is to be found in a similar passage (Ex. 3c) from Trabaci's *Canzona Cromatica* of 1603, in which the initial note G represents a departure from the regular chromatic fourth.[25] This initial note was probably looked upon by Trabaci as a variant since elsewhere in the canzona he employs the usual succession D-G. The variant was of a type Trabaci frequently introduced into his melodic lines and that he himself

Ex. 3a   Luzzaschi: *Quivi Sospiri* (Book II a5, 1576)

Ex. 3b   Frescobaldi: *Ricercare dopo il Credo* (Fiori Musicali)

Ex. 3c   Trabaci: *Canzona Franzese Settima Cromatica* (Book of 1603)

[23] Probably for reasons of tuning Frescobaldi was unable to duplicate Luzzaschi's inflection of A-flat on his keyboard.

[24] "Girolamo Frescobaldi," *The Music Review*, XIV (1953), 269.

[25] Fabrizio Fillimarino, a Neapolitan contemporary with or shortly prior to Trabaci, composed a *Canzon cromatico* using also this version of the theme: G-Eb-E-F-F♯-G. For a transcription see *Neapolitan Keyboard Composers* (Corpus of Early Keyboard Music, Vol. XXIV), ed. Roland Jackson, p. 23.

labeled in certain of his ricercari as an *inganno*. What exactly is meant by an *inganno?* In the words of Giovanni Maria Artusi it occurs "whenever one theme is succeeded by another that does not use the same melodic intervals yet retains the same names of hexachord syllables." [26] In Trabaci's canzona, for example, the note G (or re in the soft hexachord) could be considered as a substitute for the normal D (re in the natural hexachord). And in Frescobaldi's ricercare the note B-flat would be considered as equivalent to E-flat (i. e., mi for mi, since chromatic alterations at this time did not necessarily affect the basic hexachord syllables).[27]

Frescobaldi, then, seems to have adopted in this example a technique of change that had previously figured prominently in the keyboard music of Trabaci, and that offered fascinating new possibilities of freedom in the handling of melodic themes, and in particular of the stereotyped chromatic themes that had been inherited from late Renaissance composers. As such it represents a peculiar fusion of tetrachordal and hexachordal theory, of antiquity and the Middle Ages.

The application of *inganni* to chromatic subjects was by no means limited, however, to the keyboard music of Trabaci and Frescobaldi. It seems to have been characteristic also of certain madrigals by Gesualdo and of works by other experimental composers of the the time.[28] Gesualdo in *Moro lasso* (Book VI, 1611), for example, sets the text "mi da morte" to a twisting melodic subject, E-D-E♭-E (subsequently imitated A-G-G♯-A).[29] This subject (Ex. 4a) seems to have been intended as a transformation of Vicentino's tetrachord, B-D-D♯-E, whereby the initial note E (i. e., mi) became a substitute or *inganno* for what would have been the regular note B (also mi). This switch of notes much alters the character of the original pattern by bringing into it a contrary or contradic-

[26] *Seconda parte Dell'Artusi* ... (Venice, 1603), p. 45. See Roland Jackson, "The *Inganni* and the Keyboard Music of Trabaci," *Journal of the American Musicological Society,* XXI (1968), 204.

[27] According to Robert Stevenson, *Juan Bermudo* (The Hague, 1960), p. 45, Bermudo warns (in 1555) that "beginners must eventually learn that even mi-fa does not always signal a semitone." Further in *Riemann Musiklexikon,* III (Mainz, 1967), 23, "Nicht jede angezeigte Erhöhung oder Erniedrigung musste zwangsläufig eine Hexachord-Transposition veranlassen."

[28] Among whom may be mentioned Saracini, whose "Il Lamento della Madonna" (Musiche, 1614-24) includes a chromatic succession from A to C-sharp, but then shows the substitution of the note F in place of the expected D. The example is cited in *The New Oxford History of Music,* IV, 542.

[29] Carlo Gesualdo, *Madrigali Libro VI,* ed., Annibale Bizzelli, Istituto Italiano per la Storia della Musica (Rome, 1958), p. 71.

tory melodic movement. That such a change was meant by Gesualdo to call forth something strange or highly irregular to the mind of the listener of the time seems to be implied here by its textual association. In a recent study devoted to the chromaticism of Gesualdo Carl Dahlhaus suggests that the more radical features of this composer's style should be thought of as linearly, rather than chordally, conceived as has been customary.[30] If, as the present example suggests, Gesualdo frequently made use of *inganni,* this would tend also to support such a linear interpretation.

Several scholars have sensed a musical connection between Gesualdo and Frescobaldi. Redlich, for instance, feels that the *Toccata di durezze e ligature is* "reminiscent of Gesualdo's madrigals," [31] and Bukofzer that "the iridescent harmonic language of Frescobaldi can be compared with that of Gesualdo." [32] A passage by Frescobaldi such as the one cited in Ex. 4b,[33] that makes use of the same kind of *inganno* as does Gesualdo's, offers tangible support for such a relationship. On the other hand, Frescobaldi's theme seems even more intimately bound, in both its pitch and durations, to one (Ex. 4c) found in Trabaci's book of 1615 (here presumably the priority belongs to Frescobaldi). The connotation the motive

187

Ex. 4a   Gesualdo: *Moro lasso* (Book VI, 1611)

Ex. 4b   Frescobaldi: *Fantasia Ottava* (Book of 1608)

Ex. 4c   Trabaci: *Verso undecimo primo tono* (Book of 1615)

[30] "Zur chromatischen Technik Carlo Gesualdos," *Analecta musicologica,* IV (1967), 77.

[31] Redlich, *op. cit.,* p. 268.

[32] Bukofzer, *op. cit.,* p. 48.

[33] Frescobaldi, *op. cit.,* I, 31.

had in Gesualdo's madrigal (i. e., of anguish) may shed new light on the emotional content of purely abstract instrumental works such as those of Trabaci and Frescobaldi.

If the speculations of Vicentino served as a fountainhead for late Renaissance experimentation with chromaticism, he himself also provided an intriguing example in the polyphonic fragment entitled *Jerusalem convertere* (Ex. 5a). According to Edward Lowinsky, the piece is a Lamentation that "starts with the motif of the Greek chromatic tetrachord: A, B-flat, B-natural, D and its inversion: G, E, E-flat, D."[34] Such a juxtaposing of different chromatic directions in close proximity must have seemed exceptionally daring in 1555, for it strikingly forecasts similar passages encountered in the considerably later madrigals of Luzzaschi or Gesualdo.

Ex. 5a   Vicentino: *Essempio del genere cromatico, & delle sue spetie a cinque voci*

Ex. 5b   Frescobaldi: *Capriccio Cromatico* (Book of 1624) transposed down a second

Ex. 5c   Trabaci: *Canto Fermo Quarto* (Book of 1603)

Frescobaldi makes use of a similar series of entries (Ex. 5b) in the opening of his *Capriccio Cromatico*,[35] which (if transposed down a second)

[34] *Tonality and Atonality in Sixteenth-Century Music* (Berkeley, Calif., 1962). p. 41. The example by Vicentino appears on p. 42. Strictly speaking, the answer is not an inversion but a retrograde.

[35] Frescobaldi, *op. cit.*, II, 34.

even corresponds in part with Vicentino's voice parts — the second entry, in fact, is identical. An important difference, however, may be seen in Vicentino's faithful retention of the pattern of two half steps and a minor third he described in his treatise, as opposed to Frescobaldi's expressive departures from this pattern. These alterations of certain tones are again explicable as chromatic *inganni*, as the following diagram will illustrate (here the conventional notes are placed in parentheses above the notes Frescobaldi substituted for them):

(G)   (C)
D B♭ B C   G E E♭ D   G E E F

In his insertion of *inganni* Frescobaldi appears to have relied upon an earlier and quite similar passage (Ex. 5c) found in Trabaci's *Canto Fermo Quarto* of 1603. Trabaci's point of imitation (here against the Spagna theme in breves) shows a remarkable likeness to that of Frescobaldi's capriccio, even in the durational values of the first measure and a half. Trabaci, however, by relating his entries with the repeated quarter-notes makes his melodic changes — in themselves more drastic than Frescobaldi's — stand out more conspicuously. These changes involve a reshaping of the basic tetrachords by moving the lines in continually unexpected directions, as may be indicated by this diagram:

189

(G)   (D)   (D)
D B♭ B C   G E E♭ C   G E E♭ F

Gesualdo places at the very outset of his madrigal *Languisce al fin* (Book V, 1611) one of his most peculiar and oblong melodic lines (see Ex. 6a),[36] which in its prominent downward leap and ensuing half-step descent represents an extreme departure from the accepted vocal norms of the Renaissance. A rationale emerges, however, if the first two entries — E-G♯-G-F♯ and B-D♯-D-B — are considered in the light of the *inganni*, for simply by reversing the initial notes of these entries (tonic for dominant), each would be reduced to a conventional Greek tetrachord: *B*-G♯-G-F♯ answered by *E*-D♯-D-B. Gesualdo has distorted these conventional forms in a manner not unlike the elongation of objects or figures in the works of mannerist painters, e. g., El Greco (1548?-1625), who is nearly contemporary with Gesualdo.

Gesualdo's curious opening may have provided the animus for Tra-

[36] Cited in Lowinsky, *op. cit.*, p. 44. Bizzelli, *op. cit.*, transcribes the opening erroneously.

baci's even more exaggeratedly disproportionate theme (Ex. 6b) in the
Verso Undecimo Sesto Tono (1615). The most immediate resemblance
would be in the initial leap downwards (here a diminished fifth!) followed once again by descending melodic movement, a succession of notes,
moreover, whose rhythm is identical to Gesualdo's.

Ex. 6a   Gesualdo: *Languisce al fin* (Book V, 1611)

Ex. 6b   Trabaci: *Verso Undecimo Sesto Tono* (Book of 1615)

190

Ex. 6c   Frescobaldi: *Recercar Cromaticho* (Fiori Musicali)

And yet Trabaci actually exceeds Gesualdo in audaciousness by embody-
ing within a single theme two contrarily moving chromatic inflections —
apparently an innovation on his part, although intimated, certainly, by
Vicentino's chromatic inversions in different voice parts. Can Trabaci's
peculiar theme be explained in terms of *inganni?* Not as readily, to be
sure, as can Gesualdo's. The last part of the theme, F-Eb-E-F, seems
comparable to Ex. 4, above, in that the initial note, F, could be considered a substitute for the normal c. The first part, however, C-F♯-F-Eb
(partially overlapping the second), would require two note substitutions;
both the first and fourth notes would have to have been altered: A (or
G?) to C, and E (or D?) to Eb! Here, to be sure, if this be an application of the technique, it has crossed over the boundary lines of recogniz-
ability.[37]

[37] Further support for an interpretation of this sort is lent by a theme in Trabaci's
Ricercare Cromatico (1615), one actually marked "inganni" by the composer, in
which the first two notes of a descending tetrachord appear a sixth lower than normal: (**D C♯**)

    F E C A D G

$$\begin{array}{ll} \text{(A)} & \text{(E)} \\ \text{C F\# F E\flat E F} \\ \text{(C)} \end{array}$$

This brings us to the most apparently baffling of all Frescobaldi's themes (Ex. 6c), that of his *Recercar Cromaticho*,[38] which in the words of Bukofzer "seems to defy in its bold intervallic progressions any constriction of a mode or key."[39] Again one notices, as in Gesualdo's theme and in Trabaci's, the strange angularity and the downward leap (here B-F♯) followed directly by descending motion. But what connects it especially with Trabaci's is the inclusion of two contrary inflections within the one theme, A-B♭-B and F♯-F-E. Does this theme also lend itself to an interpretation based on the Greek tetrachords? Ambros perhaps already sensed such a relationship when he wrote that Frescobaldi here "composed what must be called a harshly irregular and quite gigantic ricercare on the unwieldy ancient Greek tetrachord of the chromatic genus."[40] As in Trabaci's theme, two overlapping tetrachords might be implied: A-B♭-B would require a completion by the note D, while F♯-F-E would require a preceding note A:

$$\begin{array}{c} \text{(D)} \\ \text{A B\flat B F\# F E D} \\ \text{(A)} \end{array}$$

If this interpretation is the accurate one, then Frescobaldi's theme (and perhaps Trabaci's, too) should be experienced in a manner similar to Gesualdo's, that is, as an elongation or exaggeration of an accepted musical pattern. As such the theme acquires an added dimension of expressivity wrought by the unexpected lengthenings and abrupt shifts of direction that result from the *inganni*. And the answer: D-F-F♯-C♯-C-B-A, would be heard differently from the subject since its alterations (presumably C-sharp for G and F-sharp for E) stand in marked contrast to it. Thus throughout the ricercare the theme is continually shifting in its implied *inganni* as well as its tonal degrees, like a great shimmering facade. Frescobaldi has here used chromaticism as the main basis of a lengthy musical work. A different kind of total chromatic composition, no less fascinating, will now be discussed as the third part of this paper.

[38] Frescobaldi, *op. cit.*, V, 34.
[39] Bukofzer, *op. cit.*, p. 49.
[40] *Op. cit.*, IV, 441.

191

III

Frescobaldi's *Toccata Duodecima* of Book One [41] has been a source of unceasing bewilderment to music historians, who have generally sought to comprehend it in terms of the usual figural toccata. Armand Machabey has simply declared it "an object of astonishment," [42] while Pirro has written that in it "the mode is obscured beginning with the second measure, and chromatic motives hold together propitious and strange harmonic progressions." [43] Its almost complete absence of figuration and continual chromaticism would seem to relate it, however, to earlier experimental pieces of a similar nature, pieces sometimes called *Consonanze Stravaganti* or *Durezze e Ligature* by composers such as Macque, E. Pasquini, or Trabaci. Trabaci's pieces, rather than those of other composers, probably served as the most direct model for Frescobaldi, in that his compositional procedure, like Frescobaldi's, consisted of reiterating a particular chromatic pattern (i. e., using the pattern "motivically") as the basis of a brief section, thereby defining it as distinct from the next (even though cadences rarely appear as dividing points in the form). This principle of construction is actually not far removed from that of a toccata; for in place of contrasting figural patterns the composer has merely substituted chromatic patterns, such as the ascending or descending Greek tetrachords, the chromatic fourths, chromatic *inganni*, interrupted syncope cadences, each of which is distinctive from the others.

In Trabaci's *Consonanze Stravaganti,* for example, the form seems to fall into the following sections:

Measures
1-3	slowly ascending chromatic line, G-Bb-B-C-C#, resolving irregularly to the note A (see Ex. 1b, above)
4-9	altered syncope cadences with *durezze* (augmented triads)
10-11	contrasting diatonic passage
12-15	return to the altered syncope cadences

Frescobaldi's toccata, although carried out on a vaster scale, actually obeys a very similar principle of design:

Measures
1-9	altered syncope cadences and rising inflections
10-13	descending Greek tetrachord and chromatic fourth

[41] Frescobaldi, *op. cit.*, III, 43.
[42] *Gerolamo Frescobaldi* (Paris, 1952), p. 55.
[43] "L'Art des organistes," p. 1252.

13-17	ascending chromatic patterns of a minor third
17-23	ascending and descending chromatic patterns simultaneously
23-32	descending chromatic patterns
32-38	ascending chromatic patterns
38-44	slowly ascending chromatic patterns against a more rapid figure (characteristic of a normal toccata)
44-49	descending chromatic patterns
49-60	ascending and descending chromatic patterns in close proximity and with overlapping entries (a kind of climax)

Thus the distance of Frescobaldi's piece from a regular toccata is not as great as may have been supposed. Perhaps one should call this a "chromatic toccata."

In the present paper we have taken cognizance of a number of musical correspondences between Frescobaldi and earlier composers, particularly Trabaci. This raises some important questions concerning Frescobaldi's creative process. How extensively did he draw upon the music of other composers? How may he have used borrowed materials — the excerpt from *Toccata Cromaticha*, for example, suggests a process of transforming (or even of disguising)? To what extent are the musical correspondences we have noted here simply to be considered common material at the time?

If, then, Frescobaldi adapted earlier materials this would accord with the image of him as "famed all over the world for his virtuosity and rare gift of improvisation," [44] for improvisers usually have a special facility with the musical ideas of others. In those passages that correspond with Trabaci's one notices, however, that the borrowings are quite brief, consisting usually of little more than a melodic phrase, a few chords, etc. These seem mostly to have served as a stimulus to his imagination. And in this regard it may be significant that he selected those very aspects of Trabaci's style that were most innovative at the time, such as contrary chromatic inflections, altered syncope patterns, chromatic *inganni*. These Frescobaldi transformed, of course, according to the dictates of his own style. And comparing his version with those of the earlier composer, we are provided with a more certain means than hitherto of gaining insight into the style of Frescobaldi, who until now has been perhaps the most inscrutable of all the early Baroque composers.

193

---

[44] Lang, *op. cit.*, p. 363.

The *Vespero delli Cinque Laudate* and the Role of *Salmi Spezzati* at St. Mark's*

By JAMES H. MOORE

DURING THE LAST YEAR of his life, Francesco Cavalli, then *maestro di cappella* of St. Mark's in Venice, published a collection of double-choir Vespers psalms and Magnificats. The print was issued by Gardano in 1675 and entitled simply *Vesperi a otto voci*.[1] On first examination, the collection seems to be just one more of those comprehensive Vespers publications designated *per tutte le solennità dell'anno* that were common in the late sixteenth and seventeenth centuries—collections from which a chapel master, with a certain amount of choosing and juggling, could assemble the five required Vespers psalms for all major feasts of the church year.[2] Indeed, the first two-thirds of Cavalli's collection contain material that is entirely familiar (see Table 1). The first section, called *Vespero della Beata Vergine Maria*, comprises those texts used on feasts of the Virgin or other female saints, which Monteverdi set in his monumental print of

* Research for this study was supported by grants from the Gladys Krieble Delmas Foundation, the National Endowment for the Humanities, and the American Council of Learned Societies. A shorter version of this paper was presented at the national meeting of the American Musicological Society, New York City, 31 October 1979.

[1] The full title page of Cavalli's 1675 collection reads as follows: CANTO Primo Choro/VESPERI/A OTTO VOCI/DI FRANCESCO CAVALLI/Maestro Di Capella della Serenissima Republica in S. Marco/CONSACRATI/AL SERENIS.mo PRENCIPE/NICOLO SAGREDO/DOGE DI VENETIA/(printer's device)/IN VENETIA. 1675 Stampa Del Gardano (RISM C 1566). The print consists of nine partbooks: canto, alto, tenore, and basso for each of two choirs, and a part for organ. The sole surviving set of partbooks is in the Civico museo bibliografico musicale, Bologna; fortunately, the set is complete.

[2] At the moment, scholars of seventeenth-century music lack a complete bibliography of printed *geistliche Vokalmusik* to parallel Vogel's bibliography of *weltliche Vokalmusik*. However, a bibliography of prints of Vespers polyphony before 1700 is now being assembled by Jeffrey Kurtzman and James Armstrong. A number of these prints were discussed in a paper given by Armstrong at the national meeting of the American Musicological Society, Washington, D.C., 1976: "Italian Vesper Music in the 1580s: A View from the Perspective of Giacomo Vincenti's Music Catalogue of 1591." For a summary of the contents of such prints between *ca.* 1600 and 1620, see Jeffrey Kurtzman, *Essays on the Monteverdi Mass and Vespers of 1610*, Rice University Studies, LXIV, 4 (1978), pp. 124–31.

1610. The second section, entitled *Vespero delle Domeniche, et altri salmi*, contains the five Sunday psalms as well as eight additional psalm texts which, when assembled in various permutations, will create the correct sets of Vespers psalms for all other major feasts of the church year. These two sections include all the psalms generally found in Vespers collections of the period. However, Cavalli's collection is a bit more comprehensive than most, for he includes a third section entitled *Vespero delli Cinque Laudate ad uso della Capella di San Marco*, or the "Vespers of the Five *Laudate* for the use of the chapel of St. Mark's," a service that has puzzled scholars of Venetian music in recent years.[3]

TABLE 1

Francesco Cavalli. *Vesperi a otto voci.* (Venice: Gardano, 1675)
Contents

196

Vespero della B.V.M.	Vespero delle Domeniche, et altri Salmi	Vespero delli Cinque Laudate	
Dixit	Dixit	Laudate pueri	[Psalm 112]
Laudate pueri	Confitebor	Laudate Dominum	
Laetatus sum	Beatus vir	omnes gentes	[Psalm 116]
Nisi Dominus	Laudate pueri	Lauda anima mea	[Psalm 145]
Lauda Ierusalem	In exitu	Laudate Dominum	
Magnificat	Laudate Dominum	quoniam bonus	[Psalm 146]
	Credidi	Lauda Ierusalem	[Psalm 147]
	In convertendo	Magnificat	
	Domine probasti		
	Beati omnes		
	De profundis		
	Memento		
	Confitebor		
	Angelorum		
	Magnificat		

The service is a unique one; it is made up of psalms 112, 116, 145, 146, and 147 (in the Vulgate numbering), each of which begins with a form of the verb *laudare*. Three of the psalms are normal items in published Vespers collections; *Laudate pueri*, *Laudate Dominum omnes gentes*, and *Lauda Jerusalem* are almost always set, for they form part of Vespers for feasts of Our Lord, of the Virgin, and of the saints. The

[3] While the service is specified only as *Vespero delli Cinque Laudate* in the *tavola* of the collection, the subtitle *ad uso della Capella di San Marco* is included on a title page for the service, which precedes the actual music in each of the nine partbooks. For previous inquiries into the significance of the service, see Denis Arnold, "Cavalli at St. Mark's," *Early Music*, IV (1976), 273–74 and Jane Glover, *Cavalli* (New York, 1978), p. 147, n. 14.

remaining two psalms, however, *Lauda anima mea* and *Laudate Dominum quoniam bonus est psalmus* do not usually appear in collections of this period, nor is a service consisting of five *Laudate* psalms found in the standard modern sources for Catholic liturgy or in the post-Tridentine Roman sources.[4]

A survey of the Vespers prints of composers who worked at St. Mark's in the sixteenth and seventeenth centuries, however, reveals that Cavalli is by no means the only figure to have published a *Vespero delli Cinque Laudate*, although he does seem to be the only one to have given the service a specific name. Giovanni Rovetta, who succeeded Claudio Monteverdi as *maestro di cappella* in 1644 and was himself succeeded by Cavalli in 1668, brought out an extensive collection in 1662 entitled *Delli Salmi a 8. voci* and subtitled *Secondo l'uso della Serenissima Capella Ducale di San Marco*;[5] it opens with a special Vespers service segregated from the rest of the collection, which consists of the very five *Laudate* psalms set by Cavalli, plus a Magnificat.

Moreover, in 1675, Natale Monferrato, the *vice-maestro* of St. Mark's, who would soon succeed Cavalli as *maestro di cappella*, published a set of *Salmi brevi a otto voci* which, like Rovetta's print, begins with the five *Laudate* psalms and a Magnificat.[6] Several other collections contain the service in a hidden form; while it is not set as a unit, the two unusual *Laudate* psalms, *Lauda anima mea* and *Laudate Dominum quoniam bonus est psalmus*, are included in collections containing the standard psalms for major feasts of the church year, so that by combining the two unusual *Laudate* psalms with the three more common ones, the "Vespers of the Five *Laudate*" could be assembled for performance. Such hidden sets occur in Rovetta's *Salmi a otto*

197

[4] The service is absent from all three of the major post-Tridentine breviaries, i.e., those of Pius V, Clement VIII, and Urban VIII. For a discussion of the breviary reforms and the connections between these breviaries and the liturgy of St. Mark's, see my doctoral dissertation, "Vespers at St. Mark's, 1625–1675: Music of Alessandro Grandi, Giovanni Rovetta, and Francesco Cavalli" (Ph.D. diss., Univ. of California at Los Angeles, 1979; forthcoming in the series *Studies in Musicology*, [Ann Arbor, 1981]), pp. 185–88.

[5] CANTO/PRIMO CHORO/DELLI SALMI/A OTTO VOCI/Accommodati da cantarsi alla Breve/Secondo l'uso/DELLA SERENIS.ma CAPELLA DUCALE DI S. MARCO/DI GIO: ROVETTA/Maestro di detta Capella./Opera Duodecima./ (printer's device)/IN VENETIA M. DC. LXII. Apresso Francesco Magni detto Gardano A (RISM R 2980).

[6] Canto Primo Choro./SALMI/BREVI/A OTTO VOCI/A DUE CHORI/DI D. NATALE MONFERRATO/Vice Maestro di Capella della Serenissima Republica/di Venetia/DEDICATI/All'Illustrissimo Signore/IL SIG. COLOMBANO/ZANARDI/OPERA NONA./(printer's device)/In Bologna per Giacomo Monti. 1675. Con licenza de' Superiori (RISM M 3045).

voci of 1644,[7] in *vice-maestro* Antonio Sartorio's *Salmi a otto voci* of 1680,[8] and in the *Vespertina omnium solemnitatum psalmodia* published in 1597 by Giovanni Croce, the last *maestro di cappella* but one before Monteverdi himself.[9] We have evidence, moreover, that this service was set by both earlier and later composers at St. Mark's. In the 1573 and 1589 editions of the *Istitutioni harmoniche*, Zarlino cites a number of psalms by Willaert as examples of *cori spezzati*, among which he lists, in order, settings of the five texts that make up the *Cinque Laudate*.[10] Furthermore, in the surviving musical archives of St. Mark's, now housed in the cloister of Sant'Apollonia, there are

---

[7] CANTO Primo Choro/SALMI A OTTO VOCI/DI GIO: ROVETTA/ Maestro di Capella della Serenissima Republica,/OPERA OTTAVA/DEDICATI/ All'Illustrissimi, et Eccellentissimi Signori/PROCURATORI/DELLA CHIESA DI S. MARCO./CON PRIVILEGIO./(printer's device)/IN VENETIA, A/Apresso Alessandro Vincenti. MDCXXXXIIII (RISM R 2972).

[8] Canto Primo Choro/SALMI/A OTTO VOCI/A DUE CHORI/Accomodati all'uso della Serenis.ma Capella Ducale di S. Marco/DI ANTONIO SARTORIO/ Vice Maestro della medesima/DEDICATI/A GL'ILL.mi et ECC.mi SIG.ir. [sic]/ PROCURATORI/DI SUPRA/CASSIERE/L'Illustrissimo, et Eccellentissimo Signor Procurator/LEONARDO/PESARO/OPERA PRIMA/IN VENETIA, M. DC. LXXX./APPRESSO Gioseppe, [sic] Sala (RISM S 1074).

[9] CANTUS/PRIMI CHORI/VESPERTINA/OMNIUM SOLEMNITATUM/ PSALMODIA/OCTONIS VOCIBUS DECANTANDA,/AUCTORE IOANNE A CRUCE CLODIENSE/In Ecclesia Divi Marci Musices Vice Magistro./CUM PRIVILEGIO./(printer's device)/VENETIIS,/Apud Iacobum Vincentium. M D XC VII. A (RISM C 4449–52). Copies of this print were purchased at St. Mark's as late as 1645; see Archivio di Stato di Venezia (hereafter, A.S.V.), San Marco, Procuratia de Supra, Registro 12, entry of 31 March 1645: "Per spese per la chiesa//à Cassa *ducati* cinque *denari* 5, contadi al mastro di Cappella per due copie vespri a 8. voci in stampa del Chiozotto."

[10] The three principal editions of the *Istitutioni harmoniche* all contain slightly different versions of this passage. The five *Laudate* psalms are mentioned only in the editions of 1573 (pp. 329–30; see also Guy A. Marco and Claude V. Palisca, eds., *Gioseffo Zarlino, The Art of Counterpoint* [New Haven, 1968], p. 245) and 1589 (see Roman Flury, *Gioseffo Zarlino als Komponist* [Winterthur, 1962], pp. 27–28). Flury's claim that the psalms were composed by Zarlino is based upon a misreading of the text. The text from the 1573 edition reads as follows: "et tale difficultà si farà alquanto più facile, quando si haverà essaminato le dotte compositioni di esso Adriano; come sono quelli Salmi: Confitebor tibi d*o*mine in toto corde meo in consilio iustor*um*. Laudate pueri dominum: Lauda Ierusalem dominum; De profundis; Memento Domine David, et molti altri; tra i quali sono i Salmi; Dixit Dominus Domino meo: Laudate pueri Dominum: Laudate Dominum omnes gentes: Lauda anima mea Dominum: Laudate Dominum quoniam bonus est Psalmus: Lauda Ierusalem Dominum; et il Cantico della Beata Vergine; Magnificat anima mea Dominum, il quale composi già molti anni à tre Chori." Surely, the connective *il quale* in the final sentence refers to the three-choir Magnificat setting alone, and not to the psalms that precede it.

settings of the two unusual *Laudate* psalms by Baldassare Galuppi, dated 1780 and 1789.[11]

That the service had a special position in St. Mark's is clear.` After all, Cavalli had specified that the service was "ad uso della Capella di San Marco," and Rovetta had made the same claim for his print of 1662. Indeed, a number of documents link Rovetta's collection even more firmly with the *cappella marciana*. The composer's dedication suggests that the collection was actually printed for the private use of the ducal chapel and not for commercial distribution, for in describing his motives for publication, he states that "since these psalms would easily be lost and worn out if they existed in just a few manuscript copies, and since these texts are used and needed very frequently . . . I have decided to put them into print, so we will have the benefit of many copies of longer durability."[12] Moreover, the collection is dedicated to the Procurators of St. Mark's, and on 7 January 1663, they voted to pay for the printing of the collection, a most unusual act for them.[13] Similar documents suggest that Rovetta's collection of 1644 was also printed for the private use of St. Mark's, for he dedicated the collection to the Procurators just after they appointed him *maestro di cappella* and informed them in the dedication:

> Scarcely had I been honored by the Kindness of Your Excellencies with this noble position than, feeling within myself the stimulus of gratitude

199

[11] There is no published catalogue of this archive, but I have assembled a manuscript catalogue of its contents. Four settings of *Laudate* psalms, all for double choir, are shelved alongside a number of other works of Galuppi. They are located on the shelves which look out onto the Bridge of Sighs and the back of the ducal palace, on the next-to-bottom shelf, on the right side. The two crucial settings are labeled as follows: 1) Laudate Dominum quoniam bonus à 8 voci e Violini di Baldassare Galuppi Anno 1780; and 2) Lauda anima mea Dominum à due cori di *Baldassare Galuppi da Burano* 1789.

[12] Giovanni Rovetta, dedication to *Delli Salmi a 8. voci* (Venice: Magni, 1662): "E perche di facile rimarrebbono smarriti, e consunti, se solamente ad alcuno esemplare di penna fossero raccommandati: cadendo molto frequente l'uso, e necessità di quelli . . . propria perciò resolutione m'è parsa rassegnarli alle stampe: dalle quali s'ha il beneficio e di molteplici copie e di durabilità più costante."

[13] A.S.V., San Marco, Procuratia de Supra, Registro 146: "Adi 7. Genaro 1662 [*more veneto*] Havendo il Maestro di Capella Giovanni Rovetta fatta stampare alcune messe, et salmi necessarij per la Capella di San Marco: mentre gl'antichi manuscritti erano dal tempo consunti, et impossibile à più servirsene. Pero essendo conveniente oltre il rimborsarlo della spesa considerabile di riconoscere il suo diligente impiego gl'Ill*ustrissi*mi et Eccel*lentissi*mi Signori Procura*tor*i. . . . Hanno terminato, *che* de danari della Cassa della Chiesa siano al medesimo dati ducati cento e cinquanta, nei quali il sopra più della spesa serva *per* testimonio del gradimento, e *per* aletamento à chi serve la Chiesa, et questa procuratia."

and of duty, I finished up several compositions of which I thought the service of the Most Serene Chapel of St. Mark's had the greatest need.[14]

Furthermore, on 3 January 1644, the Procurators had given Rovetta special permission to publish certain unnamed materials, in a document which, because of its date and the remote dates of Rovetta's other sacred publications, almost certainly refers to the 1644 collection of psalms.[15]

These documents connecting the *Cinque Laudate* with the ducal chapel hint at the core of the problem of identifying the service: as the private chapel of the Doge, St. Mark's had its own liturgy, which it retained through the reforms of the Council of Trent, the breviary reforms of the seventeenth century, and the fall of the Venetian Republic, right up to 1807, when St. Mark's became the cathedral of Venice and was forced to adopt the Roman rite. This is a factor that has been largely overlooked in studies of Venetian sacred music of the High Renaissance and early Baroque and, as we shall see below, it is crucial to an understanding of the musical repertoire.[16]

That St. Mark's had a viable liturgy which differed from that of Rome is recorded in many documents from the late sixteenth and seventeenth centuries. In the preface to his *ceremoniale* of 1564, master of ceremonies at St. Mark's Bartolomeo Bonifacio warned the reader not to be surprised at finding descriptions of a number of ceremonies that did not correspond with the Roman rite.[17] And canon Giovanni Pace reported in the preface to his *ceremoniale* of 1678 that St. Mark's

200

[14] Preface to Giovanni Rovetta's *Salmi a otto voci* (Venice: Vincenti, 1644): "Appena honorato dalla benignità dell'Eccellenze Vostre di questa nobilissima carica, sentendo in me lo stimolo della gratitudine, e del debito, hò dato fine ad alcune compositioni, delle quali hò pensato haver più di bisogno il servitio della Serenissima Real Capella di San Marco." It is worth noting that Cavalli's collection had a similar dedication, addressed to Doge Nicolò Sagredo.

[15] A.S.V., San Marco, Procuratia de Supra, Registro 144: "1643. 3 Genaro [*more veneto*] Che sia concessa licenza à D: *Giovanni* Rovetta *Vice* Mastro di Capella di poter stampar le cose nominate nella sua supplica hoggi presentata."

[16] The early literature on the special rite of St. Mark's is broader than one might expect. See Flaminio Corner, *Ecclesiae venetae antiquis monumentis* (Venice: J. B. Pasquali, 1749), IX–X, 204–15; Marco Foscarini, *Della letteratura veneziana* (Venice: Manfrè, 1752), p. 192, n. 254; Giovanni Diclich, *Rito veneto antico detto patriarchino* (Venice: Rizzi, 1825); Antonio Pasini, "Il rito antico ed il cerimoniale della Basilica di San Marco," in Camillo Boito, ed., *La Basilica di S. Marco in Venezia* (Venice, 1888); more recently, see Mario dal Tin, "Note di liturgia patriarchina e canti tradizionali della Basilica di S. Marco a Venezia," *Jucunda Laudatio*, I–IV (1973), 90–131; and David Bryant, "Liturgia e musica liturgica nella fenomenologia del 'Mito di Venezia'," in *Mitologie*, ed. Giovanni Morelli (Venice, 1979), pp. 205–14.

[17] A.S.V., Consulatore in Jure, Registro 555, fols. 1[v]–2[r]: "Quare diligens lector, si quid invenerit in descriptione hac rituum, et cerimoniarum Ecclesiae. Sanctae Divi

had taken full advantage of the loophole in Pius V's bull *Quod a nobis*, which said that any church with a distinct liturgical tradition over two-hundred years old did not have to adopt the Tridentine breviary.[18] On 1 January 1613, Doge Marc'Antonio Memo emphasized that the rite of St. Mark's was to be used not only in the church itself but also in the four small churches under ducal jurisdiction and in any church visited by the Doge during one of his ceremonial *andate* around the city on major feasts.[19] On 27 June 1628, Doge Giovanni Cornaro ordered that the Mass and Divine Office be celebrated in St. Mark's "according to the rite, form, and ancient use of this church, without the slightest innovation."[20] However, the decree of Doge Nicolò Contarini on 10 June 1630 was the most precise; it specified that "in the celebration of the Divine Office in this church, one must observe

---

Marci Evangelistae Civitatis Illustris Venetiarum, diversum a ritibus aliarum Ecclesiarum non debet mirari, praesertim cum nostra haec Ecclesia in praecibus orariis, non omnino Ecclesiam sequatur Romanam id quod et multae aliae faciunt: non solum praesbyterorum Secularium, verum etiam Monacorum, ac diversorum ordinum Regularium: deviant enim in celebrandis officiis divinis ab Ecclesia Romana, ejusdem permissione vel etiam concessione."

[18] Milan, Biblioteca ambrosiana, MS A. 328 inf., unpaginated folio in the preface: "In questa Ducal Basilica si stabilì il suo Clero con ammirabile direttione, et con ordine hierarchica e perche ogni chiesa possiede e le sue Cerimonie, et il suo Rito, da sommi Pontefici anche tolerato nell'officiatura, giusto la Bolla di Pio 5.o 1568, quando però eccedi il corso di anni 200—Resta stabilir, et decretar per regola propria perpetua, et immutabile della medesima Ducal Capella, e risvegliare al Mondo nuovo Ceremoniale secondo il Rito di San Marco."

[19] In A.S.V., Cancelleria Inferiore, Registro 79, fols. 87ᵛ–88ʳ, the Doge instructs *maestro di coro* Cesare Vergaro to oversee the ceremonies "che giornalmente occoreno farsj non solo nelle chiese alla capella nostra di San Marco annesse, et dipendentj, ma in altre ove per publiche ordinationj, o votj, o per particolare divotione siamo solitj andare con publica pompa." Vergaro is to supervise these ceremonies "ordinando intorno le sacre ceremonie nella medesima maniera, et coll'istessa facoltà, che solete et che dovete nella predetta chiesa di San Marco nostra capella, dall'uso et dal cerimoniale della quale non intendemo, che vi dobbiate in modo alcuno discostare." The decree was reiterated by the Collegio in 1660; see A.S.V., San Marco, Procuratia de Supra, Busta 88, Processo 195, fascicolo 1, fol. 105ʳ, entry of 3 January 1659 (*more veneto*).

The chapels that are "annexed" to St. Mark's are the four Venetian churches under ducal jurisdiction: Santa Maria in Broglio, SS. Filippo e Giacomo, San Giacomo di Rialto, and San Giovanni Nuovo di Rialto. On the various *andate* of the Doge to different churches in Venice, see Francesco Sansovino–Giustiniano Martinioni, *Venetia città nobilissima* (Venice: Curti, 1663), pp. 492–525, and Ellen Rosand, "Music in the Myth of Venice," *Renaissance Quarterly*, XXX (1977), 524–25.

[20] A.S.V., Cancelleria Inferiore, Registro 81, p. 47: "ordinando et operando che tutte le sacre Ceremonie sijno fatte, et osservate secondo il rito, forma et uso antico di detta Chiesa senza pur minima inovatione." See also canon Giovanni Pace's explanation of this decree, Biblioteca ambrosiana, MS A. 328 inf., fol. 71ᵛ.

201

the rubrics, rites, uses, and ceremonies described in the book called the *Orationale*."[21]

This is not the only reference to the *Orationale* in contemporary documents. It is mentioned by Sansovino, who states that the two major guides to the liturgy of St. Mark's are "the book of ceremonies and that other one called the *Orationale*, and its rubrics."[22] The large ceremonial books of St. Mark's also mention it prominently.[23] The *Orationale* was, in fact, the special breviary of St. Mark's. A copy in the Bodleian library has been known for some time,[24] but I have located two additional copies in the Biblioteca del Civico Museo Correr in Venice, which are almost certainly the volumes copied and illuminated between 1565 and 1567 by the Brescian priest, Giovanni Battista Vitale.[25] The *Orationale* is only the most important of a large

[21] A.S.V., Cancelleria Inferiore, Registro 81, p. 70: "Che nel Celebrar li Divini Offitij in detta Chiesa siano Osservate le Rubriche, Riti, Usi, et Cirimonie descritte nel libro chiamato Orationale."

[22] Sansovino–Martinioni, *Venetia città nobilissima*, p. 517: "il libro delle ceremonie et quell'altro detto Orationale nelle sue rubriche."

[23] See, *inter alia*, the 1564 *ceremoniale* of Bartolomeo Bonifacio, A.S.V., San Marco, Procuratia de Supra, Registro 98, fol. 3ᵛ: "Antiphona Tecum principium cum suis psalmis ut in Orationali"; fol. 6ᵛ: "vide Rubricam in Nostro Orationali"; fol. 22ʳ: "vide ibi Antiphona ad Magnificat, ut in Orationali"; fol. 22ᵛ: "Hodie Vespere dicuntur, cum Deus in adiutorium meum intende etc., omnia ut in Orationali"; and the 1678 *ceremoniale* of Giovanni Pace, Milan, Biblioteca ambrosiana, MS A. 328 inf., fol. 74ʳ: "Rubrica Generale circa l'Uffitio cavata dal Orational."; Pace also includes an "Index Rerum obsoletarum, quae non sunt in usu ex antiquo Ceremoniali exerptarum," which contains the following excerpts: fol. 69ʳ: "In Octavis Sancti Stephani, et Sancti Ioannis Evangelistae dicebatur Offitium B.M.V. Hoc est contra Rubricas Orationalis Sancti Marci"; fol. 70ᵛ: "Duobus diebus ultimis ante Vigiliam Pentecostes dicebatur Offitium B.V.; hoc est contra Rubricas, et Orationale nostrum, cui debet convenire Ceremoniale."

[24] On the Bodleian copy of the *Orationale*, see Madan Falconer, *A Summary Catalogue of Western Manuscripts in the Bodleian Library at Oxford* (Oxford, 1897), IV, 381; Walter Howard Frere, *Bibliotheca musica liturgica* (London, 1901), p. 24; and Stephen Joseph Peter Van Dijk and Joan Hazelden Walker, *The Origins of the Modern Roman Liturgy: The Liturgy of the Papal Court and the Franciscan Order in the Thirteenth Century* (London, 1960), p. 325. The volume is used as a liturgical source in Joan Ann Long, "The Motets, Psalms, and Hymns of Adrian Willaert: A Liturgico-Musical Study" (Ph.D. diss., Columbia Univ., 1971) and Jane Weidensaul, "The Polyphonic Hymns of Adrian Willaert" (Ph.D. diss., Rutgers Univ., 1978). While Falconer's Bodleian catalogue dates this volume as 1514, no explanation is given for the date. Indeed, the manuscript appears to be much later than the sixteenth century, and I would tentatively identify the Bodleian *Orationale* as the copy ordered in 1668 by the Procurators of St. Mark's. See A.S.V., San Marco, Registro 15, entry of 23 February 1667 (*more veneto*): "Per spese per la Chiesa//à Cassa ducati vinti contadi à Padre Domenico Buli à conto di rescriver l'Orational della Chiesa di San Marco d'ordine dell'Eccellentissimo Signor Procurator Cassier."

[25] The two copies of the *Orationale* in the Biblioteca Correr are catalogued as Codici Cicogna 1602 and 163. Cicogna 1602 is a complete breviary, with the addition

cache of liturgical books connected with St. Mark's outlining a liturgy that differs from that of Rome in many areas. The volumes include manuscript antiphonaries, graduals, missals, and Marian supplications, as well as prints of the rites of Holy Week, Christmas Matins, the Blessing of the Waters on Epiphany, the Office for the three great feasts of St. Mark, and the special litanies and special psalter of the basilica.[26]

---

of an eighteenth-century title page and a number of supplementary folios at the end, containing the liturgy for feasts added to the Venetian calendar after the volume was originally copied. Cicogna 163 is only a *pars aestivalis* of the *Orationale*; the remainder of this copy has not come to light.

The identification of Cicogna 1602 with the volumes copied by Vitale is suggested by Emmanuele Cicogna in his prefatory notes attached to the volume; and, indeed, the volume is signed on fol. 152[r] as follows: "Presbyter Ioannes de Vitalibus Brixianus scripsit, notavit, et miniavit hunc librum Anno Domini M. D. LXVII." The identification of Cicogna 163 as a work of Vitale is less certain. However, we know that two volumes, one large and one small, were commissioned at this time and that Vitale was paid a fixed sum for each page copied and for each initial illuminated (see A.S.V., San Marco, Procuratia de Supra, Registro 130, entry of 20 February 1564 [*more veneto*]). It seems highly probable that Cicogna 163 is the smaller of these two volumes. On Vitale's dealings with the Procurators over the copying of the *Orationale*, see also A.S.V., San Marco, Procuratia de Supra, Busta 76 (Culto ed oggetti relativi), processo 176, fascicolo 3, fols. 11[r]–14[v]. The two copies of the text are cited here as the *orationale festivo* and *orationale feriale*. For a more detailed study of these breviaries and the relationship of the manuscripts, see Moore, "Vespers," pp. 192–95.

[26] The liturgical sources that preserve texts from St. Mark's are discussed in detail in Moore, "Vespers," pp. 192–204. The most important surviving manuscript sources after the *Orationale* include the large fifteenth-century antiphonaries (A.S.V., San Marco, Procuratia de Supra, Registri 113–18); the graduals of the basilica, which are housed, uncatalogued, in the *loggia dei cavalli* in St. Mark's; a missal that preserves the special rite of the church (Biblioteca nazionale marciana, Cod. lat. III–111 [= 2116]); the eighteenth-century manuscript of "Supplicationes ad gloriosissimam virginem Mariam pro variis necessitatibus ad usum Ducalis Basilicae Sancti Marci Venetiarum" copied in 1788 (Biblioteca Correr, Codice Cicogna 596); a copy of the Office for the three feasts of St. Mark (Biblioteca nazionale marciana, Cod. lat. II–93 [= 2925]); and a number of miscellaneous manuscripts (A.S.V., San Marco, Procuratia de Supra, Registri 119, 122; Biblioteca Correr, Codici Cicogna 1595, 1605, 1006).

The most important prints are Giovanni Stringa's *Psalterium Davidicum* (Venice: Rampazetto, 1609), the *Officium hebdomadae sanctae, secundum consuetudinem ducalis ecclesiae S. Marci Venetiarum* (Venice: Rampazetto, 1597), the *Officia propria festi Sancti Marci apostoli, et evangelistae cum octava: necnon translationis, et apparitionis corporis eiusdem* (Venice: Patrianus, 1602), as well as a number of miscellaneous prints: *Officium in nocte nativitatis Domini ad matutinum, secundum consuetudinem ducalis ecclesiae Sancti Marci Venetiarum* (Venice: Poleti, 1722), *Benedictio aquae quae sit in nocte Epiphaniae, juxta consuetudinem ecclesiae ducalis Sancti Marci Venetiarum* (Venice: Poleti, 1722), *Litaniae secundum consuetudinem ducalis ecclesiae Sancti Marci Venetiarum* (Venice: Pinelli, 1719), the *Supplicationes ad Sanctissimam Virginem Mariam tempore belli secundum consuetudinem ducalis basilicae S. Marci Venetiarum* (Venice: Pinelli, 1695 and 1719), and *Officia propria sanctorum civitatis, dioecesis, et totius dominii Venetiarum* (Venice: Recurti, 1765). Emmanuele Cicogna's *Saggio di bibliografia veneziana* (Venice, 1847) cites some of these prints as well as certain others that seem to be no longer available; these may have

203

If one compares the *Orationale* with pre-Tridentine Roman sources,[27] beginning with Advent, they correspond with minor variants right up to the services for Christmas Eve. They begin to diverge, however, with Vespers for the Christmas Vigil. The antiphons listed in the *Orationale* for this feast are the ones we expect from our knowledge of Roman liturgy, although the third and fifth are exchanged from their position in the Roman rite; but the psalms are a surprise. Instead of the texts from the Roman rite (*Dixit Dominus*, *Confitebor*, *Beatus vir*, *Laudate pueri*, and *Laudate Dominum omnes gentes*), we find the very five psalms that Cavalli dubbed the *Vespero delli Cinque Laudate*.[28] (See Figure 1; the liturgy for Vespers of Christmas Eve is in the column at the far right.) The remainder of the *Orationale* reveals that the *Cinque Laudate* were used not only on the Vigil of Christmas but on a bewilderingly large number of other feasts (which are tabulated in the first part of Table 2): the Vigils of Epiphany, of Ascension, and of Pentecost, Second Vespers for Corpus Christi and for its Octave, First Vespers for the Purification, and the Vigils of the Assumption, of the Nativity and Conception of the Blessed Virgin, and of All Saints' Day. At one time, the sequence had also been used for Vespers on Holy Saturday. Thus, the service would have been one of the most prominent sequences of Vespers psalms of the entire church year at St. Mark's.[29]

The origins of the *Cinque Laudate* are not difficult to trace. Antonio Pasini and Giovanni Diclich, the two prominent nineteenth-century scholars who attempted to unravel the mysteries of the rite of St. Mark's, found its origins in the rite of Aquileia, the patriarchate just east of Venice in which, according to one tradition, St. Mark actually wrote his gospel. During the late Middle Ages political and ecclesiastical struggles reigned between Venice and Aquileia until 1451, when the patriarchate was finally transferred to Venice.[30] Two printed breviaries of the Aquileian rite, published in 1481 and 1496, are

---

been a part of his personal collection that never found its way into the public Venetian collections.

[27] The major source used for this purpose has been the *Breviarium romanum* (Venice: Variscum, 1562), published just before the Trent reforms, and incorporating a certain number of specific Venetian feasts alongside the Roman rite.

[28] Biblioteca Correr, Codice Cicogna 1602, fol. 13[r].

[29] See Biblioteca Correr, Codice Cicogna 1602, fols. 19[v], 57[r]–57[v], 64[r]–64[v], 81[v], 108[r], 112[v]–113[r], 74[v]–75[r], 121[r]–121[v], 51[v] (in the order of the feasts cited above).

[30] On the relations between Venice and Aquileia, see Otto Demus, *The Church of San Marco in Venice* (Washington, D.C., 1960), and Pasini, "Rito antico ed il cerimoniale della Basilica di San Marco."

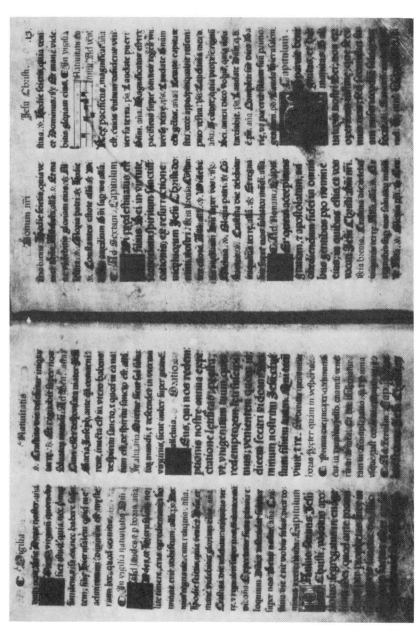

Figure 1. *Orationale* of St. Mark's, with the liturgy for the Vigil of Christmas. Venice, Biblioteca del Civico Museo Correr, Codice Cicogna 1602, fols. 12ᵛ–13ʳ

TABLE 2

Variants in the Psalm Sequences for Vespers between St. Mark's (*Orationale*) and
the Roman Rite (*Breviarium romanum*, Venice: Variscum, 1562)

Feast	St. Mark's	Rome	Aquileia
Vigil of Christmas	Cinque Laudate	Male *cursus*	Cinque Laudate
Vigil of Epiphany	Cinque Laudate	Male *cursus*	Cinque Laudate
Vigil of Ascension	Cinque Laudate	Male *cursus*	Cinque Laudate
Vigil of Pentecost	Cinque Laudate	Male *cursus*	Cinque Laudate
Corpus Christi, Second Vespers	Cinque Laudate	Dixit Confitebor Credidi Beati omnes Lauda Jerusalem	Dixit Confitebor Credidi Beati omnes Lauda Jerusalem
Purification, First Vespers	Cinque Laudate	Female *cursus*	Cinque Laudate
Vigil of Assumption	Cinque Laudate	Female *cursus*	Cinque Laudate
Vigil of Nativity of B.V.M.	Cinque Laudate	Female *cursus*	Cinque Laudate
Vigil of Conception of B.V.M.	Cinque Laudate	Female *cursus*	Cinque Laudate
Vigil of All Saints' Day	Cinque Laudate	Male *cursus*	Cinque Laudate
Holy Saturday (formerly)	Cinque Laudate	—	—
Holy Saturday (at present)	Laudate Dominum omnes gentes	Laudate Dominum omnes gentes	Laudate Dominum omnes gentes
Feast of the Holy Trinity, First Vespers	Levavi oculos meos Ad te levavi De profundis Memento Laudate nomen Domini	Male *cursus*	Cinque Laudate
Dedication of the Church of St. Mark's, Second Vespers	Credidi Laetatus sum Nisi Dominus Confitebor Angelorum Lauda Jerusalem	Dixit Confitebor Beatus vir Laudate pueri Lauda Jerusalem	Credidi Laetatus sum Nisi Dominus Confitebor Angelorum Lauda Jerusalem
SS. Hermagoras and Fortunatus, Second Vespers and St. Clement, Second Vespers	Dixit Confitebor Beatus vir Credidi Eripe me Domine	—	Dixit Beatus vir In convertendo Eripe me Domine Lauda Jerusalem

206

TABLE 2, continued

Feast	St. Mark's	Rome	Aquileia
Epiphany, Second Vespers, and Octave of Epiphany, First and Second Vespers	Dixit Confitebor Beatus vir De profundis Memento	Sunday *cursus*	Dixit Confitebor Beatus vir De profundis Memento
Purification, Second Vespers	same psalms as above	Female *cursus*	same psalms as above
St. Agatha, First Vespers	Dixit Confitebor Beatus vir Laudate pueri Lauda Jerusalem	Female *cursus*	ferial psalms
Vigil of Nativity of St. John the Baptist	Dixit Confitebor Beatus vir Laudate pueri Memento	Male *cursus*	Cinque Laudate
Feast of the Transfiguration, Second Vespers	Sunday *cursus*	Male *cursus*	Credidi Laetatus sum Nisi Dominus Confitebor Angelorum Lauda Jerusalem
Feasts of St. Mark and of SS. Peter and Paul, First Vespers	Dixit Laudate pueri Credidi In convertendo Domine probasti me	Male *cursus*	Cinque Laudate

207

extant,[31] and a comparison of the *Orationale* with these volumes reveals that a sizeable proportion of the liturgical idiosyncrasies of the rite of St. Mark's can be traced to Aquileia. Among these is the *Vespero delli Cinque Laudate*, which was used in Aquileia on all but one of the occasions when it was used in St. Mark's. As one can see from Table 2, it formed First Vespers of the feasts of the Holy Trinity, the Annunciation, SS. Philip and James, the Finding of the Holy Cross, St. John before the Latin Gate, St. John the Evangelist, the Apostles

[31] These two volumes are the *Breviarium secundum ritum et consuetudinem alme ecclesiae Aquileiensis* (Venice: Franciscus de Hailbrun, 1481) and the *Breviarium secundum usum Aquileiae* (Venice: Andreas de Torresanis de Asula, 1496). Both are cited in Hans Bohatta, *Liturgische Bibliographie des XV. Jahrhunderts* (Vienna, 1911), p. 51.

Peter and Paul, the Visitation, the Transfiguration of Our Lord, and St. Laurence. Moreover, the additional use of the *Cinque Laudate* for First Vespers of the Common of Apostles, the Common of Martyrs, and the Common of Virgins means that it served on virtually every important saint's day of the year. In fact, a rubric states that the five *Laudate* psalms are to be used for First Vespers of any feasts for which no other psalms are specified, making them a sort of general Common for First Vespers throughout the year.[32]

A survey of pre-Tridentine breviaries, however, reveals that the rites of Aquileia and St. Mark's were not the only early liturgies to include the *Cinque Laudate*; in fact, the service was very widespread.[33] It is found in the three principal English liturgies, the rites of Sarum, Hereford, and York, as well as in a number of monastic and special liturgies; the Dominicans, Augustinians, and Carmelites all used the *Cinque Laudate*, as did the special rite of the church in Salzburg.[34] The psalms are always used for First Vespers in these liturgies, although the specific occasions of their appearance during the church year vary with the different rites. Nor was St. Mark's the only rite to retain them after the Trent reforms; they continued to be used by the Dominicans and the Carmelites, among others. Indeed, the large Carmelite breviary published in Antwerp in 1672 lists the *Cinque Laudate* on fifteen occasions during the church year,[35] and two collections of Vespers psalms composed by Lorenzo Penna and published in Bologna in 1669 and 1677 contain the psalms *Lauda anima*

208

[32] See *Breviarium secundum usum Aquileiensis*, fol. 129ᵛ: "In super notandum quasi semper in primis vesperis festorum duplicium et cum pleno officio psalmi infrascripti videlicet. Laudate pueri dominum. Laudate dominum omnes gentes. Lauda anima mea. Laudate dominum quoniam. Lauda hierusalem."

[33] See Ludwig Eisenhofer and Joseph Lechner, *The Liturgy of the Roman Rite* (London, 1961), p. 470; the service is described briefly here, but no details are given about its use.

[34] The uses of the *Cinque Laudate* in early liturgies can be documented through the following books, among others: Francis Procter and Christopher Wordsworth, *Breviarium ad usum insignis ecclesiae Sarum* (Cambridge, 1882); Walter Howard Frere and Langton E. G. Brown, *The Hereford Breviary: Edited from the Rouen Edition of 1505 with Collation of Manuscripts* (London, 1904, 1911, 1915), see especially the large comparative liturgical table, III, 266–68; *Breviarium augustanum* (Augsburg: Ratdolt, 1495); *Breviarium ad usum alme ecclesiae salzburgensis* (Salzburg, Venice: Giunta, 1518); *Breviarium secundum ordinem sancti dominici* (Venice: Joannis de Colonia, Nicolai Jenson sociorumque, 1481); Benedict Zimmerman, *Ordinaire de l'ordre de Notre-Dame du Mont Carmel par Sibert de Beka (vers 1312)* (Paris, 1910).

[35] See Biblioteca Apostolica Vaticana, R. G. Liturgia V. 476: *Breviarium carmelitarum* (Antwerp: Parys, 1672).

mea and *Laudate Dominum quoniam bonus est psalmus* along with several other unusual texts under the rubric "all'uso Carmelitano."[36]

Nonetheless, it seems clear from the published Venetian collections, with their rubrics and dedications, that in the minds of the composers connected with St. Mark's, the service was the exclusive property of the ducal chapel, and they included the service only in those collections which seem to have been designed for the private use of the *cappella marciana*.

It is really beyond the scope of this article to discuss other items of the Venetian liturgy; indeed, a complete tabulation of the variants between the Vespers liturgies of St. Mark's, Rome, and Aquileia could easily fill a volume.[37] Suffice it to say that the *Cinque Laudate* was not the only Vespers service in which St. Mark's differed from Rome. As one sees in Table 2, the combination of psalms used for First Vespers of the Feast of the Holy Trinity (Psalms 120, 122, 129, 131, and 134 in the Vulgate) was unique and did not even stem from Aquileia.[38] Composers seem not to have set this service in *canto figurato* until Rovetta set the three unusual psalms of the service— *Levavi oculos meos* (Psalm 120), *Ad te levavi* (Psalm 122), and *Laudate nomen Domini* (Psalm 134)—in his collection of 1662, and Antonio Sartorio set them in his *Salmi a otto voci* of 1680. Indeed, we know quite specifically that these psalms were not set before 1600, for in an inquest during August of 1600 to decide whether or not Rocco da Bruni should be reappointed to his post of *maestro di coro*, Giovanni Croce made a statement regarding the performance of Vespers on Trinity Sunday. When asked whether or not Bruni had ever altered the ceremonies of the Divine Office, Croce responded:

209

> He made changes in the ceremonies for First Vespers of the Most Holy Trinity, which he wanted sung with two choirs; but we do not have settings of these psalms, nor were they ever composed by any of the *maestri di cappella*; so as not to cause a scandal, we sang them in

[36] Lorenzo Penna, *Psalmorum totius anni modulatio* . . . (Bologna: Monti, 1669); *idem, Il Sacro Parnaso delli salmi festivi e brevi* . . . (Bologna: Monti, 1677). I am indebted to Jeffrey Kurtzman for drawing my attention to these collections and for providing me with photocopies of their contents. On the stability of the Dominican liturgy after the Council of Trent, see William R. Bonniwell, *A History of the Dominican Liturgy* (New York, 1944), pp. 279–80.

[37] For a comparison of the texts of psalm antiphons, Magnificat antiphons, and hymns, see Moore, "Vespers," pp. 234–56. For a discussion of the liturgical calendar and of the special psalter used in the basilica, see *ibid.*, pp. 207–17 and 217–21.

[38] See Biblioteca Correr, Codice Cicogna 1602, fol. 61ᵛ; see also A.S.V., San Marco, Procuratia de Supra, Registro 98, fol. 24ʳ: "Sabbato post Pentecostes. In hac Vigilia et in die Psalmi cantantur cum omni pompa . . . Psalmi in primis Vesperis sunt: Levavi oculos meos, Ad te levavi, De profundis, Memento, Laudate nomen Domini."

falsobordone, and a senator, whose name I do not now remember, spoke to me and asked me about this innovation of singing *falsobordone* in the chapel of St. Mark's.[39]

Another set of psalms unique to St. Mark's is that for Second Vespers on the Feast of the Dedication of the Church of St. Mark, 8 October (*Credidi, Laetatus sum, Nisi Dominus, Confitebor tibi Domine . . . quoniam audisti*, and *Lauda Jerusalem*).[40] This set can be traced to Aquileia, where it was used for both the Dedication of the Church of Aquileia and for the Feast of the Transfiguration. Although settings of these psalms appear in collections by Rovetta (1662), Cavalli (1675), Monferrato (1675), and Sartorio (1680), the service was not set for double choir by composers connected with St. Mark's before Giovanni Croce's *Vespertina omnium solemnitatum psalmodia* (1597). Indeed, this service was the subject of an extended inquiry in 1589 concerning the entire problem of single-choir versus double-choir performance, an inquiry that will be discussed further below, since it has great significance for the role of double-choir Vespers psalms in the ceremonies of St. Mark's.

A fourth set of psalms used in St. Mark's and not in the Roman rite is that for Second Vespers on the Feasts of SS. Hermagoras and Fortunatus, the two legendary Aquileian saints, 12 July, and of St. Clement, 23 November (*Dixit Dominus, Confitebor, Beatus vir, Credidi*, and *Eripe me Domine ab homine malo*). The unusual psalm in the group, *Eripe me Domine*, seems never to have been set by the composers of the basilica in their published Vespers collections.

A number of other sets of psalms were used on different occasions in St. Mark's than in the Roman rite; these are all listed in Table 2. One set, however, should be noted in particular; the psalms for Second Vespers of Christmas (*Dixit Dominus, Confitebor, Beatus vir, De profundis*, and *Memento Domine David*) were used more extensively at St. Mark's than in the Roman rite, for the *Orationale* directed that they be performed every day between Christmas and the Octave of Epiphany; they were also to be used at Second Vespers of the Feast of the Purification.[41] These occasions include four important feasts for

---

[39] A.S.V., San Marco, Procuratia de Supra, Busta 88, fol. 60^r: "ha alterato nell'officiatura del primo Vespero della Santissima Trinità, quale lui voleva che si cantasse à doi chori, et non vi sono li salmi, ne mai sono statti fatti da alcuno delli Maestri di capella, et noi per non far scandolo li cantassimo in falso bordon et fui chiamato da un senator, che hora non mi soviene et mi interogò di questa novità, che si cantasse in Capella di San Marco falso bordon."

[40] See Biblioteca Correr, Codice Cicogna 1602, fol. 119^r; see also A.S.V., San Marco, Procuratia de Supra, Registro 98, fol. 53^r.

[41] See the statement in the *Orationale* at the end of Vespers on Christmas Day,

which the Roman rite specifically prescribes other sets of psalms: Second Vespers of Epiphany, First and Second Vespers of the Octave of Epiphany, and Second Vespers of the Purification. These uses are especially significant, for the service was included as a whole— psalms, antiphons, hymn, Magnificat antiphon, and Magnificat—in Adrian Willaert's *Sacri e santi salmi* of 1555, a collection that, as we shall see below, seems to clash with certain ceremonial rubrics of the basilica.

Of all of these variants between St. Mark's and Rome, however, only the *Vespero delli Cinque Laudate* seems to have assumed a sufficient identity in the minds of the composers of the basilica to warrant a special name as well as a special place in a number of Vespers prints, segregated from the rest of the psalms.

II

If one examines the musical collections in which the *Cinque Laudate* are found, one is struck immediately by a single facet of musical style. Every printed setting of the service that has come down to us is for eight voices, divided into two four-part choirs—or, in those settings published after 1597, two four-part choirs plus basso continuo. Moreover, the relative simplicity of the style, the exclusion of obvious soloistic writing, the setting of the texts as *salmi brevi*, and the inevitable changing of choirs at the ends of verses or at their mediant or flex immediately recalls the most famous Vespers collection in this style, the print of Willaert and Jachet of Mantua, published by Gardane as *Di Adriano e di Iachet. I Salmi appertinenti alli Vesperi per tutte le feste dell'anno, parte a versi, et parte spezzadi. Accomodati da cantare a uno et a duoi chori* . . . (Venice, 1550).[42] These works are, in short, *salmi spezzati* and are the clear descendants of those *salmi spezzati* of Willaert that formed the backbone of the monumental Gardane print.[43]

211

Biblioteca Correr, Codice Cicogna 1602, fol. 14ᵛ: "Praedictae antiphonae cum psalmis suis dicuntur in vesperis quotidie usque ad octavam Epiphaniae inclusive excepto quod in vigilia Epiphaniae dicitur antiphona O admirabile commercium." This rubric is also alluded to in one of the *ceremoniali* of St. Mark's; see A.S.V., San Marco, Procuratia de Supra, Registro 98, fol. 3ᵛ, in a statement about Vespers on Christmas Day: "Ad Vesperis: Antiphona Tecum principium cum suis psalmis ut in Orationali, quae in festivitatibus, quam in Octavis Natalis, Sancti Stephani, Sancti Ioannis, Sanctorum Innocentorum, iuxta ritum antiquum Nostrae Ecclesiae, et est Rubrica in Nostro Orationali sub: Tecum principium."

[42] The most recent study of this collection is contained in Mary Stuart Lewis, "Antonio Gardane and his Publications of Sacred Music, 1538–1555" (Ph.D. diss., Brandeis Univ., 1979), pp. 257–62.

[43] On the survival of *salmi spezzati* in the seventeenth century, see Jerome Roche's

Such uniformity and simplicity of style is, of course, highly unusual in the seventeenth century, when a bewildering variety of styles and media come to be used for Vespers psalms: the large-scale *stile concertato*, with its soloists, obbligato instruments, and choirs; small-scale *concerti;* and even virtuoso settings for solo voice and basso continuo.[44] And yet, the *Cinque Laudate* do not exhibit this variety, hinting that there was perhaps some rule, stricture, or tradition requiring that these psalms be set for double choir, in a retrospective musical style that would ally them with the earlier traditions of St. Mark's.

It is now over a quarter-century since Giovanni d'Alessi drew our attention to the "precursors of Willaert in the practice of *coro spezzato*," demonstrating that a tradition of double-choir singing was already current in the Veneto at the time of Willaert's print of 1550, and that the exclusive connection of double-choir psalms with Willaert and St. Mark's was simply a myth.[45] Like many myths, however, there is a grain of truth to this one, and the validity of the popular pairing of double-choir Vespers services with St. Mark's becomes clear if one examines the *ceremoniali* of the basilica.

Since these volumes are not generally known by musical scholars, perhaps a word about them is in order.[46] While there are over a dozen *ceremoniali* in Venice and Milan that describe the ceremonies of St.

212

---

discussion of the three such works by Monteverdi, "Monteverdi and the *Prima Prattica*," *The Monteverdi Companion*, ed. Denis Arnold and Nigel Fortune (London, 1968), pp. 186–89; *Idem*, "Northern Italian Liturgical Music in the Early Seventeenth Century, Its Evolution around 1600, and Its Development until the Death of Monteverdi" (Ph.D. diss., Cambridge Univ., 1967), pp. 200–12.

[44] For an exhaustive survey of these idioms, see Roche, "Northern Italian Liturgical Music in the Early Seventeenth Century"; for a more focused survey, see Jeffrey Kurtzman, "Some Historical Perspectives on the Monteverdi Vespers," *Studien zur italienisch-deutschen Musikgeschichte*, X, Analecta Musicologica, 15 (1975), 29–86; revised version published in Kurtzman, *Essays*, pp. 123–82.

[45] Giovanni d'Alessi, "Precursors of Adriano Willaert in the Practice of 'Coro Spezzato'," this JOURNAL, V (1952), 187–210; see also Anthony Carver, "The Psalms of Willaert and His North Italian Contemporaries," *Acta musicologica*, XLVII (1975), 270–83.

[46] The major *ceremoniali* of St. Mark's have been cited in a few studies on Venetian music; see Denis Arnold, "Vivaldi's Church Music," *Early Music*, I (1973), 66–74; Mario dal Tin, "Le cerimonie di Pasqua a Venezia nel 1564," *Jucunda Laudatio*, I–IV (1973), 132–42; and Bryant, "Liturgia e musica liturgica." From the literature in other areas of the humanities, see, *inter alia*, Staale Sinding-Larsen, *Christ in the Council Hall: Studies in the Religious Iconography of the Venetian Republic* (Rome, 1974); and Edward Muir, "The Doge as *Primus Inter Pares*: Interregnum Rites in Early Sixteenth-Century Venice," *Essays Presented to Myron P. Gilmore*, ed. Sergio Bertelli and Gloria Ramakus (Florence, 1978), I, 146–60.

Mark's,[47] a comparison of them reveals that they are almost all copies of just two major texts, which were composed in the sixteenth and seventeenth centuries. The first of these texts, the *Rituum ecclesiasticorum caerimoniale*, was assembled by master of ceremonies Bartolomeo Bonifacio in 1564. It was recopied sometime in the 1590s, and plans were made to publish it; it was then copied again in 1646 and presented for inspection to the Roman inquisition, possibly in preparation for another attempt at publication; and a final copy was made in 1752, this time more as an historical document than for actual use. The signatures in the front of the original copy show that it was handed from one master of ceremonies to the next until 1677. These signatures, as well as the presence of the volume in liturgical inventories and other church documents, suggest that it served as the ecclesiastical authority for the last part of the sixteenth and the first half of the seventeenth century.[48] In the following year, 1678, canon Giovanni Pace finished the other major text, the *Ceremoniale magnum sive Raccolta universale di tutte le ceremonie spettanti alla ducal regia capella di San Marco*, which he had been compiling since the 1640s. Later copies of Pace's text were made in 1695, 1732, and 1745.[49]

213

    Throughout both *ceremoniali* we find directions for the performance of Vespers by two choirs on specific days of the year, generally on those feasts with the rank of Greater Doubles in the liturgical calendar of the *Orationale*.[50] It is clear that this sort of service was not

[47] For a discussion of these volumes, see Moore, "Vespers," pp. 109–19.

[48] There are at least five copies of Bonifacio's *ceremoniale* in Venetian libraries: Biblioteca nazionale marciana, Cod. lat. III–172 (=2276); A.S.V., Consulatore in Jure, Registro 555; A.S.V., San Marco, Procuratia de Supra, Registri 98 and 99; and Biblioteca Correr, Codice Cicogna 2768. For the bibliographic details on the manuscripts and their interrelationships, see Moore, "Vespers," pp. 110–12 and 114–17.

[49] There are at least six copies of Pace's text in Venice and Milan: Milan, Biblioteca ambrosiana, MS A. 328 inf.; Venice, Biblioteca nazionale marciana, Cod. it. VII–1269 (=9573) and Cod. it. VII–396 (=7423); Venice, Biblioteca Correr, Codici Cicogna 2769, 2770, and 1295. For bibliographic details, see Moore, "Vespers," pp. 110–13.

[50] In his own *cerimoniale*, Pace quite specifically states that he is speaking of two polyphonic choirs of four voices each; see, *inter alia*, Biblioteca ambrosiana, MS A. 328 inf., fol. 44ʳ: "La Vigilia del Corpus Domini s'apre la Palla, si canta Vespro in 5.0 da un Canonico cui *per Turnum*, et dalli Cantori à due Cori li Salmi à 8." Bonifacio's standard statement might seem ambiguous at first, for he does not specify the number of voice parts involved but only describes the performance as being by two choirs; see A.S.V., Consulatore in Jure, Registro 555, fol. 68ᵛ (ceremonies for the Feast of the Assumption): "In primis Vesperis psalmi omnes Laudate. In secundis Vesperis psalmi de Dominica, qui cantantur in utrisque Vesperis a Cantoribus in duobus Choris." However, since he elsewhere specifies *alternatim* performance between a polyphonic choir and a plainchant choir (*ibid.*, fol. 26ᵛ: "et cantato Magnificat per

to be performed at the whim of the *maestro di cappella* or whenever the *Orationale* specified the psalms for which we have double-choir settings. It was, rather, a liturgical necessity for certain feasts of the church year. Of about one hundred fifty Vespers services per year that demanded the presence of the singers of the *cappella*, approximately fifty are specified as double-choir services in the *ceremoniali*.[51]

There are several attempts within Bonifacio's *ceremoniale* to gather the feasts demanding double-choir Vespers into lists. For example, at the end of the tome, a number of these feasts are assembled into a list entitled "Days on which Vespers are sung in two choirs."[52] This list is described as part of the *tariffa cantorum* of Gioseffe Zarlino, and it is in the hand of Nicolò Fausti, Zarlino's *maestro di coro*; however, since it does not include all the feasts for which the body of the *ceremoniale* specifies double-choir music and, moreover, is not copied into the later exemplars of the *ceremoniale*, it is difficult to tell how accurate it is or how long it was in effect. Clearly, no one felt the need to preserve it on the numerous occasions when the volume was re-copied. A more important list is in Bonifacio's own hand. It contains all the feasts for which the *ceremoniale* specifies double-choir Vespers, but its title is somewhat different: "Days on which the *Pala* is opened, when psalms

214

Cantores et Chorum alternatim") and also describes plainchant performance (*ibid.*, fol. 46ᵛ: "Olim fiebat cum Cantoribus, et Organis hodie vero in Cantu plano sine Organis") as well as contrasting single-choir and double-choir performance (*ibid.*, fol. 48ᵛ: "Vesperi cantantur in duobus Choris Cantorum si possunt quod non sint impediti ad Convivium Domini Ducis, sin autem in uno Choro cantantur"), it seems fair to say that his prescription of performance "a duobus Choris Cantorum" refers to performance by two polyphonic choirs, most likely in settings for eight voices.

[51] These figures are approximate; I have calculated the number of Vespers services at which the singers of St. Mark's were to be present in the basilica from several lists of musicians' duties. The most important lists are those from 1515, copied over again in 1564 and in 1646 (A.S.V., San Marco, Procuratia de Supra, Registro 98, fols. 68ʳ–70ʳ); from 1677 (Biblioteca Correr, Codice Cicogna 3118, fascicoli 44–50); from 1678 (Biblioteca ambrosiana, MS A. 328 inf., fols. 163ʳ–165ᵛ); from 1755 (A.S.V., San Marco, Procuratia de Supra, Registro 99, fols. 409ʳ–413ʳ); and 1761 (A.S.V., San Marco, Procuratia de Supra, Busta 91, large unpaginated folio; manuscript copies of this list are in A.S.V., San Marco, Procuratia de Supra, Registro 100, fols. 358ʳ–361ʳ).

The days on which double-choir Vespers were required were originally listed on a large *Tariffa cantorum* that was kept in the sacristy of St. Mark's and has not survived. Nonetheless, a fairly accurate count of these feasts can be gathered by paging through the *ceremoniali* of Bonifacio and Pace feast by feast, although because of the elaborate detail which both provide, neither can be counted upon to be completely accurate.

[52] Biblioteca nazionale marciana, Cod. lat. III-172 (=2276), fol. 114ʳ: "Dies in quibus cantantur ad vesperas duobus choris. . . . Trata dalla tarifa del Maestro di capella Messer Iseppo Zerlino."

are sung by the singers."[53] At first this title seems somewhat enigmatic; just what is the connection between the opening of an altarpiece and the performance of psalms by singers of the *cappella?* The situation is clarified, however, in Giovanni Pace's *ceremoniale;* for at the end of a list of the days and services at which the singers must be present in St. Mark's, Pace writes the following rubric: "Every time the *Pala* is opened, the singers must sing Vespers in two choirs, with psalms set for eight voices."[54]

The *Pala* to which Bonifacio and Pace refer is, of course, the famous *Pala d'oro,* the large gold altarpiece that is the central jewel of the basilica. (See Figure 2). Constructed in Constantinople in 976, the *Pala* was enlarged by gold panels in the twelfth century, decorated with jewels after the sack of Constantinople in the thirteenth, and placed in its present frame in the fourteenth. On *feriae* and minor feasts, the *Pala d'oro* was not visible; it was hidden behind a special ferial altarpiece, painted by Paolo Veneziano and his sons in 1345. On the major feasts of the church year, however, the *Pala d'oro* was opened by an impressive mechanism that folded up the ferial altarpiece and lifted it above the *Pala d'oro,* at the same time as it unfolded the *Pala d'oro* for the populace to see.[55]

Just when the practice began of pairing the opening of the *Pala d'oro* with the performance of Vespers for eight voices in two choirs is difficult to say. Pace gives only a very vague explanation: "The singers used to be obligated to sing the *Te Deum.* The Most Excellent Procurators freed them from this duty on the condition that they should sing psalms for eight voices, in two choirs, every time the *Pala d'oro* was opened."[56] It must have been before Bonifacio compiled his *ceremoniale* of 1564, however, for he states that while psalms had once been performed in plainchant on major feasts, they are now done in two choirs.[57] Moreover, he alludes briefly to this agreement between singers and Procurators in a document dealing with ceremonies on the

215

---

[53] *Ibid.,* fols. 46^v–47^r: "Diebus quibus Palla aperitur. Quando cantant*ur* Psalmi p*er* Cantores."

[54] Biblioteca ambrosiana, MS A. 328 inf., fol. 164^v: "Ogni volta, che si apre la Palla sono obligati Cantare à due Chori con li Salmi à 8. li Vesperi."

[55] On the *Pala d'oro* and the mechanics of opening it, see Rodolfo Gallo, *Il Tesoro di S. Marco e la sua storia* (Venice, n.d.).

[56] Biblioteca ambrosiana, MS A. 328 inf., fol. 208^r: "Li Cantori erano obligati à cantar il Te Deum. Furono licentiati dalli Ecc*ellentissi*mi Proc*urat*ori da questo obligo, cum hoc, che cantassero li Salmi à Otto, in due Chori, ogni volta, che fosse aperta la Palla."

[57] A.S.V., San Marco, Procuratia de Supra, Registro 98, fols. 70^r–70^v, 30^v.

216

Figure 2. The *Pala d'oro* of St. Mark's

feasts of the Apparition of the Body of St. Mark and the Nativity of
St. John the Baptist.[58]

[58] A.S.V., Consulatore in Jure, Registro 555, fol. 63^r: "Quando vero Cantores
sunt licentiati propter Te Deum laudamus a Dominibus Procuratoribus loco Te Deum

We have several lists from different periods of the days on which the *Pala d'oro* was opened and, hence, double-choir music performed.[59] And while there are a number of discrepancies between them, the majority agree on one point: every service for which the *Orationale* prescribes the *Cinque Laudate* is also a service for which the *Pala d'oro* was opened and a double-choir Vespers required.[60] Thus, according to the liturgical strictures of the basilica, it would not have been possible to perform the *Cinque Laudate* in any manner other than an eight-voice setting for two choirs, the very medium for which it is set in the printed collections.

The most important implication of the relationship between the liturgical calendar, the *Pala d'oro*, and double-choir Vespers psalms is, of course, not merely the light shed upon the *Vespero delli Cinque*

---

cantant*ur* a duobus Choris psalmi in primis Vesperis; psalmi vero de Apostolis, ut quando*que* accidit, sed nunc in choro in utris*que* Vesperis san*cti* Joan*ni*s psalmi ca*n*tant in duobus Choris."

The habitual pairing of the opening of the *Pala d'oro* with the performance of double-choir psalms set for eight voices is mentioned in a number of other documents as well. In his description of Vespers on Ascension Day, Pace states that "s'apre la Palla, e si canta Vespro in 5.o, e con li Cantori à due Chori con li Salmi à 8., cosi anche si fà ogni volta, che s'apre la Palla" (Biblioteca nazionale marciana, Cod. it. VII–1296 [=9573] fol. 45ʳ). Moreover, an act of the Procurators of 14 June 1615, which details fines for musicians who miss services of various types, establishes special fines for certain days of the year when the Signoria is not present in church but the *Pala d'oro* is still opened and double-choir psalms are sung: "nell'altre festività, o giorni, che la Seren*issi*ma Sig*no*ria non viene in Chiesa, et che si apre la Palla et si canta a doi Chori" (A.S.V., San Marco, Procuratia de Supra, Busta 91, Processo 208, fascicolo 1).

[59] These overlap with the lists of days and services cited above in note 51, for a number of these lists include designations for the opening of the *Pala d'oro* and for double-choir Vespers performance. The lists with this information are Biblioteca nazionale marciana, Cod. lat. III–172 (=2276), fol. 114ʳ, dated 1588–91; A.S.V., San Marco, Procuratia de Supra, Registro 98, fols. 69ᵛ–70ʳ, dated 1646; Biblioteca Correr, Codice Cicogna 3118, fascicoli 44–50, dated 1677; Biblioteca ambrosiana, MS A. 328 inf., information collated from the entire volume, dated 1678; A.S.V., San Marco, Procuratia de Supra, Registro 99, fols. 409ʳ–13ʳ, dated 1755; and A.S.V., San Marco, Procuratia de Supra, Busta 91, large unpaginated folio, dated 1761.

[60] A number of these sources are rather casual affairs which do not seem to have been put together with much care and are replete with additions and marginal notes. Nonetheless, taking the feasts for which the *Cinque Laudate* are prescribed in the *Orationale*, the opening of the *Pala d'oro* and a double-choir Vespers service is prescribed for each feast in at least half of the six sources listed above in n. 59, as follows: Vigil of Christmas (prescribed in 3 sources); Vigil of Epiphany (3 sources); Vigil of Ascension (4); Vigil of Pentecost (6); Second Vespers of Corpus Christi (4); First Vespers of the Purification (6); Vigil of the Assumption (5); Vigil of the Nativity of the B.V.M. (5); Vigil of the Conception of the B.V.M. (5); Vigil of All Saints' Day (3); Holy Saturday (not included in the sources).

Laudate, but that shed upon the entire tradition of *salmi spezzati* at St. Mark's. There was clearly a great demand for eight-voice Vespers psalms in two choirs, for Bonifacio's *ceremoniale* lists over fifty services per year on which the *Pala d'oro* was opened, and the Doge, the Procurators, or the Senate could request a double-choir Vespers on other days if they wished.[61] It seems certain that the prints of *salmi spezzati* by the *maestri* of St. Mark's, which begin with Willaert and last through three-quarters of the seventeenth century, were printed for these occasions and that, far from being works for minor feasts, which their retrospective style might suggest, they were probably used on some of the most important days of the year.

At this point, one should note that the documents seem to clash with our traditional view of the most famous Vespers repertoire from the Seicento at St. Mark's: the large works in the *stile concertato* in Monteverdi's *Selva morale e spirituale* (Venice: Magni, 1640) and *Messa a quattro voci e Salmi* (Venice: Vincenti, 1650), as well as the equally elaborate compositions in Giovanni Rovetta's *Messa e Salmi* (Venice: Vincenti, 1639) and Francesco Cavalli's *Musiche sacre* (Venice: Vincenti, 1656). It is difficult to believe that these elaborate works were not written for major feasts. Moreover, if we look for genuine, retrospective *salmi spezzati* among Monteverdi's works for St. Mark's, we come up with only three compositions: the *Credidi* and *Memento a otto voci da capella* from the *Selva morale* and the *Dixit Dominus a 8 voci alla breve* from the *Messa a quattro voci e Salmi*. Are we to assume that these small works were written for major feasts while the elaborate *concertato* repertoire was performed on unimportant days? Not quite. The *concertato* pieces certainly could have been used on the numerous saints' days throughout the year when the *Pala d'oro* was not opened; indeed, it is probably significant that both Monteverdi and Cavalli included the hymns from the *Commune sanctorum* in their large Venetian Vespers prints. At this point, however, we could certainly do with an *explication du texte* from Pace himself, telling us exactly what he meant by the phrase "singing Vespers in two choirs with the psalms set for eight voices." He seems to imply that the entire service is to be sung in this manner, and the collections of *salmi spezzati* are the

218

---

[61] See A.S.V., Consulatore in Jure, Registro 555, fol. 64ᵛ: (on the Feast of the Visitation) "In secundis vero Vesperis cantantur psalmi a duobus Choris Cantorum si placet Magistro Chori, id est ad petitionem Serenissimi Principis vel Dominicorum Procuratorum." *Ibid.*, fol. 67ʳ: (on the Feast of the Transfiguration) "In secundis Vesperis aliquando cantantur psalmi a duobus Choris Cantorum ad petitionem Dominorum Procuratorum seu Senatorum, sed ordinarie non cantantur psalmi a Cantoribus nisi ut supra."

only ones that could satisfy this requirement. Furthermore, there is no evidence from any of the ceremonial books or documents that mixed performances, with some psalms in *canto figurato* and others in plainchant or *falsobordone*, were a feature of St. Mark's as they were of such provincial centers as San Petronio in Bologna or Santa Maria Maggiore in Bergamo.[62]

By the mid-seventeenth century, however, there may have been another way around this regulation. There are, of course, large *concertato* works by both Monteverdi and Cavalli set for two choirs. *Dixit Dominus, Laudate Dominum omnes gentes*, and the Magnificat are set for two choirs in Monteverdi's *Selva morale*, and those three items plus *Lauda Jerusalem* are set for two choirs in Cavalli's *Musiche sacre*. Thus, it may be that the performance of the first and last psalms of a service, plus the Magnificat, in settings for two choirs constituted enough of a gesture to satisfy liturgical requirements and to allow the large *concertato* works to be used on the days when the *Pala d'oro* was opened, even if the intermediate psalms were sung in smaller settings.[63] We must recognize, however, that there are a number of important Vespers services for which the seventeenth-century repertoire provides only settings of *salmi spezzati*: Second Vespers of Christmas and Pentecost, Easter Vespers, First Vespers of Corpus Christi, as well as all of those occasions when the *Cinque Laudate* were used.

219

The import of this discussion should be clear. It seems that the most important feasts at St. Mark's did not necessarily require the most elaborate music. On the contrary, on many of the most solemn days of the year, the pull of tradition seems to have been more telling than the desire for lavish display, and the finest tribute the *cappella marciana* could pay the city of Venice was to invoke the brilliant days of Willaert, Rore, and Zarlino and, as Pace puts it, "cantare à due Chori con li Salmi à 8. li Vesperi."

While Pace's rubric on the correlation of double-choir Vespers services with the opening of the *Pala d'oro* was undoubtedly operant during the seventeenth century, there are signs that it might not yet have been strictly enforced at the time of Bonifacio's *ceremoniale*; for

---

[62] See James Armstrong, "The Vespers and Magnificats of Maurizio Cazzati" (Ph.D. diss., Harvard Univ., 1969); and Jerome Roche, "Music at Santa Maria Maggiore in Bergamo, 1614–43," *Music and Letters*, XLVII (1966), 296–312.

[63] Denis Stevens has also noted that the only items to receive large double-choir settings in the *stile concertato* are the first and last psalms of a service plus the Magnificat. See Stevens, *Monteverdi: Sacred, Secular, and Occasional Music* (Rutherford, N.J., 1978), p. 83.

there are a number of inconsistencies in Bonifacio's volume as well as some points where Pace's rubric seems to clash with extant sixteenth-century repertoire. For example, on Second Vespers for Corpus Christi, one of the feasts for which Bonifacio himself states that the *Pala d'oro* is to be opened,[64] he also states that the *Cinque Laudate* are to be sung in plainchant.[65] Moreover, we have the problematic example of Willaert's large compendium of 1555 for Vespers and Compline: *I sacri e santi salmi che si cantano a vespro et compieta, con li suoi hinni, responsorii, et benedicamus, composti da l'eccellentissimo musico Adriano Vvillaert a uno choro et a quatro voci* (Venice: Gardane, 1555 and 1561; Rampazetto, 1565; "li figliuoli di Antonio Gardano," 1571). This collection contains two complete Vespers services, one for Second Vespers of Christmas and the other for the B.V.M.; for each of the services, only alternate psalm verses are set for a single four-part choir.

While there would have been plenty of use at St. Mark's for a single-choir setting of the Vespers of the Blessed Virgin, the publication of a single-choir version of Christmas Vespers is strange. For, as I documented above in note 41, Second Vespers of Christmas had a special place in the liturgy of St. Mark's, and the service was repeated every day for both feasts and *feriae* through the Octave of Epiphany. Moreover, of all the days on which it was used, only the feasts of the Holy Innocents and St. Silvester as well as the ferial days would have required a service for a single polyphonic choir; the other days demanded double-choir settings, at least in theory. Thus, it may be that the tradition of pairing a double-choir Vespers service with the opening of the *Pala d'oro* was not strictly followed at this early a date. It is also possible, of course, that the print was not destined for St. Mark's; after all, the publication of four editions in a little over a decade points to a large commercial market.

At any rate, we do know that by the end of the century the liturgical schedule of double-choir Vespers was taken seriously and was not just an abstract plan in the ceremonial books. For we have records of an inquest that took place in 1589, which show not only that the schedule was followed strictly, but that musicians were quite conscious of the appropriateness of different styles of music for

220

---

[64] A.S.V., San Marco, Procuratia de Supra, Registro 98, fol. 70ʳ.

[65] A.S.V., San Marco, Procuratia de Supra, Registro 98, fol. 35ᵛ: (on Second Vespers for Corpus Christi) "In *secundis Vesperis Antipho*na Cenantibus cu*m* reliquis, psalmi omnes Laudate in cantu plano."

different feasts.[66] It seems that a liturgical calendar (the *tariffa cantorum*) hung in the sacristy of St. Mark's, on which were noted the obligations of the singers; and a red cross was placed beside those days on which a double-choir Vespers was to be sung. However, on 8 October, the feast of the Dedication of the Church of St. Mark, no red cross appeared on the calendar, and a dispute arose between the master of ceremonies and the singers over whether double-choir settings were to be used;[67] this was a particular problem, since the service was unique to St. Mark's, and it seems that one psalm, the *Confitebor angelorum*, had never been set for two choirs. When the master of ceremonies asked the singers to sing four psalms in double-choir settings and the missing one in *falsobordone*, they refused and walked out of the church. During the inquest, they explained that *falsobordone* was only used during Lent at St. Mark's and was otherwise a style of music not fitting for the chapel of the Most Serene Prince. Furthermore, they were not pleased to be asked to perform double-choir music on a day they insisted was outside the canon. As one of them testified:

> It is not the custom to sing this service in two choirs, nor does one of the psalms exist [in a double-choir setting] as do those for all the other Vespers services set by the hand of Messer Adrian. If this had been the custom, he would have set it. However, his successor Messer Ciprian did not set it either; nor did the present Maestro Messer Padre Isepo Zarlino, and if he had wanted it sung by two choirs, he would have set it.[68]

If documents reveal that *salmi spezzati* were connected with the liturgical practices of St. Mark's to a startling degree, they have some equally surprising revelations about the manner in which these pieces were performed. The popular concept is, of course, one of equal choirs of singers tossing the psalm verses back and forth between the double choirlofts of St. Mark's. There is evidence, however, that this concept may be wrong on all counts; that is, that the choirs were not

221

[66] The records of the inquest of 1589 are in A.S.V., San Marco, Procuratia de Supra, Busta 91, Processo 208, fascicolo 1.

[67] The terminology used in the inquest contrasts psalms described as *ugnolo*, a Venetian term which is the equivalent of *unico* or *singolo*, and psalms described alternately as *canto doppio* or *à dui chori*.

[68] A.S.V., San Marco, Procuratia de Supra, Busta 91, Processo 208, fascicolo 1, fol. 20[v] [16 Ottobre 1589]: "perche non è solito il cantarlo doppio ne manco vi è il salmo si come sono tutti li altri vespori a dui cori fatti *per* mano de Messe*r* Adria*n* che se questo fosse statto ordi*n*ario mancandovi un sol salmo lo havrebe fatto ne manco lo ha fatto Messe*r* Ciprian successor suo ne il *pre*sente Maestro Messe*r* Padr*e* Isepo perche se l'havesse voluto che'l se cantasse a dui cori lo haverebbe fatto."

equal and that the psalms were often sung from a structure other than the lofts. On the first point, our information comes from Bonifacio, who writes the following passage:

> On the singing of psalms in all solemnities: In all solemnities, the psalms used to be sung by the small chapel and by singers who sang from memory. It is thought, and it is said that they were sung in the Gregorian manner. Today this mode of singing has gone out of use, and the singers of the large chapel sing all the psalms and all the other items; and they sing these psalms divided into two choirs, namely, four singers in one choir and all the rest in the other, since the small chapel no longer exists.[69]

This is not the only document to describe this sort of performance. In a description of Vespers on the Vigil of Pentecost, Bonifacio writes:

222

> After the midday meal, at the usual hour, when the *Pala d'oro* has been opened ceremoniously, Vespers are sung with the greatest decorum, as is indicated in our books. The psalms all begin with *Laudate* and are said under this antiphon: *Veni Sancte Spiritus*; and the singers sing these psalms divided into two choirs, namely four singers in one choir, and all the rest in the other, as is the custom in solemnities.[70]

While the evidence is not airtight, these documents, plus a host of others which describe the same phenomenon, do suggest that the practice of pitting a solo quartet against a large *ripieno* choir was not the invention of the early seventeenth century but was practiced in St. Mark's well before the *concertato* works of Croce and the late works of Giovanni Gabrieli. Indeed, the prints of Croce and Gabrieli may merely make explicit a practice that was already considered a tradition in 1564 and may well have been used as early as the 1550 *salmi spezzati* of Willaert.[71]

---

[69] A.S.V., San Marco, Procuratia de Supra, Registro 98, fol. 70ʳ–70ᵛ; also fol. 30ᵛ: "De psalmis canendis in omnibus solemnitatibus. In omnibus solemnitatibus, olim psalmi cantabantur a capella parva, et a cantoribus qui ex practica cantant, si habeantur sic dicebantur cantare, more Georgiano, hodie hic mos canendi abijt in dissuetudinem et Cantores maioris capellae cantant omnes Psalmos, et reliqua, et psalmos cantant divisi in duobus choris, videlicet quatuor cantores in uno choro, et reliqui omnes, in altero, quia capella parva non extat."

[70] A.S.V., San Marco, Procuratia de Supra, Registro 98, fol. 26ᵛ: "Post prandium hora solita aperta solemni Palla, Vesperi cantantur cum omni pompa, ut in Nostris Libris. Psalmi omnes Laudate, sub hac Antiphona: Veni Sancte Spiritus, et Psalmi cantant Cantores divisi in 2. Choris, videlicet 4 Cantores in uno Choro, et reliqui omnes in altero ut moris est in solemnitatibus."

[71] While Bonifacio's "quatuor cantores in uno choro et reliqui omnes in altero" might seem at first to echo the "a uno choro et a quatro voci," which forms part of the

Another point that must be re-examined is the placement of musicians for *salmi spezzati*. The structure mentioned most often in the documents is, surprisingly enough, not the choirlofts, but an octagonal platform on the floor of the church called the *bigonzo* or "tub," the very structure drawn by Canaletto in his famous sketch of the singers of St. Mark's.[72] The most striking statement regarding the *bigonzo* is the one given by Giovanni Pace for Vespers on the Vigil of Epiphany:

> The *Pala d'oro* is opened on this day as well as on both offices of the feast itself. Vespers are celebrated by five priests, and psalms in eight parts are sung in two choirs in the *bigonzo*.[73]

Moreover, on a large ecclesiastical calendar, first drawn up in 1515 and printed a number of times through 1761, several feasts have the description "Vespero à due Cori con Palla nel Bigonzo."[74] Canaletto's famous sketch shows the capacity of the structure. Eleven people are squeezed into the space—probably not enough to perform a double-choir Vespers with ease if two equal choirs were demanded. However, if one choir is to consist of only four voices, the eleven or twelve people who could fit into the *bigonzo* might well suffice for a performance.[75]

The manner in which *salmi spezzati* were performed at St. Mark's, their relationship to the *Pala d'oro*, and the control that the liturgical calendar exerted on both—all of these factors hint at a broader artistic principle: that musical style at St. Mark's in the late Cinquecento and the Seicento was not the result of free artistic design but, on the

223

---

descriptive title of Willaert's *I sacri e santi salmi*, I do not think that the two are related. On the contrary, I would see Willaert's title as a mere variant of the designation "a quattro voci a uno choro," as Gardane described his 1555 publication of the psalms of Dominico Phinot, a collection which, like Willaert's, consists of alternate psalm verses set for a single four-part choir. Bonifacio, on the other hand, is always careful to differentiate between true double-choir performance (i.e., two polyphonic choirs) and *alternatim* performance (see above, n. 50), and I think he is describing two four-part choirs here, one of soloists, and one with many singers per part.

[72] See W. G. Constable, *Canaletto: Giovanni Antonio Canal, 1697–1768* (Oxford, 1962), item 558.

[73] Biblioteca ambrosiana, MS A. 328 inf., fol. 14ʳ: "La Vigilia dell'Epifania si apre la Palla hoggi, et à tutti due li offitij di dimani. Si cantano li Vesperi in 5.0 et dalli Cantori à due Chori li Salmi à 8 in Bigonzo."

[74] A.S.V., San Marco, Procuratia de Supra, Busta 91, large unpaginated folio.

[75] Perhaps the most exact description of the use of the *bigonzo* for *salmi spezzati* comes in a passage from one of the eighteenth-century *ceremoniali* in which the singers are directed to sing double-choir psalms in the *bigonzo* every time the *Pala d'oro* is opened; the only option they are given is to sing the psalms from either side of the

contrary, was highly dependent on liturgical function and on past Venetian tradition. Indeed, when the *Vespero delli Cinque Laudate* was performed before the *Pala d'oro* in settings for *cori spezzati*, three cornerstones of the Venetian cultural heritage were on display. A liturgy from Aquileia was performed before an altar from Byzantium in an idiom that recalled the greatest days of the Venetian musical establishment. And surely, in the minds of Venetians, for whom the seventeenth century was an age of uncertainty and decline, the entire service was a majestic symbol of the past glories of the *Serenissima Repubblica*.

The University of Chicago

224

---

altar of St. Clement during the summer when the *bigonzo* is too hot. See A.S.V., Consulatore in Jure, Registro 557, fol. 358ᵛ: "Ogni volta che si apre la Palla li Cantori cantano à due Cori li Salmi à Otto nel Bigonzo, senza istrumenti; nell'estate, si è introdotto un'uso di cantare all'Altare di S. Clemente divisi mettà per parte, per aver qualche respiro dal caldo, che li tormenta nel Bigonzo. Ma prima di far questo dimandano permissione al Maestro di Coro."

The Descending Tetrachord:
An Emblem of Lament

ELLEN ROSAND

DURING the fourth and fifth decades of the seventeenth century, a particular bass-line pattern, the descending minor tetrachord, came to assume a quite specific function associated almost exclusively with a single expressive genre, the lament. In the present study we shall explore the reasons behind this association — leaving aside, for the moment, the complicated issue of the origins of the pattern itself and its relation to the terms *passacaglia* and *ciaccona*.[1] These reasons involve the aesthetic premises of early opera and the attempts by composers to underscore the dramatic centrality of the lament within the context of a continuous dramatic-musical flow.

At least since the drama of Greek antiquity, the lament had enjoyed a special status; an emotional climax followed by a resolution of the action, it was a soliloquy, a moment of particularly intense expression within the movement of a narrative structure. And in later, nontheatrical literature, the lament *topos* retained its distinct identity. In the poetry of Ovid or Ariosto, to cite two influential

An earlier version of this paper was presented at the Annual Meeting of the American Musicological Society in Los Angeles in November, 1975. It is part of a larger study of the lament, a project undertaken with the aid of a Younger Humanist Fellowship from the National Endowment for the Humanities (1974-75).

[1] Several investigations of the origins and meaning of *passacaglia* and *ciaccona* have touched upon the relationship of these terms to the descending tetrachord bass pattern. See especially Wolfgang Osthoff, "Die frühesten Erscheinungsformen der Passacaglia in der italienischen Musik des 17. Jahrhunderts," *Atti del congresso internazionale di musiche popolari mediterranee e del convegno dei bibliotecari musicali* (Palermo, 1959), pp. 275 ff.; Thomas Walker, "Ciaccona and Passacaglia: Remarks on their Origin and Early History," *Journal of the American Musicological Society*, XXI (1968), 300 ff.; and Richard Hudson, "Further Remarks on the Passacaglia and Ciaccona," *Journal of the American Musicological Society*, XXIII (1970), 302 ff.

examples, it provided the occasion for special formal development, the display of particularly expressive rhetoric and affective imagery. Whether devised as a series of independent emotional epistles, as in Ovid's *Heroides*, or as an intensely moving outburst controlled by Ariosto's sophisticated poetic art, as in Olympia's plaint in *Orlando Furioso* (X, 20-34), the lament was set apart.

The librettists and composers of early opera, as heirs to this tradition, continued to acknowledge the special position of the lament and to distinguish it from the narrative flow of its dramatic context. Librettists imposed greater formality on the lament through the use of more strongly metered and rhymed texts in which especially affective lines often recurred as refrains. And composers interpreted these texts with greater freedom, repeating or otherwise enhancing the most affective words or phrases through melodic sequence, dissonance, or textural conflicts, and often providing an overall tonal coherence in order to create structural self-sufficiency.[2]

227

One of the most effective, and certainly the most influential, of early operatic laments was Monteverdi's lament of Arianna, found in his opera *Arianna* with a libretto by Ottavio Rinuccini, performed in Mantua in 1608. The musical isolation of this lament from its narrative context was recognized almost immediately, as we know from a contemporary description of the opera's performance, which singled out for special notice the abandoned Arianna's moving lament.[3] This perception was confirmed by the publication of a number of monodic Arianna laments, beginning in 1613,[4] and, most

---

2 Cf., for example, the settings by Peri and Caccini of Orfeo's lament, "Non piango e non sospiro," in scene 2 of Rinuccini's libretto for *Euridice*, and Monteverdi's setting of the parallel passage from Striggio's libretto for *Orfeo*, Act II, "Tu sei morta." For modern transcriptions of the Peri and Monteverdi settings, see Nino Pirrotta, "Monteverdi e i problemi dell'opera," *Studi sul teatro veneto fra Rinascimento ed età barocca*, ed. Maria Teresa Muraro (Florence, 1971), pp. 325 ff. Caccini's lament appears in the excerpt from *Euridice* edited by Robert Eitner, *Publikationen älterer . . . Musikwerke* (Berlin and Leipzig, 1873-1905), X, 59.

3 "[*Arianna*] being performed by both men and women who excelled in the art of singing, succeeded most admirably in the lament that Ariadne, abandoned by Theseus, sang on the rock; it was performed with so much feeling [*affetto*] and in such a pathetic manner [*si pietosi modi*] that not a single listener remained unmoved, nor did a single lady fail to shed some small tear at her plaint." Federico Follino, *Compendio . . .* (Mantua, 1608), quoted in Angelo Solerti, *Gli albori del melodramma* (Milan, Palermo, and Naples, 1904), II, 145.

4 Monodic settings of Rinuccini's text were published by Severo Bonini (1613) and Francesco Costa (1626). Pellegrino Possenti's "Pianto d'Arianna" (1623), is a

conclusively, by the composer's own reworking of the piece as a madrigal,[5] his publication of the monody,[6] and his adaptation of this madrigal to a sacred text.[7]

Arianna's lament derives its structure from a variety of elements, both textual and musical: from refrains, from recurrent rising and falling of intensity, from shifting between sections of opposition and coordination of voice and bass line, from sequences and other literary and musical patterns. The principal source of its extraordinary affective power lies in Monteverdi's projection of Arianna's thoughts through flexible control of a number of musical elements in unpredictable combinations of contrast and recurrence. The lament is self-contained but it is not closed; it is not an aria. Its organization develops out of the internal exigencies of the text, and no superimposed formal structure determines its shape. Arias, on the other hand, being fixed, predetermined musical structures, were inappropriate to the expression of the uncontrolled passion of a lament.

Indeed, a clear distinction between lament and aria persisted for some time. This is particularly apparent in the fourth and fifth monody books of Sigismondo d'India, published in 1621 and 1623. Primarily, these volumes contain pieces marked "aria," pieces which are characterized by strophic structure, brevity, and a simple melodic and rhythmic style; a number of them utilize preexistent patterns such as the *romanesca*. In addition to these arias, however, there are five pieces labeled "lamento in stile recitativo" (laments in dramatic style) which are highly expressive and irregular musical settings of lengthy narrative texts written by the composer himself.[8]

228

---

setting of a text by Giambattista Marino, evidently inspired by Rinuccini's example. In addition to these laments of Arianna, Monteverdi's inspired a large number of monodic laments for other characters including Olympia, Dido, Apollo, Jason, Orpheus, Erminia, and the Virgin Mary. See Nigel Fortune, "Monteverdi and the 'Seconda Prattica,'" *The Monteverdi Companion*, ed. Denis Arnold and Nigel Fortune (London and New York, 1968), pp. 203 ff.

[5] *Il sesto libro de madrigali* (Venice, 1614).

[6] *Lamento d'Arianna . . . con due Lettere Amorose in genere rappresentativo* (Venice, 1623); modern edition by Gian Francesco Malipiero, *Tutte le opere di Claudio Monteverdi* (Asolo, 1926-42), XI.

[7] "Iam moriar filli," in *Selva morale e spirituale* (Venice, 1640).

[8] For a discussion of these laments, see Nigel Fortune, "Sigismondo d'India, An Introduction to his Life and Works," *Proceedings of the Royal Musical Association*,

But perhaps only one other lament of the early Baroque period approaches Arianna's in affective impact, as well as in significance for the development of the genre. That is Monteverdi's setting of another Rinuccini text, the "Lament of the Nymph," published in the eighth book of madrigals in 1638.[9] As in Arianna's lament, the affective exigencies of its text determine its musical development. However, it is constructed over a descending tetrachord ostinato pattern, which contributes a new dimension: its clearly perceptible shape imparts a firm foundation to the bass line, thus increasing the opportunities for conflict with the voice, one of the principal means of affective intensification in recitative. In exploiting the possibilities of opposition between voice and bass line, Monteverdi's setting of the "Lament of the Nymph" illuminates the expressive implications of the descending tetrachord pattern and demonstrates its suitability for association with lament.

The most significant, potentially affective, feature of the pattern is its strong harmonic direction, reinforced by stepwise melody, steady, unarticulated rhythm, and brevity. Harmonically, it suggests one of two possible realizations, either a modal sequence of root position triads or a more tonal succession involving two first-inversion triads: i, v_6, iv_6, V. Denial of these tonal implications creates a frustration of expectation and results in a heightening of tension.

229

Fully aware of the dramatic possibilities inherent in the tetrachord, Monteverdi deliberately and irregularly contradicts the strong implications of the pattern; by employing suspensions, syncopation, and phrase overlapping, he creates affective dissonances of harmony, melody, rhythm, and texture. In addition, he achieves structural dissonances by exploiting the ambiguity of phrase length, the double function of the tonic note as the beginning or ending of a phrase, which is increased by ostinato repetition of the pattern. The resulting phrase overlap demands extraordinary breath control from the singer, frequently pushing her to physiological limits in order to express the corresponding extremity of her psychological state.

LXXXI (1954-55), 41 ff.; Federico Mompellio, *Sigismondo d'India, musicista siciliano* (Milan, 1956), pp. 48 ff.; and Fortune, "Monteverdi and the 'Second Prattica,'" pp. 205 ff. Fortune indicates a number of similarities between the laments of d'India and Monteverdi's lament of Arianna.

9 Modern edition in Malipiero, *Tutte le opere*, VIII, 288 ff.

Two other features of the tetrachord ostinato of the "Lament of
the Nymph" further establish the appropriateness of its association
with lament. Its strongly minor configuration, emphasizing two of
the most crucial degrees of the mode, invokes the full range of somber affects traditionally associated with minor since the Renaissance;[10] and, in its unremitting descent, its gravity, the pattern offers
an analogue of obsession, perceptible as an expression of hopeless
suffering.

The almost seamless texture of Monteverdi's setting virtually
obscures the strophic structure of Rinuccini's text, creating a con-
tinuously affective, unpredictable, open lament, comparable in
emotional power to Arianna's lament.[11] But the "Lament of the
Nymph" represents a further stage in the development of the genre.
Its affect, epitomized by the tetrachord ostinato, is built into the
music itself in a new way. The tetrachord supplants the most important source of affect in recitative laments like that of Arianna —
the interpretation of the singer. In laments with freer bass lines,
the singer's declamation of the text, rhythmically more flexible,
ornamented according to the tastes of the individual performer,
created the affect. Indeed, contemporary descriptions of *Arianna*
specifically praise the power of the singer, Virginia Andreini Ram-
poni, whose performance of the lament moved the audience to
tears.[12]

In this connection it is relevant to recall that the composers
of most early seventeenth-century laments were singers themselves —
Jacopo Peri, Giulio Caccini, Marco da Gagliano, d'India — and
that they could communicate the full affective implications of their

230

10 See Leonard B. Meyer's discussion of the affective implications of the minor
mode in *Emotion and Meaning in Music* (Chicago, 1956), pp. 222 ff.

11 A sharp contrast to Monteverdi's treatment is provided by two canzonette-style
strophic settings of the Rinuccini text: one by Antonio Brunelli, *Scherzi, arie, canzonette e madrigali. Libro secondo* (Venice, 1614), with a modern transcription in
Putnam Aldrich, *The Rhythm of Seventeenth-Century Italian Monody* (New York,
1966), p. 166; the other by Giovanni Battista Piazza, *Canzonette. Libro secondo*
(Venice, 1633), pp.10 f.

12 ". . . And all the performers, well-dressed, played their roles very well, but
best of all [was] Ariadne *comediante* [i.e., Ramponi], . . . who in her musical lament
accompanied by violas and violins [*viole et violini*] made many cry for her misfortune;
there was one musician, Raso [Francesco Rasi], who sang divinely; but next to
Ariadne, the eunuchs and all the others seemed like nothing." Follino, *Compendio*,
quoted in Solerti, *Albori*, I, 99.

written music through their own performances. Monteverdi, however, did not sing his own laments, although he wrote them for performers with whom he worked closely and whose capabilities he knew well. Indeed, although the "Lament of the Nymph" probably was written for a particular singer, Monteverdi's music, when compared to laments with freer bass lines, leaves less room for interpretive license. Through its tetrachord structure the composer exercised a higher degree of control over its performance.[13]

Monteverdi published the "Lament of the Nymph" in the second part of his eighth book of madrigals, balancing the "Combattimento di Tancredi e Clorinda" in the first part of the volume.[14] Both of these madrigals are distinguished by the rubric "in genere rappresentativo" (representational style). The meaning of the term with regard to "Combattimento" is clear. It refers to the dramatic structure of the work, the participation of a narrator and two characters, and to its performance with movement and gesture. But it also refers to the mimetic musical setting of the text, the imitation of the passions of the poetry ("ad immitatione delle passioni dell'oratione"), to quote Monteverdi himself,[15] the pictorialism, the musical representations of battle sounds and of galloping horses, which are so crucial to the total dramatic effect of the work.

The "Lament of the Nymph" offers an analogous situation: "stile rappresentativo" refers not only to its dramatic form — a scene in which a shepherd's chorus frames and comments on the nymph's plaint — but also to the specific musical means by which the form achieves its full expressive representation, in this case of an emotional state rather than a narrative action. It is precisely the descending tetrachord ostinato, as an appropriate mimetic gesture,

231

13 Monteverdi still intended a certain amount of flexibility in the performance of the "Lament of the Nymph." In a rubric at the beginning of the three-part madrigal, he distinguishes between the lament itself and its framing choral sections: they are to be sung regularly ("al tempo della mano"), while the lament should be sung more freely ("a tempo del'affetto del animo, e non a quello de la mano"). Indeed, this distinction, by specifically encouraging the singer to oppose the regular bass line, affirms the function of conflict between bass and voice, between regularity and irregularity, as the chief source of affective power in the lament.

14 Denis Stevens, "Madrigali Guerrieri, et Amorosi," *The Monteverdi Companion*, pp. 238 ff., demonstrates the parallel construction of the two sections of Book VIII.

15 Preface to the "Combattimento di Tancredi e Clorinda," *Tutte le opere*, VIII, 132.

that embodies the representational element in the "Lament of the Nymph," that signifies its affect.

Although distinguished by its intense dramatic style, the "Lament of the Nymph" is only one of a number of works of the 1630s based on the descending tetrachord. Several aria and cantata books printed before the "Lament of the Nymph" — by composers such as Gerolamo Frescobaldi, Giovanni Felice Sances, Martino Pesenti, Benedetto Ferrari, and Francesco Manelli — contain at least one tetrachord piece.[16] But in these collections, in which variety of expression is a primary goal, the tetrachord provides but one of several options for bass-line organization. Others include the so-called *ciaccona*, and longer patterns such as the *romanesca* and *ruggiero*. In addition, many of the bass lines are freely composed.

Unlike the "Lament of the Nymph," the tetrachord pieces of these composers, as well as their settings of other bass lines, are in fact arias. Lacking the variety, the unpredictability, and musical tension of Monteverdi's treatment, they follow the closed, strophic structure of their texts. Moreover, these composers seem to have

232

[16] Pieces based on a descending tetrachord ostinato that were published before 1638 include: Fasolo, "Lamento di Madama Lucia," *Il carro di Madama Lucia . . .* (Rome, 1628), minor tetrachord; Girolamo Frescobaldi, "Aria di Passacaglia: Così mi disprezzate," *Primo libro di arie musicali* (Florence, 1630), minor tetrachord; Giovanni Felice Sances, "Usurpator tiranno," *Cantade e arie a voce sola. Libro secondo, parte prima* (Venice, 1633), minor tetrachord; Martino Pesenti, "O mio thesoro ascolta," from the cantata "O Dio che veggio," *Arie a voce sola . . . con una cantata . . . sopra il passacaglio . . . Libro secondo* (Venice, 1633), major tetrachord; Nicolò Fontei, "Gran follia di pittor," *Bizzarrie poetiche. Libro secondo* (Venice, 1636), major tetrachord; Francesco Manelli, "La Luciata," *Musiche varie* (Venice, 1636), major tetrachord; and Benedetto Ferrari, "Questi pungenti spini," *Musiche varie* (Venice, 1637), major tetrachord.

Whether or not these pieces were actually written before the "Lament of the Nymph" is difficult to ascertain because its date of composition is uncertain. A number of works published in the eighth book of madrigals were certainly written earlier — the "Combattimento di Tancredi e Clorinda," for example, was performed in 1624 — so that the "Lament of the Nymph," too, may well date from an earlier period in Monteverdi's career. Indeed, since concise patterns like the descending tetrachord had begun to replace the longer *romanesca* or *ruggiero* patterns in the late 1620s and early 1630s, it seems likely that the "Lament of the Nymph" was written around that time. I would suggest a date close to 1632, the year of publication of Monteverdi's *Scherzi musicali,* which contains the *ciaccona* "Zefiro torna," using a similarly abbreviated bass pattern. For an attempt to place the "Lament of the Nymph" much earlier, in Monteverdi's Mantuan years, see Stevens, "Madrigali Guerrieri, et Amorosi," p. 253; but cf. as well the editors' comment in the *Monteverdi Reader,* p. 253, n. 3.

made little distinction between the major and minor forms of the tetrachord. They did use the minor form in conjunction with sad texts, exploiting some of the expressive devices implied by the pattern — suspensions, phrase overlap and syncopation — but they rarely labeled their settings laments. And for equally plaintive texts they even adopted the major tetrachord as well as other kinds of bass lines.[17] Not until the 1640s, and particularly in opera, does a definitive association between lament and descending minor tetrachord ostinato become explicit.

Although the music of many operas of the late 1630s and early 1640s is lost, the prominence of lament texts in many of the surviving librettos suggests that they received special attention.[18] And to judge from the contemporary aria books of the composers whose operas are lacking — particularly Manelli, Ferrari, and Sances — the descending minor tetrachord probably offered one option for setting these texts.

The first substantial evidence of a recurrent relationship between lament and the descending minor tetrachord occurs in the operas of Francesco Cavalli.[19] Like those of his much earlier predecessors, Cavalli's laments stand out clearly from their contexts, albeit for different reasons. They are generally distinguished by their slow tempo, heavily stressed triple meter, and string accompaniment, as well as by their heightened affective style. The scores themselves —

17 Fasolo's "Lamento di Madama Lucia": "O sfortunata chi mi consola" (cf. n. 16 above) offers an exceptional — and possibly significant — example of a minor tetrachord piece bearing the title "lamento." But Manelli's "La Luciata," a setting of the identical text, bears no such title. It, in fact, is based on the major descending tetrachord. The Fasolo and Manelli settings are compared in Elena Ferrari Barassi, " 'La Luciata' di Francesco Manelli. Considerazioni su una perduta stampa della Biblioteca Municipale di Breslavia, l'esemplare di un manoscritto berlinese e un componimento del 'Fasolo,' " Atti del convegno di studi italo-polacchi, Bologna, 1970 (in press).

For evidence of the probable lascivious connotation of the descending major tetrachord, see Wolfgang Osthoff, Das dramatische Spätwerk Claudio Monteverdis (Tützing, 1960), p. 87.

18 The libretto of Ermiona, for example, by Pio Enea degli Obizzi, which was set by Sances for a performance in Padua in 1636, contains elaborate descriptions of four laments. Pierluigi Petrobelli, "L'Ermiona di Pio Enea degli Obizzi ed i primi spettacoli d'opera veneziana," Quaderni della rassegna musicale, III (1965), 134 f., suggests that they were modeled on Rinuccini's lament of Arianna.

19 Each of Cavalli's twenty-seven extant operas contains at least one lament, and many of them contain two or three; their total number exceeds fifty. All Cavalli manuscripts hereafter cited are located in Venice, Biblioteca Marciana, Classe IV.

many of them autographs — are generally quite free of specific performance indications; yet often their laments are identified by title ("lamento") or by mode of performance ("adagio," or "con violini"). Cavalli's librettists also recognized the special status of the lament; not only did they contribute to its definition through standardization of its dramatic position and text form, but they even occasionally prefaced lament texts with the same performance indications In *Veremonda*, for example, a libretto of 1652, a lament text carries the rubric "con viole."[20]

In addition to their slow tempo or string accompaniment, most of Cavalli's laments are marked by a clear relationship to the descending minor tetrachord as ostinato. Frequently an unaccompanied statement of the pattern in the bass at the outset signals the association. This framing device distinguishes the piece from its surrounding narrative context; the tetrachord pattern sounds the mood, a declaration of "lament" that sets the piece apart, as if in quotes.

Although he consistently refers to the pattern, Cavalli rarely treats it as strictly as Monteverdi did in the "Lament of the Nymph," either with regard to its persistence or its physiognomy. With Cavalli, when the pattern is simple, it usually modulates or is combined with another pattern; or else it is completely abandoned during the course of the lament. More commonly, however, the pattern itself undergoes modification: it may be inverted (Ex. 1), chromaticized (Ex. 2), arpeggiated (Ex. 3), or otherwise embellished melodically or rhythmically. Occasionally Cavalli uses the tetrachord with even greater freedom: some laments exploit the harmony or the possibilities of phrase overlap suggested by the tetrachord, or the affective language, the suspensions and syncopations associated with its realization, but lack any discernible pattern in the bass.[21] Finally, in a

234

20 Luigi Zorzisto, *Veremonda, L'Amazzone di Aragona* (Venice, 1652), Act II, scene 7, pp. 83 f. (For the identification of Luigi Zorzisto as Giulio Strozzi and the redating of the Venetian libretto of *Veremonda* to 1653, see Lorenzo Bianconi and Thomas Walker "Dalla 'Finta Pazza' alla 'Veremonda': Storie di febiarmonici," *Rivista italiana di musicologia*, X [1975], 449 and n. 71.) A traditional association of lament with strings ("violini" and/or "viole") extends at least as far back as *Arianna* (cf. n. 12 above). Europa's lament from *Ermiona*, too, was enhanced by the sound of strings (cf. Petrobelli, "L'Ermiona," p. 133).

21 Cf. Artemisia's lament, "Affligetemi," in *Artemisia* (1656), II, xii [cod. 352 (9876), fol. 79f.].

few instances, specific tetrachord reference occurs solely in the ominous announcement of the opening ritornello.[22]

Ex. 1: *Hipermestra* (1658) III, xi [cod. 362 (9886), fol. 118]

Ex. 2: *Egisto* (1643) II, vi [cod. 411 (9935), fol. 41]

Ex. 3: *Eliogabalo* (1667) I, xvi [cod. 358 (9882) fol. 48]

The descending minor tetrachord was clearly not the only compositional pattern available to Cavalli, and his operas contain several pieces based on other patterns. The descending major tetrachord, for example, occurs as an ostinato in several love duets,[23] and occasionally a fast-moving ostinato of a different kind underlies a comic aria.[24] In adopting a single pattern as a framing reference for his laments and in the particular selection of the descending minor tetrachord, Cavalli was evidently motivated by a number of factors, musical and dramatic, affective and structural.

Originally, his conception of *dramma per musica* did not allow for formal music that interrupted narrative flow. Supernatural or comic characters, because of their peripheral relation to the main plot, could lapse into song, but serious characters were required to behave more realistically in order to maintain dramatic convic-

235

---

[22] Cf. Alindo's lament, "Disperate pupille," in *Artemisia*, III, xix [fol. 138f.], and Romilda's lament, "Che barbara pietà," in *Xerse* (1654), III, viii [cod. 374 (9898), fol. 157ᵛff.].

[23] Cf. Diomeda's and Trasimede's duet, "Sperando me'n vò," in *Oristeo* (1651), I, ii [cod. 367 (9891), fol. 11], and Deinira's and Licco's duet, "Figlio, figlio," in *Ercole amante* (1662), III, vii [cod. 359 (9883), fol. 78ff.]. The prototype for such duets is, of course, the final duet of Monteverdi's *Incoronazione di Poppea*. For new evidence questioning the attribution of the duet to Monteverdi see Alessandra Chiarelli, " 'L'Incoronazione di Poppea' o 'Il Nerone.' Problemi di filologia testuale," *Rivista italiana di musicologia*, IX (1974), 150. Concerning the affective implications of the descending major tetrachord, cf. n. 17 above.

[24] Cf. Oristeo's aria, "Tu d'amore," in *Oristeo*, I, vi [fol. 19]; Orsede's aria, "Occhi belli," in *Oristeo*, I, ix [fol. 26ᵛ], and Ceffea's aria, "Nudo arciero," in *Scipione affricano* (1664), I, xiv [cod. 371 (9895), fol. 38ᵛf.].

tion and verisimilitude. Therefore, from the outset of Cavalli's
career, the major protagonists of his operas generally expressed
themselves in flowing, open recitative, sliding briefly into more
measured sections at particularly dramatic moments, or even occasionally into full arias when the situation permitted (i.e., if the
text suggested some kind of formal song or if a character was irra-
tional and subject to unrealistic behavior).[25]

Always responsive to such occasions for increased musical expression, Cavalli could hardly have ignored the central affective climax
of an opera, the lament. Yet, setting the lament as a formal aria
would have deprived the situation of its dramatic impact; for, even
though the extreme emotional state of the character might have
justified it, superimposing a closed, preexistent musical structure
on an essentially spontaneous situation would have obscured the
audibility and weight of the text, thereby diminishing its impact.
Indeed, two of Cavalli's earliest laments, like the great laments in
Monteverdi's operas, were essentially continuous recitatives heightened by dissonance and affective text repetition and structured only
by refrains.[26]

For many reasons, the descending tetrachord ostinato offered an
ideal solution to this dramatic and musical problem. It was a means
for setting the lament apart from its context and at the same time
maintaining its intense emotional power. Whatever the loss of
spontaneity such patterning entailed, it was more than compen-
sated for by the intrinsic affective implications of the tetrachord
ostinato.

Some of these implications in reference to the "Lament of the
Nymph" have already been discussed. The pattern offered the possibility of consistent, yet unpredictable conflict between voice and
bass line, creating dissonances of melody, rhythm, and texture; and
the effect of this conflict was increased by the nonverbal impact of
reiterated descent in the minor mode as a fitting expression of
endless suffering.

---

[25] The problems of verisimilitude and their effect on the aria in early opera are
discussed by Nino Pirrotta, "Early Opera and Aria," *New Looks at Italian Opera:
Essays in Honor of Donald J. Grout*, ed. William W. Austin (Ithaca, 1968), pp. 93 ff.

[26] Cf. Teti's lament, "Pure orrecchi sentiste," in *Le nozze di Peleo e di Teti* (1639),
III, vi [cod. 365 (9889), fol. 88ᵛff.], and Procri's lament, "Volgi, deh volgi il piede," in
Gli amori di Apollo e di Dafne (1640), I, vii [cod. 404 (9928), fol. 45ff.].

Moreover, the structural implications of the tetrachord did not essentially diminish the affect. Its brevity may have increased its perceptibility as a pattern, but it also limited its large-dimension formal function. In fact, this brevity rendered it ideally suitable for measured sections of indeterminate length, restricted or extended, facilitating the fluidity of dramatic expression — that flexible shifting back and forth between more and less measured music so essential to Cavalli's style. The pattern easily lent itself to interruption after a few statements or else to repetition indefinitely extended. It could be expanded in longer phrases without losing its identity through cadential extension (Ex. 4) or through combination with its inversion (Ex. 5). It also provided a ready formula for modulation as a means of increasing the dimensions of a lyrical statement. Particularly in such strophic texts as the "Lament of the Nymph," the tetrachord could even be exploited expressly to obscure formal outlines by creating ambiguities between phrase and strophe endings.[27]

237

Ex. 4: *Ormindo* (1644) III, xi [cod. 368 (9892) fol 166ᵛ]

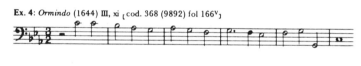

Ex. 5: *Statira* (1655) III, iv [cod. 372 (9896) fol. 78ᵛ]

For Cavalli, then, the descending tetrachord ostinato essentially offered a compromise between the spontaneous expressivity of recitative and the lyrical expressivity of aria, providing a means of affective structuring without necessarily imposing closure. He illustrates the importance of this compromise most explicitly in those early tetrachord laments which are interrupted or concluded by excited recitative exclamations[28] and in those freer recitative laments heightened by brief tetrachord passages.[29]

27 Cf. Mandane's lament, "Deh, sia l'ultimo," in *Ciro* (1654), II, ix [cod. 354 (9878), fol. 68ᵛff.].

28 Cf. Apollo's lament, "Misero Apollo," in *Gli amori di Apollo e di Dafne*, III, iii [fol. 85ᵛff.], and Tigrane's lament, "Con infocati teli," in *Doriclea* (1645), II, ii [cod. 356 (9880), fol. 44ff.].

29 Cf. Isifile's lament, "Infelice ch'ascolto," in *Giasone* (1649), III, xxi [cod. 368 (9887), fol. 159ᵛff.].

But by shortly after the middle of the seventeenth century such compromise was no longer necessary; the formal reasons for Cavalli's use of the descending tetrachord ostinato had lost their relevance. The number and dimensions of closed forms in opera had shown a marked increase after 1650, reflecting a more relaxed and casual attitude toward dramatic verisimilitude. Cavalli's laments had in fact become full arias, standardized in both the form and expressive content of their texts. At the same time the lament lost something of its original dràmatic position as the central affective climax of an opera; occasions for laments instead proliferated to the point where a number of librettos of the 1650s and 1660s contain as many as three, distributed over their three acts.[30]

The increasing frequency and formal self-sufficiency of the lament obviated an original function of the descending tetrachord ostinato; yet even after it had outlived its structural usefulness, Cavalli continued to employ the pattern in his laments. Such commitment suggests that the function of the descending tetrachord had become primarily symbolic, for now mere reference to the pattern sufficed to identify the genre, to define a plaintive aria as a lament.

The pattern had assumed a clear meaning of its own; it was an unambiguous sign of lament, and Cavalli's use of it involved both exploration and confirmation of that meaning. The accumulated tradition of references in such a large body of works as his helped to establish the symbolic status of the pattern in the fullest sense. Repeated identification of the descending tetrachord with the lament reinforced this meaning, and subsequent use of the pattern depended as much on this tradition of association, this acquired affective significance, as on any intrinsic musical quality.

The descending minor tetrachord continued to provide the basis for lament arias of later Baroque composers, among them Purcell, Handel, and Bach. Yet perhaps the most revealing statement of the tetrachord-lament equation occurs in an instrumental work, the "Lament" from Bach's Capriccio in B-flat Major "on the departure of his dearly Beloved Brother," of 1704 (Ex. 6).

238

---

[30] *Statira* (1655) [cod. 372 (9896)] contains laments in II, x, III, iv, and III, x. *Scipione affricano* contains laments in I, vi, II, xvii, and III, xv.

Ex. 6: Bach: *Capriccio in B♭* (1704) "Ist ein allgemeines Lamento der Freunde" [*Bach Gesellschaft* XXXVI, p. 192]

Here, in a keyboard work based on the descending tetrachord ostinato, without text, the lament affect is projected by a purely musical figure: the pattern itself declares its precise iconographic significance, an emblem of lament.

239

THE ITALIAN CANTATA
OF THE BAROQUE PERIOD*

GLORIA ROSE

In the baroque period, the Italian cantata was treated as a category of vocal chamber music. It took many forms in the long course of its history. But it always retained the essential marks of chamber music. This was what distinguished the cantata from the other newly developing categories of opera and oratorio, notwithstanding many features in common[1].

Throughout the baroque period, Italian musicians were keenly aware of the differences between music composed for different functions and places. Quite early in the 17th century they set up a distinction between church music, theater music and chamber music. The three divisions are named or described by Cesare Crivellati in 1624; by Giovanni Battista Doni in about 1635; in a testimonial for four Italian musicians, in 1646; by Angelo Berardi in 1681 and again in 1689; and by Pier Francesco Tosi in 1723[2]. The same three divisions of church, theater and chamber music are also implied by Severo Bonini in about 1650[3]; and the divisions of church and chamber music are mentioned by Giacomo Antonio Perti in the Dedication to his *Cantate morali, e spirituali* (Bologna, 1688). Johann Mattheson showed in 1739 that he knew very well what belonged to « die wahre Natur einer Cantate »[4].

241

The true nature of the cantata is governed by its character as chamber music. It is this which moved the composers of Italian cantatas in their choice of poems, and in evolving their musical forms and styles. They sometimes wrote cantatas more dramatic than usual, just as they sometimes wrote operas more intimate than usual, or oratorios more theatrical than usual. But basically, they developed the cantata as chamber music to be performed by skilled musicians, before an audience of knowledgeable listeners.

It is well known that cantatas developed from the monodies of early 17th-century Italy, i.e. from Italian songs composed for solo voice and basso continuo.

* This chapter was finished and submitted in February 1967.

[1] I am grateful to the American Council of Learned Societies for a Grant-in-Aid in support of my latest research on the Italian cantata.

[2] Cesare Crivellati, *Discorsi musicali*, Viterbo 1624, 196; Giovanni B. Doni, *Trattato della musica scenica* in *Trattati di musica* II, ed. A. F. Gori, Florence 1763, 69/70; Testimonial in Modena, Archivio di Stato, Musica Bª2ª; Angelo Berardi, *Ragionamenti musicali*, Bologna 1681, 155–156; id. *Miscellanea musicale*, Bologna 1689, 41; Pier Francesco Tosi, *Opinioni de' cantori antichi, e moderni*, Bologna 1723, 41/42, 58.

[3] Severo Bonini, *Prima parte de' discorsi e regole sovra la musica:* Florence, Biblioteca Riccardiana, Ms. 2218, fol. 70, 80'–88, 91'–101'.

[4] Johann Mattheson, *Der vollkommene Capellmeister*, Hamburg 1739, 214/215.

Monody and cantata are essentially the same thing at different stages of development. Monodies, in turn, were preceded by earlier solo songs with instrumental accompaniment. The composers of monodies were fond of stressing the novelty of their achievements; but monodies were heavily indebted to the accompanied solo songs, the improvisatory solo singing, and the polyphonic madrigals of the 16th century[5]. Nevertheless, monodies were novel in that they were intended originally and exclusively for solo singers, and in that they developed a musical style of their own[6].

It was, therefore, quite legitimate for Giulio Caccini to publish his songs under the proud title of *Le nuove musiche* (Florence, 1602). Caccini's collection may not have been the first actually to appear in print[7], but it was unquestionably a most important and influential work. *Le nuove musiche* not only started a fashion in published collections of solo songs[8]; it also provided a model for them. The twelve *madrigali* and the ten *arie* in Caccini's *Nuove musiche* represent the main forms of monody as it was cultivated in the early decades of the 17th century. The madrigals (named after their poetry, and not after the polyphonic variety of madrigal) tend to have an arioso type of melody, with elaborate ornamentation at cadences, and a fairly slow-moving bass. The arias tend to have less florid melodies and more active bass lines; with one exception, they are strophic songs or strophic variations, i.e. each strophe is set to the same or a slightly modified bass, over which the melody varies.

The various musical forms and styles found in Caccini's *Nuove musiche* are fundamental to the development of monody and therefore of cantata. The arioso, in particular, was a new and distinctive style of music; it was adopted by the composers of monodies far more widely than strict recitative. But strophic songs were

242

[5] Important discussions of the background to monody occur in Alfred Einstein, *The Italian Madrigal* II, Princeton 1949, Chapter 11, «Concerto and Concento», and Chapter 12, «Pseudo-Monody and Monody»; Otto Kinkeldey, *Orgel und Klavier in der Musik des 16.Jahrhunderts*, Leipzig 1910, Chapter 6, «Klavier und Orgel in der Haus- und Theatermusik»; Claude V. Palisca, «Vincenzo Galilei and Some Links Between ‹Pseudo-Monody› and Monody», *MQ* XLVI (1960), 344–360; Federico Ghisi, «La tradition musicale des fêtes florentines et les origines de l'opéra», *Musique des intermèdes de «La Pellegrina»*, ed. D. P. Walker, Paris 1963, xi–xxii. The most thorough treatment of the subject occurs in a work outstanding for detail and insight: William V. Porter, *The Origins of the Baroque Solo Song: A Study of Italian Manuscripts and Prints from 1590 to 1610*, Diss. Yale University, 1962 (ms.).

[6] This is clearly brought out by Porter, op. cit., especially pages 8–12, and 165–170.

[7] The *Musiche* of Domenico Maria Melli (or Megli) was probably printed before Caccini's collection. Melli's Dedication is dated 26 March 1602, in Venice. Caccini's Dedication is dated 1 February 1601 in Florence (Florentine old style calendar, i.e. 1602), but the printing was delayed until the end of June 1602. This delay of publication is explained by the printer, at the end of Caccini's preface. The title page of Caccini's *Nuove musiche* bears the date 1601, but the actual date of printing – 1602 – is given on the reverse of the title page and on the last page of the volume.

[8] A chronological, annotated and up-to-date list of these publications has been prepared by Nigel Fortune: «A Handlist of Printed Italian Secular Monody Books, 1602–1635», *Royal Musical Association Research Chronicle* III (1963), 27–50.

also important, where the voice and the bass are mostly in simultaneous motion, and there are often rhythmic patterns based upon dances[9].

Monody found immediate success. It was quickly taken up in such centers as Florence, Rome and Venice, and soon monodies were being written and sung all over Italy. Amateur and professional musicians alike were attracted to monody. Its composers include some who are now remembered especially for their operas: Jacopo Peri, Marco da Gagliano, Stefano Landi and Claudio Monteverdi. Many composers wrote polyphonic madrigals as well as monodies[10]. Duets and, to a lesser extent, trios were included in some collections of monodies.

For the most part, monodies, duets and trios were set to the verses of contemporary poets, and often to the verses of such famous poets as Ottavio Rinuccini, Gabriello Chiabrera, Giovanni Battista Guarini and Giambattista Marino. The poetic forms are madrigals, sonnets, ottavas and strophic pieces. The literary style is intentionally and successfully artificial. The subjects are usually variations on the theme of unrequited love. Italian lyric poetry of the 17th century is usually dismissed by musicologists with a few derogatory comments[11]. But literary scholars have studied it seriously and have placed a much higher value on it[12].

There was a considerable exchange of music and musicians among the various centers of monody. Although the composers of each center tended to emphasize different aspects of monody, they were also influenced by the monodies composed at other centers. Monodies were printed and reprinted in large numbers; they reached a wide public within and beyond Italy; they were responsible, more than any other category, for disseminating the latest styles of music[13].

Monodies were given a variety of names by their composers and publishers. Sometimes they were named after their poetic forms, e.g. *madrigali, sonetti,*

243

---

[9] See the penetrating discussion, and the anthology of complete songs, in Putnam Aldrich, *Rhythm in Seventeenth-Century Italian Monody*, New York 1966.

[10] Cf. Gloria Rose, « Polyphonic Italian Madrigals of the Seventeenth Century », *ML* XLVII (1966), especially 158/159.

[11] Perhaps the most unfortunate of these is « Some poems are little more than amorous baby-talk », under « Song » in *Grove's Dictionary of Music and Musicians* VII, [5]London 1954, 926.

[12] For a sound and appreciative study of this poetry, see Carlo Calcaterra, *Poesia e canto*, Bologna 1951, Chapter 4, « La melica italiana dalla seconda metà del Cinquecento al Rolli e al Metastasio ». Calcaterra also demonstrates the continuity of Italian lyric poetry from the 16th to the 18th centuries. James V. Mirollo presents a survey of literary criticism on Marino and the Marinists, together with fresh insights of his own, in his excellent book, *The Poet of the Marvelous: Giambattista Marino*, New York and London 1963.

[13] A full treatment of the subject of monody appears in Nigel Fortune, *Italian Secular Song from 1600 to 1635: The Origins and Development of Accompanied Monody*, Diss. (Gonville & Caius College), University of Cambridge 1953 (ms.). For a shorter and more accessible discussion, see id., « Italian Secular Monody from 1600 to 1635 », *MQ* XXXIX (1953), 171–195. Jan Racek, *Stilprobleme der italienischen Monodie*, Prague 1965, was difficult to procure and reached me too late to use in the present essay. I regret this because Racek's book is outstanding in scholarship and perceptiveness; it is a prime work in this field.

ottave; sometimes they were published under such fanciful titles as *Ghirlandetta amorosa* or *Giardino musicale;* still more often they appeared as collections of *Le varie musiche* or simply *Musiche.* The terminology of the period was not, however, entirely indiscriminate. *Madrigali* (in one musical section) and *sonetti* and *ottave* (in several sections) were usually composed in a free, arioso style. *Arie, ariette, canzonette, scherzi* and *villanelle* are usually strophic songs in a lighter vein.

It has often been stated that the word «cantata» originally meant nothing more than a piece of music to be sung, as opposed to «sonata», a piece of music to be played. I have found no evidence to support this notion. The word «cantata» was used, at different times and places in the baroque period, to designate different kinds of compositions. But is was used in almost every instance to designate a particular kind of composition. Paradoxically, the word «cantata» was seldom used to designate cantatas of the decades around 1650, most of which are not designated at all; and these if any are the cantatas which, by their very diversity, might just be called «pieces of music to be sung».

244The earliest known use of the word «cantata» to designate a piece of music occurs in Alessandro Grandi's *Cantade et arie à voce sola*, which was reprinted, with corrections and additions, at Venice in 1620 (the original date of publication is not known). This collection has been lost since World War II; but from descriptions by earlier scholars we know that it contained *cantade, sonetti* and *madrigali*, which were in strophic variation form, with some distinctions among the three groups; and *arie*, which were strophic songs[14].

The one piece entitled «cantata» in Carlo Milanuzi's *Quarto scherzo delle ariose vaghezze* (Venice, 1624) is in strophic variation form, with an introduction and ritornello for continuo[15]. In Giovanni Pietro Berti's *Cantade et arie* (Venice, 1624), the *arie* are mostly simple strophic songs, whereas the one *cantata* is again in strophic variation form, with a ritornello for continuo between the strophes[16].

But already in the 1620's the word «cantata» was being used to designate sectional pieces other than strophic variations, as well as continuous recitatives, and simple little arias. All these belonged to the category of vocal chamber music, as did the strophic songs, strophic-rondo songs, duets and dialogues of the 1620's.

At this time, too, the element of contrast was becoming more pronounced within these compositions. Sections of contrasting meter and melodic style within

[14] The collection is described by Eugen Schmitz, *Geschichte der weltlichen Solokantate,* ²Leipzig 1955, 67/68; and in somewhat more detail by Hugo Leichtentritt, «Der monodische Kammermusikstil in Italien bis gegen 1650», in A.W. Ambros, *Geschichte der Musik* IV, ed. Leichtentritt, Leipzig 1909, 876/877. Schmitz gives a few music examples; others may be seen in Manfred Bukofzer, *Music in the Baroque Era,* New York 1947, 52, and in Henry Prunières, «La cantate italienne à voix seule au dix-septième siècle», *Encyclopédie de la musique et dictionnaire du conservatoire* V.2, Paris 1930, 3395/3396.

[15] Schmitz, op. cit., 69.

[16] Ib., 69/70.

a piece had already appeared in the earliest known collection of monodies in Rome, Ottavio Durante's *Arie devote* (Rome, 1608), and in many other early collections in Rome and elsewhere[17].

By the second decade of the century, there are pieces which contain sections in recitative and aria styles, e. g. in Sigismondo d'India's *Le musiche ... Libro quinto* (Venice, 1623); G. P. Berti's *Cantade et arie* (Venice, 1627)[18]; and Stefano Landi's *Il secondo libro d'arie musicali* (Rome, 1627). Since Berti worked in Venice, Landi in Rome, and d'India mainly in Turin, it is evident that the latest musical styles were practiced in various centers of Italy. And not every musician spent his entire creative life in one center. Giovanni Felice Sances, for instance, started work in Rome, then went on to Bologna, Venice, Padua and Vienna. The surviving publications of Sances include his *Cantade ... à voce sola* (Venice, 1633); *Cantade ... à doi voci* (Venice, 1633); and *Il quarto libro delle cantate et arie à voce sola* (Venice, 1636). These publications present a survey of Italian vocal chamber music in the 1630's. There are strophic variations for solo voice; strophic songs and ensembles; solo songs with recitative and aria sections; solos and duets built upon ostinato basses; solos and ensembles in rondo form; dialogues ending with duets. A similar survey is presented by a manuscript compiled evidently in the third decade of the 17th century: Bologna, Civico Museo Bibliografico Musicale, Q. 49. Here the musical structures are not quite so varied; but the manuscript is of particular interest because it contains the music of composers working in different centers – Florence, Rome and Parma[19].

245

Printed anthologies (produced especially in the 1620's and occasionally thereafter) and manuscript anthologies (numerous from the 1640's) sometimes contain the work of composers from different parts of Italy. More often, however, they show what was being composed in one center around a certain time. Thus the *Raccolta d'arie spirituali à una, due, e tre voci di diversi eccellentissimi autori* (Rome, 1640) contains pieces by Orazio Michi (dell'Arpa), Domenico Mazzocchi, Loreto Vittori, Marco Marazzoli, Giacomo Carissimi (whose piece is marked «d'incerto») and other musicians working in Rome. The *Ariette di musica, à una, e due voci di eccellentissimi autori* (Bracciano, 1646) likewise contains the

[17] Jacopo Peri, *Le varie musiche à una due, e tre voci*, Florence 1609; Giovanni Girolamo Kapsberger, *Libro primo di arie passeggiate à una voce*, Rome 1612, *Libro secondo d'arie à una e più voci*, Rome 1623 and *Libro terzo di villanelle* à 1.2. *et* 3. *voci*, Rome 1619; Antonio Cifra, *Scherzi sacri ... à una, à due, à tre, et quattro voci. Libro primo*, Rome 1616; Giovanni Francesco Anerio, *Diporti musicali. Madrigali* à 1.2.3. & 4. *voci*, Rome 1617, and *Selva armonica ... madrigali, canzonette, dialoghi, arie à una, doi, tre & quattro voci*, Rome 1617 – to name only some of the collections I have myself seen.

[18] See the music examples by d'India and Berti in Fortune, «Italian Secular Monody», 191/192. Additional examples by d'India appear in Federico Mompellio, *Sigismondo d'India*, Milan 1956.

[19] The manuscript is discussed, and its contents listed, by Nigel Fortune, «A Florentine Manuscript and Its Place in Italian Song», *AMl* XXIII (1951), 124–136.

music of composers working in Rome: Carissimi, Luigi Rossi, Mario Savioni, Giovanni Marciani, both Virgilio and Domenico Mazzocchi, and others. Luigi Rossi's splendid *Gelosia* is the most complex of the solo pieces in this anthology, but other pieces also show a contrast of musical styles between the sections. Most compositions of this kind in the first half of the 17th century are still quite short: they are individual compositions with contrasting sections, rather than large works with distinct arias and recitatives.

Manuscript anthologies of cantatas started to become numerous in the 1640's; and from the middle of the century, they represent the chief means by which cantatas were transmitted. This change from prints to manuscripts may be due to the economics of publishing. By 1650 at the latest, cantatas had become so popular and numerous that they dominated the field of vocal chamber music. But while cantatas multiplied, musicians did not; and no one edition could hope to capture enough of the market to show much profit.

In Rome, few cantatas were printed, but hundreds of cantata manuscripts were compiled. Cantatas were published chiefly in Bologna and Venice, where there were important music publishers, but where composers of cantatas also seem to have been fewer and less prolific (we need more investigation of the publishing firms and systems of patronage in Bologna and Venice especially).

So numerous and so dispersed are the cantata manuscripts which have survived (to say nothing of those which have disappeared) that we can hardly estimate their total number. I have found cantatas by Carissimi in about 170 manuscripts of the 17th and 18th centuries; Eleanor Caluori has found cantatas by Luigi Rossi in over 200 manuscripts[20]; and Edwin Hanley has found cantatas by Alessandro Scarlatti in approximately 3000 *(sic)* manuscripts[21]. These figures exclude the many additional cantata manuscripts which we searched, and also 19th and 20th century copies. When we take into account that the number of cantatas in each manuscript may average somewhere from twenty to forty, we begin to get the measure of the output.

A large number of the sources can be seen listed in the *Wellesley Edition Cantata Index Series*, a project currently being carried out under the very able direction of Owen Jander[22]. The project is vast in conception and ambitious in aim, but is no more so than the subject requires. For it is on the musical manuscripts of the 17th and 18th centuries that our knowledge of the Italian cantata must rest.

[20] cf. infra, 662 n. 27.
[21] cf. infra, 672 n. 61.
[22] The Series is published by Wellesley College, Wellesley, Massachusetts. Already available are Fascicle 1 on Antonio Cesti, compiled by David Burrows (1964); Fascicle 2 on Mario Savioni, compiled by Irving Eisley (1964); Fascicle 3 on Luigi Rossi, compiled by Eleanor Caluori (1965); Fascicle 4 on Alessandro Stradella, compiled by Owen Jander and Fascicle 5 on Giacomo Carissimi, compiled by Gloria Rose (1966). In preparation are fascicles on Francesco Tenaglia, Carlo Caproli, Alessandro and Atto Melani, and others yet to be announced. The Series is hereafter abbreviated as *WECIS*.

The category of the cantata is a broad one, since it includes such diverse pieces as short strophic songs; long arioso laments; compositions for one, two or three voices containing recitatives, arias and ariosos in any number and order. But such are the pieces appearing side by side in the manuscripts; and they were regarded in the 17th century, not as separate species, but as varieties of vocal music all suitable for performance in a more or less private setting. For the decades around 1650, a broad, flexible and inclusive definition of «cantata» is historically the most accurate [23].

In the cantata manuscripts of this period, designations are sparse and inconsistent. Occasionally a piece is headed «aria», «arietta», «recitativo», «duetto», or «dialogo». The heading «cantata» or «cantata à voce sola» appears seldom before the 1670's. In most cantata manuscripts, there are no such designations at all (indeed, we are lucky if the composers are named). And in other kinds of contemporary sources, such as letters, diaries, treatises, etc., there are few references to cantatas. When we can trace these references to cantatas existing in manuscripts, we find the same sort of terminology as in the titles of cantata publications. We find that the great variety of pieces which were called «arie» or «ariette» or «canzonette» in the 1640's, were later, from the 1650's or so, called «cantate» as well. There is also one charming reference by Carissimi himself to a «cantatina» he was sending to a patron [24]. Giovanni Maria Crescimbeni was writing from a later period and in connection chiefly with poetry, but his discussion of «Cantate» is relevant here [25]:

Besides entertainments *(feste)*, they introduced for music certain other kinds of poetry, which now are generally called Cantatas, which are composed of verses and little verses rhymed without rule, with a mingling of arias, and sometimes for one voice, sometimes for several; and they have made and do make these also compounded of dramatic and narrative [elements]. This sort of poetry is an invention of the 17th century, since in the preceding [century] madrigals were used for music, and other regulated compositions.

A list of the cantata composers from about 1640 to the end of the baroque period would include almost every name of importance in Italian music of that period. Some composers were more attracted than others to the cantata; and cantatas

247

---

[23] I do not think, however, that the word «cantata» should be used for pieces with Latin texts. In the contemporary sources, *cantate* have Italian texts (whether secular or sacred), and *motetti* have Latin texts. This distinction is clearly indicated in the works of Bassani, for instance, whose publications are conveniently listed in Richard Haselbach, *Giovanni Battista Bassani*, Kassel & Basel 1955, 18–59. In all the publications entitled *Cantate*, the texts are in Italian; in all the publications entitled *Motetti*, the texts are in Latin. Haselbach indiscriminately and incorrectly describes *cantate* and *motetti* alike as «Kantaten» or «Solokantaten», in his otherwise admirable book.

[24] Draft of an undated letter, Rome, Archives of the German College, Busta Ecclesiae S. Apollinaris, Carte appartenente a Giacomo Carissimi ..., 16. I am grateful to the Reverend Peter Henrici, S. J., for very kindly granting me access to these Archives.

[25] Giovanni Maria Crescimbeni, *L'istoria della volgar poesia* I, [3]Venice 1731, 299/300.

were cultivated more actively in some centers than in others. But cantatas were written all over Italy, by composers holding all sorts of musical posts. The same kinds of poems were set, the same kinds of musical structures and styles were employed. There seem to be no essential or consistent differences between the cantatas produced in Rome, Bologna, and Venice, to name three of the main centers. The differences are associated not so much with the place as with the date and personality of the composer.

Luigi Rossi (ca. 1598-1653) produced close to 300 cantatas, but only two operas and a few oratorios. At the opposite extreme, Francesco Cavalli (1602–1676) produced over 40 operas but only a small number of cantatas. Rossi worked in Rome and Cavalli in Venice, which offered different opportunities. They were officially employed in different capacities. But the decisive factor seems to have been that the lyrical nature of the cantata appealed more to Rossi, and the dramatic nature of opera appealed more to Cavalli[26].

The work of Rossi includes virtually every species of the contemporary cantata[27]. There are strophic songs; strophic variations; rondo forms; compositions made up of recitatives, ariosos and arias, alone or in different combinations; and a variety of pieces for two, three and four voices. His arias are handled with a direct and sure touch, as in this aria from *Se non corre una speranza*[28]:

[26] This is an expansion of the parallel drawn by Prunières, «Cantate italienne», 3405. Prunières' essay is well worth reading in its entirety. It is not comprehensive in scope and not always correct in details; I am furthermore bound to disagree with Prunières' judgment of Carissimi's secular cantatas as «very cold» (3407). Nevertheless, the essay is correct in its main lines, and it includes passages of fine insight.

[27] A doctoral dissertation on the cantatas of Luigi Rossi, for Brandeis University is now (1970) being written by Eleanor Caluori. Miss Caluori has provided a valuable introduction to her fascicle on Luigi Rossi, *WECIS*, fasc. 3.

[28] Rome, Biblioteca Casanatense, Ms. 2466, fol. 210–212 – In the texts of the music examples, capitals, accents, and punctuation marks have been added.

ri. S'in-gan-na, sì, sì, s'in-gan-na, sì, sì, chì fol-le. sì cre-de che sta-bil la fe-de gli ser-bi chì

vi-ve lon-ta-no i suoi dì. S'in-gan-na, sì, sì, s'in-gan-na, sì, sì, s'in-gan - - - - -

- - - - - na, s'in-gan-na, sì, sì, s'in-ganna, sì, sì, s'in-gan - na, sì, sì, s'in-gan - - -

- - - - - - - na, s'in-ganna, sì, sì,_____ s'in-gan-na, sì, sì.

249

Some of Luigi Rossi's finest compositions are his laments, of which the most famous is probably *Un ferito cavaliero*, on the death of King Gustave of Sweden[29]. Similar cantatas – long, serious works, in a style of expressive recitative or arioso throughout – were written by other composers. It is interesting, however, that Rossi is known to have been familiar with the *Lamento d'Arianna* from Monteverdi's opera: he copied this entire magnificent lament into a manuscript which he prepared early in his career (under the heading « Dell'Arianna del Monte Verde »)[30]. Certainly Rossi was not the only composer to be influenced by the *Lamento d'Arianna*. Severo Bonini wrote, about 1650, that « there was not a house which, possessing harpsichords or theorbos, did not have the lament of that [opera] »[31]. The *Lamento d'Arianna* was composed as part of an opera; but when it was taken up as a separate piece, it was given the function of a piece of vocal chamber music, in the same manner as a cantata.

Another prolific composer of cantatas was Marco Marazzoli (ca. 1619–1662). On the whole, however, Marazzoli's compositions do not rank with the best work of his contemporaries[32]; and few of his cantatas are musically distinguished.

[29] See *WECIS*, fasc. 3a, No. 196.

[30] London, British Museum, Add. Ms. 30491, fol. 39–41'.

[31] Severo Bonini, *Prima parte de' discorsi e regole sovra la musica*: Florence, Biblioteca Riccardiana, Ms. 2218, fol. 87'.

[32] Despite the extravagant claims (and misleading references) of Piero Capponi, in «Marco Marazzoli e l'oratorio ‹ Christo e i Farisei›», *La scuola romana*, Siena 1953, 101–106; and in the commentary to the recordings, *Storia della musica italiana* II, ed. Cesare Valabrega,

Cantatas of a much finer character appear in the work of Domenico Mazzocchi (1592–1665), in his *Dialoghi e sonetti* (Rome, 1638) and his *Musiche sacre e morali* (Rome, 1640), and scattered through manuscripts of the 17th century. Mazzocchi's output of cantatas, or of any other music, was relatively small; but it is of very high quality[33]. His cantata *S'io mi parto, ò mio bel sole* is a *Ciaccona*, as it is headed; and all three of the musical sections conclude with the same textual and musical phrase. Here is the third and last section of the cantata[34]:

250

30. Volume II, disc 5 of these recordings is intended to illustrate the 17th-century Italian cantata. It contains a preponderance of examples by Marco Marazzoli. It gives but one short duet attributed to Luigi Rossi by Capponi, who has been unwilling to identify his source either here or in response to letters. And it includes nothing by Carissimi or Savioni. There is, however, a cantata by Carissimi (there called an oratorio) on disc 10 of volume I.

[33] This observation is based upon my examination of Mazzocchi's cantatas, madrigals, motets, and his one surviving opera. It seems to be confirmed in a dissertation recently completed: Wolfgang Witzenmann, *Domenico Mazzocchi (1592–1665): Dokumente und Interpretation*, Tübingen 1965. The dissertation is summarized in *Mf* XIX (1966), 322/323.

[34] Rome, Biblioteca Casanatense, Ms. 2472, fol. 9–10.

Ma par-ten-do io mo-ri - rò, ma par-ten-do io mo-ri - rò.

With Giacomo Carissimi (1605–1674), the level of artistic quality is conspicuously high in his approximately 150 surviving cantatas. Carissimi, like Luigi Rossi, cultivated all species of the cantata and was a master of its many forms and styles[35]. In structure, his cantatas are at once varied and unified. His melodies are shapely and glowing with fresh invention. His harmony is a blend of diatonic smoothness and chromatic affectiveness, built upon a variety of keys predominantly in the minor mode. His declamation is unsurpassed for its skilful joining of words and music. The following example is from *Ferma, lascia ch'io parli*, a Lament of Mary Queen of Scots, which was greatly admired and quoted from by Dr. Charles Burney[36]:

Fer-ma, fer-ma, las-cia, las-cia ch'io par - li. Ma, ma, che di - rò? Pur -

trop-po hoggi fa-vel-la· a mio pro l'In-no - cen - za, e di sì rea sen-ten-za a Dio s'ap-pel -

la. Vi - - li-pe - sa, vi - - li - pe - sa In-nocen - za. S'u-na Re - gi-na a

te sal-var non li - ce, cui l'In - vi-dia fa guer - ra, a chi ri-cor-rer de-ve in Inghil-

251

[35] For a general survey, see my article, «The Cantatas of Giacomo Carissimi», *MQ* XLVIII (1962), 204–215. For representative cantatas see, Giacomo Carissimi, *Six Solo Cantatas*, ed. Gloria Rose, London 1969.

[36] Charles Burney, *A General History of Music* IV, London 1789, 142–144 (in the reprint [Baden-Baden] 1958, 608–610). My example is from Münster, Bibliothek des Bischöflichen Priesterseminars, Santini Ms. 868, fol. 155'–157. The entire cantata is recorded in *Storia della musica italiana* I, disc 10. It is included there, erroneously, as an oratorio, as is Carissimi's motet for 2 voices, *Tolle sponsa*. The manner of performances, directed by Lino Bianchi, is equally arbitrary. In the cantata, the accompaniment shifts from harpsichord alone, to harpsichord with cello, to organ alone, and these over again. There is no evidence that single cantatas were performed in any such manner.

Some of Carissimi's cantatas are single (and sometimes long) arias, composed in a variety of forms. Others are sectional pieces, composed entirely in arioso style. But the majority of Carissimi's cantatas are composite works, containing a succession of recitatives, ariosos and arias. This is true generally of the cantatas from this period. In Carissimi's work, however, the difference between recitative, arioso and aria styles is frequently a matter of degree; the styles are not sharply distinct from one another, and one style will often merge smoothly into another style.

Recitative and aria are more clearly differentiated in the cantatas of other contemporary composers. This is so, for instance, in the approximately 175 cantatas of Mario Savioni (ca. 1608–1685)[37]. Savioni's cantatas are notable for the high proportion of arias they contain: about two-thirds of his cantatas consist entirely or almost entirely of arias[38]. The following example, from *Spiega amor, deh, per pietà*, shows how Savioni repeated the words of one short phrase, to build a musical section of flowing melody and varied sequences[39]:

[37] Confirmed by Irving Eisley, *The Secular Cantatas of Mario Savioni 1608–1685*, Diss. University of California, Los Angeles 1964 (ms.), especially pages 107, 213/214.

[38] Ib., 131 – Eisley gives an incomplete list of the cantatas and sources of cantatas by Savioni, here and in *WECIS*, fasc. 2. But his dissertation presents a lively evaluation of Savioni's musical style. Eisley also makes some perceptive comments on the poetry of 17th-century cantatas.

[39] Rome, Biblioteca del Conservatorio di Musica S. Cecilia, Ms. G. 885, fol. 77.

Savioni was further unusual in favoring trios over duets[40]. Some of his trios might be more accurately classed as madrigals, rather than as cantatas; but there was no sharp distinction between these two categories[41]. Although Monteverdi's Seventh (1619), Eighth (1638) and Ninth (1651, posthumous) Books of Madrigals were published in the traditional form of part books, they include pieces which are the same in substance as many of the duets and trios found in cantata manuscripts, customarily presented in score. For the most part, however, cantatas for two or three voices are larger, composite works, in which ensembles alternate with recitatives and arias for solo voices.

About fifty-five cantatas by Antonio (born Pietro) Cesti (1623–1669) are preserved – not a very large number for those times. But Cesti's cantatas were highly esteemed by at least one distinguished composer of the next generation. Giacomo Antonio Perti wrote in the preface to his *Cantate morali, e spirituali* (Bologna, 1688), «I have endeavored to follow, as best I have known, the three greatest lights of our profession, Rossi, Carissimi, and Cesti». Cesti's cantatas, like Savioni's, are more notable for their arias than for their recitatives. Lilting melodies in triple meter and long melismata over a wide range are characteristic of many cantatas by Cesti[42].

Luigi Rossi and Carissimi were singled out by Cesti himself, who alluded to them in his cantata *Aspettate, adesso canto*. This cantata is a parody of the very cantatas that Cesti and his colleagues were writing at the time. It is a vivid, first-hand comment on the manner of writing cantatas and on the insatiable demand for new cantatas[43]. *Aspettate, adesso canto* is a brilliant but not unique

253

---

[40] Eisley, *Secular Cantatas*, 131–134.

[41] Cf. Rose, «Polyphonic Madrigals», 158/159.

[42] Cf. *Tu m'aspettasti al mare* in the *Handbuch der Musikgeschichte*, ed. Guido Adler, Frankfurt 1924, 379–382; [2]Berlin 1930, I, 439–442. See also the seven solo cantatas by Cesti, ed. David Burrows, *The Wellesley Edition* No. 5, Wellesley 1963 and Antonio Cesti, *Four Chamber Duets*, ed. David Burrows, Madison 1969. For further discussion see Burrows, *The Cantatas of Antonio Cesti*, Diss. Brandeis University 1961, (ms).

[43] *Aspettate, adesso canto* is included in Burrows' Wellesley edition 70–93. It is the subject of Burrows' interesting article, «Antonio Cesti on Music», *MQ* LI (1965), 518–529. Burrows wishes us (ib., 522) «not to read it as an objective report on the state of music in Italy in the

example of self-parody in the Italian cantata. *Se voi vi credete sentirmi cantare* contains such phrases as «Non attendete accenti, messe di voce ò trilli, forte, e piano, Lamento sopra di Clori, ò Filli, nemen vago passaggio»[44]. There are further examples, and more may come to light as the cantata repertory continues to be explored[45].

We are only now beginning systematically to investigate the cantatas of such outstanding composers as Carlo Caproli (or Caprioli), Antonio Francesco Tenaglia, Pier Simone Agostini, Bernardo Pasquini[46]. Some composers, for example Alessandro Stradella, Giovanni Legrenzi, Giovanni Maria Bononcini, are known chiefly for their operas or instrumental music. But Stradella wrote around 200 cantatas[47].

We have as yet few complete Italian cantatas in modern editions. The modern anthologies include mainly excerpts or single arias from cantatas or, mistakenly, from operas; they present thereby a misleading picture of the cantata. The Wellesley Edition, in its sub-series, «The Italian Cantata», is making a valuable contribution. Each volume contains a selection of whole cantatas by one composer.

Humor of other kinds than self-parody appears occasionally in the texts of cantatas. There are some delightfully gay works by Carissimi, such as the solo cantatas *Allegria vuol' Amore* and *Amor mio, che cosa è questa?*[48]; the duet «A piè d'un verde alloro», sung by the philosophers Democritus and Heraclitus[49]; the trio «Poiche lo sdegno intese», with a charlatan love-doctor as protagonist[50]. But these are rather exceptional cases in the cantata repertory as a whole, where the texts are more likely to be gloomy than cheerful.

Composers seemed never to tire of poems expressing the sorrows and torments of an unlucky lover; it is much the commonest theme. The lover's distress may be described in narrative, or, more frequently, it may be uttered by himself. The lady may be depicted as cruel, heedless or relentless. The lover may hope to

mid-17th-century». But this cantata, like so many satires, is a revealing document; it is more realistic than exaggerated. I think that Burrows is closer to the truth when he says: «In the course of being amusing, however, Cesti leaves very little out of his account of mid-17th-century musical practice» (loc. cit.).

[44] Anonymous in Paris, Bibliothèque Nationale, Ms. Vm⁷. 2, fol. 10'–11.

[45] Cf. Burrows, «Antonio Cesti on Music», 519 n. 3.

[46] Because of much anonymity and many conflicting attributions in the sources, it is often very difficult, if not impossible, to ascertain the composers of certain cantatas. Earlier scholars, working from a limited number of sources, have sometimes assigned cantatas to the wrong composers. It is now possible to check individual cantatas against *WECIS*, rather than accepting uncritically the composers named in Schmitz, *Solokantate;* in *MGG* under composers' names and under the relevant section of «Kantate» (by Hans Engel); and in general histories of music.

[47] See *WECIS*, fasc. 4.

[48] Printed in Giacomo Carissimi, *Six Solo Cantatas*, ed. G. Rose.

[49] Printed in *Alte Meister des Bel Canto. Italienische Kammerduette des 17. und 18. Jahrhunderts* II, ed. Ludwig Landshoff, Leipzig 1927, 52–65.

[50] Printed in *L'arte musicale in Italia* V, ed. Luigi Torchi, Milan 1897, 238–265.

be rewarded for his constancy, or may be resigned to die for it. All these and many more variations are woven round this central theme of unrequited love. There are also poems which deal with love in a general or contemplative manner; poems which stress the beauty of a pastoral scene; and poems which treat historical or mythological characters.

A smaller but not insignificant number of cantatas are set to poems of a moral or spiritual nature. In publications, these may be called « cantate morali » or « arie spirituali » or some such title, as in Perti's work cited on p. 667 above. In a group of cantata manuscripts at the Biblioteca Estense in Modena, the cover of each manuscript bears a title and the word « Amor » or « Moral », according to the subject matter of the cantata. These moral or spiritual texts were set to music in the same manner as the amorous poems.

With regard also to literary structure and style, there is no difference between the amorous and the spiritual poems. The texts of cantatas show a great diversity of structures. They range from short strophic forms with regular rhyme schemes to long, complicated forms with a variety of internal poetic schemes. In some poems the distinction is quite clear between narrative portions in irregular verse, intended for recitatives; and lyrical portions in regular rhyme schemes, intended for arias. But poetic structures were sometimes treated quite freely by the composers of cantatas.

The literary style of the period is characterized by an abundant use of rhetorical figures and conventional images, and by a delight in the sheer sound of words and verses. The cantata composers had at their disposal a heritage of poetry by such masters as Petrarch, Ariosto and Tasso. If they preferred to set the verses of Marino's followers, who were minor poets, it is because they felt that these verses best suited their own kind of music. Indeed, most of the poems used in cantatas may have been specially written for the purpose.

Apart from an occasional sonnet by Tasso or madrigal by Guarini, the cantata texts are by such lesser known poets as Domenico Benigni, Francesco Balducci, Francesco Buti and Giovanni Lotti. Cantata texts were written also by aristocrats, and by aristocratic ecclesiastics, such as Cardinal Fabio Chigi, later Pope Alexander VII; Cardinal Giulio Rospigliosi, later Pope Clement IX; Cardinal Benedetto Pamfili; Cardinals Francesco and Antonio Barberini. Many of these poets are known for the opera and oratorio librettos they wrote as well. Finally, some composers of cantatas, such as Domenico Mazzocchi and Loreto Vittori, wrote some of their own texts.

In the cantata manuscripts, poets are seldom named; and only exceptionally can their work be traced to collections of poetry. It is probable that most of the cantata poets, whether identified or anonymous, were known personally to the cantata composers. Some of the poets named above are known to have been in regular association with the composers of cantatas; and there is a letter by Carlo

255

Caproli to Cardinal Antonio Barberini, from Lyon, 5 January 1654, in which Caproli begs Barberini «to spur Sig. Lotti on to send me short *ariette* of verses because thus they want them»[51]. Another report testifies, surely with some truth behind its mock-modesty, to a similar collaboration between poet and composer. Crescimbeni relates, in his *L'arcadia* (Rome, 1708), an occasion when Alessandro Scarlatti wanted to present some «Canzoni» with texts by Giovanni Battista Zappi. Zappi objected to Scarlatti[52]:

> You know very well that such compositions, done only for the sake of music, are little suited to the refined taste of the eminent men of letters who are the Shepherds of this gathering. And especially must this be said of mine, since they are produced by me without any preparation, extemporaneously, and for the most part at the very same table of the composer of the music, as you yourself have many times seen and experienced.

There is some evidence that the word «cantata» took on a more uniform meaning in course of the 1670's. From this decade the heading «cantata» appears in the sources with increasing frequency, and sometimes in distinction to the pieces called «ariette» or «canzonette». In Giovanni Legrenzi's *Cantate, e canzonette a voce sola* (Bologna, 1676), each piece bears one or the other of these designations. In Legrenzi's *Echi di riverenza di cantate, e canzoni* (Bologna, 1678), the *canzoni* are strophic songs, whereas the *cantate* are more extended and varied compositions[53]. Giovanni Bassani's many publications of *Cantate amorose*, from 1680 to 1703, contain compositions built variously of recitatives, arias, and ariosos[54]. In many sources from the 1670's, and in some earlier ones, the individual components of cantatas are headed «recitativo» or, more frequently, «aria».

Clearly, by the seventh decade of the 17th century, the cantata was understood to mean a more or less extended composition, built of contrasting sections. The recitatives and arias in any one cantata might vary in number and in arrangement; but they were now quite separate components within the whole work. This was the kind of cantata known (in 1703) to Sébastien de Brossard[55]:

> It is a large piece, of which the words are in Italian; varied with *Recitatives*, *Ariettas*, and different tempos; usually for solo Voice and a basso continuo, often with two Violins or several Instruments, etc. When the words are *pious*, or moral, they are named *Cantate morali ò spirituali;* when they speak of *love*, they are *Cantate amorose* etc.

[51] The entire letter is printed in Henry Prunières, *L'opéra italien en France avant Lulli*, Paris 1913, 154/155; transcribed from Paris, Bibliothèque Nationale, nouv. acq. françaises Ms. 2113, fol. 191.

[52] op. cit., 289.

[53] Schmitz, *Solokantate*, 116/117.

[54] See the musical analyses in Haselbach, *Giovanni Battista Bassani*, 238–248. See Bassani's compositions in *I classici della musica italiana* II; and the collection recently published though prepared years ago, *Cantate a voce sola*, ed. G.F. Malipiero, Fondazione Giorgio Cini, Venice ca. 1964 (?).

[55] *Dictionaire de musique*, Paris 1703, «CANTATA».

By the time Johann Mattheson and Jean-Jacques Rousseau came to write their definitions, the cantata had become more stereotyped in structure. In 1739 Mattheson wrote[56]:

From arias, recitatives, ariosos, etc. results the fifth category of our vocal music, namely V. the Cantata, which can be of two kinds: 1) when it begins and ends with an aria; 2) when it presents both [arias] or only the beginning [aria] with a recitative. Further, cantatas can be sacred or secular, according to their contents.... That arrangement of cantatas which is begun with one aria, centered with the second [aria], and concluded with the third [aria], is the most agreeable. The intermingling of recitatives is understood.

According to Rousseau (in 1768), « *Cantatas* are generally composed of three Recitatives, and as many Arias »[57].

It was not, however, before the end of the 17th century that cantatas had become so prescribed in structure. And then, notwithstanding Mattheson and Rousseau, they were most commonly built of two arias, each preceded by a recitative. But there are also many cantatas of this period with additional recitatives and arias, or with the shorter form of aria–recitative–aria. The arias within cantatas became similarly prescribed in structure; and by the first decade of the 18th century, relatively few arias were composed in forms other than the da capo. A great many, perhaps a majority, of the arias show a feature which is called, in English, a « motto beginning » and, in German, a « Devise »: the voice sings the initial phrase, then rests while the continuo plays alone, then repeats the initial phrase and continues with the rest of the aria[58]. The initial phrase is sometimes introduced by the continuo alone, and it is then sometimes repeated by the continuo while the voice is resting. Altogether the continuo is more active in arias than it had been in cantatas of the earlier 17th century. The same features are to be found in the arias of contemporary operas, which, after all, were being composed in the same centers and largely by the same musicians.

257

Although the majority of cantatas continued to be accompanied by basso continuo alone, additional instruments were employed more often from the last decades of the 17th century. Thus parts were sometimes written for one or especially two violins, or occasionally for flutes or trumpets. A cantata with such additional parts is still a chamber work, and not to be confused with the serenata, a different though related category of music. It is true that some cantatas were headed « Serenata », and that some serenatas were headed « Cantata ». In practice, however, the two categories differed in musical resources and function[59]. Sere-

---

[56] Mattheson, *Capellmeister*, 214.
[57] *Dictionaire de musique*, Paris 1768, 71.
[58] Cf. p. 673/674.
[59] For the distinction between cantatas and serenatas made by 18th-century writers, see Crescimbeni, *Poesia* I, 300; Mattheson, *Capellmeister*, 216/217; Burney, *History of Music* IV, 140/141 (reprint 606/607); the letters about a serenata of Alessandro Scarlatti, printed in

natas called for larger instrumental forces; they were performed to larger audiences, and they were frequently composed for specific occasions of importance. They do not have the function of chamber music, and they sometimes took place out of doors. There seems to be no evidence for any outdoor performance of Italian cantatas, nor is it probable.

Italian cantatas of the 17th and 18th centuries were performed in private and usually aristocratic houses, to small and musically cultivated audiences. Cantatas with moral or spiritual texts were probably performed mainly, though not exclusively, in religious circles. But whether secular or sacred, the cantatas were generally performed, as well as composed, by trained, professional musicians.

The singers were predominantly sopranos, both female and male. The accompanists were predominantly players of the lute and harpsichord in their various sizes. Many other instruments, however, were also used to accompany monody and cantata: guitar, double harp, clavichord, organ, violoncello. In the 18th century there was a certain change of fashion. Cantatas were then accompanied chiefly by a keyboard instrument (especially the harpsichord), frequently doubled by a melodic bass instrument (especially the violoncello). The accompaniment was conceived with imagination and variety. The singing was managed with refinement and expressiveness. The performances were altogether suited to the audiences of musical connoisseurs [60].

The Italian cantata at the turn of the 18th century is illustrated in the work of Alessandro Scarlatti (1660–1725), the most prolific of all the cantata composers. The number of known cantatas by Scarlatti stands now at 802, according to the latest research of Edwin Hanley [61]. This number, high as it is, includes only the chamber cantatas, and not the serenatas and single arias of Scarlatti. In writing cantatas, Scarlatti used the same kinds of texts and the same musical forms as did his contemporaries. His cantatas, along with his musical works in general, are grounded in the rich traditions of his musical heritage [62]. Scarlatti's music is

258

Mario Fabbri, *Alessandro Scarlatti e il Principe Ferdinando de' Medici*, Florence 1961, 66/67. The terminology of « serenata » is discussed by Owen Jander, *The Minor Dramatic Works of Alessandro Scarlatti*, Diss. Harvard University 1962 (ms.), 85–95; Stradella's serenatas are discussed there on 95–133.

[60] I shall give details in my forthcoming book on the chamber cantata.

[61] Communication from Dr. Edwin Hanley, 22 September 1968. Hanley has found almost 20 more cantatas by Scarlatti since the completion of his work, *Alessandro Scarlatti's Cantate da Camera: A Bibliographical Study*, Diss. Yale University 1963 (ms.). The main part of this dissertation is a thematic, analytical catalogue of the cantatas by Scarlatti. Hanley's catalogue, now in course of publication, is a masterly work of fundamental importance.

[62] Scarlatti's links with the past, and the differences between his music and that of the following generation of composers in Naples, were pointed out so long ago as 1905, by Edward J. Dent, *Alessandro Scarlatti: His Life and Works*, London 1905, revised edition, ed. Frank Walker 1960, 196–198. This aspect of Scarlatti's music has also been well demonstrated by Edwin Hanley, in his articles on Scarlatti in *MGG* XI (1963), 1482–1506, and *Enciclopedia della musica* IV, Milan 1964, 132–137.

original, however, by the sheer force of his genius. The majority (though certainly not all) of Scarlatti's later cantatas are in the form of recitative–aria–recitative–aria (i. e. two of each). Yet within the basic outline of each cantata, the arias are usually contrasted sharply in key, meter, and the kind of material employed; the recitatives are flexible and expressive sections, which frequently include passages in arioso style; and there is throughout an abundance of melodic and harmonic inspiration[63]. The freedom and boldness of harmony in Scarlatti's cantatas have long been recognized. But Scarlatti was an equally great master of musical declamation. Notice, for instance, the telling intervallic leaps and rhythmic patterns in this example, taken from a recitative in Scarlatti's *Dove una quercia annosa*[64]:

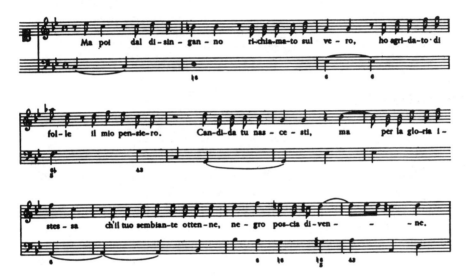

The following example is from Scarlatti's *Al fin m'ucciderete;* it shows the ending of the first recitative and the (motto) beginning of the first aria[65].

[63] For a more detailed musical analysis, see the interesting article by Malcolm Boyd, «Form and Style in Scarlatti's Chamber Cantatas», *Music Review* XXV (1964), 17–26. Boyd is also the author of an M.A. thesis, *Alessandro Scarlatti and the Italian Chamber Cantata*, Durham University 1962 (ms.).

[64] Dresden, Sächsische Landesbibliothek, Ms. Mus. 1/I/2,1, fol. 72'–73.

[65] Washington, D.C., Library of Congress, Ms. M 1620. S 287 Case, fol. 6'–7'.

The generation of composers following Scarlatti continued to write chamber cantatas, though in decreasing numbers. Cantatas, like operas, of the early 18th century have been assigned to what has been called «the Neapolitan School». But this is an unfortunate and misleading term. A geographical name has been misapplied to a chronological stage of development. There is no such thing as a «Neapolitan cantata». There are only cantatas of a more or less uniform kind which were written all over Italy in the first half of the 18th century. As Schmitz points out, what he nevertheless persists in calling «the Neapolitan School» includes composers working not only in Naples, but in Bologna, Rome, Florence and especially Venice.[66] The cantatas of the Venetian Benedetto Marcello, for instance, belong to the mainstream of 18th-century Italian cantatas.[67]

This 18th-century form of the cantata consists of alternating recitatives and arias, most commonly arranged as recitative–aria–recitative–aria. The recitatives are relatively short, the arias relatively long. The arias are almost invariably in da capo form; they frequently start with a motto beginning; they may include elaborate figuration for the voice; and they are supported by an active, sometimes

[66] Schmitz, *Solokantate*, 163.

[67] For a selection of Marcello's cantatas, see Giacomo Benvenuti's edition in *I classici musicali italiani* II, Milan 1942; for further discussion, see Caroline Sites, *Benedetto Marcello's Chamber Cantatas*, Diss. University of North Carolina 1959 (ms.).

a running, bass. By now, in the 18th century, there are also cantatas accompanied by strings and sometimes other instruments, in addition to the continuo.

It is to this stage in the development of the Italian cantata that Handel's cantatas belong. Handel had good opportunities to hear, for instance, Alessandro Scarlatti's cantatas in Rome and Francesco Gasparini's cantatas in Venice; and in his Italian duets, he also followed the excellent lead of Agostino Steffani. But a full-scale study of Handel's cantatas, based upon the original sources, has not yet been published[68].

By the middle of the 18th century, cantatas were no longer written in significant numbers by the leading Italian composers. Nor did they furnish the main staple of vocal music performed in private homes. Jean-Jacques Rousseau wrote in his *Dictionnaire de musique*, « it is not without reason that *Cantatas* have gone out of Fashion, and that they have been replaced, even in Concerts, by Scenes of Opera »[69]. Dr. Burney, a connoisseur and great admirer of the Italian cantata, wrote in his *General History of Music*[70]:

> But cantatas, which were composed with more care, and sung with more taste and science than any other species of vocal Music, during the latter end of the last century and beginning of the present, seem to have been wholly laid aside, after the decease of Pergolesi, till revived by Sarti, who has set, in the manner of cantatas, several of Metastasio's charming little poems, which he calls *canzonette....*

> Indeed, it is to be lamented that a species of composition so admirably calculated for concerts as the *cantata*, should now be so seldom cultivated.... Opera scenes, or single songs, now supply the place of cantatas in all private concerts.

The substitution of opera arias for cantatas is well documented in the musical sources. A certain number of pieces from operas had always been sung as chamber music: the *Lamento d'Arianna* was a favorite piece, and arias from various other operas are found in cantata manuscripts of the 17th century. But from the 1670's an increasing number of manuscripts were compiled of opera arias, alone or together with cantatas. And by the middle of the 18th century, opera arias had usurped the position of cantatas[71].

261

[68] For introductory studies, see Anthony Lewis, «The Songs and Chamber Cantatas», *Handel: A Symposium*, ed. G. Abraham, London 1954, 179–199; and Julian Herbage, «The Secular Oratorios and Cantatas», ib., 132–155 – Lewis presents an excellent survey, which (with some material from Herbage) forms the basis of Paul H. Lang's discussion in his *George Frideric Handel*, New York 1966, 63–67; but Lang introduces some inaccuracies; and Lang's account (55–60, 63/64) of the cantata before Handel includes more numerous and serious mistakes, showing insufficient acquaintance with the secondary literature as well as with the original sources. Lang does, however, start with the excellent idea of treating the 17th-century cantata as an important background to the cantatas of Handel. Ursula Kirkendale presents much documentary material in her fine article, «The Ruspoli Documents on Handel», *JAMS* XX (1967), 222–273. See also Rudolf Ewerhart, «Die Händel-Handschriften der Santini-Bibliothek in Münster», *Händel-Jb.* VI (1960), 111–150.

[69] Rousseau, *Dictionnaire*, 72.

[70] Burney, *History of Music* IV, 179 (reprint 637/638).

[71] No major work on the 18th-century Italian cantata has been published since Schmitz,

In the course of its history, which coincides with the baroque period, the cantata exercised an influence second to no other category of music. It developed alongside of opera, and the two categories show similar traits at the various stages of their development. But the performance of cantatas, unlike that of operas, demanded no elaborate preparation or production. Cantatas were circulated and sung all over Italy. They were sought after in France, Germany and England. The number and dispersion of the surviving sources shows that some cantatas enjoyed phenomenal popularity. Luigi Rossi's solo cantata *Anime, voi che sete dalle furie* survives in 16 contemporary manuscripts, in 5 countries[72]. Constantine Huygens wrote in a letter of 1 May 1670, from The Hague, « As for *Anime*, the famous production of Sr. Luiggi, it is a very long time since we have possessed it. And how could you believe that till now we have been able to live without anime?»[73] The pun (*anima* can mean soul or spirit) is a nice touch to an already striking testimony. Luigi Rossi's duet *Dite, o cieli* survives in 16 contemporary manuscripts; it was printed in 4 French collections from 1701 to 1708, in an English collection of 1688, and in an English collection of about 1790[74]; it served as the direct model for John Blow's also very popular *Go, perjur'd man*[75]. Carissimi's cantata for 3 voices, *Sciolto havean dall'alte sponde*, is preserved in 14 contemporary manuscripts; its final trio survives in 13 further manuscripts, in 4 French collections printed from 1701 to 1708, and in Roger North's *Memoires of Musick* (1728)[76]. Alessandro Scarlatti's solo cantata *Al fin m'ucciderete* survives in 35 copies from the 18th century, plus 5 copies from the 19th century[77].

As the example of Blow's song shows, Italian cantatas were imitated as well as admired in England. Some of the songs by Henry Lawes and Henry Purcell are virtually cantatas: extended pieces with contrasting sections, or lengthy ariosos. In Germany, the native *Lied* was similarly influenced by the Italian cantata; the songs of Heinrich Albert, Adam Krieger and Philipp Heinrich Erlebach, for instance, include sections in recitative, arioso and aria styles. In France, the earliest known cantatas are by Marc-Antoine Charpentier, who had studied in Rome with Carissimi. (There are also some Italian cantatas by Charpentier[78].) Nicolas Bernier,

Solokantate, 156–188. But Helmut Hucke has added some interesting new material in his section of the «Kantate» entry in *MGG* VII (1958), 563–575.

[72] *WECIS*, fasc. 3a, No. 17.

[73] W.J.A.Jonckbloet and J.P.N. Land, ed., *Musique et musiciens au XVIIᵉ siècle: Correspondance et oeuvre musicales de Constantin Huygens*, Leyden 1882, 54.

[74] *WECIS*, fasc. 3a, No. 221; and fasc. 5.

[75] Sir John Hawkins, *A General History of the Science and Practice of Music* IV, London 1776, 488–490, where it is attributed to Carissimi. It is attributed to Carissimi also in *Apollonian Harmony* II, London ca. 1790, 30/31, where it is headed «NB. This was the Model on which Dr. Blow composed the preceeding Song.»

[76] *WECIS*, fasc. 5; and John Wilson, *Roger North on Music*, London 1959, 120–122.

[77] Information from Edwin Hanley, 22 September 1968.

[78] Paris, Bibliothèque Nationale, Ms. Vmʳ. 8, fol. 17; Ms. Vmʳ. 18, pages 70–72; Ms. Vmʳ. 55, pages 74–77.

who began publishing French cantatas in 1703 or shortly thereafter, had studied in Rome with Caldara. Jean-Baptiste Morin stated plainly in the preface to his first book of *Cantates françoises*[79] that he had based his cantatas upon Italian examples. Indeed, the French cantatas themselves show that they were written in imitation of Italian ones[80].

The influence of the Italian cantata both abroad and at home was great and far-reaching. The beauty of the music was worthy of its reputation.

[79] Paris 1706.
[80] See the fine articles by David Tunley, «The Cantatas of Louis Nicholas Clérambault», *MQ* LII (1966), 313–331; and «The Emergence of the Eighteenth Century French Cantata», *Studies in Music* I (1967), 67–88.

[1967]

263

Music and the Claims of Text: Monteverdi, Rinuccini, and Marino

Gary Tomlinson

The composer of vocal music writes as poet and scholiast. His message is autonomous but not wholly his own. He sets to work with a preexistent artwork before him—a poem or passage of prose, often written without thought of musical setting—and fashions his song under its constraints. He welcomes to his work a second, distinct language, one which corresponds to his own at most only partially in syntax and significance.

The composer's unique act of accommodation, structuring his setting after certain requisites of his text, may have far-reaching implications for his musical style—implications too often ignored in today's musical analysis and criticism. Which particular textual characteristics the composer chooses to emphasize will depend on much beyond the text itself: on his view of the nature and capabilities of musical discourse, shaped internally by musical procedures developed from the canon of his predecessors, externally by general expectations and aspirations of his culture; and on his equally rich conception of the tradition behind his text. The text-music interface is therefore a provocative area of exploration for critic and historian alike. It points to the expressive aims of a composer in a given work, and it elucidates broader cultural assumptions concerning the nature of musical and poetic discourse.

Claudio Monteverdi, champion of novel musical idioms—a *seconda pratica musicale*—which aimed to make the words the "master of the harmonies," cultivated a shrewd ear for contemporary poetic styles and a quick appreciation for their aptness to musical setting. The texts he chose (or was assigned) to set so shaped his music that the development of his style may be understood as a succession of readings—some profoundly exegetic, others more superficially so—of the varied poetic idioms he approached. And the rich diversity of his large secular output, consisting mainly of twelve collections of madrigals and other short works published from 1587 to 1651 and of numerous operas and dramatic entertainments, gains coherence from an understanding of his poets.

Monteverdi's long career spans decades marked in the history of Italian poetry by sweeping changes in taste and fashion. The arbiter of new trends and, from around 1610, the darling of the *stilnovisti* was the Neapolitan Giambattista Marino (1569–1625). His name has come to denote a group of related seventeenth-century poetic styles, "Marinist" styles, and his works will serve as one focal point for my discussion. Largely (though by no means completely) supplanted by Marinism were more traditional idioms, many of them stemming from Petrarchan tendencies of the earlier sixteenth century. One poet with deep roots in earlier Petrarchism, and a crucial figure in Monteverdi's development, was the Florentine Ottavio Rinuccini (1562–1621), author of many of Monteverdi's texts, including his second opera, *L'Arianna*.

266

1

Rinuccini had his own view of the difference between his style and Marino's, which we may glean from an anecdote related years later by the Florentine *letterato* Carlo Dati:

> I remember hearing that Cavalier Marino, reading Ottavio Rinuccini's noble tragedy *L'Arianna,* and admiring it, came to the verses
>
> > O Teseo, o Teseo mio,
> > se tu sapessi, o Dio,
> > se tu sapessi, ohimè, come s'affanna
> > la povera Arianna,
> > forse, forse pentito
> > rivolgeresti ancor la prora al lito . . . ,
>
> and asked the author why he had chosen *povera* instead of *misera,* which seemed to him more regal. To which Rinuccini answered, "Begging your pardon, Sig. Cavalier: you ask this question because you are a foreigner. You should know that for us *povera* is much

Gary Tomlinson, assistant professor of music history at the University of Pennsylvania, is the author of articles on Monteverdi, early opera, and Verdi. He is currently writing a book on Monteverdi and late-Renaissance culture.

more affective, full of pathos, and appropriate than *misera;* and that in this passage it signifies not destitute of riches but deprived of all happiness. We use it in this sense even in the case of a powerful monarch, to describe his sorrows, and not to call him a beggar."[1]

To us Rinuccini's self-conscious *toscanità* consists in more than just this native linguistic precision; it speaks first in his clarity of language and simplicity of imagery, evoking a Florentine poetic past marked by the proximity of popular and patrician styles. Croce saw Poliziano's vernacular works behind Rinuccini's limpid elegance (and certainly the poet's second music-drama, *L'Euridice,* owes much to Poliziano's *Festa d'Orfeo*).[2] Rinuccini's plain-speaking style springs more directly, however, from a long line of sixteenth-century intermediaries, including Luigi Alamanni, Lodovico Martelli, Antonfrancesco Grazzini detto il Lasca, and Remigio Nannini.[3]

Also typically Florentine is the strain of colloquial piety running through Rinuccini's works. Some of his lyrics rely in their straightforward contrition on the popular devotional verse of Girolamo Benivieni;[4] while in others Rinuccini develops a *fin de siècle* urgency of sentiment rarely encountered in his predecessors:

267

> O miei giorni fugaci, o breve vita,
> ohimè! già sei partita.
> Già sento, ò sentir parmi
> la rigorosa Tromba
> davanti à te giusto Signor chiamarmi.
> Già nel cor mi rimbomba
> il formidabil suono;
> miserere di me, Signor perdono.[5]

[Oh fleeting days, oh too short life, alas! you are gone. Already I hear, or seem to hear, the relentless trumpet call me before you, just Lord. Already the dread sound echoes in my heart; have mercy on me, Signor, pardon me.]

1. Carlo Dati, ed. *Prose Fiorentine raccolte dallo Smarrito Accademico della Crusca,* 6 vols. (Venice, 1735–43), 1. i:17; here and elsewhere, all translations from the Italian are my own, unless otherwise indicated. The first volume of this collection reproduces the edition of Florence, 1661, the only volume published by Dati during his lifetime.

2. See Benedetto Croce, *Storia dell'età barocca in Italia* (Bari, 1967), p. 346.

3. For lyrics of these poets, see *Opere Toscane di Luigi Alamanni* (Venice, 1542); *Opere di M. Lodovico Martelli* (Florence, 1548); *Rime di Antonfrancesco Grazzini detto il Lasca, parte prima* (Florence, 1741); and *I fiori delle rime de' poeti illustri,* ed. Girolamo Ruscelli (Venice, 1586). An important modern anthology with works by all four poets is *Lirici del cinquecento,* ed. Luigi Baldacci (Milan, 1975).

4. See *Opere di Girolamo Benivieni Firentino* (Florence, 1524).

5. *Poesie del Sr. Ottavio Rinuccini* (Florence, 1622), p. 292; all further references will be included in the text.

But if the cutting desperation of Rinuccini's madrigal is rarely matched by his Florentine forebears, nevertheless its language, attuned to the weightiness of its subject in its persistent rhetorical parallelisms, its dark vowels, and its sonorous double consonants, echoes the tortured idiom of Giovanni Battista Strozzi the Elder:

> Ria lagrimosa tromba
> di spavento s'ha posto a bocca Morte;
> e sì grave e sì forte
> suona dall'oscurissima sua tomba,
> che 'nsino al ciel rimbomba: udite belva
> spietata, voi che per quest'atra selva
> pur traviate lassi;
> e volgete lassù, volgete i passi.[6]

[Death has put to its mouth an awful, woeful trumpet of fear; and so loud and low it sounds from his darksome tomb that it echoes even to the heavens: heed the pitiless beast, all you who wander lost through this obscure wood, and turn your steps toward heaven.]

268

In their care to gauge their linguistic and rhetorical structures to the *gravità* of their subject, Rinuccini and Strozzi place themselves squarely in a poetic tradition extending well beyond the walls of their native city, that is, in the sixteenth-century tradition of Petrarchan revival and emulation.

Gravità was a central term in this tradition from 1525, when Pietro Bembo, in his influential *Prose della volgar lingua,* opposed it to *piacevolezza* ("pleasantness") in an expressive dialectic he considered vital to all literary utterance. From the mixture of these contrasting elements, Bembo sought a diversity of expression *(variazione)* which would insure against tedium; their balance in each composition was determined by the weightiness (or slightness) of the content. Bembo enumerated linguistic and syntactic techniques for the achievement of both *piacevolezza* and *gravità,* and later writers, Torquato Tasso among them, enlarged upon his precepts. In the verse of Petrarch (and the prose of Boccaccio), Bembo saw an ideal matching of style to content, an interplay of *piacevolezza* and *gravità* appropriate at every moment: "Petrarch realized both of these parts so wondrously that we cannot decide in which he was the greater master."[7]

Sixteenth-century Petrarchism is not simply a matter of Bembo's Ciceronian accommodation of style to subject, though this aspect bears rich potential for musical elaboration. More obviously, Petrarchism im-

6. Giovanni Battista Strozzi, "Ria lagrimosa tromba," in *Lirici del cinquecento,* p. 333.
7. Pietro Bembo, *Opere in volgare,* ed. Mario Marti (Florence, 1961), pp. 321–22.

plies the imitation and development of the abundant stock of themes, *topoi*, and images in the *Canzoniere,* borrowed elements which echo through the poetry books of the entire century.[8] Dominant among these is the Petrarchan opposition of secular longings and the injunctions of faith, that self-conscious ambivalence summed up in the closing verse of the great *canzone* "I' vo pensando, et nel penser m'assale": "et veggio 'l meglio et al peggior m'appiglio [and I see the better but I lay hold on the worse]." The poet's realization that the ends of his love for Laura are not reconcilable with his Christian beliefs creates an ever present tension in the *Canzoniere,* announced already in the opening sonnet (set, incidentally, by Monteverdi in his *Selva morale e spirituale* of 1640):

> Voi ch'ascoltate in rime sparse il suono
> di quei sospiri ond' io nudriva 'l core
> in sul mio primo giovenile errore,
> quand' era in parte altr' uom da quel ch' i' sono:
>
> del vario stile in ch' io piango et ragiono
> fra le vane speranze e 'l van dolore,
> ove sia chi per prova intenda amore
> spero trovar pictà, non che perdono.
>
> Ma ben veggio or sì come al popol tutto
> favola fui gran tempo, onde sovente
> di me medesmo meco mi vergogno;
>
> et del mio vaneggiar vergogna è 'l frutto,
> e 'l pentersi, e 'l conoscer chiaramente
> che quanto piace al mondo è breve sogno.

269

[You who hear in scattered rhymes the sound of those sighs with which I nourished my heart during my first youthful error, when I was in part another man from what I am now:

for the varied style in which I weep and speak between vain hopes and vain sorrow, where there is anyone who understands love through experience, I hope to find pity, not only pardon.

But now I see well how for a long time I was the talk of the crowd, for which often I am ashamed of myself within;

and of my raving, shame is the fruit, and repentance, and the clear knowledge that whatever pleases in the world is a brief dream.][9]

8. For a probing discussion of sixteenth-century views and uses of Petrarch, see Luigi Baldacci, *Il Petrarchismo italiano nel cinquecento,* rev. ed. (Padua, 1974).

9. I quote the translation of Robert M. Durling, *Petrarch's Lyric Poems: The "Rime sparse" and Other Lyrics* (Cambridge, Mass., 1976), pp. 432, 36.

Rinuccini, along with dozens before him, opened his own *canzoniere* in the same penitential vein:

> Quanto in rime cantai dettando Amore,
> che nel cor giovenil gran tempo accolsi,
> all'hor che gli occhi e più la mente volsi
> a quella, cui donar mi piacque il core.
>   Scrissi nè già per acquistarmi onore,
> cercato in van da chi cantando duolsi,
> ma scoprendo 'l mi' error mill'altri volsi
> trar con l'esempio mio d'inganno fuore.
>   E forse fia che 'l cieco e van desio
> (queste Rime leggendo alma gentile)
> spento, in foco più bel s'infiammi, e incenda;
>   e quanto 'l Mondo ha in se posto in oblio,
> disdegnando beltà terrena e vile,
> altro à cantar più degn'oggetto prenda.

[P. 40]

270

[How often I sang rhymes of love!—love, which I long welcomed into my youthful breast, turning my eyes and still more my mind to her to whom it pleased me to give my heart. ¶ I wrote not to acquire honor, sought in vain by those who lament in song; rather, uncovering my error, I hoped to draw a thousand others away from falsehood by my example. ¶ And perhaps it will happen that some gracious soul, purged of blind and empty desire, will read these rhymes and kindle a truer flame, ¶ and, forgetting this world, disdaining its vile and earthly beauty, will take more worthy subjects for his song.]

To be sure, sixteenth-century poets viewed Petrarch's crisis through a haze of more recent ideologies. Especially important was the Platonizing theory of love expounded in the fifteenth century by Marsilio Ficino and his followers and diluted for popular consumption in countless *trattati d'amore* throughout the next century (Bembo, with his dialogues on love entitled *Gli asolani* [1505], figures centrally in this trend).[10] Ficino's amorous casuistry granted legitimacy to sensual passion—in its visual and auditory if not its tactile manifestations—as a necessary stimulus to a higher, divine passion. His distinction of sacred and profane love thus eased the Petrarchan impasse at the same time as it exhorted sixteenth-century Petrarchists to an ever more self-conscious examination of their

---

10. See Eugenio Garin, *Storia della filosofia italiana,* 3 vols. (Turin, 1966), 1: chaps. 2. v and 3. ii, for a good overview of Ficino's theory of love and its dissemination in the *trattati.* For a more extended discussion of Ficino's theory, see Paul Oskar Kristeller, *The Philosophy of Marsilio Ficino* (Gloucester, Mass., 1964), esp. chap. 13; and for Ficino's own words, see his commentary on Plato's *Symposium, De amore* (the work was published in Ficino's Italian translation in 1544 as *Sopra lo amore).*

own earthly desires. The union of Petrarchan and neo-Platonic themes in sixteenth-century poetry resulted in a fundamentally inward-looking artistic stance, less profoundly searching than Petrarch's but striving still for the self-knowledge which characterizes the *Canzoniere*. Again Rinuccini may set the tone (cf. Petrarch's sonnets 118 and 122):

> Per l'eterno cammin già l'anno quinto
> fornito ha 'l corso, e l'incomincia 'l sesto,
> da che servo d'Amor dolente, e mesto
> me'n vo con volto di pallor dipinto.
> E per veder che naturale instinto
> quell'alma indura, di pregar non resto,
> nè rompo il duro laccio, e non mi desto
> d'amoroso letargo oppresso, e vinto.
> Anima che farem, piangerem sempre
> servi infelici di beltà sì frale,
> in così dure, e dolorose tempre?
> O pur rivolti al Regno alt'immortale,
> pria che morte ne assalga, o 'l duol ne stempre,
> per più nobil sentier batterem l'ale?
>
> [P. 231]

271

[Already the fifth year has run its course, and the sixth has begun, since first I went about with pallid face, a miserable servant of love. ¶ And, because natural instinct hardens her soul, I do not cease my pleas, nor break the cruel ties, nor awaken from this oppressive lethargy of love. ¶ Soul, how will it be? Shall we weep forever, wretched servants of such frail beauty, in pitiless and lamentable bonds? ¶ Or, turning toward the immortal Kingdom on high, before death assails us or sadness maddens us, shall we wing our way along a nobler path?]

Petrarchan introspection, Bembian accommodation of style to content, and a native Florentine predilection for simplicity and straightforward contrition—all of these components of Rinuccini's idiom merge in his four music-dramas. The result is melodrama in the best sense: short plays focused in plot and language on the vivid portrayal of human suffering and passion. In writing these simple Ovidian dramatic fables—from *La Dafne* (1594) through *L'Euridice* (1600) to *L'Arianna* (1607–8) and *Narciso* (1608?)—Rinuccini gradually mastered an unadorned yet lyrical rhetoric ideally suited to the frank sorrows of his protagonists. Compare the stolid plaint of Apollo over the transformed Daphne,

> Dunque ruvida scorza
> Chiuderà sempre la beltà celeste?
> Lumi, voi che vedeste

> L'alta beltà, che a lagrimar vi sforza,
> Affisatevi pure in questa fronde: . . .

[Will rough bark, then, enclose forever your heavenly beauty?
Eyes, you who saw her high beauty, which makes you now weep,
turn your gaze to these leaves: . . .]

with the fluid sorrow of Ariadne abandoned by Theseus,

> Lasciatemi morire,
> Lasciatemi morire;
> E che volete voi che mi conforte
> In così dura sorte,
> In così gran martire?
> Lasciatemi mòrire.[11]

[Leave me to die, leave me to die; what would you have comfort
me, in such cruel straits, in such great martyrdom? Leave me to
die.]

272

Rinuccini's modest claim to our attention rests in his achieving this direct
projection of unequivocal psychological states in a language at once "af-
fettuosa, compassionevole, e propria," as he reportedly described it to
Marino. This achievement goes far to explain the special significance
Rinuccini's verse held for Monteverdi and other composers of the early
seventeenth century.

Introspection finds no place in the new poetics of Marino. His vision, as Carlo Calcaterra has argued, turns decisively outward, to the
world of sensory experience, and his inability "to transcend the image of
life proffered by his five senses" forms the foundation of his artistic
experience.[12] He transforms the neo-Platonic legitimation of sensual
perception into its exaltation, and in his emphasis on tactile delight, he
strikingly inverts the Ficinian hierarchy of the senses.[13] Love becomes
little more than the simultaneous gratification of all five senses; the care-

11. Rinuccini, *La Dafne* and *L'Arianna*, in Angelo Solerti, *Gli albori del melodramma*, 3
vols. (Milan, 1905), 2:96, 175; for modern editions of Rinuccini's music-dramas, see 2:65–
239. All further references to this edition of Rinuccini's music-dramas will be included in
the text.

12. Carlo Calcaterra, *Il parnasso in rivolta* (Bologna, 1961), p. 34. Calcaterra's discussion of Marino remains fundamental; his view has been modified but not altered in its
essentials by the work of younger generations of scholars, including Giovanni Getto and
Franco Croce. A useful introduction to Marino's life and works in English is James V.
Mirollo, *The Poet of the Marvellous: Giambattista Marino* (New York, 1963).

13. See Calcaterra, *Il parnasso*, pp. 13, 18, and 35.

ful neo-Platonic distinction of sacred and profane desires, which had endowed Petrarchan themes with new vitality in the sixteenth century, collapses in a spiritual vacuum.

In the poetic exordium of Marino's *Rime* of 1602, the Petrarchan spiritual dilemma, which we have seen also in the opening sonnet of Rinuccini's *canzoniere*, has already vanished:

> Altri canti di Marte, e di sua schiera
> gli arditi assalti, e l'onorate imprese,
> le saguigne vittorie, e le contese,
> i trionfi di Morte orrida, e fera.
>   I' canto, Amor, da questa tua guerrera
> quant'ebbi a sostener mortali offese,
> come un guardo mi vinse, un crin mi prese:
> istoria miserabile, ma vera.
>   Duo begli occhi fur l'armi onde trafitta
> giacque, e di sangue in vece amaro pianto
> sparse lunga stagion l'anima afflitta.
>   Tu per lo cui valor la palma, e 'l vanto
> ebbe di me la mia nemica invitta,
> se desti morte al cor, dà vita al canto.[14]

273

[Let others celebrate the daring attacks, famous deeds, bloody victories and struggles of Mars and his legions, and the crude and horrid triumphs of Death. ¶ I sing, Love, how I suffered mortal wounds at the hands of your she-warrior, how a glance defeated me, a wink captured me—a wretched story, but true. ¶ Two lovely eyes were the weapons that ran through my broken spirit and left it to shed bitter tears in place of blood. ¶ You, through whose valor my unscathed foe won from me both palm and pride: if once you killed my heart, now quicken my song.]

Petrarch's soul-searching and Rinuccini's angst are here replaced by a more superficial play of ideas, lacking altogether in psychological tension: an extended allegory of love as war (one of Marino's favorite images) turned in the final verse to an epigrammatic pretext for the poet's song. Marino's heart is withering, his life miserable, we must believe, from no deeper ill than sexual frustration.

Marino's treatment of nature also reveals the new despiritualized outlook and bears comparison with that of his compatriot, Tasso. The bedewed nocturnal vistas of Tasso's best lyrics live as much in poetic fantasy as in reality and typically function as an organic projection onto the landscape of a vividly human emotion:

14. Giambattista Marino, *La lira: Rime del Cavalier Marino* (Venice, 1638), pt. 1, p. 1; all further references will be included in the text.

Qual rugiada o qual pianto,
quai lacrime eran quelle
che sparger vidi dal notturno manto
e dal candido volto de le stelle?
E perché seminò la bianca luna
di cristalline stille un puro nembo
a l'erba fresca in grembo?
Perché ne l'aria bruna
s'udian, quasi dolendo, intorno intorno
gir l'aure insino al giorno?
Fur segni forse de la tua partita,
vita de la mia vita?[15]

[What dewdrops or what tears, what humors were those that I saw
fall from the nighttime mantle and from the soft-white face of the
stars? And why did the argent moon sow a limpid cloud of crystal-
line drops in the womb of the fresh grasses? Why did we hear the
breezes, almost weeping, turn round and round in the darkness till
dawn? Were these perhaps portents of your leaving, life of my
life?]

274

Marino, in contrast, strikes no profound resonance in his juxtaposition
of natural and human realms. Nature is for him merely the perversity of
an overly bright moon, impediment to his nighttime amorous escapades
(in the sonnet "Né tu pietosa dea, né tu lucente"). Or it serves in all its
splendor as an "ornamental pretext," to use Giovanni Getto's phrase, for
conceits contrived to make the reader marvel (here in ll. 11 and 14):[16]

Pon mente al mar, Cratone, or che 'n ciascuna
riva sua dorme l'onda, e tace il vento,
e Notte in ciel di cento gemme e cento
ricca spiega la vesta azzurra, e bruna.
Rimira ignuda, e senza benda alcuna,
nuotando per lo mobile elemento,
misto, e confuso l'un con l'altro argento,
tra le ninfe del ciel danzar la Luna.
Ve' come van per queste piagge, e quelle
con scintille scherzando ardenti e chiare,
volte in pesci le stelle, i pesci in stelle.
Sì puro il vago fondo a noi traspare,
che fra tanti dirai lampi e facelle,
"Ecco in ciel cristallin cangiato il mare".

[*La lira,* pt. 1, p. 60]

15. Torquato Tasso, *Aminta e rime,* ed. Francesco Flora, 2 vols. (Turin, 1976), 1:165.
16. Giovanni Getto, "Introduzione al Marino," in *Barocco in prosa e in poesia* (Milan, 1969), p. 37; on nature in Marino, see esp. pp. 37–41.

[Look to the sea, Crato, now that the waves sleep on every shore, the wind quiets, and Night unfurls in the sky its dark and bluish cloak, rich with a hundred hundred gems. ¶ See there nude, without a single veil, swimming in the mobile element where one silver mixes with another, the Moon dance among the stellar nymphs. ¶ See how, in this realm and that, sparkling clear and playful, the fish swim turned to stars, the stars to fish. ¶ So clearly the bottom shines through to us, amid so many fires and flashes, that we might say—"Here is the sea changed to a crystal heaven!"]

"È dal poeta il fin la maraviglia," writes Marino, proclaiming the stimulation of surprise in the reader as a central goal of his art. But his notorious metaphors, studied epigrammatism, jarring employment of scientific or technical jargon (a modest example is the "mobile elemento" in l. 6 above), and unending enumerations and descriptions of flowers, trees, gems, and the like—all of these arise from a deeper source than the simple urge to strike wonder in his readers. They spring from the poet's need, in the absence of an inner wellspring of artistic subjectivity, to enrich with poetry the impersonal reality around him. Marino seeks, through the novel relationships between commonplace objects and ideas struck up in his imagery and epigrammatic twists, to create an illusion of subjectivity within an essentially objective world view. While Tasso's landscape is a rich extension of lover and beloved, of intersecting psyches, Marino's waits in vain to be artificially enlivened in astonishing arabesques of technical virtuosity.

275

Calcaterra has written that "the sensual beauty of the word, beloved in and of itself as form and music, was the primary motivation of Marino's art"; and in this love of a luxuriant verbal music independent of his subject, Marino again distances himself from the Petrarchan tradition.[17] Earlier poets as diverse as Tansillo and della Casa or as Rinuccini and Tasso had learned from Bembo the expressive dividends of a language and style matched to content. But Marino's much-vaunted musicality at times uses language as so many sonorous fragments, full of sound, signifying nothing, as in the listings and descriptions of natural objects which lard *L'Adone* (1623) and the "idylls" of *La sampogna* (1620).[18] Occasionally Marino employs verbal virtuosity as an expressive end in itself, to dazzle his reader; usually, however, the language is not warranted by the subject. In this madrigal to Saint Francis, the miracle of the stigmata moves Marino to no more dignified stylistic *gravità* than a witty word play:

17. Calcaterra, ed., intro. to *I lirici del seicento e dell'Arcadia* (Milan, 1936), p. 12.
18. The rarity of such listings in *Le rime* and *La lira* is probably mainly a function of the brevity of the lyrics listed here.

Amasti amato amante,
e qual vero amatore,
ti trasformasti nell'amato Amore.
Ed amante, ed amato,
Amor innamorato
de le sue piaghe sante
l'amoroso sembiante
ne le tue membra impresso
in te sol per amor stampò se stesso.

[*La lira,* pt. 2, p. 117]

[You loved, beloved lover, and, as a true lover, you transformed yourself into beloved Love. And, loving and loved, enamored Love, marking your limbs with the loving semblance of His holy wounds, in you for love alone impressed Himself.]

Most often, perhaps, Marino's lush musicality arises in the poet's forced attempt to forge a rhetoric of impassioned emotion, and from several moments in his oeuvre it is evident that he looked to Rinuccini's music-dramas as one source for this idiom.[19] But Marino never knew Rinuccini's restraint. His delight in shimmering sonorities leads him well beyond the bounds of genuine sentiment in this exchange of Venus and Adonis from *L'Adone:*

"Non sono," egli ripiglia "or non son questi
gli occhi, onde dolci al cor strali mi scocchi?
Gli occhi, onde dolce il cor dianzi m'ardesti?
Begli occhi . . ." E 'n questo dir le bacia gli occhi.
"Begli occhi," ella soggiunge "occhi celesti
cagion che di dolcezza il cor trabocchi.
Core ond'io vivo senza cor, tesoro
ond'io povera son, vita ond'io moro!"[20]

["Are these not," he replies, "now are these not the eyes whence sweet shafts pierce my heart? The eyes whence my heart just now was enflamed? Beautiful eyes . . ." and saying this he kisses her eyes. "Beautiful eyes," she takes up, "heavenly eyes, which make my heart overflow with joy!—heart whence I live without a heart, treasure whence I am poor, life whence I die!"]

19. In *L'Adone,* for example, the lament of the nymphs and of Venus for the dead Adonis (canto 18) is reminiscent at several points of Rinuccini's *Dafne* and *Euridice;* and a few of the more vital locutions in Marino's *Arianna* (on which see below) recall clearly Rinuccini's lament of Ariadne.

20. Marino, *Opere,* ed. Alberto Asor Rosa (Milan, 1967), p. 741; all further references will be included in the text.

Rinuccini's favored word, *povera,* carefully gauged in his usage to capture Ariadne's anguish, recurs here in Marino's last verse. Typically, however, Marino prefers its objective sense, "destitute of riches," to a more subjective meaning and deprives it of any emotional significance. Also typically, he deploys it in the series of hackneyed love conceits in which the passage culminates. Cleverness and claptrap in a world devoid of authentic passion mark the Marinist vision.

Inspired by Rinuccini's famous and greatly admired example, Marino included in *La sampogna* his own version of the abandoned Ariadne's woes. Marino's *Arianna* elaborates on the main classical tellings of the story—those of Ovid (*Heroides* 10), Catullus (64), and especially Nonnos (*Dionysiaca* 47)—and for the most part studiously avoids direct borrowings from Rinuccini's *Arianna*. It also points up some important adjuncts of Marino's expressive frigidity.

Most striking is Marino's predilection for minute description, for dwelling on objective particulars which can only hinder the projection of Ariadne's grief. We come upon the sleeping heroine, and for sixty-five lines the poet details her gown, earrings, necklace, hair, feet, and body (this last most lingeringly and with the delectation of a voyeur: Ariadne's undergarments lie open almost to the point of exposing "l'ultime bellezze, ove natura / vergognosa s'asconde"). Marino misses few opportunities to parade his erudition. Standing over Ariadne, Bacchus is moved by her beauty to think her a goddess; so for fifty lines he muses on her identity, rehearsing emblem-book fashion the characteristics of Venus, Pasithea, Cynthia, Thetis, Diana, and Minerva (the passage is modelled after *Dionysiaca* 47, ll. 275–94). Such catalogs are not restricted to the emotionally restrained portions of the story. Ariadne retains throughout her lament the presence of mind to enumerate the winds which may have helped Theseus on his way, to list the services she could render her lover as his handmaid (both themes borrowed from Nonnos), and to analyze the alternatives left to her if he does not return.

Through such devices Marino inflates Ariadne's lament to a bloated 300 lines, as compared to eighty-one lines in Rinuccini's version. But nowhere in all this rampant verbiage does Marino duplicate the simple passion captured by his predecessor. At the height of Rinuccini's lament, Ariadne lashes out at her faithless lover, summoning the wrath of heaven against him. Still in love with Theseus, however, she immediately repents her outburst:

> Che parlo, ahi! che vaneggio?
> Misera, ohimè! che chieggio?
> O Teseo, o Teseo mio,
> Non son, non son quell'io,

277

Non son quell'io che i fêri detti sciolse:
Parlò l'affanno mio, parlò il dolore;
Parlò la lingua sí, ma non già 'l core.

[What words, alas! what ravings? Wretch, alas! what request? Oh Theseus, oh my Theseus, it was not, was not I, it was not I who spoke such wicked words: my woes spoke, and my anguish spoke; my tongue spoke, yes, but not my heart.]

In her wretched state she reconciles herself to death:

Misera! ancor do loco
A la tradita speme, e non si spegne
Fra tanto scherno ancor d'amore il foco?
Spegni tu, Morte, omai le fiamme indegne.
[2:177–78]

[Wretch! Still I entertain betrayed hopes, and is the fire of love in such mockery not spent? Extinguish, Death, the unworthy flames.]

Marino's Ariadne, at the climax of her plaint, also contemplates death; but only, it seems, as a pretext for a series of tortured conceits in which various means of suicide are shown to be ineffective after love's sorrows (and which well exemplifies the rhetorical lifelessness so often the corollary of the Marinist search for *acutezza*):

Potrò nel mar gittarmi,
e dentro il salso umore
estinguere in un punto
e la vita e l'ardore:
ma s'io verso da' lumi
e mari e fonti e fiumi,
né mi sommergo in essi,
come morir tra l'acque
esser può mai ch'io speri?
Se col focile accendo
fiamma ingorda e vorace,
per distruggermi in foco
questo mi giova poco;
ché da maggior fornace
sento ognor consumarmi,
né può cenere farmi. . . .
[Pp. 492–93]

[I could throw myself in the sea, and in the briny deep extinguish at once both life and love: but if my eyes spill forth founts and rivers and seas, and these do not submerge me, how can I hope to die in the waters? If I light a greedy, voracious flame to consume me, this avails me little; for a brighter fire burns me at every moment, yet turns me not to ash. . . .]

Eavesdropping throughout Ariadne's lament, Bacchus feels no compassion. He "takes delight in her sorrow," and we can scarcely blame him. Marino too, undoubtedly, would have us marvel at his own witticisms and ornamental rhetoric rather than shed a heartfelt tear for his heroine.

2

Monteverdi never set Marino's *Arianna*. But in his setting of Rinuccini's lament, the only surviving fragment of his complete opera *L'Arianna* (1607–8), he touched emotional depths previously unknown to the nascent style of recitative and set an expressive standard for dramatic laments which endured for over a half-century. His success was due in part to the nature of his text. Rinuccini's impassioned rhetoric—the exclamations and affective repetitions, the syntactic parallelisms sculpted to express now agitation, now dejection, the mournful or barbed assonance underlining the ever changing emotions, all evident even in the brief excerpts quoted above—accorded perfectly with the ideal of a musical language of explicit dramatic power. Thus in the famous opening of his setting (fig. 1), Monteverdi accentuates the somber assonance of Rinuccini's verse through dissonance on the first "La*scia*temi" and a yearning chromatic ascent at its repetition; the melodic drop of a fourth to the first "morire" expands into a despondent falling sixth at its return in line 2. Monteverdi captures the expressive crescendo of Rinuccini's next lines in his melodic and rhythmic structure, as the interval outlined in quarter-note declamation at "che mi conforte" is widened from a third to a leapt fourth in line 4 and finally a fifth in line 5, both leaps "sprung" by quickened eighth-note declamation. Note that Monteverdi is careful also to project the syntactic parallelism of lines 4 and 5 and to emphasize again Rinuccini's dark assonance at "gran." In Monteverdi's sensitive reading, Rinuccini's passionate Tuscan idiom rediscovered onstage the dramatic birthright it had claimed more than a century before, in Poliziano's *Orfeo*.[21]

279

21. *Orfeo* too was a music-drama, though none of the improvised setting of Poliziano's verse has come down to us; see Nino Pirrotta, *Li due Orfei: da Poliziano a Monteverdi* (Turin, 1975), esp. chap. 1. For a more detailed discussion of the novelties of Monteverdi's *Arianna* and their relation to Rinuccini's text, see my "Madrigal, Monody, and Monteverdi's 'via naturale alla immitatione,' " *Journal of the American Musicological Society* 34 (Spring 1981): 60–108.

1. Lascia _ te _ mi mo _ ri _ re, 2. la _ scia _ te _ mi mo _

_ ri _ re; 3. e che vo _ le _ te voi che mi con _ for _ te

4. in co _ sì du _ ra sor _ te, 5. in co _ sì gran mar _ ti _ re?

280

FIG. 1.—Monteverdi, *Ariadne's Lament,* beginning. Used by permission of European American Music Distributors.

Most of Monteverdi's voluminous dramatic output between *L'Arianna* and his last two operas, *Il ritorno d'Ulisse in patria* (1641) and *L'incoronazione di Poppea* (1642), is lost. But in his *Concerto: Settimo libro de madrigali* of 1619, Monteverdi published two works in this so-called *genere rappresentativo,* long works in recitative style for solo voice and *continuo,* which help clarify the effect of Marinist idioms on Monteverdi's style. The first, "Se i languidi miei sguardi," is a poetic love letter (it was printed with the subtitle *Lettera amorosa*) of seventy-eight mostly unrhymed seven- and eleven-syllable lines. It is the work of Claudio Achillini (1574–1642), a friend and epigone of Marino, immortalized by Manzoni's citation in *I promessi sposi* of his grandiloquent sonnet "Sudate, o fochi, a preparar metalli" (literally "Sweat, o fires, to temper metals").[22] The second work, "Se pur destina e vole / il Cielo," is termed a *Partenza amorosa* and, though a later printing of both pieces erroneously renames it a *Lettera amorosa,* it clearly sets forth not a letter but the parting words of a lover to his beloved. Its author is revealed by a mid-seventeenth-century manuscript in the Florentine Biblioteca Nazionale to be Rinuccini;[23] thematic and stylistic links between this poem and Rinuccini's other lyrics and music-dramas confirm the ascription. The poem is a *frottola* of a sort written a century earlier by Benivieni, among others, and

22. The author of the poem was identified by Claudio Gallico in "La 'Lettera amorosa' di Monteverdi e lo stile rappresentativo," *Nuova rivista musicale italiana* 1 (July/August 1967): 287–302. The poem appears in *Rime e prose di Claudio Achillini* (Venice, 1680), pp. 100–104.

23. Ms. cl. 7.902; the poem appears on folios 99v–100r.

revived by a number of Florentine poets of the early seventeenth century: a long succession of *settenari* arranged in rhyming couplets.[24]

There is little of the poet in Achillini. His letter is marked throughout by the rhythmic lifelessness of its opening lines:

> Se i languidi miei sguardi,
> se i sospir interrotti,
> se le tronche parole
> non han sin hor potuto,
> o bel idolo mio,
> farvi de le mie fiamme intera fede,
> leggete queste note,
> credete a questa carta,
> a questa carta, in cui
> sotto forma d'inchiostro il cor stillai.

[If my languid gaze, if my broken sighs, if my halting speech have not by now, oh my lovely idol, revealed to you in full my passion, read these words, believe this letter, this letter which distills my heart in ink.]

281

Grammatical units correspond with disconcerting regularity to the versification (even the infrequent *endecasillabi* are used only to accommoderate phrases of extra length), and the strict parallelisms of lines 1–3 and 7–8 are therefore ploddingly emphasized. Monteverdi dutifully reflects these parallel locutions in his music, producing harmonic stasis and melodic redundancy (see fig. 2). The good Marinist, Achillini here con-

Fig. 2.—Monteverdi, "Se i languidi miei sguardi," beginning. Used by permission of European American Music Distributors.

24. See Benivieni, *Opere* (n. 4 above). The 1622 edition of *Poesie del Sr. Ottavio Rinuccini* preserves another *frottola* on pp. 173–76. Other seventeenth-century *frottole* by Maria Guicciardini and Anna Capponi are reproduced in *Poesie italiane inedite di dugento autori*, ed. Francesco Trucchi, 4 vols. (Prato, 1847), vol. 4; the *viluppi* of Michelangelo Buonarroti *il giovane* published there show the same form.

centrates his energies on enumerating the lover's sighs, glances, and broken speech and on the climactic image of line 10, instead of working for a vivid depiction of his lover's loneliness. His poetics, like Marino's, emphasize conceits and images at the expense of impassioned rhetorical structure. Monteverdi can do little to project in dramatic music such images and conceits, such figures of thought not clearly embodied in the form of the text. He retreats to an emblematic treatment of line 10, matching a long melisma to the word "cor."

Rinuccini's opening, even within the metric strictures he has set himself, speaks a more passionate language:

> Se pur destina e vole
> il Cielo, almo mio sole,
> ch'in tenebre mi viva,
> ascolta alma mia diva
> ciò che potrà ridire
> fra cotanto martire
> di sconsolato Amante
> lingua fredda e tremante.

282

[If indeed Heaven destines and wills, my beloved sun, that I live in darkness, hear, my dear goddess, what the cold and trembling lips of a desolate lover may say amid such misery.]

The impetuous enjambment of lines 1–2 staves off from the outset the debilitating coordination of grammar and prosody of Achillini's poem and blurs and enriches the parallelisms of lines 2 and 4. Monteverdi tailors his melodic phrases not to the line units but to the enjambment (the unstressed rhyme "vole"-"sole" remains to assert subliminally the metric shape of the poetry); and he underlines Rinuccini's parallelism ("almo mio sole . . . alma mia diva") through fleeting rhythmic similarities (see fig. 3). The rhythmic and harmonic variety of this example depends directly upon the rhetorical vitality of Rinuccini's verse.

Fig. 3.—Monteverdi, "Se pur destina e vole il Cielo," beginning. Used by permission of European American Music Distributors.

As in Ariadne's lament, Rinuccini's lively rhetoric allows Monteverdi to pursue an emotion-laden style unattainable in setting a poem like "Se i languidi miei sguardi." Rinuccini forgoes Achillini's conceits in favor of the direct, anguished idiom we have seen above in his madrigal "O miei giorni fugaci":

> O pensier vani e folli!
> Che speri? ohimè! che volli?
> Già dibattendo l'ale
> giunge l'ora fatale
> dell'aspra dipartita.

[Oh vain and foolish thoughts! What do you hope? Alas, what do you want? Already high on wing the fatal hour of bitter departure approaches.]

Monteverdi responds with an agitated, exclamatory recitative (see fig. 4).

283

FIG. 4.—Monteverdi, "Se pur destina e vole il Cielo," excerpt. Used by permission of European American Music Distributors.

Even Rinuccini's parallel locutions are structured in a livelier fashion than Achillini's: instead of repeating a full grammatical unit (as in Achillini's "Se i languidi miei sguardi, / se i sospir interrotti," etc.), Rinuccini suggests syntactic identity with a brief anaphora, then moves off in a new grammatical direction (note Rinuccini's enhancement of his false parallelism with the assonance "tre*mante*"-"di*mando*"): "a voi, tremante e muto, / a voi dimando aiuto [to you, to you, trembling and mute I sue for aid]." At times even literal anaphora is suppressed in favor of a carefully wrought play of assonance (my italics):

> O *del* cor luce e speme,
> *odi le* voci estreme,
> *odile* e del bel seno
> una lagrima almeno
> bagni la viva neve.

[Oh light and hope of my heart, hear my last words, hear them and bathe the living snow of your breast with at least one tear.]

Such "developing parallelisms," in contrast to Achillini's static repetition, elicit from Monteverdi progressive, forward-moving settings, in keeping with the aroused emotions of the protagonist (see fig. 5).

284

FIG. 5.—Monteverdi, "Se pur destina e vole il Cielo," excerpt. Used by permission of European American Music Distributors.

The rhetorical shortcomings of Achillini's poem, of course, mask a more basic inadequacy of the work: emotional frigidity. Like Marino in *L'Arianna,* Achillini shows scant interest in a vivid portrayal of his lover's sentiments. He devotes himself instead to a long central apostrophe to the hair, eyes, and mouth of the beloved, a passage bristling with conceits and metaphors, which occupies more than three-quarters of the original 141 lines of his composition.

Monteverdi saw the problems posed in setting such a text to music in the *genere rappresentativo.* To overcome them, he deleted the sixty-three lines describing the eyes and mouth of the beloved; but the remaining forty-four lines praising her hair still proved excessive. Here Achillini's conceits, extended metaphor, and kaleidoscopic imagery offered little to the composer of *L'Arianna:*

> Dolcissimi legami,
> belle mie piogge d'oro
> qual hor sciolte cadete
> da quelle ricche nubi
> onde raccolte sete,
> e cadendo formate
> preziose procelle
> onde con onde d'or bagnando andate
> scogli di latte e rivi d'alabastro . . .

[Sweetest bonds, my beautiful rains of gold, when you fall loose from those rich clouds where you are gathered, and falling form a precious tempest whence milk-white reefs and shores of alabaster are bathed in waves of gold . . .]

Monteverdi set this text to lifeless declamation over harmonies of a tiresome immobility not encountered in "Se pur destina": no fewer than eight measures of D minor followed by three of A minor before the harmonic rhythm resumes a less moribund pace. The *genere rappresentativo* has no power to enliven the cold *concettismo* of Achillini's poem.

These recitatives from the *Seventh Book of Madrigals* define in their contrast a fundamental expressive dilemma confronting Monteverdi during the second decade of the seventeenth century. In the 1590s and the first years of the new century, he had explored (and, it has been argued, exhausted) the dramatic potential of the madrigal for five unaccompanied voices, taking as his starting material stirring passages from Tasso's epic *Gerusalemme liberata* and Giambattista Guarini's pastoral tragicomedy *Il pastor fido*. In Alessandro Striggio's *Orfeo* (1607) and especially in *L'Arianna*, he had merged techniques from his polyphonic styles with the recitative of earlier Florentine opera composers in a musico-dramatic language of unprecedented power.[25] These crucial developments in Monteverdi's style had depended upon poets whose primary goal, at least in the texts Monteverdi chose, was the expression of human passion through vivid rhetorical structure. Now the face of Italian poetry was changing, the rhetoric of heightened emotion ceding to rhetoric per se, to ornamental description and wit. Faced with the overlong *acutezze* of Achillini's love letter, Monteverdi had discovered one solution to their setting: his music assumes the inexpressive role of a bland and neutral conveyance for the text. It was not a solution, we may guess, that could long satisfy the composer.

285

3

The richer solutions which Monteverdi hit upon in the last twenty-five years of his career are too varied to be recounted in any but cursory fashion here. They reveal a general tendency in Monteverdi's music toward an overtly pictorial response to the text's prominent images, that is, a reliance on pictorial madrigalisms as an important means of text expression.[26] Inevitably, the close bond between music and text

25. See my "Madrigal, Monody."
26. A "madrigalism" is a musical device constructed to reflect the meaning of the word or phrase it sets. The term was derived by musicologists from the polyphonic madrigal of the sixteenth century, where such devices frequently occur. As the related descrip-

that Monteverdi had forged in his earlier dramatic styles is loosened in these works. A new, less profound interaction of text and music originates in the texts themselves: the madrigalisms of the music arise as a logical response to the image-oriented Marinist verse.

This trend is evident already in the two- and three-voice *continuo* madrigals of Monteverdi's *Seventh Book*, frothy, delightful works emphasizing words and images which allow for virtuosic roulades in their depiction: "you sing, I sing," "smile," and the like. Four of these works set madrigals by Marino himself, while five others set lyrics by Guarini, whose madrigal verse was an important precursor of Marino's *concettismo*.[27]

Pictorial depiction of text characterizes as well Monteverdi's famous *stile concitato* ("agitated style"), developed in the *Combattimento di Tancredi et Clorinda* (1624). Here Monteverdi gives dramatic rationale to the madrigalisms depicting the wary circling of the combatants, the clashing of their swords, and so on: he instructs the singers representing Tancredi and Clorinda to mime the actions as they are depicted in the music. In most of Monteverdi's later uses of the *stile concitato,* however, and especially in many of the madrigals of his *Madrigali guerrieri et amorosi* (1638) this representational aspect is lacking. In these works, the devices of the *stile concitato*—rapid-fire repetition of a single chord, fanfarelike triadic melodies over static harmonies, and the like—are reduced to pictorial madrigalisms plain and simple, and uninteresting madrigalisms at that.

The pictorialism of Monteverdi's late works is evident also, finally, in his operas of the 1640s, *Il ritorno d'Ulisse in patria* and *L'incoronazione di Poppea.* Here again it arises in response to the conceits and images of

286

---

tive phrase "word painting" suggests, many madrigalisms depend for their significance on the listener's perception of a more or less straightforward visual correlation between musical gesture and textual meaning (e.g., an ascending scale at the words "He rose to Heaven"). Such madrigalisms I qualify as "pictorial." In their static, iconic character, pictorial madrigalisms are inimical to musical idioms of heightened emotion. Other madrigalisms depend on no such visual adjuncts but constitute a direct translation of the emotional charge carried by the text into musical terms (e.g., unprepared dissonances or harsh harmonic juxtapositions at a word like "alas!"). Such "affective madrigalisms" always played an important role in Monteverdi's most impassioned styles; a famous example is the beginning of Ariadne's lament (fig. 1 above).

27. These works mark Monteverdi's first approach to Marino's epigrammatic, conceit-ridden madrigal verse. For his earlier settings of Marino's poetry (there are five in his *Sesto libro de madrigali* of 1614) Monteverdi had sought out the most conservative side of the poet's personality: ecloguelike sonnets and *canzoni* incorporating pastoral dialogues easily adapted to semidramatic musical settings. For the stylistic similarities of Marino's and Guarini's madrigal verse, see Pirrotta's wide-ranging "Scelte poetiche di Monteverdi," *Nuova rivista musicale italiana* 2 (1968): 10–42 and 226–54, esp. p. 239, and Ulrich Schulz-Buschhaus, *Das Madrigal: Zur Stilgeschichte der italienischen Lyrik zwischen Renaissance und Barock* (Bad Homburg, 1969), pp. 214–18.

Marinist poetic styles. Gian Francesco Busenello, the author of *Poppea,* aligned himself early with the *Marinisti* by publishing in 1624 a collection of sonnets in defense of Marino's *Adone.* With an eye cast over his shoulder to Rinuccini and Marino, he wrote his own version of Ariadne's lament; like Marino's, it is a frigid exercise in strained imagery. This proclivity for *concettismo* carries over into Busenello's librettos and, as Francesco Degradà puts it, "constitutes [their] most debilitating fault."[28] *Poppea,* for all its diversity of character and action, is no exception. And Busenello's excessive image-making in this work, combined with a discursive, prosaic dialogue reminiscent of Italian spoken drama of the period, posed a formidable challenge to the composer of Rinuccini's lyrical *Arianna.*

Monteverdi's brilliant solution, a song style shifting easily from simple declamation to sections of heightened melodic interest with relatively frequent madrigalisms, is successful through much of the score. Its pictorial devices, lively *arioso* sections, and clear strophic forms with instrumental *ritornelli* inject a much-needed variety into Busenello's long dialogues and soliloquies. Only in the most impassioned moments of the drama (moments like Ottone's discovery of Poppea's faithlessness, or Octavia's monologues in acts 1 and 3) is the inadequacy of the style apparent. At these points, the union of music and poetry in a single affective idiom is essential to the projection of the protagonist's emotions, and Monteverdi's settings strikingly invoke the style of Ariadne's lament. But the occasional intrusion even here of the new-style madrigalisms distances the music from the text, disrupting the fundamental illusion that the character onstage naturally speaks a musical idiom of heightened expressive power. This disruption is apparent in Octavia's first soliloquy, "Disprezzata regina," where the thunderbolts she calls down on her faithless husband Nero are matched to extended melismas in the music. It is clearer still in the despondent stammering which opens her speech "A dio Roma" (fig. 6). We can accept such bald musical imitation of reality in a comic figure, for example the stuttering glutton Iro of *Il ritorno d'Ulisse* (exposure of theatrical pretense, after all, has always been a stock-in-trade of comedy). But Octavia's mimetic stutter undermines the illusion that her language of sorrow is real speech, and the remainder of her soliloquy, though cast in the heartfelt declamation of Ariadne, rings hollow.

There is a certain poignancy in Monteverdi's bold attempt, in his

287

28. "Gian Francesco Busenello e il libretto della *Incoronazione di Poppea,*" in *Claudio Monteverdi e il suo tempo,* ed. Raffaello Monterosso (Verona, 1969), pp. 81–102; see also p. 95 n. Degradà published Busenello's lament of Ariadne for the first time in an appendix to his article.

Fig. 6.—Monteverdi, *L'incoronazione di Poppea*, act 3, sc. 7, beginning. Used by permission of European American Music Distributors.

mid-seventies, to forge a new dramatic style to accommodate the pedestrian verse of a poet thirty-two years his junior. Certainly Monteverdi recognized Busenello's weaknesses, and he probably looked back with nostalgia to the poet of *L'Arianna,* his most renowned work. (In 1633, at any rate, he had written of the "natural means to [musical] imitation" which he had discovered in composing Ariadne's lament, and in 1640 he had revived the thirty-two-year-old *Arianna* for the Venetian theater San Moisé.) Busenello was the product of a new generation, with new ideals of poetic expression. He and his mentor, Marino, could little enhance the dramatic style of a composer whose first maturity was nourished by Rinuccini, Tasso, and the Guarini of *Il pastor fido.*

And this dramatic style, adumbrated in the early settings of Tasso and Guarini and in *Orfeo,* fully realized in *L'Arianna,* echoed in the recitatives of the *Seventh Book* and the late operas—this language remained the expressive heart of Monteverdi's achievement, whatever the novelties of his late works. It is the last and greatest monument to the Renaissance insistence that music and words be but two aspects of a single syntax of human emotion. In his later works, Monteverdi is often constrained by his poets to acknowledge a different view in which music is seen as an emblematic language, working by independent means toward the same expressive goals as the poetry it sets. But he is rarely at ease with this view; his most basic expressive impulses remained those of his formative years. In the most compelling moments of Monteverdi's artistry, from his first works to his last, text and music are joined as one.

All the more striking, then, is the variety of musico-poetic conjunction in the works of his last years. This variety reveals a curiosity, an urge to explore new areas of the music-text interface, which remained as vigorous in the composer's seventy-fifth year, when he composed *Poppea,* as it had been in his twenty-fifth, when he published his first settings from Tasso's *Liberata.* (And I have omitted much of the variety of Monteverdi's late works here, from the autobiographical *Secretum,* which Nino Pirrotta has discerned in his settings of Petrarch's poems, to the "emblematic" use of the descending tetrachord in the *Lament of the Nymph* described by Ellen Rosand, in which the repeating bassline tran-

288

scends in its inherent expressive potency a purely pictorial role.)²⁹ The unflagging vigor of Monteverdi's imagination, comparable in his era perhaps only to the boundless curiosity of Galileo, allowed him to span, as few other artists, two decisively different cultural moments. In *L'Arianna* and related works, he is the last Renaissance composer, the greatest musical arbiter of the expressionistic outgrowths of sixteenth-century Petrarchism. In the late settings of Marino and Guarini, he is spokesman for a new world view, impersonal, objective, and stylized. In the final operas, he labors, heroically, to be both.

29. See Pirrotta, "Scelte poetiche di Monteverdi," pp. 230–33 and 251–54, and Rosand, "The Descending Tetrachord: An Emblem of Lament," *Musical Quarterly* 65 (July 1979): 346–59.

THE INFLUENCE OF *MUSIQUE MESURÉE À L'ANTIQUE,* PARTICULARLY ON THE *AIRS DE COUR* OF THE EARLY SEVENTEENTH CENTURY

D. P. WALKER.

Many French *airs de cour* of the early 17th century, when compared, for example, with English lute–songs, have certain striking rhythmical peculiarities which cannot easily be accounted for. These airs can be divided into two groups. Both have a very free rhythm in which there can be no regular beat, the time signature, if there is any, being quite meaningless; each syllable is usually given only the value of a minim or a crotchet or of their equivalent in notes of smaller values. But the first group obeys a principle in accordance with which the metre of the text is emphasized by long notes at the *coupe* and at the end of the line; whereas the rhythm of the second group is completely free and has no intelligible plan.

It has often been asserted that these peculiarities are due to the influence of *musique mesurée à l'antique* [1]. This is a useful, and in the case of the first group, a very likely conjecture; but it is not a proven fact, as many musicologists seem to suppose, nor a complete explanation. To assess it at its true value we must consider the general relation of *musique mesurée* to the music surrounding it.

This relation is an unusual one. The theories which produced *musique mesurée* closely resemble those of numerous other humanist writers and musicians [2]. Yet the music itself seems to have little connection with any style that preceded it. The theory of *musique mesurée* fits easily into a general historical setting, but Baif's musicians put this theory into practice in such a complete and uncompromising manner that their work stands quite outside the general developement

291

---

[1] e. g. Masson in *Bericht über d. II. Kongress d. I. M. G.*, 1907, 182; Warlock, *Preface to French Ayres from Gabriel Bataille*, Oxford, 1926; Rolland in *Encyclopédie de la Musique*, ed. Lavignac & La Laurencie, Pt. I, T. III, Paris, 1921, 1344; Gérold, *L'Art du Chant au xviie siècle*. (Publ. de la Faculté de Lettres de l'Université de Strasbourg, fasc. I), 1921, 25 seq.

[2] v. Walker, "Musical Humanism in 16th & early 17th centuries," *Music Review*, Cambridge, 1941–2.

of musical language. The double restriction of syllabic homophony[3] and the — = $\downarrow$, ⌣ = $\downarrow$, rule[4] left only a very small field in which the composers' traditional habits of musical thought could operate. The violent change in rhythm and texture which resulted from these restrictions was not due to the sudden development of some already existing aesthetic tendency but to the ruthless application of two principles of composition that were quite foreign and opposed to any contemporary style.

We have this most unusual situation. By its unswerving obedience to theoretical principles *musique mesurée* was almost completely cut off from the styles and traditions of the music preceding it; but, unlike similar pedantic experiments[5], it did not die after a short and miserable life, but flourished vigorously for over fifty years. It was neither a reaction against, nor a developement of any earlier music. Therefore, apart from its theoretical background, which links it up with earlier and contemporary thought, and regarded simply as music, *musique mesurée* began its history abruptly in 1570[6]. But, once it had become successful appreciated music, it entered the general flow of musical history and may have influenced its course.

That *musique mesurée* should exercise some influence on ordinary music is at least probable. The general rhythm of *musique mesurée* was as clear and easy to hear as that of a dance tune, yet it was as free from an isochronous beat as any individual voice of a polyphonic work, and, inspite of this freedom, it conformed to a regular metrical pattern. These qualities of rhythm and texture made *musique mesurée*

---

[3] i. e. every syllable of the text is always sung simultaneously by all parts, though any amount of independent figuration is allowed from the beginning of one syllable to the beginning of the next.

[4] i. e. a long in the text is always set with a minim (or its equivalent in notes of smaller value) and a short by a crotchet. The principle is of course the same if — = $\downarrow$, ⌣ = $\downarrow$, or — = $\downarrow$, ⌣ = $\downarrow$.

[5] e. g. the revival of the genera (v. Walker, *op. cit.*, II, 114 seq.), or *vers mesures* apart from their music (v. Augé–Chiquet, *La Vie, les Idées & l'Œuvre de J. A. de Baïf*, Paris, 1909).

[6] This statement needs perhaps some qualification. The texture, for example, of some of Le Jeune's *musique mesurée* attains, inspite of syllabic homophony, a surprising degree of rhythmic independence in individual parts, a quality due to the polyphonic habits natural to his period. It might also be claimed that the syllabic homophony of *musique mesurée* was derived from earlier homophonic or partly homophonic songs. This is perhaps partially true, but there is no doubt that the chief reasons for its adoption were theoretical ones.

strikingly different both from learned polyphony and from dance tunes or popular monody. In some measure it combined the good points of both: the rhythmic freedom of the former with the clear texture and regular rhythmic pattern of the latter. Therefore, also taking into account the high aesthetic standard of much *musique mesurée*, it seems natural that there should be a vogue for such unusual yet attractive music, and that, owing to this, the style of ordinary music should be affected by some of these peculiarities of rhythm and texture and by another of its salient qualities, its excellent treatment of text.

There is indeed considerable evidence for the vogue of *musique mesurée* [7]; but the evidence of its influence is of a much more doubtful kind. With the exception of Fabrice Marin Caietain and possibly Monteverdi, no composer nor writer of this time remarks on this influence. One can only point out certain peculiarities in settings of *vers rimés* which may be due to the influence of similar peculiarities in *musique mesurée*. These peculiarities which distinguish *musique mesurée* from other contemporary styles are: its homophonic texture, its " unbarrable " but schematized rhythm, and its excellent treatment of text.

That the texture of *musique mesurée* influenced contemporary and later music has been suggested, even affirmed, by several historians [8]. Some of these were misled by the assumption that *musique mesurée* was performed monodically. Since it was meant to be and was in fact usually performed polyphonically [9], that is, in parts, their views need no refutation. It is, however, likely that *musique mesurée* was an important influence in the general change from a predominantly fugal to a predominantly monodic or homophonic style. This change, which had been slowly developing all through the 16th century, reached its climax at the beginning of the next century, when in France, as in England and Italy, large quantities of lute–songs began to appear. In all countries accompanied solos were immediately preceded by simple 3, 4 or 5 part airs of homophonic texture. These were often arranged as lute–songs, and in some cases it is difficult to decide whether

293

---

[7] e. g. the publication of large collections of Le Jeune's and du Caurroy's *musique mesurée* between 1594 and 1610, or v. d'Aubigny's account of du Caurroy's conversion to *musique mesurée* (Œuvres, ed. Réaume & Caussade, Paris, 1883-92, I, 453, III, 271-274).

[8] e. g. Masson, *ibid.*; Rolland, *ibid.*

[9] The evidence for this is too bulky to be given here and must form the matter of another article. The few *chansons mesurées* in the Bataille series of lute-songs are of course an exception.

the composer originally conceived his work as a homophonic part song or as an accompanied solo[10]. It was during the last stages of this continuous and gradual change that *musique mesurée* was published. *Musique mesurée* did not hasten the change; for in England, where there was no humanist movement in music, the publication of lute-songs began just as early. But, since the vogue for *musique mesurée* occurred at this crucial time, one would expect it to have some effect on the style of early French monody. The texture of *musique mesurée* was in no way a cause of the triumph of monodic style; homophonic songs began to appear before *musique mesurée* was invented and continued to do so quite independently of it[11]. But, chiefly owing to its homophonic texture, *musique mesurée* slipt into its place in the general development of musical language and became capable of being a source of later styles.

One would expect both the other distinguishing characteristics of *musique mesurée* to affect contemporary and subsequent styles. In fact, with a few exceptions, the excellent treatment of text in *chansons mesurées* is not to be found in the *airs de cour*, but only the beatless ¦ and ¦ rhythm. In two earlier non–monodic works, however, the Airs of Fabrice Marin Caietain[12] and the Balet de la Royne[13], the rhythm of the text is preserved to a remarkable degree, and there is good reason to suppose that the composers were consciously imitating *musique mesurée*.

Fabrice's Airs are a miscellaneous collection: his own settings of *vers mesurés* et *rimés*, *chansons mesurées* by Courville, and ordinary airs by Beaulieu and Nicolas de la Grotte. In the dedication he writes:

... et pour ce que je suis de nation & langue estrangere je pourroy manquer à bien approprier les Airs sur les lettres Françoises, mais come ceux qui veullent profiter aux estudes hantent les lieux ou s'en fait la profession, Moy pareillement me defiant de mes forces, (car je n'ay aucune honte de le declairer), ay frequenté

[10] v. e. g. Gérold, *op. cit.*, p. 23.

[11] e. g. numerous songs of Jannequin, or the Chansons of Nicolas de la Grotte, Paris, 1569.

[12] *Airs Mis en Musique à quatre parties* ... *sur la Poësie de P. de Ronsard, & autres excellens Poetes.* Premier Livre, Paris, Le Roy & Ballard, 1578; Second Livre, 1578. (Superius and Tenor of both books are in the British Museum; the Bassus should be in the Bibl. Royale at Brussels, but is lost.).

[13] *Balet Comique de la Royne Faict aux nopces de Monsieur le Duc de joyeuse Et de Mademoyselle de Vaudemont, sa sœur, Par Baltazar de Beaujoyeulx* ..., Paris, Le Roy & Ballard et Mamert Patisson, 1582. (There is an unreliable reprint of the music by Weckerlin; the text, without music, will be found in P. Lacroix, *Ballets et Mascarades de Cour*, Genève, 1868-70, I, 1-87).

l'escole de Messieurs de Courville & Beaulieu, l'ung Orphee l'autre l'Arion de France, leur vertu & nostre amitié me permettant de les appeller ainsi, car ilz ne sont seulement excelents aux recits de la Lyre, mais tres doctes en l'art de Musique, & perfaits en la composition des airs, que les Grecs appellent Melopee, suivant leurs auertissements & bons auis J'ay corrigé la plus part des fautes que J'auoy peu faire en n'observant les longues & breues de la lettre.

Of Beaulieu little is known; four of his songs are in this collection [14], and he wrote some of the music for the Balet de la Royne [15]. Courvile at this period was the principal musician of Baïf's movement. Fabrice, then, under the influence of Courvile, not only wrote *chansons mesurées*, but also, when setting *vers rimés*, may have followed his " bons auis " and observed the " longues & breues de la lettre ". In fact, in his settings of *vers rimés* one finds the same lavish use of coloured notes as in his *musique mesurée*, the same homophonic texture, and also the same careful attention to the " quantity " of syllables. Even the vices as well as the virtues of *musique mesurée* appear in these settings of *vers rimés*. In examples one and two [16]

295

Ex 1

Qui veut sçauoir A - mour   et sa na-tu - re, Son arc ses

feux ses traits et sa poin-tu - re,   que o'est qu'il est et que o'est

qu'il de - si - re,   Li - se oes vers je m'en vay le de-cri - re eto.

Ex 2

Ma gran - de et lon - gue   ami - tié plus gran - de fauenr ` me -

ri - te. Il faut aymer jusqu'au bout etc.

[14] Three of these are also in Le Blanc's Airs, 1579, repr. Expert, *Monuments de la Mus. fr. de la Ren.* No. 3, pp. 8, 54, 57.

[15] v. infra p. 7.

[16] Fabrice, *op. cit.*, Livre I, text of Ronsard and Bertaut.

19

the natural accentuation is followed closely except at " au ", " en "
and the two " ses ", where the false longs give the effect of a misplaced
tonic accent.

These remarks are also true of the homophonic songs in the Balet
de la Royne [17].   In some respects these songs resemble normal *musique
mesurée* even more closely than Fabrice's do.   Fabrice's airs and his
chansons mesurées [18] are either absolutely " note contre note "
throughout [19] or else they contain occasional slight differences of rhythm
between parts which prevent a syllable being sung simultaneously [20];
also, he uses such groups as ♩. ♩ with a syllable under each note.   In
the homophonic songs of the Balet de la Royne all parts always sing
each syllable simultaneously.   Each syllable is worth ♩ or ♪ (or ♩ or ♪);
no other values are used and rhythmic variety is obtained by splitting
♩ into ♫♫ or ♩. ♪ etc.   Indeed, except that they lack a regular
poetic metre, these songs are undistinguishable from *musique mesurée*.
Unfortunately there is no certain external evidence connecting the
Balet with Baif's movement.   There are, however a few indications,
which combined with the internal evidence just given, justify the sup-
position that the peculiar style of these songs is due to this influence.

Baif and Le Jeune are known to have helped with some of the
festivities for the marriage of the Duc de Joyeuse; the Balet de la Royne
was a part of these festivities.   Although the verse of the ballet is
written by the Sieur de la Chesnaye [21], and the music by Beaulieu and
Salmon [22], Baïf and Le Jeune may well have been able to affect the
way in which some of the text was set.   Baïf hoped to extend his

[17] e. g. the first two choruses ("Chant des Sereines " and " Reponse de la
Voute Doree ").

[18] With one exception, his setting of " Une puce j'ay dedans l'oreille ", which
has independent entries to illustrate the words " je cour de ça, je cour de la ".

[19] e. g. the first song quoted above.

[20] e. g. " Je ne l'ay dict qu'à moy " (*Op. cit.*, Livre II).

[21] This may possibily be a pseudonym for d'Aubigné, who says (*Œuvres*, ed.
Réaume & Caussade, I, 23) that he " dressa le project de la Circé que la Royne mere
ne voulut pas executer, pour la depense: & depuis le Roy Henri troisiesme l'executa
aux nopces du Duc de Joyeuse "; but Prunières (*Le Balet de Cour*, Paris, 19:4,
pp. 86-7) is probably right in thinking that this does not necessarily imply that
d'Aubigné wrote the verse.

[22] For Beaulieu v. supra p. 144, "Maistre Salmon " was Chantre et Valet
du Roi; apart from this little is known of him (v. Prunières, *op. cit.*, p. 88). Gérold
(*op. cit,*, p. 4) suggests that Savornin, who played, the part of Jupiter, may be
Savorny, one of whose chansons mesurées ("Chanvallon les Roys ") appeared in
Livre V of the Bataille series. This would be another link with *musique mesurée*.

THE INFLUENCE OF MUSIQUE MESUREE A L'ANTIQUE   147

movement to drama and was particularly interested in the project of a " ballet mesuré "[23]. The verses at the beginning of the printed description of the ballet, although they may merely refer to the classical subject of Circé, seem also to hint at a more precise and literal imitation of antiquity[24]. Finally, one can see from his remarks " au Lecteur " that Beaujoyeux, the creator of the ballet, had humanist ideals:

... je me suis advisé qu'il ne seroit point indecent de ... diversifier la musique de poësie, et entrelacer la poësie de musique, et le plus souvent les confondre toutes deux ensemble: ainsi que l'antiquité ne recitoit ses vers et Orphee ne sonnoit jamais sans vers.

Fabrice and the Balet de la Royne belong to the first period of *musique mesurée*, from the foundation of the Academy, 1570, to the publication of Mauduit's Chansonettes, 1586. The success of *musique mesurée* in these early years was not great enough, and too little had been printed, to encourage many imitators. There are no other signs of ordinary music being affected by it until the early years of the 17th century, when all Le Jeune's and Du Caurroy's *musique mesurée* was published. It is at this time that *airs de cour* begins to appear in great quantity[25]. If we assume that their rhythmical peculiarities are in some measure derived from *musique mesurée*, then it seems likely that those of the first group (where the metre of the text is emphasized in the setting) are the product of intelligent, conscious imitation of *musique mesurée*, and those of the second group (where the irregular rhythm follows no perceptible plan) the product of superficial or unconscious imitation. From a casual hearing of many *chansons mesurées* one might easily gain the impression of completely unplanned, uncontrolled ♩ and ♩ rhythm. A knowledge of the principles of *musique mesurée*, or a quick perception of long, complicated metrical schemes, would reveal a strictly ordered rhythmical plan.

297

[23] v. My article on the Academy, Vol. I, No. 2 of this periodical.

[24] Anonymous verses adressed to Beaujoyeux, which claim that he has revived the « Balet composé en son tour mesuré ... " " des cendres de la Grece ", that he has shown " la façon, tant estimee De nos poëtes anciens, Les vers avec la musiquè, Le Balet confus mesuré ".

[25] The largest series of these is: *Airs de differents autheurs, mis en tablature de luth par Gabriel Bataille*, Paris, Pierre Ballard, 1608 & 1612; Second Livre, 1609 & 1614; 3ieme, 1614; 4ieme, 1614; 5ieme, 1614; 6ieme, 1614; 7ieme, 1617; 8ieme, 1618. A few of these have been transcribed by Peter Warlock, Oxford Univ. Press, 1926.

An isolated and doubtful example of intelligent imitation has been found by M. Prunières [26] in the Italian music of this period. In the "Dichiaratione di una lettera" at the back of Monteverdi's Scherzi (1607) [27] the composer's brother asks:

> ... Il canto alla francese in questo moderno modo che le stampe da tre o quattro anni in qua si va mirando, hor sotto a parole de mottetti, hor de madrigali, hor di canzonette & d'arie, chi fu il primo di lui che lo riportasse in Italia di quando venne da li bagni di Spa l'anno 1599 [28]? Et chi incomincio a porlo sotto ad orationi latine o a vulgari nella nostra lingua prima di lui? Non fece questi scherzi all'hora?

Prunières' assertion that " il canto alla francese in questo modo " means *musique mesurée*, or a style modelled on it [29], is on the whole born out by the rhythm of several of the Scherzi. But, in his enthusiasm for his discovery, he finds far more certain indications of this influence than actually exist. With a few exceptions in each case, it is true that the airs in question are all homophonic, have only two note values (usually ♩ and ♪) for each syllable, and have a rhythmic scheme which recurs from line to line and from stanza to stanza. Also, the ending ◡ – – is very frequent, an unusual one in normal music, but extremely common in *musique mesurée* [30] (example 3) [31].

298

Ex 3

Da-mi - gel - la Tut - ta   bel - la Ver-sa,   ver - sa quel bel

Da-mi - gel - la Tut - ta   bel - la Ver-sa,   ver - sa quel bel.

[26] *La Vie E L'Œuvre de Claudio Monteverdi*, Paris, 1926, pp. 20–26, 54–58, and article "Monteverdi and French Music" in *The Sackbut*, Vol. III, 1922, pp. 98 seq.

[27] Reprinted in Malipiero's edition of his complete works, Asolo, 1926.

[28] He spent a month in Spa and a month in Brussels. Prunières (*La Vie*, etc., p. 295) tries to prove that he was likely to hear *musique mesurée* in Belgium because works of Le Jeune & du Caurroy appear in collections published in Belgium; but in none of the three he cites is there any *musique mesurée*.

[29] Previously this was supposed to refer to the style of Jannequin or di Lasso.

[30] cf. Prunières, "Monteverdi and French Music", *op. cit.*, p. 99.

[31] *Tutte le opere*, ed. Malipiero, X, 40.

vi - no Fa che ca -da la ru - gia - da Di-stil- la - ta di . ru - bi - no.

vi - no Fa che ca -da la ru - gia - da Di-stil -la - ta di ru - bi - no.

But Prunières also claims that, like *musique mesurée*, many of the Scherzi and some of the airs in the *Orfeo*[32] have no regular beat.   In fact most of them have an extremely obvious one; he can only point to several airs which change frequently from $\frac{3}{4}$ to $\frac{6}{8}$[33].   This alternation between two kinds of triple rhythm is foreign to *musique mesurée*, but quite common in other 16th century music[34].   Prunières also believes that the harmony of the Scherzi is like that of *musique mesurée*.   He says: "of 15 scherzi 13 are in G major, one in D minor, one in C major "[35].   This is quite true, but it proves the exact opposite of his contention, since all the composers of *musique mesurée* were extremely conservative in their harmony and only wrote in the major when, occasionally, they used the 11th or 12th ecclesiastical modes.

The conscious, intelligent imitation of *musique mesurée* is certainly the most probable cause of the rhythmic structure of our first group of French *airs de cour*.   These airs, in addition to their free ♩ and ♩ rhythm, resemble *musique mesurée* in that the metre of their text is musically underlined[36].   The text is ordinary syllabic verse, and its metre is emphasized in this manner.   Long notes, usually minims as opposed to crotchets, are put under the last two syllables of every kind of verse; in decasyllabics and alexandrines a long note is also put under the fourth and sixth syllables respectively that is, at the *Coupe*.   The last two syllables of a feminine line are often ♩♩ instead of ♩♩, and of a

[32] ed. Malipiero, XI, 43 seq.: « Vi ricordo o boschi ombrosi », « Ecco purche voi ritorno ».

[33] e. g., Scherzo quoted above, and airs cited in note (32).

[34] e. g. *Chansons au luth et Airs de Cour français du XVIᵉ siècle*, ed. La Laurencie, Mairy & Thibault, Paris (Publications de la Société française de Musicologie), 1934, pp. 142, 147, 160.

[35] Prunières, "Monteverdi and French Music", *op. cit.*, p. 106.

[36] This was first noticed by Gérold, *op. cit.*, pp. 27 seq.

masculine ♩ ♩. Variants which still obey the same principle substitute a minim for any of the crotchets. Number 4 is an example of alexandrines [37],

and the air of Guédron (Ex. 5) of decasyllabics [38] (but for the first line).

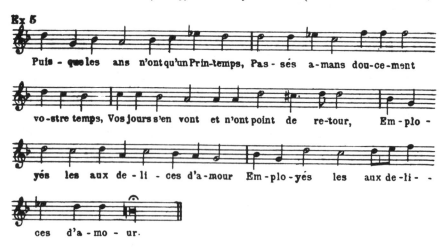

300

---

[37] "A la Reyne", *Bataille*, Libre IV.

[38] From *Bataille*, Livre VII, taken from the Ballet "La Délivrance de Renaud", 1617 (Vide Prunières, *Le Ballet de Cour*, appendice).

Difficulties arise with octosyllabics; in this metre, by far the most common in the airs de cour, there is no fixed *coupe* or caesura which can be underlined with a minim. The composers of these airs, however, set this type of verse as if there were a *coupe* after the fourth syllable, as in decasyllabics. Thus the ideal scheme of an octosyllabic line is: ♩♩♩♩♩♩♩♩ for a feminine line, and: ♩♩♩♩♩♩♩♩ for a masculine. The number of airs in, for example, the *Bataille* series which conforms to these schemes from beginning to end is quite small; but the tendency to do so more or less completely is strong enough to justify the assumption that these composers were in fact trying to model the rhythm of their airs on the metre of their text[39]. The two airs[40] (Exs. 6 and 7) will serve as examples, the first of exact conformation to the above scheme, the second of a typical variant.

301

Occasionally they follow the scheme until it involves the first of the three minims falling on an *e* feminine; a minim is then put on the third or fifth syllable instead of the fourth[41]. They do not however

[39] Cf. other examples in Gérold, *op. cit.*, pp. 28 seq.
[40] From *Bataille*, Livres I & II (both octosyllabics).
[41] e. g., *Bataille*, ed. Warlock, p. 25 (note last line).

always shrink from accenting an *e* feminine in this way, and, with this
exception, the metrical scheme is allowed to distort the natural rhythm
of the text to any extent, as in example 8 [42],

Ex 8

Si trai - tre et si plein de ma - li - ce,

or in the second line of " C'est un amant " quoted above [43]. As in
Monteverdi's Scherzi, the frequent ending ♩ ♩ ♩ is a particularly striking resemblance to *musique mesurée.*

Our second group of *airs de cour* are like those just described in
their lack of a regular beat and in their tendency to set each syllable
with one of two time values, usually ♩ or ♩. But no attempt is made to
follow the real or imaginary metre of the text. In one respect only,
then, are these airs similar to *musique mesurée.* They have the same
" unbarrable " ♩ and ♩ rhythm. But they have no metrical plan and
their text is set with a complete disregard for natural verbal rhythm.
The notation of these airs is usually like that of *musique mesurée.* No
changes from duple to triple time are indicated. There is often no time
signature [44], and if, as often in *musique mesurée,* $\mathbb{C}$ or $\mathbb{C}\!\!\!|$ is put at the

302

Ex 9   (from Airs à 4 parties, 1619)

Nous sommes, ou ne som-mes pas, ces beaux bal - le -teurs pleins d'ap-

pas, dont le re - nom court par la Fran - ce Peut estre aus - si qu'on

n'en dit rien: mais pour le moins, nous sçauons bien que tou-jours

va ce - luy qui dan - ce.

---

[42] From " Suiuray—je toujours cet enfant ", *Bataille,* Livre III.

[43] p. 151.

[44] This is in accordance with Mersenne's statement: " . . . l'on met le nombre 3 . . .
lorsqu'on chante en mesure ternaire . . . ou bien l'on n'y met nul signe, afin que la
mesure soit libre " (*Harmonie Universelle,* Paris, 1636, V, xi).

beginning, it has no possible meaning. But in later airs the changes of rhythm are shown by a rapidly changing time signature [45]. Many of the airs of Jehan Boyer [46] have two notations: one in the version for four voices and another in the version for voice and lute. The soprano parts (Exs. 9 and 10) from the two versions show how the same irregular rhythm, for which there was no traditional notation, may appear in different disguises.

Ex 10   (from **Airs en Tablature de Luth, 1621**)

Nous sommes etc

303

Examples of this type of air are not as numerous as appears at first sight. In many airs the rhythmic irregularity is only apparent. They have a regular triple rhythm except at cadences, where they change to duple. These changes can be explained as written–out ritardandos or pauses on the final note. For example, the air "Vostre humeur est par trop volage" [47] has a straightforward triple rhythm [48] up to the refrain, except for the final bar of each line, which is one crotchet too long. The effect when this is sung is certainly that of a recurrent ritardando. The modern notation, for instance, of the second line might be as in example 11 or in example 12 instead of the original (Ex. 13).

[45] e. g. nearly all those of Boesset, Rigaud and Boyer.
[46] *Airs à 4 parties*, Paris, Ballard, 1619; *Airs de Jean Boyer, Parisien, mis en tablature de luth par luy-mesme*, Paris, Ballard, 1621.
[47] *Bataille*, ed. Warlock, p. 4.
[48] As Warlock indicated by dotted bar-lines.

304

The first three phrases of "Si le parler et le silence"[49] are also in triple time except for the ends of the phrases. Here the transcription 𝅗𝅥𝄐 for 𝅗𝅥𝅗𝅥 is born out by the third phrase, which is a very slightly altered version of the first, with the same harmony, and which ends 𝅗𝅥𝅗𝅥 instead of 𝅗𝅥𝅗𝅥. The same effect of ritardando is given in "Cessez mortels"[50], (Ex. 14) in which the time changes are marked.

49 *Ibid.*, p. 34.
50 *Bataille*, Livre IV.

305

The first of these changes at (i) would be transcribed 𝟑/𝟒 ♩♪. The second is more odd; the rhythm at (ii) is obviously still triple, and the change to 2 is only put in so as to have an unhurried 4–3 suspension on the penultimate note. Similarly Boesset's "Divine Amarillis "[51] (Ex. 15)

Ex 15

is quite regular except at (iii), which in modern notation would probably be 𝟑/𝟒 ♪♪♪♪ ♩♩ ♩. That pauses were written out in this way with notes of longer value is proved by the many songs with repeats and second time bars[52]; that ritardandos were sometimes written out is shown by the ending of Fabrice's " Je ne l'ay dict " (Ex. 16)[53].

306

Ex 16

Sometimes also an apparently irregular air will fit easily into a triple or duple scheme if a rest is inserted at the beginning. For example, Guédron's " Puisque les ans " has no time signature in the

[51] In Mersenne, *Harm. Univ.*, Livre I des Instrumens; he gives both the lute version and the version à 4.

[52] e. g. in the Boesset air just cited the final note in the first time bar is a dotted minim, in the 2nd time bar a long.

[53] Fabrice, *op. cit.*, Livre II.

Bataille version [54] and would make nonsense if it were barred in 𝄴 or 𝄵; but in the polyphonic version [55] it begins with a crotchet rest, has a 𝄴 signature, and fits well into duple time.

Nevertheless, even when these only apparently irregular airs have been subtracted, there remains a considerable number whose rhythm resembles that of *musique mesurée* except that it is not based on a metrical scheme, as in the charming setting (Ex. 17) of a poem by Desportes [56].

Ex 17

1. De mes ans la fleur se des - teint,
2. Ma vi - gueur peu à peu se fond,

J'ay l'oeil cave et pasle le teint
Maint sillon re - plis - se mon frond,

Ma prunel le est tou - te es - blu - oïe,
Le sang ne bou - st plus dans mes

Lute

307

[54] Quoted above p. 154.
[55] Reprinted in Appendix of Prunières, *Ballet de Cour*.
[56] *Bataille*, Livre VI. Cf. *Bataille*, ed. Warlock, pp. 13, 18.

De gris blanc ma te - ste se peint,
vei - nes: Com - me un tra - it mes beaux

Et n'ay plus si bon - ne l'ouïe
jours s'en vont, Me laissant faible entre les pei - nes

All musical measure or beat is lacking and there is apparently no rhythmic principle to take its place; as Rolland says, there was at this time " une veritable ivresse de rythmes libres "[57]. This freedom is not even controlled by the natural verbal rhythm of the text, which is distorted to a remarkable degree note, for instance, in the air just quoted, the stress on " se " in the first line and on " est " in the third[58]. As an English contemporary, Ed. Filmer Gent., remarked[59],

" the *French* when they compose to a ditty in their owne Language being led rather by their free Fant'sie of Aire (wherein many of them do naturally excell) then by any strict and artificiall scanning of the Line, by which they build, doe often, by disproportion'd Musicall Quantities, inuert the naturell Stroke of a Verse, applying to the place of an *Iambicke* Foot, such modulation as Iumps rather with a Trochay ".

[57] Rolland, " L'Opéra au XVIIe siècle ", in *Encyclopédie*, ed. Lavignac & La Laurencie, Pt. I, T. III, Paris, 1921, p. 1344.
[58] cf. *Bataille*, ed. Warlock, pp. 13, 18.
[59] *French Court Aires, with their Ditties Englished, Of foure and five Parts. Together with that of the Lute. Collected, Translated, Published by Ed. Filmer Gent*, London, 1629, Preface.

Filmer explains this distortion of the text by the " lack of metrical feet ", that is, syllabic versification, and by the weak, rare tonic accent in French [60]. These do very adequately account for the considerable distortion of verbal rhythm in most French settings of all kinds, and of all periods up to the 19th century. But in French popular song the distortion arises naturally because a weak verbal accent, unsupported by metre, is dominated by a strong and regular musical rhythm. And in all polyphony there is an inherent tendency to do violence to the text, both because of its inaudibility and because of the rhythmic variety necessary in different voices. This tendency is strengthened by the weak nature of French accentuation. In these *airs de cour*, on the other hand, the composer had no reason or excuse for " applying to the place of an *Iambicke* Foot, such modulation as Iumps rather with a Trochay ", since he had abandoned any regular musical or metrical beat; whereas, in our first group of airs, the equally bad treatment of text can be partially explained by the practice of emphasizing the fourth syllable in octosyllabics [61]. Filmer was not the only contemporary to notice this characteristic of the *airs de cour*. Mersenne remarks on it, but without disapproval or explanation [62].

309

We have supposed that the peculiarities of rhythm in these *airs de cour* were due to the influence of *musique mesurée*. A striking quality of *musique mesurée* is its inevitably good treatment of text. Such distortions as an accented *e* feminine never occur. Like all humanistic musical movements one of its chief aims was to ensure that in every way the text should dominate or condition the setting [63]. It is therefore necessary to give some adequate explanation of the bad treatment of text in these *airs de cour*. It is interesting to note in this connection that a striking exception to these generalizations is Pierre Guédron, who in nearly all his songs shows great respect for the verbal rhythm of his text [64]. This may well be due to the direct influence of *musique mesurée*. Guédron wrote both the music and the words for the Balet du Roy, of which Mauduit, one of the chief musicians of *musique mesurée*,

---

[60] Filmer, immediately after passage quoted: " And this without much violence to their *Poems*, since the disorder and confusion of *metricall* Feet in their Verse is as Inoffensive as Indiscernable, by reason. . . of the Euen Pronunciation of their Tongue ".

[61] cf. supra.

[62] *Harm. Univ.*, II, xxiii.

[63] cf. Walker, " Musical Humanism ", 1, 6, & passim.

[64] See e. g. air quoted supra p. 150.

was the *chef d'orchestre* [65].   Moreover he set to music some *vers mesurés* of Rapin [66], and was the successor of Le Jeune as *Compositeur de musique de la chambre du Roi* [67]. Guédron, however, is only an isolated, though important, exception; we have still to find an explanation of the distortion of verbal rhythm in the great majority of *airs de cour*.

This explanation can perhaps be found in the use of couplets.   In an English or German poem the tonic accents tend to fall in the same places in all verses; in verse written to be sung they invariably do. The use of couplets, therefore, though perhaps aesthetically unsound,

310

Ex 18

1. Les dieux   tant seu-le-ment   Peu-uent ay - mer   si

hau - te - ment.   2. Car   les dieux   seu-le-ment

Peu-uent ay-mer   si   hau - te - ment.   8. D'obte -

nir   en l'ay-mant   Si-nonqu'un glo - ri - ux   tour - ment.

does not necessarily result in misplaced accents.   If changes in the music are necessary to fit different verses, they need only be slight ones, often only such as a good singer would make spontaneously; they do not seriously alter the musical rhythm.   In French, owing to syllabic versification, couplets almost invariably result in misplaced accents. If the tune were altered for each couplet the changes would often completely transform the musical rhythm, and therefore could not reasonably be left to the singer's discretion.   Yet in this period there is only one isolated case of an air in which different versions of a tune are given for

[65] v. Michel Brenet, *Musique et Musiciens de la Vieille France*, Paris, 1911, p. 230.

[66] " Lorsque Leandre " in Guédron's *Airs de Cour à 4 et 5 parties*, Paris, 1608 (also in *Bataille*, Livre I)

[67] v. M. Cauchie, Note on Le Jeune, in *Revue de Musicologie*, 1927, p. 162.

different couplets: an anonymous song in the *Bataille* series.   In this it is only for the last two lines of each stanza that the tune is varied (Ex. 18)[68].

There are also the remarks of Mersenne[69], in quoting the settings of two odes of Horace by Nicolas du Chemin, of which he gives only the first verses:

Il n'y a point d'autres differences dans les couplets qui suiuent le premier, sinon qu'en tous les seconds vers la premiere syllabe est longue, & partant doit estre d'une demie mesure; mais parceque la syllabe fa de fauete du premier couplet est briefve, il y a un soupir deu ant pour faire paroistre ladite briefve, en gardant neantmoins le mesme temps[70].

And on the second ode:

Quant aux autres couplets de cet Ode, ils se peuvent chanter sur ce mesme chant, pourveu que l'on allonge les syllabes de l'un qui se trouent briefves dans l'autre.

These two passages from Mersenne and the song from *Bataille* are the only evidence of any attempt to reform this abuse.   Hence, as M. Prunières remarks[71], it is not surprising that composers made little attempt to follow the rhythm of a first verse when in any case the subsequent verses were bound to be violently distorted.

It is true that couplets were in use long before these lutesongs appeared; but they are much less frequent in the earlier polyphonic songs of di Lasso, Costeley or Le Jeune.   Short texts, often of a popular and frivolous kind, were chosen, or a whole long poem was set without making use of the couplet system[72].   Whereas in the *airs de cour* couplets were always used; M. de la Laurencie concludes[73] that " l'allure simple et la constitution strophique " are the only characteristics common to all *airs de cour*.   Moreover most of the *airs de cour* have, as it were, couplets within couplets.   A verse of four lines is often set with only two phrases, either *aabb* or *abab*.   This ancient musical form naturally intensifies the effect of couplets, since its use makes nearly impossible any attempt to set even a first stanza justly.   It is of course possible that good singers, when a first verse was set justly, altered the melody

311

---

[68] The beginning of this air, "Cessez mortels ", is quoted above, p. 159.

[69] *Harm. Univ.*, VI, xxiii & xxix.

[70] Thus: (first verse) fauete linguis;   (2nd verse) arbusta sulcis.

[71] Prunières, *Le Ballet de Cour*, pp. 232 seq.

[72] e. g., Le Jeune, « Le Printemps, " ed. Expert, I, 1.

[73] Introduction to *Chansons au Luth* (v. supra note 34), p. xxvii.

to fit subsequent ones.   But, apart from the isolated example in *Bataille* there is no evidence that melodic alterations from couplet to couplet were ever anything more than " diminutions ", which, judging from this example given by Mersenne [74], made matters still worse (Ex. 19).

Air de Monsieur Boesset. Chant simple

Ex 19

N'es-pe - rez plus mes yeux   De re - uoir en ces

lieux la beau - té   que j'a - do - re,   -re,

Le ciel ja - loux   de mon bonheur, A ra - uy ma

nais-sante au - ro - re   par sa ri - gueur.

Diminution de Monsieur le Bailly

(2nd couplet)

Les pleurs n'ont plus de lieu. Dans   le coeur

de   ce dieu Dont le feu   me de-uo - re.

Le ciel ja-loux de mon bonheur, A ra

uy ma nais-sàn-te au-ro - re par sa ri-gueur.

74 *Harm. Univ.*, VI, xxiii. 21

Autre diminution de Monsieur Boesset

We have now examined the three main characteristics of *musique mesurée* which may have influenced contemporary music, its texture, rhythm and treatment of text; and we have seen signs of an influence exercized by the latter two in many *airs de cour* of the early 17ᵗʰ century. It must again be emphasized that these signs are by no means a certain indication of this influence and may well be due to quite other causes. Moreover, until the problems of interpretation raised by the notation of *musique mesurée* and the *airs de cour* are fully solved, that is, until we know more exactly what their rhythm was when performed, all discussions on the subject of this article must run the risk of being founded on wrongly interpreted documents.